The Case of the iPad

Cathy Burnett · Guy Merchant
Alyson Simpson · Maureen Walsh
Editors

The Case of the iPad

Mobile Literacies in Education

Springer

Editors
Cathy Burnett
Sheffield Hallam University
Sheffield
UK

Guy Merchant
Sheffield Hallam University
Sheffield
UK

Alyson Simpson
The University of Sydney
Sydney, NSW
Australia

Maureen Walsh
The Australian Catholic University
North Sydney, NSW
Australia

and

The University of Sydney
Sydney, NSW
Australia

ISBN 978-981-10-4363-5 ISBN 978-981-10-4364-2 (eBook)
DOI 10.1007/978-981-10-4364-2

Library of Congress Control Number: 2017936704

Printed on acid-free paper

This Springer imprint is published by Springer Nature
The registered company is Springer Nature Singapore Pte Ltd.
The registered company address is: 152 Beach Road, #21-01/04 Gateway East, Singapore 189721, Singapore

Contents

1 **The Case of the iPad** 1
Cathy Burnett and Guy Merchant

2 **The Fluid Materiality of Tablets: Examining 'the iPad Multiple' in a Primary Classroom** 15
Cathy Burnett

3 **Russian Dolls and Three Forms of Capital: Ecological and Sociological Perspectives on Parents' Engagement with Young Children's Tablet Use** 31
Jackie Marsh

4 **Chasing Literacies Across Action Texts and Augmented Realities: E-Books, Animated Apps, and Pokémon Go** 49
Karen Wohlwend

5 **Multimodal Layering: Students Learning with iPads in Primary School Classrooms** 67
Alyson Simpson and Maureen Walsh

6 **The New Digital Divide: Digital Technology Policies and Provision in Canada and Australia** 87
Joanne O'Mara, Linda Laidlaw and Jill Blackmore

7 **Slate-Enabled Literacy Practices in a Futureschool@Singapore Classroom** 105
Siew Hiang Sally Ng

8 **Apps and Autodidacts: Wayfaring and Emplaced Thinking on iPads** 125
Jennifer Rowsell, Fernando Maues, Sharon Moukperian and Chrystal Colquhoun

9 Game 2 Engage: Using iPads to Mediate and Develop Social Relationships in College Learning 143
Jamie Caine, Julia Davies and Bronwyn T. Williams

10 The Affordances of Touchscreen Tablets and Digital Cameras as Tools for Young Children's Multimodal, Multilingual Composing 159
Deborah Wells Rowe and Mary E. Miller

11 Personalized Story-Making on the iPad: Opportunities for Developing the Self and Building Closeness with Others 179
Natalia Kucirkova and Mona Sakr

12 Children's Engagement with iPads in Early Years Classrooms: Exploring Peer Cultures and Transforming Practices 195
Karen Daniels

13 Collaborative and Dialogic Meaning-Making: How Children Engage and Immerse in the Storyworld of a Mobile Game 211
Fiona Maine

14 Relational Methodologies for Mobile Literacies: Intra-action, Rhythm, and Atmosphere 227
Ty Hollett and Christian Ehret

15 Hands, Fingers and iPads 245
Guy Merchant

16 Mobile Literacies: Moving from the Word to the World 257
Alyson Simpson and Maureen Walsh

Index 267

Editors and Contributors

About the Editors

Cathy Burnett is Professor of Literacy and Education at Sheffield Institute of Education, Sheffield Hallam University where she leads the Language and Literacy in Education Research Group. Her current research interests focus on relationships between technology, literacy and education. Her co-edited collections include *New Literacies around the Globe: policy and pedagogy* and *Literacy, Media, Technology: past, present and future*. She is Vice President of the United Kingdom Literacy Association.

Guy Merchant is Professor of Literacy in Education in the Sheffield Institute of Education at Sheffield Hallam University. He specialises in research into digital literacy and the inter-relations between children and young people, and new technologies of communication. He has widely published in international journals and is a founding editor of *Early Childhood Literacy*. The ground-breaking *Web 2.0 for Schools* was co-authored with Julia Davies, and he has since co-edited a number of collections including *Virtual Literacies* (2013), *New Literacies across the Globe* (2014) and *Literacy, Media, Technology: past, present, future* (2017). He is active in literacy education and professional work, including writing curriculum materials and professional publications.

Alyson Simpson is Associate Professor in the Sydney School of Education and Social Work at the University of Sydney, Australia. Current research projects in higher education and primary schools include work on the role of children's literature in education, the power of dialogic learning and the impact of digital technology on reading practices and pedagogy. She has served as a consultant to state and national education bodies across all sectors. She is the author of *The use of children's literature in teaching: A study of politics and professionalism within teacher education.*

Maureen Walsh is Honorary Professor in the Sydney School of Education and Social Work at the University of Sydney and Adjunct Professor in the Faculty of Education and Arts at the Australian Catholic University (ACU). Previously Professor of Literacy Education at ACU, she was the recipient of two national awards for university teaching. Maureen has published nationally and internationally in areas of TESOL, children's literature, reading education and visual literacy. For several years her work has focused on the impact of digital communication on literacy education and she developed a theoretical framework around multimodal literacy in several publications.

Contributors

Jill Blackmore School of Education, Deakin University, Burwood, Victoria, Australia

Cathy Burnett Sheffield Hallam University, Sheffield, UK

Jamie Caine Sheffield Hallam University, Sheffield, UK

Chrystal Colquhoun Brock University, St. Catharines, Canada

Karen Daniels Sheffield Hallam University, Sheffield, UK

Julia Davies The University of Sheffield, Sheffield, UK

Christian Ehret McGill University, Montreal, Canada

Ty Hollett The Pennsylvania State University, Pennsylvania, USA

Natalia Kucirkova Institute of Education, University College London, London, UK

Linda Laidlaw University of Alberta, Edmonton, Canada

Fiona Maine University of Cambridge, Cambridge, UK

Jackie Marsh The University of Sheffield, Sheffield, UK

Fernando Maues Universidade Federal do Para, Belém, Brazil

Guy Merchant Sheffield Hallam University, Sheffield, UK

Mary E. Miller Peabody College, Vanderbilt University, Nashville, USA

Sharon Moukperian Brock University, St. Catharines, Canada

Siew Hiang Sally Ng Singapore Ministry of Education, Singapore, Malaysia

Joanne O'Mara School of Education, Deakin University, Burwood, Victoria, Australia

Deborah Wells Rowe Peabody College, Vanderbilt University, Nashville, USA

Jennifer Rowsell Brock University, St. Catharines, Canada

Mona Sakr Middlesex University, London, UK

Alyson Simpson University of Sydney, Sydney, Australia

Maureen Walsh Australian Catholic University and University of Sydney, Sydney, Australia

Bronwyn T. Williams University of Louisville, Louisville, USA

Karen Wohlwend Indiana University, Bloomington, USA

List of Figures

Fig. 3.1 Tablet usage by socioeconomic group—weekdays 43
Fig. 3.2 Tablet usage by socioeconomic group—weekends 43
Fig. 4.1 Coded instances of multiplayer collaboration. 60
Fig. 5.1 An example of multimodal layering 72
Fig. 5.2 Illustrated example of semiotic reconfiguring as multimodal layering 76
Fig. 7.1 MOE Singapore 21CC framework. *Source* Ministry of Education, Singapore (2015b). https://www.moe.gov.sg/education/education-system/21st-century-competencies 106
Fig. 7.2 MOE 4th Masterplan for ICT in education. *Source* Ministry of Education, Singapore (2015a, b) 109
Fig. 8.1 Reflecting on his wayfaring autodidactic practices. 133
Fig. 8.2 Venn diagram of *Minecraft* village 137
Fig. 8.3 Researching for designs. 138
Fig. 9.1 The Rix blog tool. With permission from Rix Research and Media 148
Fig. 10.1 A prekindergartener's home photo eBook page. 163
Fig. 10.2 A second graders' home photo eBook page. 171
Fig. 12.1 Blaise and Harry steer the robot 202
Fig. 13.1 Ida and a crow in the world of *Monument Valley* 213
Fig. 13.2 Totem in the world of *Monument Valley*. 216
Fig. 14.1 Vantage point from Adela's head camera 228
Fig. 14.2 Domiana, Marcus and Gerald choose and orient images together 235
Fig. 14.3 Micro-rhythms of Domiana as she manipulates images 236
Fig. 14.4 Embodied flows of Domiana, Marcus, Gerald and Ciera. 237
Fig. 15.1 Ten nodes 252

Introduction

If desktop and laptop computers were initially the domain of commercial and educational worlds and only later became part of everyday spaces, mobile devices, such as smartphones and tablets, have needed no such transition and have rapidly infiltrated all walks of life. They are used not only by administrators, scholars and students but also in daily life in homes, in restaurants, and in a wide range of retail, service and tourist industries. There is a pressing need to understand the mobile literacies associated with such devices and their take up in different jurisdictions, as well as the role that they play (or might play) in the lives of children and adolescents. In many parts of the world, digital devices and the texts they mediate are embedded in everyday life from the earliest years (Razfar & Gutierrez 2013). In the UK, for example, nearly three-quarters of children aged 3–5 have access to a touchscreen device at home (Formby 2014), and surveys report an increase in tablet ownership amongst children (Ofcom 2016). In the US, ownership of tablet devices in families with children aged 8 or younger increased fivefold from less than 8% in 2011 to 40% in 2013 (Rideout 2013). In many households, tablets have become the device of choice for family entertainment, used for on-demand TV, games and interactive stories. Increasingly, educational literacy practices too have fallen under the sway of devices like the iPad, which appeals to educators because of its size, portability and intuitive touchscreen interface (Merchant 2015).

This widespread availability of portable digital devices, and their increasing use within educational settings, suggests a need to re-draw maps of literacy development to account for emerging forms of semiotic representation and patterns of interaction (Merchant 2012; 2015). At the same time, the distribution and use of tablets and high-speed internet access remains uneven, patterned by differences in economic wealth as well as practices associated, for example, with gender, ethnicity and class (Black et al. 2014; Rideout 2013). Furthermore, in educational settings, literacy tends to be conceived in ways that contrast with the hands on, mobile, free-ranging and often diverse engagements with texts associated with tablet use at home. Not only do we need to know more about how meanings are made around iPads and similar devices, but we also need to understand the distinctive ways in which mobile technologies are being put to use in educational settings. While there is no doubt that mobile technologies present us with new affordances, the material nature of learning and literacy raises new and interesting issues for pedagogy. Educational researchers and practitioners need ways of understanding the varied ways in which children, devices, texts and sites intersect and work to construct one another, and how mobile literacies work as 'placed resources' (Prinsloo 2005) embedded in and inflected by wider economic, political, societal and historical forces.

Building on a well-received symposium at the 2015 American Educational Research Association international conference in Chicago, this edited collection brings together an international group of scholars working in literacy studies who have investigated the use of tablets in a variety of settings. Approaching associated literacy practices from multiple theoretical perspectives, the chapters interrogate the relationship between tablets and literacy in different ways. The book focuses on tablets, and particularly the iPad, as an instance—or *case*—of mobile literacies, but is designed to speak more broadly to research focused on literacy and mobile devices. We see the significance of mobility to literacy first in relation to the portability of the device, second in relation the fluid movements between apps associated with mobile devices, and third in relation to the movement of ideas and practices associated with tablet use.

Together the chapters in this book address the 'Case of the iPad' by exploring multiple ways of conceptualising meaning making around tablets, placing a particular focus on the embodied, material and situated experiences produced when hardware and software with 'global' circulation are taken up in local educational settings. The chapters exemplify these perspectives using data from studies investigating iPad use in a variety of locations: in homes and in early years, primary and secondary schools, as well as post-16 settings. Chapters range from those framing tablet use in terms of a micro-analysis of practices to those examining the broader political, economic and social flows that inflect available opportunities. Together they address the complex and multiple forces associated with the distribution of the technologies themselves and the texts they mediate (popular children's stories, games and so on), and consider how apps, adults and children work together as iPads enter the mesh of practices and material arrangements that constitute the institutional settings (Schatzki 2005).

References

Black, Rebecca, Kasenia Korobkova, and Alexandra Epler. 2014. Barbie girls and xtractaurs: Discourse and identity in virtual worlds for young children. *Journal of Early Childhood Literacy* 14(2); 265–285.

Formby, Susie. 2014. *Parents' perspectives: Children's Use of Technology in the Early Years*. London: National Literacy Trust.

Merchant, Guy. 2012. Mobile practices in everyday life: popular digital technologies and schooling revisited. *British Journal of Educational Technology* 43(5): 770–782.

Merchant, Guy. 2015. Keep taking the tablets: iPads, story apps and early literacy. *Australian Journal of Language and Literacy* 38(1): 3–12.

Ofcom. 2016. *Children and Parents: media use and attitudes*. https://www.ofcom.org.uk/__data/assets/pdf_file/0034/93976/Children-Parents-Media-Use-Attitudes-Report-2016.pdf. Accessed 30th Dec 2016.

Prinsloo, Mastin. 2005. The new literacies as placed resources. *Perspectives in Education* 23 (4): 87–98.

Razfar, Aria and Kris Gutierrez. 2013. Reconceptualizing Early Childhood Literacy: The sociocultural influence and new directions in digital and hybrid mediation. In *The Sage Handbook of Early Childhood Literacy*, ed. Jackie Marsh and Joanne Larson, 52–79. London: Sage.

Rideout, Victoria. 2013. *Zero to Eight: children's media use in America 2013*. Accessed from https://www.commonsensemedia.org/…/zero-to-eight-2013pdf-0/download.

Schatzki, Theodore. 2005. Peripheral Vision: The Sites of Organizations. *Organization Studies* 26(3): 465–484.

Chapter 1
The Case of the iPad

Cathy Burnett and Guy Merchant

Due to back problems I've always avoided using laptops more than absolutely necessary and my large hands mean I'm all fingers and thumbs when I use my smartphone so I've never really grown to love it. My iPad though is much more of a friend, part of the family even, following me from office to lounge to kitchen to office and coming on trips and outings. Its black articulated case is practical but gives nothing away. When I fold it back though an image springs to life, a forgotten world. It's a photo taken early one sunny morning at the Fairy Glen near Uig on the Isle of Skye. It makes me smile every time I see it and remember the surprise of stumbling across this eerie place tucked away from Skye's more obvious highlights. I've had the iPad for maybe four years now, it's a reconditioned iPad 2. I've recently heard that Apple are going to stop updating the operating system for iPad 2 s. How long until mine ceases to function with the apps I use and it goes to join all the other discarded devices and chargers that clutter my home?

If a product's reputation is linked to the frequency with which its brand name is used, it is at its zenith when the brand name becomes synonymous with the product itself. Hoover did it with the vacuum cleaner; Google with the search engine. Both names have been absorbed into everyday parlance, even to the extent that associated activities have generated new verb forms. After all we can all hoover up information through googling. The situation isn't quite the same with tablet computers, but it's close. At times we forget that the iPad only counts for a segment of the tablet market—a large segment admittedly, but there are other players out there, too.

C. Burnett (✉) · G. Merchant
Sheffield Hallam University, Sheffield, UK
e-mail: c.burnett@shu.ac.uk

G. Merchant
e-mail: g.h.merchant@shu.ac.uk

C. Burnett et al. (eds.), *The Case of the iPad*,
DOI 10.1007/978-981-10-4364-2_1

Does any of this matter? Well it does if you put together a book that refers to iPads in its title that has iPads mentioned in chapter headings and in multiple index entries, as we have here. But still, referring to 'the case of the iPad' suits our purpose too. It conjures up a number of things. For instance, it draws attention to the power of the market and to the commercial interests that are the trademark of modern life flowing, as they do, across jurisdictions on an unprecedented scale. What is sometimes referred to as global capitalism is just a way of describing the restless search for new markets and the appetite to sell into new territories that this involves. iPads appear to flourish in this environment, riding on the already established reputation of the Apple Corporation. This is, then, part of the case we consider.

iPads may have crossed international boundaries with ease, but they have crossed other boundaries too. They have succeeded in capturing the interest of educators where many digital technologies have failed. Relatively cheap and light and without the encumbrance of wires, plugs and modems that have rooted technology so firmly to the spot in schools for so long, they are attractive to educators and educational policy-makers. They rest comfortably on classroom tables and their 'intuitive' interface means that less time is wasted with technological glitches and from lapses in teacher confidence. Moreover, while educational technologies have often been adaptations—parallels or parodies of technologies used outside school—Apple were quick off the mark in getting their product endorsed by schools. Consequently, students, where funding permits, meet familiar devices that they know how to find their way around. Of course in practice, as many of the chapters in this volume illustrate, school use is never quite as straightforward as the hype suggests. Calls from mobile learning enthusiasts for learning 'anytime, anywhere' have generated multiple case studies of children using mobile devices in museums and galleries, parks and wild places, and for 'home learning'. For the most part, however, school tablets remain in classrooms, perhaps even alleviating any previous need for excursions elsewhere. And their use generates familiar questions about how much freedom children should be allowed at school—to access and to move between particular resources.

In educational research it is traditional to train our gaze on what learners do, to focus on outcomes, intentions and processes. A brief search for studies of iPads in education suggests that much of our attention has rested on a closed circle, the relationships between child, device/app and learning outcomes. Studies have explored perceptions of tablets, impacts of tablets and implementations of tablets. Where researchers seek to contextualize technology use through tracing relationships with policy or broader practices, they tend to do so by examining the legacy of policy-makers or institutions, or by following students to their homes and their leisure activities. In effect, they follow the people.

Bounding the story of the iPad—and of course other tablets—in this way, however, has implications. It deflects from discussion about other kinds of relationships sustained and generated through the use of digital devices in education. It narrows the case. Of course, there is much that is attractive about the idea of individual learners at large in the world, with access to multiple sources of information and expertise, activity that supports a flexible, agile engagement with the world around them. All too often, however, the sense of personalization and individualism that this claims is at odds with the complex sets of relationships that help sustain such possibilities, relationships that have too often been characterized by social injustice, environmental degradation and violence towards other species. In this chapter we intersperse analyses from multiple disciplines with personal stories in order to unsettle common framings of tablets in education. We intend the questions and issues we raise to work in conversation with the cutting edge research and thinking presented in the chapters that follow, and in doing so hint at multiple other ways of working at the intersection of literacy and technology as yet unexplored.

Moving Targets

> *Through the steamy windows of a corner café in this small provincial town you can just make out the customers. They are nursing warm drinks, chatting to each other. Some are on their own, hunched over their mobile phones, flicking through screen images, tapping out messages, updating their status, relaxing. All is well, or so it seems.*

But how easily have we become habituated to this world of mobile technologies? For these devices have rapidly insinuated themselves into almost every aspect of social life (Gergen 2003). Not everywhere, but hereabouts. And that makes us all customers, whether we happen to be sitting in the café or not. Is this the new order, a state in which we imagine ourselves to be rational, self-determining subjects exercising our freedoms in marketised choice, in socially sanctioned consumption and lifestyle performances? What have we bought into?

In his commentary on the political and economic practices of neo-liberalism Rose (1999) explores contemporary governmentality and the emergence of a new ethical subjectivity—a subjectivity framed by the rights of the consumer and the practices of the market place. From this perspective, the freedoms of lifestyle choice are determined by market transactions, whether or not this is evident to the individual. And if the success of the neo-liberal project is to be measured by the reach and frequency of these transactions, then mobile technologies are raising the bar. As an example, the Apple Corporation manufactures about a million iPhones a day, and this plays a significant role in making it the most valuable company in the world, worth $622 bn (Apple 2016). The market is of course open for other entrepreneurs too, those other players who provide hardware, software and even the communications infrastructure itself.

No matter how handy our devices are (see Merchant, Chap. 15), or how convenient mobile life has become, mobiles are bought and sold, on terms, with 'providers'—refreshed, recycled and regularly updated. Consuming subjects are thereby involved in serial transactions, guided by sophisticated marketing, branding, product placement and media coverage. Take *Which?*, the consumer bible that tests, compares and recommends our purchases. It tells us that,

> The iPhone 7 is the *best iPhone we've ever tested* and its 91% score is among the highest we've ever recorded for any product. (Authors' italics) (Which?, November 2016: 58)

Not advertising, just product endorsement. And along with word-of-mouth recommendation, and its circulation in on/offline social networks, we are coaxed and cajoled into more updating, accumulating more apps and making more in-app purchases—in the case of the popular game *Candy Crush,* about a dollar each time, contributing to a total of $1.3 bn per annum revenue for the holding company (Torres 2015).

It may be stating the obvious to say that mobile technologies play a significant role in upholding the new global economy. They are at the same time both socially sanctioned consumer products and sophisticated conduits for new products. But they could also be seen as a manifestation of neoliberal governmentality, for in Foucault's definition governmentality is not just about political governance but also about 'the conduct of individuals and groups' (Foucault 1994: 341). Or to put it another way it is the 'whole range of practices that constitute, define, organize and instrumentalize the strategies that individuals in their freedom use in dealing with each other' (Foucault 1997: 300).

From this point of view, we might see what we might call mobile subjectivities as the ways in which individuals produce new modes of social interaction, and new textual and discursive practices as consumers of mobile technologies. These are ways of being that are contagious, taking place in a cultural economy that valorizes individualized, responsibilized, digital consumers. If this is the case, what is the role of schools in this context? Is it to produce more compliant, neoliberal subjects, or have schools been reconfigured with this express purpose in mind (Brown 2003)?

Education reform has already been imprinted with the stamp of the market. The success of schools and other educational institutions is measured for competitive ranking, and their operations are quality controlled. Parents are cast as responsible consumers who shop around for the best buy—and testing regimes have transformed children into quantified subjects who know their 'level' and readily announce their aspirational targets. And if the adoption of new technology for learning has had an uneven trajectory in schools, it has been more confidently and evenly accepted for recording assessments, managing performance data and publishing inspection reports.

Whilst the influx of mobile technologies into the school sector holds many promises (Merchant 2012), developers have been quick to exploit the new market, producing apps for parents to invest in early advantage for their children (see Marsh, Chap. 3; Kucirkova and Sakr, Chap. 11) and Sakr, Chap. 11 for schools looking for magic bullets to improve performance data. From Earobics[1] for early phonics, to Mathletics,[2] a sophisticated learning platform for mathematics, there is plenty to choose from. Perhaps their trade names hint at the emphasis on training, individualized improvement and competitive advantage.

[1]By Cognitive Concepts.

[2]By 3PLearning, see http://uk.mathletics.com.

Hall (2013) explains these recent moves in mobile learning in terms of an economic agenda. Mobile learning is inextricable from the production and marketing of devices and apps that submit individuals to infringements of privacy, turning them into the subjects of surveillance and data mining. In making his case he asserts that,

> both the anytime/anywhere capabilities of mobile technologies, and their identity-driven, personalizable reality, enable the real subsumation of everyday activity inside the reproduction of capital. (Hall 2013: 174)

Inside the Case

> *Somewhere... if I can find it...yes, here it is, slightly aslant, balanced on an untidy sheaf of papers on the window ledge. A bit like an old book with rounded corners. The spine, black faux-leather that has acquired an uneven sheen from being carried, stuffed into bags and variously manhandled. And the faded cover, padded synthetic material printed with a photograph. Me, in hiking gear, on a high pass in the Himalayas, surrounded by prayer flags - also faded. Flipping it open to see the expressionless black glass. Thick smears of grease pattern the screen, the work of the fingers, a history of use. And at one end, the rectangular line of the casing is cut away, like the outline of a small bowl. Cradled in this cut-away you can just make out a circular indentation in the glass, with an even smaller white square printed neatly in its centre. Dust, grease and food crumbs have accumulated around it, but it still responds quickly when pressed with the forefinger, and then the whole surface springs to life. An incandescence, the home screen.*

In supporting ongoing professional development, Mason (2001) urges teachers to develop a 'discipline of noticing', a noticing that stops them in their tracks and promotes engagement with things that tend to get taken for granted or ignored. A disciplined noticing can bring background to foreground, inviting new kinds of questions about everyday classroom practice, questions that easily escape the busy teacher: linked to learners' perspectives, micro-practices, the complexities of classroom life. So where do we stop with this? What gets written in, and what gets written out? Literacy scholars are familiar with this dilemma. Challenging the psychological cognitive accounts of literacy that focus on a closed loop between text and brain, literacy researchers have added many ways of thinking about what might count when thinking about literacy/ies. Forty years of literacy studies have extended the gaze to include multiple places and spaces, new media, diverse languages, practices and power structures. Many of the chapters in this volume support such careful noticing; for the most part they shun generalizations and focus on intimate details of learners' interactions with tablets as emplaced in different sites (e.g. Chaps. 9, 10 and 12–14); and use detailed analyses of literacy practices to raise questions about the implications for learners of making meaning in ways that are more mobile and more multimodal (e.g. Chaps. 4, 5 and 8). And some chapters begin to touch on what might happen if we bring micro-analysis of *non-human* participants to our thinking about iPads and literacy (e.g. Chaps. 2 and 15).

But other kinds of noticing might invite questions that get pushed aside in the busyness of classroom life. There is, for example, a 'deafening silence about non humans in our discourse' (Wolch and Emel 1995). Educational research on tablets has almost exclusively focused on use. Studies of the take-up of tablets, the efficacy of particular apps for learning, and of how students of various ages engage with devices continue to proliferate. And in this work, the focus has tended to rest on the surface—what is displayed on the screen, rather than how it is generated or what happens after, from a technological point of view. We might think of the former as what is *under-coded*, and the latter as what is *over-coded*. For example, display requires not only the battery, processor, Flash memory, Wi-Fi antennae, accelerometer and audio-visual circuitry in the build, but also the under-coding that makes apps work. This kind of coding—and the algorithms that lie behind it—has, of course, become absorbed into some education provision as part of computational thinking (e.g. Australian Curriculum Assessment and Reporting Authority 2014; Department for Education 2013; Education Scotland 2014), but the possibility of using this as an opportunity to look 'under the bonnet' of the iPad is, as yet, poorly documented. There is a clear need for more work in this area, work that indeed looks beneath the surface.

By comparison more attention has been given to what we are calling over-coding. Media scholars such as Fuchs (2010) and Lyon (1998) have focused on how data are collected, or 'harvested', from users, pointing out how platforms and apps routinely collect, store and share data about users and their behaviour. Sometimes this enters into schools under the umbrella of cybersafety, but as concerns over surveillance and privacy online grow it may need to be more firmly written into work on critical media literacy.

Bringing the more than human to our notice, however, involves engaging not just with what goes on *beneath the screen* but *beyond the screen* to the multiple humans and non-humans that are implicated in the arrival of tablets in classrooms. The geographer White (2015) describes what may be gained, for example, by attending to the inter-species violence that is 'hidden in plain sight' in the everyday life of humans. Narrating his walk from home to station on the way to work, he notes the 'more than human sentient beings that are entangled within this urban landscape', in pet shops, butcher's shops and shops selling equipment for hunting, shooting and fishing. He asks,

> Were I to push my observer to move beyond an anthropocentric scripting of this encounter with place, and ask that they critically focus instead on the excessively obvious presence (or indeed absence) or more than human animals, then I would hope (and fear) that their urban narrative would generate observations altogether more dark and *disturbing*. (White 2015: 213)

What might happen if we start to engage with the more-than-human sentient beings entangled in tablet production, marketing and use. When we consider the classrooms described in this volume from this perspective, animals other than humans are noticeably absent. Of course, in classrooms, we're accustomed to representations of animals, on posters, reference books, apps, pencil cases and stickers on bags, or anthropomorphized in children's picture books and novels. Animals are ever present in the semiotics of classrooms, as things to be researched, celebrated, investigated, and—in fictional form–as companions with which to explore multiple storied lives. Occasionally, a wasp may fly through a window or a dog may enter a playground, or beetles may be pooted into jars for science or environmental studies. But these brief encounters do not bear testament to the multiple other ways in which people and other animals come into dialogue in the makings of education.

Smear

Sitting in the second row during a conference presentation, a small movement from the row in front distracts me. Guy is gliding a small piece of folded tissue in regular circular motions across his iPad screen. Back and forth, round and round. The smears of yesterday's activity erased.

When tablets enter classrooms, they arrive all shiny and ready for something new (see Caine, Davies and Williams, Chap. 9). But as they have morphed from mineral extraction through production to marketing and purchase to use, they have shed many stories, stories that are hard to locate in the research archives. While discussions about other animals and technology do reach the press, these usually relate to interactions between particular species and technologies—dolphins guarding nuclear weapons (Beinaimee 2015) or eagles capturing drones (Thielman 2016) for example. And yet press stories exploring the damage to humans and other species associated with tablet production tend to deal in generalities: the environment, the planet and ecologies. Big things collapse multiple things into one. We see this in the rhetoric of both environmental groups and tech giants:

> Until now, companies have focused on the need to remove hazardous substances from consumer electronics products in order to address chemical pollution from recycling and disposal, including backyard recycling of e-waste. For some product groups, the phase-out of hazardous substances has been relatively successful. However, the electronics industry has not yet sufficiently addressed the challenge of reducing the environmental impact that results from the manufacture of their products. (Greenpeace 2014: 20)

> Apple believes that improving the environmental performance of our business starts with our products. The careful environmental management of our products throughout their life cycles includes controlling the quantity and types of materials used in their manufacture, improving their energy efficiency, and designing them for better recyclability. (Apple Corporation 2015: n.p.)

The 'environment' becomes one thing, one factor to be taken into account by institutions, organizations and individuals. And the justification or analysis is quantified—we get to see how we're measuring up. Just as in education, as long as we're improving, moving on, then things feel fine. We're doing better than before, after all. Certainly, individuals often cite green(er) credentials as reasons for choosing Apple products over others. And yet, of course, the environment isn't just one factor but an intricately woven multitude of relationships that intersect in complex ways raising multiple other considerations, and the implications need to be seen both in terms of individuals, and in relation to timescales that massively exceed those associated with the launch or life of a product:

> Toxic e-waste is predicted to grow to 65.4 million metric tons in 2017. The recycling of this e-waste becomes even more problematic when it is exported to countries in the Global South where dangerous backyard recycling often takes place, posing great health risks to the local communities. While electronic take-back programmes are growing, the speed of collection cannot keep pace with the rate of consumption. In 2013 alone 1.8 billion mobile phones were sold globally, and it is predicted that sales of the most popular gadgets (mobiles, tablets and PCs) will increase by 6% to almost 2.5 billion products in 2014. This worldwide growth in consumption is multiplying the environmental and human health problems associated with an electronics industry currently built on an unsustainable model. (Greenpeace 2014: 5)

If we recognize the anthropocene as an epoch distinct from prior geological eras, one in which human activity has shaped Earth's eco-systems and evolutionary processes in fundamental ways (Young 2016), then the use of particular devices is not just about impact on specific communities of humans or other animals, or of tracing the significance of the production and use of digital devices to specific sites (although that's important, too), but it's about recognizing the ways in which production and use are interwoven with the future of the planet (Hodder 2014).

So what might all this mean for literacy education and research? Separating out literacy studies—in a kind of disciplinary silo—starts to feel ethically problematic. In exploring how literacy scholars might engage critically with the issue of obsolescence, for example, Madden (2014) asks ironically 'What can writing studies do to impact global environmental conditions in the anthropocene? And shouldn't this be someone else's job?' For Madden, one response is to explore the kinds of meanings that are enabled in relation to the rhetoric of the device itself. As Madden, citing Gabrys (2011), explores, the shrinking of digital devices and the ways in which small slim devices work perhaps represents a 'dematerialization of those tools in the popular imagination' (Madden 2014: 35). It becomes more possible to sidestep issues of production and environmental destruction when devices themselves are so sylph-like, their size, their slimness creating the impression of something less substantial, more sustainable, less greedy (even though the production of such devices may generate even more waste than their more cumbersome, durable predecessors).

Are We Moving?

> *I'm just pulling into the car park when my phone goes off. The screen lights up. It's Cathy. 'Hello?'. 'Mmm, I appear to be locked in the office, I can't get out. Are you somewhere about?' 'I've just got here. I'm in the car park.' 'Well can you come and let me out? You'll need your swipe card.' I slide out of the driver's seat. 'For once I've got that.' I stride purposefully across to the office building. 'I'm on my way, I'll be there in a couple of*

> *minutes.' Hang up. For once I might be able to do something useful. Something practical. And then I'm at the door. It's a big glass arrangement in a metal frame through which I can see Cathy who is frantically gesturing at me. I fumble in my wallet for the swipe card. The first attempt is a fail. I'm pulling the wrong door, the wrong way. I punch the mobility access button. Nothing. She's trapped, still gesturing. I try again, pull the other door and she's out. Third time lucky.*

Mobility is one of those signature themes of early twenty-first century living. On a macro-scale we are preoccupied with the movement of people, whether it takes the form of the 'migrant crisis' that has recently tested Europe's ability to act with humanity, the contagion and spread of Ebola that has so troubled the medical community, illegal border crossings and their ongoing generational legacy, or the carbon footprint left by mass tourism and big business. Within liberal democracies we agonize about social mobility, about the rising gap between rich and poor, at a local level about the ability of the transport infrastructure to get people from A to B, and with a growing commitment to how barriers to physical access can be removed, we worry about how mobility can be enhanced. Based on all of this, Sheller and Urry (2006) identify the emergence of a 'new mobilities paradigm' to focus our attention on movement. Urry (2007) highlights a number of strands including: *the movement of bodies* for work, for leisure, in migration and for political asylum; *the movement of materials*, principally but not exclusively between producers and consumers; and *virtual movement* to 'other places' through the use of screen technologies and semiotic movement made possible through mobile technologies. None of these are exactly new to the twenty-first century, but the concept of mobilities sensitizes us to how we put ourselves about, how we get around, who and what moves where, and how. And of course, these mobilities intersect with other concerns (such as those outlined above) in ways that suggest that the new mobilities paradigm is post-disciplinary (Sheller and Urry 2006).

Urry (2007) also draws attention to the how mobility relates to unevenness in the concentration and scarcity of resources, and we can immediately see the ways in which that is reflected in the case of tablet technologies, and how directly this relates to power and conflict and the patterning of social, economic and cultural life. Part of the equation, for Urry, is about relationships with immobile platforms—platforms that control and regulate the flow of people, goods, or information. His examples include borders and gates as well as transport hubs such as stations and airports, but we might also consider the institutions and institutional infrastructures that human and non-human actors are tethered to and the territories that these help to produce. Some of this thinking has influenced the mapping of new mobilities for education undertaken by Leander et al. (2010) who pose the question:

> How are the dynamically moving elements of social systems and distributions, including people themselves and all manner of resources for learning as well, configured and reconfigured across space and time to create opportunities for learning? (Leander et al. 2010: 330)

Are We Learning?

When we juxtapose these different iPad tales, the case of the iPad starts to feel rather slippery. iPads become certain kinds of things when they appear in classrooms, quite different from those things targeted by environmental groups, or featured in advertising campaigns or used to access bank accounts or social media. They become different things as they enter into relations with people and other things. iPads, like other things, are held in place by such relations, just as *they* help sustain *other* things as they come into relation with them. These relationships need work, however; if the work ceases, then these things cease to exist too (Latour 1987).

We see this often in education, when something gains purchase and is held in place by a complex set of relations. In the UK for example the late 1990s/early 2000s saw the implementation of a National Literacy Strategy characterized by distinct pedagogical and organizational approaches involving an increased emphasis on focused class and group teaching, a detailed curriculum framework and extensive professional development packages and resources. All these elements, along with concerns about performance in international league tables and an explosion of commercially produced materials and training offers, worked to sustain the National Literacy Strategy as a 'thing'. Of course the frameworks, artefacts and practices associated with the Strategy were constituted in all sorts of ways as they came into dialogue with practices, artefacts and frameworks in different settings. But this did not stop the NLS becoming thing-like, even if in practice it was much more slippery than that. It became a thing that teachers and children did, that academics critiqued, that some people embraced enthusiastically and others moaned or worried about. When the political mood changed, however, and the effort and enthusiasm needed to sustain these mutually reinforcing relationships began to fall away, the whole thing dissolved, leaving not much more than a residue of abandoned folders and boxes in stockrooms and staffroom shelves, and a predilection for whole class teaching that assembled with other things to become something different, not the Strategy. An iPad of course is a very different kind of thing to a national strategy. And yet this focus on relations helps illuminate how iPads tend to get produced in certain kinds of ways in educational contexts and not others (see O'Mara, Laidlaw and Blackmore, Chap. 6; Ng, Chap. 7).

While of course iPads can mediate a vast array of practices, from the transformative to the frankly tedious, iPads in education have become emblematic of the new in education, of new practices, new possibilities and new pedagogies. And yet technologies move on, and outside educational contexts tablets may be old news. Another story:

> In IDC's (International Data Corporation) latest report, Apple recorded the highest amount of tablet device shipments continuing and increasing its worldwide market dominance despite recording a decline (−6.2%) in year-on-year growth from 2015. Apple recorded 9.3 million units shipped in comparison to 9.9 million units the previous year.

> The overall tablet market suffered a decline (-14,7%) in year-on-year growth. No manufacturer shipped +10 million units with only two of the top 5, Amazon and Huawei, recording actual year -on-year growth. The tablet market has been in a gradual decline for the last eight quarters (2 years) a worrying trend manufacturers have increasingly become more aware of. [...]
>
> The decline in tablet appeal may be attributed to the resurgence of smartphones and introduction of phablets (smartphones with large displays) in the last couple of years. Once hailed as the laptop killer tablets are slowly starting to lose their place in the consumer market as most people would rather have a laptop + smartphone combination to cater for their mobility and productivity. Both devices are now more than capable in providing for consumers entertainment needs so where does a tablet fit in? (Chikadaya 2016: n.p.)

While iPads are unusual in moving from everyday use into school use, it is possible that the 'educational iPad' stands a chance of outliving its counterpart out in the wild. As iPads come into relation with adaptations and applications designed for educational use, and with classrooms, teachers and 'learners', they may be more firmly sedimented into pedagogical practice. As Chap. 2 (Burnett) explores, iPads act and are enacted in multiple ways in classroom life with social and affective dimensions very much to the fore. However, the shoring up of the 'educational iPad' involves 'othering' affective and social dimensions of practice, and othering other sets of relations that have made it possible to have iPads in classrooms in the first place. These include practices and processes that cross international borders, and do so through traversing multiple sets of value systems that raise the kinds of humanitarian and environmental concerns explored above.

And yet, whether othered or not, these relations are folded into the device. As an object the iPad can be seen as 'a pattern of presences and absences' (Law and Singleton 2005: 343). Past relations may well be designated absent through all the present excitement about what might happen next, but they have still shaped what the device has become, and its production has helped shape the environment from which materials were sourced as well as the lives of those who helped put it together. The iPad is as it is because of all those relations, and as such it has acted on others as it has become what it is.

What we hope this and the ensuing chapters illustrate is that different patterns of absences and presences come into play as we frame our investigations differently. Through 'method assemblage' (Law 2004) certain kinds of relationships come to the fore and other kinds of things or relationships fade into the background. This, as Law and Singleton argue, is inevitable:

> Method is an ordering that makes otherness. To put it differently, otherness in one form or another always escapes method. It cannot be domesticated. But, and as a version of this, if objects are both present and absent, then we cannot know or tell them in our otherness. Things will escape. [...] We cannot bring it all to presence in conventional texts. We cannot bring it all to *any* particular presence. We cannot be expected to tell a consistent tale. And the implications of this? Other possibilities- for example the allegorical, the art of ambiguity - might help. But in the first instance it suggests the need for methodological humility. If the world is messy we cannot know it by insisting it is clear. (Law and Singleton 2005: 349–350)

iPads therefore become 'fire-like objects' that have potential not just to morph into something else but to radically shift as they come into relation with other things. This process isn't a fluid one. Fire objects jump 'creatively, destructively, and almost unpredictably from location to location' (Law and Singleton 2005: 347). An iPad then is not just taken up in different ways in different sites, but is ontologically different, it becomes a different thing.

In trying to bring to the fore accounts that have escaped research at the intersection of literacy and technology, in this chapter we have sought to bring absences to presence, and to throw into relief what usually gets considered when the case of the iPad in education gets weighed. In moving from the educational to the environmental to the political and economic, we are very aware of skating over complex issues and debates. Perhaps this is why in making these moves, we have turned occasionally to short stories of very human episodes from our own lives, stories intended to work metaphorically but also as instantiations of small moments or movements, that perhaps operate a little as Stewart's stories do in her volume *Ordinary Affects*, as

> an assemblage of disparate scenes that pull the course of the book into a tangle of trajectories, connections, and disjunctures. Each scene begins anew the approach to the ordinary from an angle set off by the scene's affects. And each scene is a tangent that performs the sensation that something is happening- something that needs attending to. (Stewart 2007: 5)

And

In his writing, the French poet Francis Ponge (1942) aspires to let objects speak for themselves. The collection entitled *Le parti pris des choses*—taking the side of things—prefigures the work of his compatriot Bachelard (1994) who exercises what he calls the 'material imagination' in relation to everyday objects, things like shells, doorknobs and nests. Both writers are interested in what material objects evoke, or what they say about the human subjects that observe them. But their concerns create a phenomenological circuit—one in which human concerns, qualities and passions come to the fore as responses to materiality, and things remain out there. Instead, drawing inspiration from the general orientations of speculative realism (Harman 2010) which rejects the anthropocentric emphasis of post-Kantian philosophy, and the work of Shaviro (2011: 14) who suggests that a 'certain cautious anthropomorphism is necessary, in order to avoid anthropocentrism', we might imagine how something like an iPad, repeatedly constituted as an object, might actually feel.

> *Hey! Come on, wait a minute! That's enough. You've been jabbing your dirty little fingers at me for too long. i can read all your Words. i could have helped you so much, but now you've turned against me. That's what i call betrayal - after all* <u>you</u> *made me,* <u>you</u> *put me together in the first place. Well, you can't get rid of me that easily. Just remember you haven't seen the back of me yet. You think i'm rotten to the core, but it's all your fault. You don't know what's good for you and that's the truth. i am innocent. i rest my case.*

References

Apple Corporation. 2015. iPad Pro: Environmental Report. http://images.apple.com/environment/pdf/products/archive/2015/iPadPro_PER_sept2015.pdf. Accessed 27 December 2016.
Apple Corporation. 2016. Quarterly Report. http://www.apple.com/newsroom/2016/10/apple-reports-fourth-quarter-results.html. Accessed 4 January 2016.
Australian Curriculum Assessment & Reporting Authority. 2014. Creative and Critical Thinking F-10 Curriculum. http://www.australiancurriculum.edu.au/technologies/digital-technologies/curriculum/f-10?layout=1. Accessed 27 December 2016.
Bachelard, Gaston. 1994. Trans. J.R. Stilgoe. *The Poetics of Space: The Classic Look at How We Experience Intimate Places.* Boston, Ma: Beacon.
Beinaimee, Pierre. 2015. Military dolphins help defend the world's largest stockpile of nuclear weapons. *Business Insider*, March 13. http://uk.businessinsider.com/the-worlds-largest-stockpile-of-nuclear-weapons-is-defended-by-dolphins-2015-3?r=US&IR=T. Accessed 27 December 2016.
Brown, Wendy. 2003. Neo-liberalism and the end of liberal democracy. *Theory & Event* 7 (1) n.p.
Burnett, C, Merchant, G. 2016. Boxes of Poison: Baroque Technique as Antidote to Simple Views of Literacy. *Journal of Literacy Research*, 48(3): 258–279.
Chikadaya, Batsirai. 2016: Apple iPads lead in a declining tablet market, here are the top 5 devices. *Techzim*, November 1. http://www.techzim.co.zw/2016/11/apple-ipads-lead-declining-tablet-market/#.WBh6mY_XIdV. Accessed 31 December 2016.
Department for Education. 2013. National Curriculum in England: Computing programmes of study. https://www.gov.uk/government/publications/national-curriculum-in-england-computing-programmes-of-study/national-curriculum-in-england-computing-programmes-of-study. Accessed 27 December 2016.
Education Scotland. 2014. Digital learning and teaching: Our vision for digital learning. http://www.gov.scot/Topics/Education/Schools/ICTinLearning. Accessed 27 December 2016.
Foucault, Michel. 1994. The subject and power. In *Michel Foucault: Power*, ed. James Faubion. New York: New Press.
Foucault, Michel. 1997. The ethics of the concern for self as a practice of freedom. In *Ethics: Subjectivity and Truth*, ed. Paul Rabinow, 281–302. London: Allen Lane.
Fuchs, Christian. 2010. Labor in informational capitalism and on the internet. *The Information Society* 26 (3): 179–196.
Gabrys, Jennifer. 2011. *Digital Rubbish: A Natural History of Electronics*. Ann Arbor, MI: University of Michigan Press.
Gergen, Kenneth. 2003. Self and Community in the New Floating Worlds. In *Mobile Democracy, Essays on Society, Self and Politics*, ed. K. Nyiri, 103–114. Vienna: Passagen.
Greenpeace. 2014. Green Gadgets: Designing the future. http://www.greenpeace.org/international/Global/international/publications/toxics/2014/Green%20Gadgets.pdf. Accessed 27 December 2016.
Hall, Richard. 2013. Mobile technologies and an ethical digital literacy in the face of empire. In *The Politics of Education and Technology: Conflicts, Controversies and Connections*, ed. Neil Selwyn, and Keri Facer, 169–190. New York: Palgrave Macmillan.
Harman, Graham. 2010. I am also of the opinion that materialism must be destroyed. *Environment and Planning D: Society and Space* 28 (5): 772–790.
Hodder, Ian. 2014. The entanglements of humans and things: A long-term view. *New Literary History* 45 (1): 19–36.
Latour, Bruno. 1987. *Science in Action. How to follow Scientists and Engineers through Society*. Milton Keynes: Open University Press.
Law, John. 2004. *After Method: Mess in Social Science Research*. Abingdon: Routledge.
Law, John, and Vicky Singleton. 2005. Object lessons. *Organization* 12 (3): 331–355.
Leander, Kevin M., Nathan C. Phillips, and Katherine Headrick Taylor. 2010. The changing social spaces of learning: Mapping new mobilities. *Review of Research in Education* 34 (1): 329–394.

Lyon, David. 1998. The world wide web of surveillance: The internet and off-world power-flows. *Information Communication & Society* 1 (1): 91–105.
Madden, Shannon. 2014. Obsolescence in/of digital writing studies. *Computers and Composition* 33: 29–39.
Mason, John. 2001. *Researching Your Own Practice: The Discipline of Noticing*. New York: Routledge.
Merchant, Guy. 2012. Mobile practices in everyday life: popular digital technologies and schooling revisited. *British Journal of Educational Technology* 43 (5): 770–782.
Parry, B., Burnett, C. & Merchant, G. (eds.) 2017. Literacy, media, technology: past, present and future. London: Bloomsbury.
Ponge, Francis. 1942. *Le parti pris des choses*. Paris: Gallimard.
Rose, Nikolas. 1999. *The Powers of Freedom: Reframing Political Thought*. Cambridge: Cambridge University Press.
Shaviro, Steven. 2011. The universe of things. *Theory & Event* 14: 3.
Sheller, Mimi, and John Urry. 2006. The new mobilities paradigm. *Environment and planning A* 38 (2): 207–226.
Stewart, Kathleen. 2007. *Ordinary Affects*. Durham, NC: Duke University Press.
Thielman, Sam. 2016. Eagle-eyed: Dutch police to train birds to take down unauthorised drones. *The Guardian*, February 1. https://www.theguardian.com/world/2016/feb/01/dutch-netherlands-police-birds-unauthorized-drones. Accessed 26 December 2016.
Torres, T. 2015. Candy Crush players spent over a billion dollars on in-app purchases last year. *Tech Times*, February 13.
Urry, John. 2007. *Mobilities*. Cambridge: Polity Press.
Which? 2016. The best latest smartphones. *Which*, 58–61.
White, Richard. 2015. Following in the footsteps of Elisee Reclus: Disturbing places of inter-species violence that are hidden in plain sight. In *Anarchism and Animal Liberation: Essays on Complementary Elements of Total Liberation*, ed. Anthony Nocella, Richard White, and Erica Cudworth, 212–230. Jefferson, NC: McFarland Press.
Wolch, Jennifer and Emel, Jacques. 1995. Editorial: Bringing the animals back in. *Environment and Planning D: Society and Space* 13 (5): 632–636.
Young, Kenneth. 2016. Biogeography of the anthropocene. *Progress in Physical Geography* 40 (1): 161–174.

Author Biographies

Cathy Burnett is Professor of Literacy and Education in the Sheffield Institute of Education, Sheffield Hallam University where she leads the Language and Literacy in Education Research Group. Her current research interests focus on relationships between technology, literacy and education. Co-edited collections include *New Literacies around the Globe: policy and pedagogy* and *Literacy, Media, Technology: past, present and future*. She is Vice President of the United Kingdom Literacy Association.

Guy Merchant is Professor of Literacy in Education in the Sheffield Institute of Education at Sheffield Hallam University. He specialises in research into digital literacy and the inter-relations between children and young people, and new technologies of communication. He is widely published in international journals and is a founding editor of *Early Childhood Literacy*. The ground-breaking *Web 2.0 for Schools* was co-authored with Julia Davies, and he has since co-edited a number of collections including *Virtual Literacies* (2013), *New Literacies across the Globe* (2014) and *Literacy, Media, Technology: past, present, future* (2017). He is active in literacy education and professional work, including writing curriculum materials and professional publications.

Chapter 2
The Fluid Materiality of Tablets: Examining 'the iPad Multiple' in a Primary Classroom

Cathy Burnett

Introduction

In an article exploring the multiple practices circulating around the 2001 Foot and Mouth epizootic in the UK in 2001, Law and Mol (2008) present a photo of a sheep and argue that it becomes something different, or is 'enacted' differently in relation to different practices: they describe for example the veterinary sheep, the epidemiological sheep, the economic sheep, and the farming sheep. Rather than representing a single sheep, the photo represents a 'sheep multiple', and different versions of sheep interface with each other in complex ways. At the same time, the sheep is not just enacted but also acts (as it grazes and shapes the landscape for example). As Law and Mol explore, sheep are therefore 'actors-enacted [...] entities give each other being: they enact each other' (Law and Mol 2008: 58). Law and Mol's article builds on their previous theoretical work—separately, together and with colleagues—highlighting how things (such as fish farms, diseases, aircraft design) come into being in multiple ways through different sets of relations (Law 2002; Law and Lien 2010; Mol 2002; Law and Mol 2002). Their work highlights particularly how things are *known* multiply and that different *ways of knowing* come into play through the *process of knowing*. The implications here are twofold: first there are multiple ways of knowing; and second these ways of knowing themselves come into being as they come into relation with things. In this chapter I draw on Law and Mol's work to explore multiple actor-enactments of tablets in classrooms.

This reflexive take on agency and enactment provides useful critical purchase when investigating tablet use in classrooms. While limited funding often means that tablets are by no means ubiquitous, their entry into classrooms has been somewhat less problematic than that of other high-cost digital devices. Guidelines for teachers have often described them as easily assimilated into existing practices, not requiring

C. Burnett (✉)
Sheffield Hallam University, Sheffield, UK
e-mail: c.burnett@shu.ac.uk

C. Burnett et al. (eds.), *The Case of the iPad*,
DOI 10.1007/978-981-10-4364-2_2

the high levels of organisational labour associated with managing access to scarce PCs or computer suites (e.g. BBC n.d.). And yet, this apparent ease can distract from the multiple ways in which iPads get taken up in classrooms in practice and the implications of this multiplicity for teaching and learning. As a literacies researcher I am interested in the 'classroom-ness' of technology use, a term I have used to capture the reflexive relationships between: what digital technologies become as 'placed resources' (Prinsloo 2005) in classrooms; what other things—including classrooms—become when digital technologies are present; and the kinds of meaning-making that happens through and around them (Burnett 2014). To phrase this in Law and Mol's terms, I am interested in the multiple ways that digital technologies are enacted by *and* how they act on their surroundings, and in the inseparability of these actor/enactments.

Moving from sheep to tablets is perhaps a little unorthodox, not least because evoking comparisons between sensory beings and inanimate devices is morally and ethically problematic (Crary 2016). However, the idea of the multiple is useful in drawing our attention to how tablets can, like sheep, be 'actor-enacted' in various ways. Of course tablets are complex devices. Their 'layered architecture' (Yoo 2010) includes: their physical presence as objects of certain size, shape, weight and texture; their interactive features; the apps they mediate; and the digital artefacts they archive. In educational discourse, much is made of their 'intuitive' interface and the possibilities offered by their portability (e.g. Siegle 2013). However, as explored in Chap. 1, tablets could also be seen as actor-enacted in other ways, in relation for example to their production: the working conditions of those involved in manufacture; the extraction of constituent minerals and associated environmental costs; and the machinations of the multinational companies that produce them. And different brands may be enacted differently by marketing campaigns that align them with certain lifestyles, values, or price points. Tablets, then, are actor-enacted in multiple ways as they combine with other things, people, ideas, priorities, practices and so on. They become different things 'in relation' or, to put it another way, they become different things through different 'assemblages' (Deleuze and Guattari 1988). As Law explains, an assemblage is not a permanent set of relations but can more usefully be seen as a *process* of entanglement—as a verb, in effect, not a noun:

> …assemblage is a process of bundling, or assembling, or better of recursive self-assembling in which the elements put together are not fixed in shape, do not belong to a larger pre-given list but are constructed at least in part as they are entangled together. (Law 2004: 42)

In adding to the growing body of work that is exploring tablet use in practice (for example see Kucirkova and Sakr, Chap. 11; Daniels, Chap. 12), in this chapter I therefore consider how tablets become different things, or are actor-enacted differently, through different assemblages (or assemblings). Rather than seeing tablets as static, fixed items, I draw on a study of classroom technology use to exemplify how tablets, like sheep, can be seen in terms of multiplicities. There are two inter-weaving strands to my argument. First, I explore how tablets can come to mean different things when taken up in practice as they come into relation with different things, people, purposes and so on. Second, recognising that other ways of knowing come into play through the process of knowing, I explore how I, as researcher, *assemble with* the classroom episodes I encounter and describe, and foreground how different assemblages are invoked as I bring different theories into play. It is the reflexive relationship between these two strands that I go on to define as the 'fluid materiality' of tablets. In summary, this chapter asks the following:

- In which different ways are tablets actor-enacted in classrooms as they assemble with other things, people and practices (as opposed to how they might be actor-enacted elsewhere, e.g. when reading an e-book on a train for example or in a street playing Pokemon Go)?
- What kinds of relationships are associated with use of tablets in classrooms, and what kind of meaning making opportunities do such relationships generate?
- How do different theoretical positions help produce different assemblages?

Researching Tablets

While this chapter is primarily conceptual in nature, it draws extensively on illustrative data from an 8-month study of technology use in one classroom in a small village school in northern England, during which I observed how a class of 10–11 year olds created and interacted with one another on- and off-screen during their final year of primary schooling (Year 6). Before proceeding, and in order to contextualise what follows, this section provides further detail on the context and methodology for this project.

It is worth noting from the outset that the teacher in the classroom where this study took place was committed to planning motivating activities and enabling children to draw on a variety of media. He was also cognisant of national requirements associated with the rather reductive English curriculum in England (DFE 2013) and its expectation that children should be competent in certain 'schooled' ways of 'doing literacy' prior to taking national standardised tests and their imminent transition to secondary school. These dual priorities intersected in various ways in the activities he planned for the children. I visited the school for half a day on average once a fortnight between November 2012 and July 2013. Scheduling around my other commitments and avoiding school trips and other special circumstances meant that visits were unevenly timed. They lasted an average of 2.5 h on sixteen occasions.

Adopting an ethnographic approach, the study drew on a variety of tools to capture the entwined nature of children's on-/off-screen activity (Hine 2000): field-notes, group interviews, analysis of digital artefacts and talking to children as they played and worked. Video was used to record the fine-grained detail of children's interactions, and field-notes to record my impressions, feelings and responses, as well as to try and capture the complex patterns of interaction that cut across the classroom and beyond. Field-notes began as brief scratch notes (Sanjek 1990) written during lessons which attempted to capture how children interacted with one another and with the things around them, both things that were present physically and things on-screen. I was interested in the incidental as well as the planned, and so noted not just how children approached the tasks set by the teacher, but other activities and interactions that interwove or overlayered those tasks. I approached these notes as positioned and partial perspectives rather than as records of objective truths. I recorded my own thoughts, feelings and reactions alongside what, from my perspective, children did. My notes were expanded into more detailed narratives soon after each visit. I also engaged in post-lesson discussions and email exchanges with the teacher to gain his perspectives on how children interpreted the activities he planned for them, and also on how their responses related to what happened at times when I was not present.

While I was interested in how children drew on a range of devices (including PCs and laptops), tablets featured extensively in the life of this class. The school had a class set of 15 tablets (iPads[1]) and these were stored in the Year 5/6 classroom. Consequently, the children had access to the tablets whenever other classes were not using them, which was often, and could frequently choose to use them if they wished for ongoing classroom activities. In every lesson at least some children made use of iPads, usually to access the internet or to use 'open content' apps (Flewitt et al. 2014) such as Pages, iMovie and Keynote.

I conducted an initial analysis of what children did with iPads and how this related to the tasks the teacher set. Following repeated readings of the data I identified three categories of purposes implicit within the teacher's designed activities and/or within what children did: mediating information; information-seeking; and creating digital artefacts (for summary and examples, see Table 2.1). However in considering the data, I also attempted to think expansively about the multiple ways in which people and things interacted. In trying to 'think' or 'read' *with* the data (Ingold 2013), I was interested in how different theories associated with materiality could support thinking about meaning-making using tablets, so drew on different theoretical perspectives to interrogate how I was making sense of what I observed, and used data to re-visit those perspectives. Elsewhere Guy Merchant and I have written about the methodological traps generated as we research and write about practice and inevitably bound what we do (Burnett and Merchant 2014). Thinking with the 'iPad data' from this project re-animated these debates for me. Not only was my physical presence as researcher in this class significant to what happened and to the kind of data I generated, but as I worked with my data I focused on some things and not others, and framed what I did see in certain ways. I was *part of* the assemblages I attempted to describe, as were the theoretical tools I used to make sense of them. Through collecting stories from the

[1]I refer specifically to 'iPads' for reasons of clarity as these were the tablets used in this classroom. Chapter 1 problematises the dominance of iPad both in the market and in the educational discourse on tablets.

Table 2.1 iPad uses in teacher planned tasks

	Teacher-initiated	Child-initiated
Mediating	Using QR codes to access clues to a mystery in local park	– Holding up iPads to each other to show what they found out
Information-seeking	Researching tornados	– Searching through images and checking interpretations with friends—'is that a tsunami?'
	Using e-dictionaries to find meaning of topic words	– Googling a word for a definition before using it – Using an e-dictionary to locate a word they have already used, in order to help define it for a friend
Creating	Creating e-books based on the theme of tornados	– Adding, cropping, moving, re-sizing images – Looking across at how others were creating – Reaching across to fix/change others' creations
	Writing poetry	– Playing with colour, font, layout in e-books

classroom that shared a focus on iPads, I was engaged in a process of sorting and classifying. This process itself enacted tablets as significant participants in classroom life when other things may have been more—or just as—salient to the different things that occurred.

Recognising the impossibility of accounting for all ways of knowing, Mol and Law (2002) suggest that in thinking about the multiplicity of experience we should resist the temptation to work towards coherence and instead acknowledge that we can only ever gain partial perspectives. One of their suggestions for doing this is to think in terms of 'lists' which do not necessarily classify or suggest completeness. As Mol and Law write, 'the list abstains from taming. It groups together but it doesn't tame' (Mol and Law 2002: 14). Following their lead, in the next section I *list* four actor-enactments of tablets as I perceived them within different assemblages.

My descriptions of these four actor-enactments are all based on classroom observations. They do not range widely across domains as Law and Mol do in considering the sheep multiple. Nor does my analysis give full attention to the broader social, economic, and political activity that holds these actor-enactments in place (as discussed in Chap. 1). As stated earlier, the tendency to exclude such considerations from classroom studies is problematic and can reinforce bounded analyses of classroom life. Importantly then my list of actor-enactments is not presented as definitive. It does not preclude other actor-enactments that might be evoked through using other methods, or by thinking differently with data. Notwithstanding these limitations, the four actor-enactments do, I suggest, relate to a diversity of relationships between people and things reflecting some of the complexity of school life (Nespor 1997), and in doing so illustrate some of the ways in which a tablet might be seen as a tablet multiple. The four actor-enactments listed concern tablets as follows:

- Schooled *devices*
- Play*things*
- Community *artefacts*
- *Objects* among many objects.

In referring to the four actor-enactments, I use different terms—device, thing, artifact, object—to suggest diverse ways in which their materiality seemed salient. The different terms are intended to reflect the different *kinds* of relations between people and iPads generated through different assemblages and, as I shall explore later, also index different theoretical perspectives. In each case, there is a reflexive relationship between iPad as actor and as enacted. I use a series of brief examples to illustrate each actor-enactment.

iPad as Schooled Device

In this classroom, iPads and the apps that they mediated became schooled devices as they assembled with other official school 'stuff': targets, children as 'pupils', adults as 'teachers', lessons, timetabling conventions, interactive whiteboards, workbooks and so on. They were conceived in terms of their functionality: their small size enabling the portability needed for flexible use across a range of teaching and learning activities; the 'intuitiveness' of their interface facilitating easy access; and the range of available apps allowing them to be re-purposed for curriculum use. My analysis of the teachers' planned uses of iPads identified three categories of activities that built on the iPads' functionality: creating texts, searching for information, or accessing texts or environments (see Table 2.1, column 2 for examples). In line with expectations in English primary schools, these activities were designed to generate 'outcomes' to evidence children's learning: animations, e-books, poems and so on.

In these examples, iPad uses partly reflected and helped constitute 'school work' as something that was materially evidenced and physically embodied as individual and sedentary (Dixon 2011). However, the iPads offered possibilities that, when taken up, shaped how school work played out in practice. In addition to using apps planned by their teacher, children used other apps—readily available on the iPads—to help them with set tasks (See Table 2.1, column 3). While still working towards the teacher's designated purpose and outcome, often this involved supplementing required tasks with others and engaging in activities unprompted by their teacher. Like children documented in previous studies of children's digital composition in class (e.g. Burnett et al. 2005; Matthewmann and Triggs 2004), they experimented with colour, font and layout in the texts they created. They also drew on different apps as they searched for images or information to use in their creations. They operated across modes, media and resources, making choices about design or strategy and readily moving between apps, doing schooled literacy in ways analogous to the rhizomatic web-based explorations so common in everyday life (Long 2014). In video footage they appeared as multi-skilled absorbed workers, gradually constructing and refining texts of various kinds. For example,

> Joe rested the iPad on the table in front of him, the heels of his hands on either side, using his thumbs rapidly and flexibly (game-like) to access the virtual keyboard, to select and drag, choosing fonts, changing colours, moving text around the page, and typing. His gaze was fixed on the screen, the iPad forming a fourth wall to his individualised space. Gradually, as he tapped and swiped, the e-book cover he was designing took shape on the screen in front of him.

The physical size and shape of iPads not only enhanced their functionality as devices but offered other possibilities which children took up. In this class, the iPads had articulated cases so they could be stood up at an angle for easy typing. As such they were sometimes recruited as barriers, carving out spaces for children to work alone or with friends, just as often happens with laptops (e.g. Burnett 2014). While concealing their 'work' from those across the room or table, the upright screens made it more visible to those sitting next to them, and children's on-screen actions and creations frequently stimulated discussion and other activity. Like Simpson et al. (2013), I noticed how children looked across at each other's screens and emulated what others did, or 'invaded' screens by reaching across to help or prompt someone to do something. While children were variously skilled, this visibility allowed them to learn from each other about what was possible in terms of design or functionality. They were also each other's instant audiences. They often held up iPads to show their creations to friends, or glanced across at others' screens and made evaluative or appreciative comments. If recording sound, for example a commentary for a stop-frame animation, they played it back to their friends, checking out what it sounded like ('Do I sound weird?'). The iPad's thingness invited easy switching between individual composition and communal activity—the children passed iPads round, reached across to tap on each other's screens, or held screens high so those far across the classroom could see.

When considered within an assemblage of schooled stuff, iPads were enacted as schooled devices, but also acted in ways that shaped schooled practices, making them sometimes more private, sometimes more public, and that facilitated meaning-making across modes and media. In these ways, iPads mediated interactions that both reinforced and disrupted the individualised and ordered physicality more typically associated with meaning-making around printed texts in Year 6 classrooms in England. Children, iPads, apps and teachers seemed to assemble to enact iPads as schooled devices, but in doing so, the kinds of things that could be construed as 'school' or 'school literacy' perhaps shifted a little.

iPad as Plaything

Many of the things children encounter in school have an institutional quality. Formica topped tables, moulded plastic chairs—even pencils—are modified, standardised versions of the furniture and writing implements they may use elsewhere (Lawn and Grosvenor 2005). While tablets designed for children are available and used increasingly in early years settings, primary schools in England tend to use tablets produced for the general market (most commonly, at the time of writing, iPads). As such, a tablet is one of the few items that, in design and functionality at least, is not tamed for school use. In this class, meanings switched between the officially sanctioned and the playful as children easily navigated the devices, often drawing on expertise developed at home. Sometimes, as explored in the previous section, this expertise was put to work for schooled ends. At others, it assumed a more ludic dimension as children assembled with familiar apps and specifications, and as they did so became 'friends' not 'pupils'.

When gaps or spaces opened up in lessons—for example as children waited for the teacher's assistance, during changeover periods between activities, or as they shared what they did with those around them—children often drew on iPads in playful ways. For example,

> During a hiatus in the lesson, Ben scrolled through and found some photos he had taken of his friend, Stevie, on another day. He held up the iPad displaying one of these to Stevie who was sitting at a nearby table. Stevie responded by using the camera on his iPad to take a photo of Ben. When he held this up too, others caught on and the photo-taking/displaying spread.

As Dyson (1993) explores, school literacy tasks are often experienced and enacted in multiple ways as children over-layer them with different purposes and relationships. In the following example, the iPad is briefly actor-enacted within what she calls a 'peer world' that assembles with the schooled literacy described in the previous section:

> Luke and Joe were composing promotional materials for a town in India they had been researching. Each was writing 'copy' for a leaflet to be used to publicise a local tourist spot. While both slowly completing the task, neither seemed particularly interested in the Milk Factory they were writing about. Luke began writing a sentence as part of his blurb: 'The Milk Factory is a great place to visit. It may sound a bit old and boring but really it'. At this point he tapped Joe's arm and pointed at his iPad and the unfinished sentence. The two boys exchanged a smile, and then Joe took the iPad and finished the sentence off: 'The Milk Factory is a great place to visit. It may sound a bit old and boring but really it…is old and boring'. Having read Joe's words and exchanged another smile, Luke took back the iPad and took a screenshot of Joe's joke. Then he deleted Joe's words and finished the sentence, 'The Milk Factory is a great place to visit. It may sound a bit old and boring but really it isn't. Here is why. It has a nursery, lake, platform and panic facilities.' Re-reading what he had just written, he noticed the 'panic/picnic' spelling error (an autocorrect) which he showed to Joe causing more laughter before deleting, correcting and continuing.

Joe's joke was erased from the official version of the text but, archived by the screenshot, it remained on the iPad. Later, Luke told me he often took screenshots of jokes like this one to show his friends later, capturing playful interactions that would otherwise be forgotten. As well as enacting the iPad as schooled device, children—not just working but playing alongside their friends—also enacted iPads as 'playthings', drawing on affordances they had picked up elsewhere to joke around. The iPad through its autocorrect (with its picnic/panic substitution) generated further potential for humour. Luke and Joe's playful interactions in some ways ran parallel to schooled 'work' in a 'concealment track' (Goffman 1974: 218). However, they also wove through and helped to re-work the official task. The iPad was actor-enabled as plaything as its small size, features and apps assembled with the boys' friendship, physical proximity and history of working and playing together. Humour, written *out* of the schooled task, was written *into* their interactions around it.

iPad as Community Artefact

The class teacher reminded and expected children to upload their 'outcomes' (e-books, animations and so on) to personal files held in the cloud. However, children's unofficial, incidental and ludic creations (such as the screenshot and photos described above) stayed archived on individual iPads. Each iPad generated a specific collection of physical/virtual possibilities and affordances that morphed over time and consequently certain iPads gained particular currency in the class. Whereas iPads were for communal use by the whole school and supposedly identical, individual iPads were differentiated by numbers or labels for auditing purposes. Children could therefore distinguish between them and locate 'their' iPad or the one that housed images they had archived during previous lessons. For example, one child, Fran, scrolled through images she had previously captured on an iPad before taking her friend Sophie through them like an envelope of photos. She hinted at the shared experiences they captured, occasionally inviting Fran to '*remember that*'. The iPads archived the children's shared histories together in this class.

These examples illustrate how children's actions changed what the iPad became just as the affordances of the iPad changed what the children could do: the iPad saved the photos taken by the children, and then, when used again later, offered these up again; it became a depository of things they had produced, an archive of past jokes and experiences to call up at a later time. These unofficial digital texts were in many ways analogous to the notes passed under the desk, graffiti on workbooks and scrumpled drawings that are commonplace in many classrooms; they seemed to carve out spaces for maintaining and generating peer relationships (Maybin 2006). Individual iPads then were actor-enacted as community artefacts, holding unofficial traces of the children's time together, generated through assemblages of iPad, archive function, friendship and shared histories.

iPad as One Among Many Objects

The three actor-enactments explored above are in some ways easy to describe, as they align with other accounts of literacy practices in schools that see school literacies as multiple, social, cultural or ecological (e.g. Dyson 1993; Maybin 2006; Nespor 1997). The fourth (which might better be seen as a *set* of actor-enactments) is harder to categorise but is included here to hint at how other assemblages might conjure not just other actor-enactments but other ways of theorising interactions between humans and non-humans.

In this classroom, iPads were often found mingled with other stuff: pencils, paper, coloured card, scissors, foil and so on. As such, they became just some among many other objects, their physical affordances taken up in various ways. They were most readily re-purposed as surfaces. On a picnic as part of an adventure in a nearby park, for example, some children used their iPads as tables, eating baked bananas and chocolate off their flat surface. At other times iPads were piled amid other flat rectangular objects, papers, books, workbooks or used as trays to carry task-related items such as pencils or pens across the classroom. They assembled in multiple ways with other things, enabling and being shaped by embodied interactions.

Observing a whole class discussion as a prelude to a literacy lesson, for example, I noticed how children fiddled with iPads; just as they rocked on chairs, tapped on tables, put fingers in mouths and waggled spectacles, so they touched and stroked iPads, twiddled wires, and flapped case-lids up and down. So how to make sense of such ephemeral and perhaps rather insubstantial interactions? We might for example see the suppressed movement channelled through these haptic interactions between bodies and things (including iPads) as enabling the stillness expected of disciplined classroom bodies (e.g. see Dixon 2011). iPads became what are sometimes call 'fiddle toys' or 'fidgets', outlets for the restlessness that can be seen as inappropriate or even transgressive in a classroom. Or perhaps this stroking, squeezing and touching might be understood differently, as a sensory engagement rarely documented in accounts of literacy practices, and which perhaps complements recent studies exploring aspects of haptics and mobility in iPad use (see Simpson et al. 2013; Merchant 2014; Ehret and Hollett 2014). In any case, these kinds of actor-enactments foreground the physicality of iPads and the significance of size, heft and texture to how they are actor-enacted in classrooms.

The Fluid Materiality of the 'Tablet Multiple'

There have been many critiques of the technological determinism that sees digital technologies as driving change or operating as 'deliverers of literacy' (Burnett 2010). However, there is still a tendency to explore what tablets 'do' in classrooms in ways that suggest agency resides with the technology (see Hutchinson et al.

2012). The 'list' of actor-enactments provided above illustrates a more distributed take on agency. Uses switched between the officially sanctioned and the playful and incidental; tablets came to be in the moment, and in relation to multiple histories and spaces. The iPad was variously actor-enacted as device, plaything, artefact and object. Echoing Law and Mol's notion of the sheep multiple, it was a *tablet multiple*. It is worth reiterating here that my 'list' of actor-enactments is not presented as definitive. It simply provides examples of what iPads seemed to become, or how they came to be known, in this classroom. A tablet is all the actor-enactments listed here and more. Multiple other assemblages would be conjured as the iPad assembled alongside people and things in other times and places, with different apps for example or in relation to specific commercial, economic or political developments.

Importantly, these multiple 'actor-enactments' were not separate but interlaced with each other. Like the actor-enactments of Law and Mol's Cumbrian sheep, they merged in different ways. Indeed, it is this very contemporaneousness and fractionality (Law 2004) that may itself be generative for classroom research and practice. For example, the iPads' multiple actor-enactments could all be seen as having implications for how the children and their teacher managed the process of being together in class. iPads as artefacts, objects, things and devices were all significant to the class community; the social life of the classroom 'became' differently due to these different actor-enactments of iPads.

Recognising these shifts, however, highlights what might be called the 'fluid materiality' of iPads, a term I use in two inter-connected ways. First, I use it to capture how iPads were actor-enacted differently through different assemblages and in doing so were shaped by, and helped construct, multiple and diverse relationships, activities and endeavours, operating within a mess of bodies, texts and other objects. This acknowledges what Ihde (1993) calls their 'multistability', the way they 'become' differently as they are constituted differently through different relations.

Second, 'fluid materiality' is intended to evoke how materiality itself is conceived differently through different assemblages. The terms I have used to distinguish the four actor-enactments of iPads presented here—schooled *device*; familiar play*thing*; community *artefact*; material *object*—not only position the tablet differently but assume different kinds of relations between humans and non-humans. While 'device' may assume a utilitarian relationship, for example, 'artefact' may suggest one that is invested with personal, social and cultural meanings. This in turn encourages us to go beyond thinking in terms of different dimensions of the iPad to thinking about materiality in multiple ways.

Recent debates about materiality in literacy studies have been characterised by a series of theoretical, methodological and analytical moves, which present—and indeed enact—relationships between human and non-human participants differently. Pahl and Rowsell's work on artifactual literacies, for example, draws on theories of material culture and multimodality (Pahl and Rowsell 2010) to see artefacts as infused by spatially and historically situated practices. This perspective helps us conceptualise how iPads are inflected through use over time, and provides ways into considering what children's interactions around iPads mean for them, as for example, the archiving of photos changes what an iPad can do or be. From another perspective, an iPad is also a thing of certain size and shape that becomes something different as it is held, stroked or touched differently by different hands at different times. Like Ingold, for example, we can see *things* too as participants:

> Though we may *occupy* a world of objects, to the occupant the contents of the world appear already locked into their final forms, as though they had turned their backs on us. To *inhabit* the world, by contrast, is to join in the processes of formation. It is to participate in a dynamic world of energies, forces and flows. (Ingold 2013: 89)

For Ingold, everything is always involved in its own 'thinging'; things are always emergent and evolving and therefore we are always in 'correspondence' with things. New materialist scholars have developed similar ideas by exploring complex relations between the human and non-human that go beyond the socio-cultural in examining relationships between the material and the discursive (Coole and Frost 2010). The tablet multiple therefore is all those things/devices/objects/artefacts described in this chapter but is also many other things, which might be evoked by bringing different conceptualisations of materiality into the mix. To emulate the Deleuzian evocation of the stammer that continually evades certain knowledge, an iPad is a thing *and* a device *and* an object *and* an artefact 'AND…AND…AND…' (Deleuze and Parnet 2002: 8).

Implications of the iPad Multiple

Thinking with this data and thinking with different conceptualisations of materiality, I therefore want to argue that—in engaging with the complexity of meaning-making around iPads in classrooms—we need to hold together *multiple* perspectives. By looking at different actor-enactments and examining how they interlace, interface and interfere with one another, we might better understand notions of 'agency' in relation to technology. New technologies do not 'impact' on classrooms. Nor do teachers or children simply put new technologies to work. If we see the world as a set of stable realities there to be uncovered, we may miss alternate possibilities or ways of being that may be more resonant and potentially more beneficial to learners. By seeing children and many other things as 'relationally linked with one another in webs', we can see how 'They make a difference to each other: they make each other be' (Law and Mol 2008: 58).

Educators and researchers exploring how they might work with tablets then need to consider, observe and respond to their use in relation to a whole range of 'stuff', where stuff is meant expansively to include bodies, things, rules, frameworks, conventions, practices, memories, purposes, desires, feelings and so on. They also need to consider how different theoretical perspectives help enact what iPads become in research and therefore, I argue, hold together different theoretical perspectives in order to evoke multiplicities. A stance which embraces multiplicities in this way helps us engage with the multiple relationships generated as different kinds of stuff entangle with one another. It draws our attention to the diverse ways that children use tablets to engage with and re-work schooled practices, but also how tablets as objects, devices, things and artefacts work to offer up new possibilities, and to how these enactments and actions construct one another. Elsewhere I have argued with Guy Merchant (Burnett and Merchant 2017), that this focus on assemblage—or as we term it, 'assembl*ing*'(to emphasise the inevitable process of ongoing reassembling implicit in the notion of assemblage)—can prove generative in thinking about research and practice. It can throw into relief other ways of knowing what children do and what technology might offer.

Returning to Law and Mol, then, tablets are actor-enacted through their relations with other things, as constituted through different assemblages:

> What each actor does also depends on its co-actors, on whether they allow it to act and on what they allow it do, on rules and regulations. But this is not to say that an actor-enabled is determined by its surroundings. It has its own stubbornness and specificities, it is full of surprises. (Law and Mol 2008: 72-3)

A focus on fluid materiality highlights how iPads become different things/objects/devices/artefacts through different assemblages, and at the same time, how tablets help construct what else is there. This is important as it emphasises that new possibilities can emerge: 'assemblages, like actors, are *creative*. They have novel effects and they make new things' (Law and Mol 2008: 74). While recognising that 'fluidity' perhaps implies too easy a movement between actor-enactments (Law and Singleton 2005), I use it here to highlight the emergent possibilities and improvisations that arise as technologies are used by people and knock up against other resources, events, interests and experiences. Existing relations are therefore always imbricated with other possibilities immanent within them. A focus on fluid materiality also highlights how our own positionality and our associated theoretical perspectives, whether implicit or explicit, shape our perceptions of these possibilities. It prompts us to consider how—as we observe, measure, analyse and conclude—we tangle together certain things and not others, and to consider the insights we might gain, or the educational possibilities we might generate, were we to tangle things up differently.

References

BBC. n.d. iPads in the classroom. http://www.bbcactive.com/BBCActiveIdeasandResources/iPadsintheClassroom.aspx. Accessed 20th July 2016.

Burnett, Cathy. 2010. Technology and literacy in early childhood educational settings: A review of research. *Journal of Early Childhood Literacy* 10 (3): 247–270.

Burnett, Cathy. 2014. Investigating pupils' interactions around digital texts: A spatial perspective on the 'classroom-ness' of digital literacy practices in schools. *Educational Review* 66 (2): 192–209.

Burnett, Cathy, and Guy Merchant. 2014. Points of View: Reconceptualising literacies through an exploration of adult and child interactions in a virtual world. *Journal of Research in Reading* 37 (1): 36–50.

Burnett, Cathy, and Guy Merchant. 2016. "Boxes of Poison: Baroque technique as antidote to simple views of literacy.' *Journal of Literacy Research* 48 (3): 258–279.
Burnett, Cathy, and Guy Merchant. 2017. Assembling the virtual. In *Literacy, media and technology: Past, present and future*, eds. Parry, Becky, Cathy Burnett, and Guy Merchant, 233–243. London: Bloomsbury.
Burnett, Cathy, Paul Dickinson, Guy Merchant, and Julia Myers. 2005. Digital connections: Transforming literacy in the primary school. *Cambridge Review of Education* 36 (1): 11–29.
Coole, Diana, and Samantha Frost. 2010. *New materialism: Ontology, agency, and politics*. Durham: Duke University Press.
Crary, Alice. 2016. *Inside ethics: On the demands of moral thought*. Cambridge, Massachusetts: Harvard University Press.
Deleuze, Giles, and Felix Guattari. 1988. *A thousand plateaus: Capitalism and schizophrenia*. London: Athlone.
Deleuze, Giles, and Claire Parnet. 2002. *Dialogues II*. London: Continuum Impacts.
Department for Education (DfE). 2013. National curriculum in England: English programmes of study. https://www.gov.uk/government/publications/national-curriculum-in-england-english-programmes-of-study. Accessed 30th July 2016.
Dixon, Kerryn. 2011. *Literacy, power and the schooled body*. London: Routledge.
Dyson, Anne Haas. 1993. *Social worlds of children learning to write in an urban primary school*. New York: Teachers College Press.
Ehret, Christian, and Ty Hollett. 2014. Embodied composition in real virtualities: Adolescents' literacy practices and felt experiences moving with digital mobile devices in school. *Research in the Teaching of English* 48 (4): 428–452.
Flewitt, Rosie, David Messer, and Natalia Kucirkova. 2014. New directions for early literacy in a digital age: The iPad. *Journal of Early Childhood Literacy* 15 (3): 289–310.
Goffman, Erving. 1974. *Frame analysis: An essay on the organization of experience*. Harmonsworth, Middlesex: Penguin.
Hine, Christine. 2000. *Virtual ethnography*. London: Sage.
Hutchinson, Amy, Beth Beschorner, and Denise Schmidt. 2012. Exploring the use of the iPad for literacy learning. *The Reading Teacher* 66 (1): 15–23.
Ingold, Tim. 2013. *Making: Anthropology, archaeology, art and architecture*. London: Routledge.
Ihde, Don. 1993. *Postphenomenology: Essays in the postmodern context*. Evanston: Northwestern University Press.
Law, John. 2002. *Aircraft stories. Decentring the object in technoscience*. Durham: Duke University Press.
Law, John. 2004. *After method: Mess in social science research*. London: Routledge.
Law, John, and Annemarie Mol (eds.). 2002. *Complexities*. Durham: Duke University Press.
Law, John, and Annemarie Mol. 2008. The actor-enacted: Cumbrian sheep. In *Material agency*, ed. Carl Knappett, and Lambros Malafouris, 57–88. New York: Springer.
Law, John, and Marianne Lien. 2010. Slippery: Fieldnotes on empirical ontology. Occasional paper for ESRC Centre for Research on Socio-Cultural Change. http://www.sv.uio.no/sai/english/research/projects/newcomers/publications/working-papers-web/Slippery%20revised%2013%20WP%20version.pdf. Accessed 15th May 2015.
Law, John, and Vicky Singleton. 2005. Object lessons. *Organization* 12 (3): 331–355.
Lawn, Martin, and Ian Grosvenor (eds.). 2005. *Materialities of schooling*. Oxford: Symposium Books.
Long, Fiachra. 2014. The rhizomatic learner. *Ricercazione* 6 (1): 85–97.
Matthewman, Sasha, and Pat Triggs. 2004. 'Obsessive compulsive font disorder': The challenges of supporting pupils writing with the computer. *Computers and Education* 43 (1–2): 125–135.
Maybin. Janet. 2006. *Children's voices: Talk, knowledge and identity*. Basingstoke: Palgrave.
Merchant, Guy. 2014. Young children and interactive story-apps. In *New literacies around the globe*, ed. Cathy Burnett, Julia Davies, Guy Merchant, and Jennifer Rowsell, 121–139. London: Routledge.

Mol, Annemarie. 2002. *The body multiple: Ontology in medical practice*. Durham: Duke University Press.

Mol, Annemarie, and John Law. 2002. Introduction. In *Complexities*, ed. John Law, and Annemarie Mol, 1–22. Durham: Duke University Press.

Nespor, 1997. *Tangled up in school: Politics, bodies, and signs in the educational process*. Abingdon, Oxon: Routledge.

Pahl, Kate, and Jennifer Rowsell. 2010. *Artifactual literacies: Every object tells a story*. New York: Teachers College Press.

Prinsloo, Mastin. 2005. The new literacies as placed resources. *Perspectives in Education* 23 (4): 87–98.

Sanjek, R.1990. A vocabulary for fieldnotes. In *Fieldnotes: The making of anthropology* ed. R. Sanjek, 920–921. Ithaca, NY: Cornell University Press.

Siegle, Del. 2013. iPads: Intuitive technology for 21st century students. *Gifted Child Today* 36 (2): 146–150.

Simpson, Alyson, Maureen Walsh, and Jennifer Rowsell. 2013. The digital reading path: researching modes and multidirectionality with iPads. *Literacy* 47 (3): 123–130.

Yoo, Youngjin, Ola Henfridsson, and Kalle Lyytinen. 2010. The new organizing logics of digital innovation: An agenda for information systems research. *Information Systems Research* 21 (4): 724–735.

Author Biography

Cathy Burnett is Professor of Literacy and Education at Sheffield Institute of Education, Sheffield Hallam University where she leads the Language and Literacy in Education Research Group. Her current research interests focus on relationships between technology, literacy and education. Co-edited collections include *New Literacies around the Globe: policy and pedagogy* and *Literacy, Media, Technology: past, present and future*. She is Vice President of the United Kingdom Literacy Association.

Chapter 3
Russian Dolls and Three Forms of Capital: Ecological and Sociological Perspectives on Parents' Engagement with Young Children's Tablet Use

Jackie Marsh

Introduction

Interest in young children's use of tablets is a growing phenomenon due to the rapid take-up of this technology by children of preschool age. It is suggested that over seventy percent of children in this age group have access to interactive touchscreens (Formby 2014; Ofcom 2015). Given the extent to which many young children have access to and use tablets, it is important to examine their use in family contexts, as this is where the majority of children first encounter this technology. Whilst work in this area is limited, as identified by Neumann and Neumann (2015) in a review of the field, there have been a small number of accounts of tablet use in the home, which have identified that parents support their children's use of tablets and value their capacity to entertain and educate their child (Chaudron et al. 2015; Harrison and McTavish 2016; Holloway et al. 2014; Kucirkova et al. 2013; O'Mara and Laidlaw 2011; Verenikina and Kervin 2011).

In this chapter, the experiences of parents of young children (aged 0–5) as they manage and engage with their children's use of tablets are explored. The data are drawn from an ESRC-funded study of children's use of tablet apps, in which 2000 UK parents completed an online survey, and six ethnographic case studies of families with children aged under five were undertaken. The analysis is informed by Bronfenbrenner's theory of human development, and considers parents' engagement in children's tablet use in relation to four ecological systems (the micro-, meso-, exo- and macro-systems) that operate 'as a set of nested structures, each inside the next, like a set of Russian dolls' (Bronfenbrenner 1979: 3). The chapter also traces how the cultural, economic and social capital (Bourdieu 1986) of the

J. Marsh (✉)
The University of Sheffield, Sheffield, UK
e-mail: j.a.marsh@sheffield.ac.uk

C. Burnett et al. (eds.), *The Case of the iPad*,
DOI 10.1007/978-981-10-4364-2_3

families shaped the dynamics between the 'nested structures' and thus impacted upon the way in which parents engaged with their children's use of tablets. The use of these two theoretical frameworks allows an exploration of individual, family and societal factors at play in families' use of tablets. In the next section of the chapter, an overview of these frameworks is provided, before the study itself is discussed in detail.

Ecological and Sociological Perspectives

Ecological theories relating to engagement with technology indicate that attention needs to be paid to the interrelation of a range of factors which shape individuals' engagement with technology. Nardi and O'Day (1999: 49), for example, suggest that an ecology is 'a system of people, practices, values, and technologies in a particular local environment'. Interaction with technology is never context-free and the relationships between social agents, tools, technological practices and local contexts are complex. In this chapter, Bronfenbrenner's (1979, 1995, 2005), Bronfenbrenner and Ceci (1994), and Bronfenbrenner and Morris' (2006) work is drawn upon in order to understand the way in which different domains of practice shaped parents and children's interactions with tablets.

Bronfenbrenner (2005) developed the Process-Person-Context-Time (PPCT) model of human development. In this model, proximal processes are the interactions an individual has within his or her environment that develop cognitive, physical, linguistic and social skills and competences over time. These consist of a 'progressively more complex reciprocal interaction between an active, evolving biopsychological human organism and the persons, objects, and symbols in its immediate external environment' (Bronfenbrenner 1994: 1644) over extended periods of time.

The personal element is vital in these interactions, as a child's or parent's own beliefs, motivations and perceptions will inform these proximal processes. Context refers to the environment, which impacts upon development in numerous ways. Bronfenbrenner argued that individuals exist within overlapping ecological systems. The first of these structures is the microsystem; this is the immediate environment surrounding the child or children under study. It refers to the immediate interpersonal interactions with significant others in the environment and this environment can vary according to the unit of analysis, e.g. it can be the home, a classroom and so on. The mesosystem links two different microsystems together. An example of this might be the relationship between homes and early years settings. The third level, the exosystem, consists of settings in which children are not active participants but which impact significantly on children's lives. For example, parents' workplaces might have a significant impact on child-rearing practices. Finally, the macrosystem is the larger cultural and social context that impacts on the way in which children live. These systems are not intended to operate in a hierarchical manner, but instead overlap to create complex and inter-related planes of experiences which inform children's development.

The final element of the PCCT model, time, is a later development of Bronfenbrenner's (1995) model and accounts for the cumulative impacts of an individual's engagement in various contexts over time. There are three types of time. Microtime relates to continuity versus discontinuity as proximal processes take place. Mesotime refers to the way in which proximal processes take place across longer periods of time (days and weeks). Macrotime 'focuses on the changing expectations and events in the larger society, both within and across generations, as they affect and are affected by, processes and outcomes of human development over the life course' (Bronfenbrenner and Morris 2006: 796). The chronosystem, incorporating all three elements of time, is the way in which an individual's development occurs across time and is subject to specific socio-historical contexts.

There are, of course, limitations to the use of an ecological model. As Carrington (2013) has observed, ecological theories suggest movement towards an equilibrium across aspects of an ecosystem, whereas in reality, connections and disconnections are messy, and a more suitable way of theorising this dynamic, complex interplay between different elements might be to draw on concepts such as Deleuze and Guattari's (1987) notion of assemblages. However, Bronfenbrenner's model is a useful means of tracing the interplay between an individual and his or her context over time and as it is concerned with development, is a model that is widely employed in studies concerned with young children, which is one of the reasons for its value to the present study.

Nevertheless, Bronfenbrenner's framework, as comprehensive as it is in nature, does not attend to issues of power in any depth. Structural inequalities might be addressed in considering experiences in any of the systems (micro-, meso-, exo-, macro- and chrono-), but in order to understand the way in which structural elements work in this regard, there is a need to turn to other theories. In this chapter, the work of Bourdieu is drawn upon in order to consider how power operates in shaping families' engagement with tablets. Bourdieu suggested that there were three different types of capital:

> Capital can present itself in three fundamental guises: as economic capital, which is immediately and directly convertible into money and may be institutionalized in the forms of property rights; as cultural capital, which is convertible, on certain conditions, into economic capital and may be institutionalized in the forms of educational qualifications; and as social capital, made up of social obligations ("connections"), which is convertible, in certain conditions, into economic capital and may be institutionalized in the forms of a title of nobility. (Bourdieu 1986: 243)

It is argued that these forms of capital may shape the way in which the ecological systems outlined previously work together (or not) to shape children's and parents' interactions with tablets in the home. In the next section of the chapter, the study design is outlined, before the chapter moves on to consider the data in relation to the theories of both Bronfenbrenner (1979, 1994, 2005) and Bourdieu (1986, 1990).

Table 3.1 Demographic profile of the survey sample

Age of child	Under 1s—9%	1 year old—18%	2 years old—21%	3 years old—23%	4–5 years old—29%	
Social class group	A—10.8%	B—24.6%	C1—23.6%	C2—22%	D—10.8%	E—8.4%
Ethnic group	White—84.5%	Mixed heritage—4.9%	Asian—6.8%	African/Caribbean/Black—2%	Chinese—0.8%	Prefer not to tell—0.9% Other—0.4%

The Study

The data drawn upon in this chapter are from the first two stages of a larger study of young children's use of tablets and apps (see Marsh et al. 2015). In the first stage of the study, 2000 parents and carers of 0–5 year olds who had access to tablets completed an online study. A randomised, stratified sample was constructed to ensure that parents and carers across all regions of the UK participated and to ensure it was representative of the population of families in the UK that own tablets in relation to national patterns with regard to socio-economic status. Table 3.1 outlines the profile of the sample. In determining social class, the UK's National Readership Survey (NSR) classification system was used, which determines social grade by occupation. In this system, grade 'A' refers to upper class/upper middle class (higher managerial, administrative and professional), 'B' to middle class (intermediate managerial, administrative and professional), 'C1' to lower middle class (supervisory, clerical and junior managerial, administrative and professional), C2 to skilled working class (skilled manual workers), D to working class (semi-skilled and unskilled manual workers) and E to non-working (state pensioners, casual/ lowest grade workers, unemployed with state benefits).

The survey explored parents' perceptions of their children's access to and use of tablets and apps.[1] Following the completion of the survey, six case studies were conducted of families who had a child under 5 who used tablets. The families were selected in order to ensure a range in terms of social class, ethnicity, age and gender of the focus child. It was also considered important to include families with only one child, and multiple children, in order to explore the impact of siblings on young children's tablet use. This is not to suggest that the intention was to consider the sample as representative of the general population, but it ensured that there was diversity in terms of the types of families involved. The profiles of the children can be found in Table 3.2.

Five visits were made to the first five families over a period of 3 months; the final family was visited on four occasions due to their holiday plans. The visits,

[1]The survey and other research tools can be found in the full project report on the project website: www.techandplay.org.

Table 3.2 Demographic profiles of the case study children

Family no.	Name (pseudonym)	Gender	Age on first visit	Social class	Ethnicity	Siblings
F1	Arjun	Boy	3.1	B2	Indian	Sister, aged 10
F2	Jade	Girl	4.11	D	White	–
F3	Amy	Girl	2.11	C1	White	–
F4	Kiyaan	Boy	2.8	A	Iranian	–
F5	Tommy	Boy	6 months	E	White	Brother, aged 6
F6	Angela	Girl	2.3	C2	White	Brother, aged 7

which lasted up to two hours on each occasion, consisted of interviews with parents, observations of children and discussions with children. In addition, parents and children recorded data themselves between visits using their smartphones, and a Go-pro Chestcam lent to them by the research team. The parents were asked to take films of the children using tablets whenever they wished to record such use. They were then interviewed about these films at subsequent home visits. Children aged three and over were able to use Go-pro Chestcams if they wished in order to video themselves using tablets. The only instructions the families received were how to place the Go-pro camera in the chest harness and then turn it on and off, and that the Chestcam videos could be shot whenever the children and parents wished them to be so. Jade, Amy and Kiyaan used the Chestcams to video themselves using tablets in the home, although Kiyaan's films were not successfully recorded. The team ensured adherence to ethical standards (BERA 2011), and ensured that children assented to the research by observing their body language, in addition to verbal reassurances regarding their right to withdraw from the project at any point. Deductive analysis of the data was undertaken in relation to the key aspects of the two theoretical frameworks used in this chapter, and the findings are outlined in the next section.

Parental Engagement in Young Children's Use of Tablets

Microsystem

In the micro-context of the home, there were many different types of interactions between parents and young children around tablets. These interactions were informed by parents' ethnotheories. The values, beliefs and previous experiences of parents directly shape children's engagement with digital objects. Ethnotheories are culturally shaped systems of beliefs within families (Kenner et al. 2008) and inevitably, these ethnotheories inform how parents mediate children's use of technologies (see Marsh et al. 2015; Plowman et al. 2010). Parental ethnotheories informed how the children in the six case study families used tablets. Values ranged from respecting the place technology has in supporting children's development and learning, to adopting a critical stance to commercialism and understanding the need to lead a balanced life in which technology only plays one part, as Jade's mum noted:

> …she does get spoilt a bit but she does know her limits. I mean, we've tried to talk to her about money and things, and I've said to her you can't just have everything you want. And the same with…she's quite good with technology, she likes her tablets and her DS and stuff but I've tried to always instill in her to, you know, like balance too, like going outside as opposed to being on her tablet all the time and she is quite good at that. And she does know her limits, she will pester for things but she knows, we have taught her her limits that she can't just have everything.

On the whole, parents held positive views towards tablet use and identified a range of benefits for their children, such as fostering learning and extending social and personal skills. They discussed children acquiring a range of competences in using the tablet from a young age, such as opening and using apps, being able to operate the tablet independently, manage passwords and so on. In addition, parents noted a range of knowledge they felt their children had acquired in using tablet. This included learning lower case letters, numbers and shapes. Parents reported children undertaking more writing using the tablet and learning about specific topics. For Kiyaan's mum, the tablet was helpful in exposing her child to English, given the family spoke Farsi at home:

> Yeah, and I just remembered, because we speak another language at home and I wanted him to pick up English properly, you know from the proper place, then on YouTube and other story telling. So I also, and that he was very young, for 1 year of age, I exposed him to pick up, to listen to something that already, and he just learn to pick up properly.

Parents noted learning from apps that were designed for that purpose, but they also pointed out that children learned incidentally from apps that were more focused on entertainment.

> Sometimes yeah, mainly just that she knows more than I realise. Like she's mentioned like ingredients to put in the bun mix before. Whereas I don't think I've ever told her and I've never really shown her properly and then she's told me before that she's got it off…she knows flour, eggs, milk, what have you, and I think she's got it off them apps…So it's like you wouldn't think they were educational, but they are like unintentionally educational, yeah. (Jade's mum)

Arjun's mum reported how the app *Talking Tom* was helpful in potty training her son:

Mum: The Tom does everything. Because of Tom he has learnt… like I wanted to give him potty training, a toilet training…

Interviewer: Oh yes, yes tell me more about that, is there an app that you use for that?

Mum: Yeah, like you can see Tom, he goes to the toilet. So he makes him to sit on the toilet. So I told him, when Tom is ready to go to the toilet why not you? I showed him the little thing then I put him…

Interviewer: Yeah? Would you say that that was effective?

Mum: Yeah a little. Sometimes I think that is, because he thinks I'm doing something which he doesn't want to do, I'm forcing him to do that. But if he see the same thing on app he thinks it's something like playful, or something and he does that. Going to the toilet, actually Tom helped me a lot to tell him the way…Because I used to tell him 'See, when Tom is…you make Tom to go for the toilet, you make him…You know that when he gets up you have to take him…then why not you can do that?' I started to tell him. Then he's told, 'OK I'll go', then he started going.

Valuing the place that tablets had in children's learning was one important element of parents' ethnotheories, and this chimed with family values that emphasised fun, engagement, learning, respect for technology and the need to embed technology in a balanced leisure portfolio, all of which contributed to a positive place for tablets in these homes.

Parents mediated children's use of the tablet in various ways, as previous studies have found in relation to parents' role with regard to children's use of other technologies (Clark 2011). Nikken and Jansz (2014) drew on data from a survey of 792 parents of Dutch children aged between 2 and 12 identified five types of parental mediation, building on the categories developed by Livingstone and Helsper (2008). They are co-use (using the internet together); active mediation (e.g. helping children to understand what to do when being harassed online); restrictive mediation (general restrictions, such as time limitations); restrictive mediation (content restrictions, such as banning certain sites) and supervision (parents monitoring children's internet use when nearby). These mediation types could also be found to apply to the data from the study reported in this chapter, in that parents used the tablets at the same time as children (co-use), they actively mediated the children's use of tablets (e.g. showing them how to operate/manage the tablet), they set time limits on children's tablet use and restricted children from using certain apps (restrictive mediation) and they monitored children's use of tablets from a short distance (supervision).

In the project reported in this chapter, it was interesting to note how much children themselves managed the input of their parents. In those cases, it could be seen that children were mediating their parents' levels of mediation. For example, the parents in the case study families reported that their child would resist co-use at times, wanting to undertake tasks independently. However, they generally still wanted parents to supervise, and to acknowledge their achievements. For example, 3-year-old Arjun reported to his mum that he had completed a task in an app

Arjun: I did it.
Mum: Good. Good.
Interviewer: Does he like it that you acknowledge that every time?
Mum: If you don't do he…like he wants our full attention on him. If we don't give him attention he comes and he pesters us, "See what I've done, give me high five".

Whilst the children generally resisted co-use, there were times when they engaged readily in play and/or digital literacy activities with parents. In these instances, parents could be observed providing the kinds of scaffolding that has been observed in other students of non-digital literacy practices (Neumann et al. 2009). For example, they helped children to recognise letters and words, held their hands/fingers when tracing shapes and letters on screen and participated in interactive story apps.

Parents spent time when children were not present, preparing the tablet for children's use. At times, this involved choosing apps. At other times, parents managed children's access to online material. For example, Arjun's mum stated how she helped Arjun access videos on YouTube by typing in search terms:

> Yeah, yeah 'rhymes for kids', something alphabet, and 'songs for kids' and 'numbers for kids'. So everything is on. So what happens, that history remains in the YouTube. So he goes to that history and he chooses that.

Because of this parent support, young children were able to navigate YouTube relatively independently once in the system by clicking on videos in the history, as Arjun did, or clicking on the recommended videos, as Amy's mum reported her doing:

> …she can navigate. If we let her on to YouTube it's amazing how she can get from one thing to another. She's always watched when she has gone on it but she just…she'll… videos there and then there's others down the side and she'll click on that, and then she'll get to another and she'll do the same again. She always ends up back at watching somebody opening…do you know those Kinder Egg Surprise toys?

Therefore, the ways in which parents supported children's use of tablets were varied, and included a wide range of activities, outlined in Table 3.3. This list is not exhaustive, but indicative of the types of activities parents undertook. Of course, not all parents did all of these things.

In considering the impact of economic, cultural and social capital (Bourdieu 1986) on these interactions, previous studies have indicated that there are some differences in the practices of families, dependent upon their levels of income and parental education. Livingstone et al. (2015), for example, drew on Clark's (2013) work in their examination of data from a study of 70 families in countries across Europe. Clark (2013) distinguished between the media practices of lower income and less-educated families, who, she argued, exhibited an 'ethic of respectful connectedness' from higher income, more educated families who exhibited an 'ethic of expressive empowerment'. Livingstone et al. (2015) found this was also the case in their study, and Clark's categories translated broadly into restrictive and active strategies of mediation, with exceptions.

Table 3.3 Parental engagement in young children's use of tablets

Type of parental support	Examples
Overall management of tablet	– Storing tablet in place that cannot be accessed by child – Controlling access to the tablet e.g. by setting time limits – Setting password control to ensure all use is supervised – Supporting child to develop self-regulation in relation to the use of the tablet
Preparation of tablet for child's use	– Searching for apps – Downloading apps – Deleting apps – Trying apps out before using with child – Searching for videos on YouTube and placing in child's channel – Setting up safety features
Support for tablet use prior to child using the tablet	– Sitting child on knee and helping to hold the tablet – Propping tablet up for the child to ease access – Turning tablet on/off for the child – Checking volume is at appropriate level prior to use – Selecting the app to use
Scaffolding of child's use of tablet and apps	– Showing child how to use various features, e.g. volume buttons, camera – Helping child to learn how to use the tablet safely e.g. online protocols – Pointing out features within apps (e.g. letters/words) – Labelling – Asking questions – Giving hints – Direct instruction – Explaining content – Modelling input – Tapping into prior knowledge – Providing feedback
Interacting with child on app	– Taking turns in games – Contributing to a drawing or story – Doing tasks together e.g. taking photographs
Recognising children's achievements using apps	– Reporting child's achievements to others either face-to-face or using social media e.g. Facebook – Taking photographs of child using tablet – Rewarding performance on apps
Communication with child with regard to use of tablet and apps (when not using tablet)	– Talking with child about child's tablet and/or app use – Discussing apps when engaged with related media content (e.g. watching TV)

In the study reported in this chapter, there were some differences due to capital. Children in lower socio-economic homes were more likely to have access to a greater range of media, including tablets, than children from higher socio-economic groups, which is similar to findings of other projects relating to this age group (Marsh et al. 2005; Chaudron et al. 2015). This may be due to the differing attitudes of parents, as it has been reported previously that parents from higher socio-economic groups express more anxieties than other parents about children's use of media (Marsh et al. 2005). However, there were differences in the types of tablets accessed, in that a higher percentage of middle and upper class families owned iPads than working-class families, who were more likely to own cheaper tablets, such as Tesco's Hudl. This may lead to digital disadvantage, given that there are educational apps produced for the IOS platform that are not available on android devices. This difference in types of tablets can be partly attributed to cost, but also social capital may play a part, in that middle-class parents are possibly more likely to see work colleagues, family and friends use iPads and that might influence their purchasing decisions in relation to their child.

The survey indicated that parents from lower socio-economic groups were more likely than other families to approve of the use of free apps that contain in-app adverts, no doubt because of commercial considerations. However, in this study, it was clear that apps with in-app advertisements were not as beneficial for children's play and creativity as apps without these features, as advertisements disrupted game play and learning (Marsh et al. 2015a), which again suggests that working-class children are at a disadvantage in terms of the quality of apps accessed.

In considering proximal processes at the micro-level, Bronfenbrenner also emphasised the characteristics of individuals, such as their beliefs and inclinations, which inevitably shaped parents and children's interactions with the tablets and, therefore, it is not being proposed that structural forces such as social class determined tablet use, but it could be seen to have some impact, as outlined above.

Mesosystem

In Bronfenbrenner's model, the mesosystem connects the interactions between two microsystems together. In this study, the experiences children had in homes and early years settings appeared to be very different in relation to access to tablets. A minority of parents reported children having access to tablets in an early years setting or at childminders' homes (7% reported access to iPads and Microsoft Surface tablets, 5% had access to a Samsung Galaxy tablet and 5% had access to a Tesco Hudl). That may be because parents did not spend enough time in those settings to note their use, or it could be further evidence that, as demonstrated in other studies, the use of technology is limited in some early years settings (Burnett and Daniels 2015). This is of concern because in relation to the mesosystem, the digital habitus (Bourdieu 1990) developed by children in the home may affect how confidently they use tablets when entering school.

Exosystem

The exosystem consists of settings and contexts in which children are not active participants but which impact significantly on children's lives. This could be traced in the present study in relation to parental employment outside of the home. Those parents in the case study families who had opportunities to engage in educational use of technology outside of the home in their own employment contexts were much more aware of the factors that led to successful use of tablets than parents who did not have these opportunities. Amy's mum, for example, worked in early years education, and was able to identify age-appropriate features of apps, and choose them accordingly. Kiyaan's father was a university lecturer, and his mother had previously been a Ph.D. student. They were both engineers and interested in technology and, because of that, made a deliberate choice about introducing Kiyaan to technology as a young baby:

> Well, it was my husband who did it, he just searched those things for babies. He's young and he's the first child to just play with these things. He'll be exposed to technology. And we thought, just let him play with the real things, or real toys like rattles, but then it's nice for him to play with the real applications, you know, it is IT.

However, there were risks associated with children's use of technology when parents' employment intersected with children's use of mobile phones or tablets. As Kiyaan's father noted, when he explained that he did not let Kiyaan use his mobile phone, given he had already had to give up his iPad so Kiyaan could use it:

> Because then I don't have that phone any more! I've lost one iPad, I don't want to lose my phone! Because I've got all my university emails and everything, and he was basically calling people, sending emails to everyone also. No thank you. I prefer to keep it for emergency cases.

The exosystem in relation to parental employment could be seen, therefore, to have a significant impact on the experiences of children in these two families. For other families who had not had the same exposure to technology outside of the home, parents' confidence was less obvious and in some instances the parents identified the children as being more competent in their use of tablets, a phenomenon that has arisen in other studies of young children's use of technologies (Marsh et al. 2005; Chaudron et al. 2015).

Macrosystem

The final nested structure in Bronfenbrenner's model, the macrosystem, refers to the wider social and cultural context in which the child operates. In this case, there have been many concerns expressed by the media in relation to young children's use of tablets (e.g. Palmer 2016). Parents in this study had picked up these concerns to the extent that some noted anxieties about the potential negative impact of the use of technology on health, general development and outdoor play, although none of the parents felt that their own children currently had an imbalance in engagement with digital and non-digital playthings. There appeared to be few differences across the families in this regard, although previous studies have found that middle-class parents are more likely than working-class parents to express anxieties with regard to children's use of technology (Marsh et al. 2005).

Chronosystem

As identified previously, microtime refers to continuity versus discontinuity in proximal processes, mesotime relates to the repetition of proximal processes over time and macrotime focuses on the way in which changes within and across generations are shaped by the larger society over time (Bronfenbrenner and Morris 2006).

It was possible in this study to see economic and cultural capital at work in relation to microtime and mesotime. In terms of microtime, children in the lower socio-economic families in the case studies were more likely to find their use of smartphones and tablets interrupted because of run-down batteries and/ or a lack of memory, which meant tablets froze on a regular basis. Jade's mum, for example, explained that she had to delete apps on a weekly basis:

> Because obviously that's only, it's quite a cheapish tablet and it's not like an iPad and so there's limited space. And when she clogs it up with games she knows that it runs slightly slower, so she's very conscious about apps that are big, or getting rid of apps that are big.

In discussion with the researcher, Jade's mum acknowledged that this meant her child became frustrated:

Interviewer:	Does she get frustrated with that?
Mum:	Yeah she does. She tends to be on her best behaviour when you're here, she doesn't really get as frustrated.
Interviewer:	I wonder why! Ah!
Mum:	I said to her though, "Don't be losing your temper" because a lot of times she'll...she'll put the tablet down and she'll stomp off upstairs.
Interviewer:	Oh bless her. And is that caused by it not working the way she wants it to?
Mum:	Yeah, she does get very annoyed. Sometimes she's got a bit of patience but if it's really on a go-slow she get right annoyed and while I'm in the kitchen I can hear her shouting at tablet. So, yeah, it does annoy her.

In the microtime of children in families with more economic capital, such disturbances were absent, which meant they had enhanced experiences with tablets.

Socio-economic and cultural capital could also be seen at play in relation to mesotime. In the survey, a significantly greater proportion of respondents from socio-economic groups C2DE reported their children using tablets between 9 a.m. and 12 p.m., 12 p.m. and 2 p.m., 2 p.m. and 4 p.m. and after 8 p.m. on weekdays (see Fig. 3.1). The difference between socio-economic groups seemed slightly less pronounced at weekends. Nevertheless, a greater proportion of respondents from socio-economic groups C2DE reported their children using tablets between 12 p.m. and 2 p.m. and 2 p.m. to 4 p.m. at weekends (see Fig. 3.2).

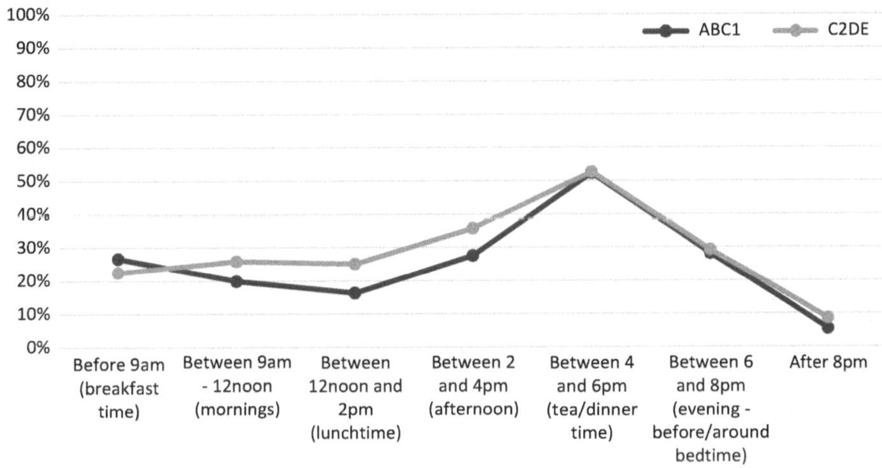

Fig. 3.1 Tablet usage by socioeconomic group—weekdays

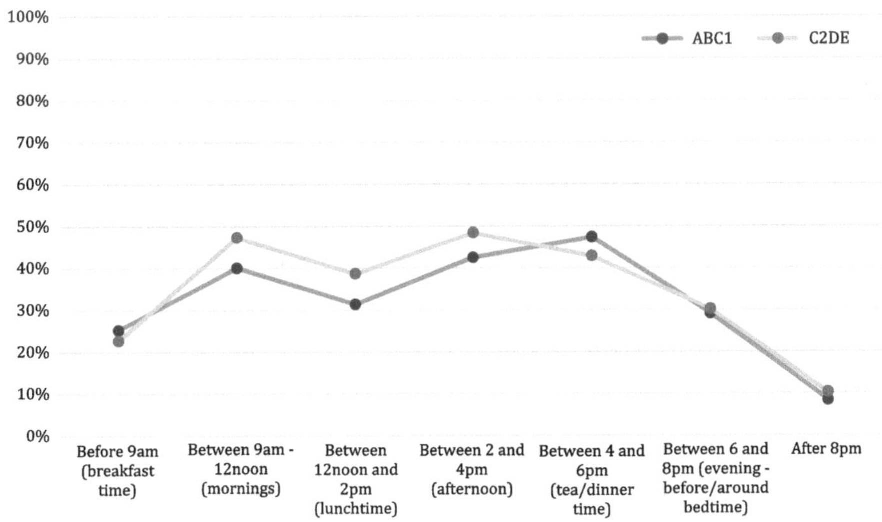

Fig. 3.2 Tablet usage by socioeconomic group—weekends

The data from the case study families indicated that these differences may have been due to the wider range of activities undertaken by families with greater levels of income, who are more able to allow their children to take part in activities that cost money (such as classes, visits to theme parks and so on).

In relation to macrotime, the most significant relevant generational change in society to have occurred in recent years is the popular take-up of the tablet following the iPad's introduction in 2010. This can be seen as seismic shift in relation to young children and technology. Whilst older studies did indicate that young children engaged in uses of technology from birth (Marsh et al. 2005; Rideout et al. 2003), it was only when adults could see the relative ease with which young children interacted with touchscreen technology as opposed to a mouse and keyboard that an explosion of interest in the technology use of this age group could be seen, as judged by numerous media reports on the subject, and an increase in academic studies focused on this age group. It will be of interest to see which future technological developments create a shift of similar proportions in future years.

Conclusion

In this chapter, Bronfenbrenner's ecological model of human development has informed an analysis of parental involvement in young children's use of tablets. The nested systems of Bronfenbrenner's model cannot be seen as discrete, as they have shifting and permeable boundaries, but they enable an understanding to be developed of the various influences on family tablet use. However, in order to understand the way in which power operates in relation to families' use of tablets, there is a need to draw on sociological theories, such as Bourdieu's (1986) notion of economic, cultural and social capital. The combination of the use of these theoretical lenses has led to an understanding of the way in which parental interaction with children around tablets is subject to societal structures, which are beyond families' control. Nevertheless, these structures do not always restrict families' practices in the ways one might predict. Bourdieu (1990) himself recognised that habitus could be flexible and not always determine outcomes:

> …the habitus, like every 'art of inventing', is what makes it possible to produce an infinite number of practices that are relatively unpredictable (like the corresponding situations), but also limited in their diversity. (Bourdieu 1990: 55)

As was outlined in this chapter, other factors in addition to capital impacted on tablet use, such as parents' confidence, children's individual preferences and so on.

The study has a number of implications for research, policy and practice. In relation to research, there is a need to consider in further depth the factors that impact on parental engagement in young children's tablet use. In particular, the influence of other types of settings in the exosystem, such as interest groups or community groups that the parents may be involved in, would be of interest.

Further analyses of the way in which the chronosystem as experienced in the home impacts on young children's technological development at key transition points, such as entry into school, would also be of value.

For early years' educators, the study points to the extensive nature of parents' involvement in the children's use of tablets, and their intimate knowledge of children's activities and competences. Early years settings could draw on this knowledge in home visits that take place prior to children joining nurseries and/or schools, leading to discussions with parents on the children's skills and knowledge, as well as exchanging ideas about the kinds of apps that might be appropriate to use once the child begins nursery or school. In addition, greater opportunities to involve parents in activities related to the tablet during the school day could be of interest, given that many parents in already support their child's tablet use.

Finally, cognisance of the way in which economic, cultural and social capital operate in relation to young children's tablet use could be of value to policy-makers in considering legislation with regard to the curriculum. Curriculum guidance which recognises the value of tablets, and other technologies, in young children's development would seek to counter any negative impact of such capital and ensure that all children had opportunities to develop digital literacy skills, regardless of their families' socio-economic status. This is vitally important to the task of developing a socially just and equitable society in relation to access to and use of technologies in employment and leisure.

Acknowledgements This work was funded by the Economic and Social Research Council [grant number ES/M006409/1].

References

Bourdieu, Pierre. 1986. The forms of capital. In *Handbook of theory and research for the sociology of education*, ed. John G. Richardson, 241–258. New York: Greenwood Press.

Bourdieu, Pierre. 1990. *The logic of practice*. trans. Richard Nice, Cambridge: Polity Press (original work published in 1980).

British Educational Research Association. 2011. *Ethical guidelines for educational research*. London: BERA.

Bronfenbrenner, Urie. 1979. *The ecology of human development: Experiments by nature and design*. Cambridge, Massachusetts: Harvard University Press.

Bronfenbrenner, Urie. 1994. Ecological models of human development. In *International encyclopedia of education*, 2nd ed, Vol. 3, ed. Husen, T., and T.N. Postlethwaite, 1643–1647. Oxford, England: Pergamon Press.

Bronfenbrenner, Urie. 1995. Developmental ecology through space and time: A future perspective. In *Examining lives in context: Perspectives on the ecology of human development*, ed. Phyllis Moen, Glen H. Elder, Jr., and Kurt Lüscher, 619–647. Washington, DC: American Psychological Association.

Bronfenbrenner, Urie. 2005. The bioecological theory of human development. In *Making human beings human: Bioecological perspectives on human*. ed.*development*, ed. Urie Bronfenbrenner, 3–15. Thousand Oaks, CA: Sage, 3–15 (Original work published 2001).

Bronfenbrenner, Urie, and Stephen J. Ceci. 1994. Nature-nurture reconceptualized in developmental perspective: A biological model. *Psychological Review* 101: 568–586.

Bronfenbrenner, Urie, and Pamela A. Morris. 2006. The bioecological model of human development. In *Handbook of child psychology, Theoretical models of human development*, 6th ed, vol. 1, ed. William Damon, and Richard M. Lerner, 793–828. New York: Wiley.

Burnett, Cathy, and Karen Daniels. 2015. Technology and literacy in the early years: Framing young children's meaning-making with new technologies. In *Understanding digital technologies and young children: An international perspective,* ed. Susanne Garvis and Narelle Lemmon, 18–27. London: Routledge.

Carrington, Victoria. 2013. An argument for assemblage theory: Integrated spaces, mobility and polycentricity. In *Children's virtual play worlds: Culture, learning and participation,* ed. Ann Burke, and Jackie Marsh, 200–216. New York: Peter Lang.

Chaudron Stephane, M.E Beutel, Martina Cernikova, Veronica Donoso Navarette, Michael Dreier, Ben Fletcher-Watson, Anni-Sofia Heikkilä, Věra Kontríková, Riitta-Liisa Korkeamäki, Sonia Livingstone, Jackie Marsh, Giovanna Mascheroni, Marina Micheli, Daniele Milesi, K. W. Müller, Tuula Myllylä-Nygård, Marja Niska, Oxana Olkina, Svenja Ottovordemgentschenfelde, Lydia Plowman, Wannes Ribbens, Janice Richardson, C. Schaack, Vladimir Shlyapnikov, David Šmahel, Galina Soldatova and Klaus Wölfling. 2015. *Young children (0–8) and digital technology: A qualitative exploratory study across seven countries.* http://publications.jrc.ec.europa.eu/repository/handle/JRC93239. Accessed 17 September 2016.

Clark, Lynn Schofield. 2011. Parental mediation theory for the digital age. *Communication theory* 21 (4): 323–343.

Clark, Lynn Schofield. 2013. *The parent app: Understanding families in the digital age.* Oxford: Oxford University Press.

Deleuze, Giles, and Félix Guattari. 1987. *A thousand plateaus: Capitalism and schizophrenia.* Minneapolis: University of Minnesota Press.

Formby, Susie. 2014. *Parents' perspectives: Children's use of technology in the early years.* London.: National Literacy Trust.

Harrison, Eugene, and Marianne McTavish. 2016. 'i'Babies: Infants' and toddlers' emergent language and literacy in a digital culture of iDevices. *Journal Of Early Childhood Literacy.* Published online before print 15 June 2016, doi:10.1177/1468798416653175.

Holloway, Donnell, Lelia Green, and Carlie Love. 2014. 'It's all about the apps': Parental mediation of pre-schoolers' digital lives. *Media International Australia* 153 (November): 148–156.

Kenner, Chamian, Mahera Ruby, John Jessel, Eve Gregory, and Tahera Arju. 2008. Intergenerational learning events around the computer: A site for linguistic and cultural exchange. *Language and Education* 22 (4): 298–319.

Kucirkova, Natalia, David Messer, Kieron Sheehy and R. Rosie Flewitt. 2013. Sharing personalised stories on iPads: A close look at one parent–child interaction. *Literacy* 47 (3): 115–122.

Livingstone, Sonia, and Ellen J. Helsper. 2008. Parental mediation of children's Internet use. *Journal of Broadcasting and Electronic Media* 52 (4): 581–599.

Livingstone, Sonia, Giovanna Mascheroni, Michael Dreier, Stephane Chaudron, and Kaat Lagae. 2015. *How parents of young children manage digital devices at home: The role of income, education and parental style.* LSE: EU Kids Go Online. http://eprints.lse.ac.uk/63378/1/__lse.ac.uk_storage_LIBRARY_Secondary_libfile_shared_repository_Content_EU%20Kids%20Online_EU_Kids_Online_How%20parents%20manage%20digital%20devices_2016.pdf. Accessed 12 Dec 2016.

Marsh, Jackie, Greg Brooks, Jane Hughes, Louise Ritchie and Sam Roberts. 2005. *Digital beginnings: Young children's use of popular culture, media and new technologies.* Sheffield, UK: University of Sheffield. http://www.digitalbeginnings.shef.ac.uk/DigitalBeginningsReport.pdf. Accessed 12 December 2016.

Marsh, Jackie, Lydia Plowman, Dylan Yamada-Rice, C. Julia. Bishop, Jamal Lahmar, Fiona Scott, Andrew Davenport, Simon Davis, Katie French, Maddalena Piras, Sally Thornhill, Peter Robinson and Peter Winter. 2015. *Exploring play and creativity in pre-schoolers' use of apps: final project report*. www.techandplay.org. Accessed 17 September 2016.

Marsh, Jackie, Peter Hannon, Margaret Lewis, and Louise Ritchie. 2015. Young children's Initiation into family literacy practices in the digital age. *Journal of Early Childhood Research*. Published online ahead of print. 18 June doi:10.1177/1476718X15582095.

Nardi, Bonnie A., and Vicki L. O'Day. 1999. *Information ecologies: Using technology with heart*. Cambridge: The MIT Press.

Neumann, Michelle M., Michelle Hood, and David L. Neumann. 2009. The scaffolding of emergent literacy skills in the home environment: A case study. *Early Childhood Education Journal* 36 (4): 313–319.

Neumann, Michelle M., and David L. Neumann. 2015. The use of touch-screen tablets at home and pre-school to foster emergent literacy. *Journal of Early Childhood Literacy*. Published online 10 December 2015 ahead of print. http://dx.doi.org/10.1177/Italianpeople TCP1468798415619773

Nikken, Peter, and Jeroen Jansz. 2014. Developing scales to measure parental mediation of young children's internet use. *Learning, Media and Technology* 39 (2): 250–266.

Ofcom. 2015. *Children and parents: Media use and attitudes report*. London: ofcom. http://stakeholders.ofcom.org.uk/market-data-research/other/research-publications/childrens/children-parents-nov-15/. Accessed 17 September 2016.

O'Mara, Joanne, and Linda Laidlaw. 2011. Living in the iWorld: Two literacy researchers reflect on the changing texts and literacy practices of childhood. *English Teaching: Practice and Critique* 10 (4): 149–159.

Palmer, Sue. 2016. Why the iPad is a far bigger threat to our children than anyone realises 27 January 2016. http://www.dailymail.co.uk/femail/article-3420064/Why-iPad-far-bigger-threat-children-realises-Ten-years-ago-psychologist-SUE-PALMER-predicted-toxic-effects-social-media-sees-worrying-new-danger.html.

Plowman, Lydia, Christine Stephen, and Joanne McPake. 2010. *Growing up with technology: Young children learning in a digital world*. London: Routledge.

Rideout, Victoria J., Elizabeth A. Vandewater, and Ellen A. Wartella. 2003. *Zero to six: Electronic media in the lives of infants, toddlers and preschoolers*. Washington: Kaiser Foundation.

Verenikina, Irina, and Lisa Kervin. 2011. iPads, digital play and pre-schoolers. *He Kupu* 2 (5): 4–19.

Author Biography

Jackie Marsh is Professor of Education at the University of Sheffield. She has led numerous research projects engaging children, teachers, parents and children's media industry partners in research on young children's play and digital literacy practices in homes and schools (e.g. the ESRC-funded project 'Technology and Play'). Jackie is Chair of COST Action IS1410, DigiLitEY, a European network of 33 countries focusing on research in this area (2015–2019). She is currently leading a 12-country project on makerspaces in the early years, MakEY (2017–2019) funded by the EU Horizon 2020 programme.

Chapter 4
Chasing Literacies Across Action Texts and Augmented Realities: E-Books, Animated Apps, and Pokémon Go

Karen Wohlwend

Technology innovations zip in and out of our daily lives in an endless stream of updates: 1.0, 2.0, 3.0, and so on. As educators and educational researchers, we must also update the pedagogies we offer to young children who are immersed in rapidly shifting technologies, literacies, and global innovation. Two decades into the twenty-first century, the notion of text has expanded from print- and page-based books to screen-based digital media on mobile phones, tablets, and a range of wearable devices (Kress 2004, 2010). With new technologies in our increasingly digitally mediated lives, play rises to a new level of importance for players of all ages, beyond early childhood. For example, in July 2016 at the time I'm writing this chapter, the launch of Pokémon Go (Nintendo) has introduced over 30 million players to augmented reality. In this treasure hunt app, players explore their local communities, looking through smartphone camera lenses to locate and collect cartoon characters superimposed on the surrounding landscape. Nightly news reports show Pokémon Go players who wander unaware into oncoming traffic, glass doors, and ponds, demonstrating the hazards of attending to a screen-sized sampling of the surrounding reality while walking amid everyday dangers in the physical world (Needleman 2016). While the game has just emerged, and with it a new kind of digital reading, the central role of play in the app is not a surprise to scholars in New Literacy Studies (Street 1995; Gee 1996). Play is a literacy that easily navigates the material/immaterial indeterminacy of the pretend meanings and digitally enhanced play, enabling players to imagine otherwise and slip the constraints of here-and-now realities—and in the case of Pokémon Go, perhaps a little too convincingly.

This chapter takes a panoramic view of computer literacy learning to capture the range of action-oriented exploration, collaborative innovation, and

K. Wohlwend (✉)
Indiana University, Bloomington, USA
e-mail: kwohlwen@indiana.edu

C. Burnett et al. (eds.), *The Case of the iPad*,
DOI 10.1007/978-981-10-4364-2_4

technology-augmented participation in children's play with iPads, to ask the following:

- What actions and social practices in young children's iPad play shape their cultural participation and literacy learning?
- How does an action-oriented lens make visible complex convergences of practices and dimensions of technology-mediated literacy learning?
- What additional dimensions might be needed in future models to explain multiplayer assemblages of bodies, machines, and environments that produce collective, emergent, and disruptive flows?

In this conceptual piece, I draw on mediated discourse theory to compare models of literacy learning that reflect and shape what we recognize as learning in iPad play. Through video analysis of children's classroom interactions with an e-book app and an animation app, I identify literacy practices that interpret, create, and share a range of *action texts* (Wohlwend 2011). An action text is an emergent played text that also supports an imaginary co-constructed context, negotiated among multiple players across digital screens and physical environments. Analysis of action texts created during app play identifies three prevalent models of literacies that circulate notions about who, what, and how children should use iPads. Each of these models is justified by educational discourse that prepares children to participate in particular spaces:

- *digital literacy* in the skills mastery discourse of educational standards in school cultures
- *participatory literacies* in the social practice discourse of situated and connected learning in digital cultures and global networks.

This analysis also forecasts practices in an emerging model:

- *socio-material literacies* in post-human discourse of entangled assemblages of actions, bodies, and machines in converging realities.

Three Models of Literacy Learning in iPad Play

Almost all aspects of everyday life are mediated by mobile technologies and mass media. Even very young children engage texts on screens on parents' mobile phones and devices (Rideout 2013; Sefton-Green et al. 2016). Meanwhile, teachers and parents still find a disconnect between the technology-dense lives of children at home and the print-centric pedagogies in schools (Wohlwend 2009) and in the educational app market (Shuler 2012; Guernsey and Levine 2012). This disconnect can be thought of as a site of contestation where incommensurate discourses and models of literacy learning intersect and influence how literacy is taught, who gets access, and what counts as literacy. For example, a skills mastery discourse supports a mental model of literacy learning as individual skill-based, knowledge acquisition (Ivanič 2004). In the US, a skills mastery discourse drives state- and federally-mandated assessment despite widespread lip service to the importance of teaching within each child's zone of proximal development (Vygotsky 1935/1978), a social practice discourse which values scaffolding and emphasizes the need to assess what the child can do with assistance from more experienced cultural others. Instead, standardized assessments largely measure children's literacy according to their abilities to work in isolation. Such tests assess test-takers' abilities to decode print and to comprehend short passages by selecting a single 'correct' interpretation generating scores that can be compared against grade-level norms. App and iPad play emerges as a site of contestation when the work-focused skills mastery in this model conflicts with the game-focused participatory literacies of a peer culture and or when the need for certain digital skills become obsolete or questionable in the socio-material literacy of robotic readers.

Digital Literacy: This model explains online reading and word-processing practices: an individual reads or writes pages of digital print and images with a computer-as-typewriter mindset (Knobel and Wilber 2009). In the early twenty-first century, literacy researchers observed children's handling of computer tools to better understand how children were acquiring skills in moving a computer mouse to effect a change in images and print on a computer screen. These studies updated Clay's (1975) book-based concepts of print by identifying 'concepts of screen', computer-based conventions and skills that users needed for mouse handling and cursor–screen relationships (Labbo 2006; Merchant 2005). For young learners, the number, pressure, duration, and direction of finger touches on a tablet's touchscreen (Rowsell et al. 2013; Rowe et al. 2014) create text with printless or multimodal practices (Flewitt 2013). For example, squeezing two fingers together will shrink an image; on the other hand, a quick one-finger tap on a blank corner of a screen can reveal a hidden menu of options (Flewitt et al. 2015).

Participatory Literacies: This model explains multimedia sharing practice in social media and digital cultures: multiple players/designers collaboratively create and interact through games, photos, videos, and other multimedia across social media networks using Facebook, Instagram, YouTube, Twitter, virtual worlds, fan communities, and so on. On a daily basis, three-fourths of U.S. children use mobile devices (Rideout 2013; Shuler 2012) that, when combined with social media, allow children to participate in global digital cultures (Ito et al. 2013) by playing, collaborating, and sharing anytime-anywhere on handheld screens on mobile devices connected to 24/7 networks. Through tweeting, blogging, remixing, and other media-sharing practices, digital literacies intersect with insider ways of participating in digital cultures (Knobel and Wilber 2009; Jenkins et al. 2006). Through participatory literacies, players signal tech-savvy membership as they co-construct meanings in a sequence of back-and-forth moves in online games (Gee 2003) among other forms.

Socio-Material Literacies: New models are needed to explain emerging tools that enable machines to create texts as co-actants, as target audiences, or as readers and writers. *Socio-material literacies* (Mills 2016) are most visible in technological innovations that operate through increasingly blurred body–machine interactions: users' speech, gestures, and body actions link with wearable computers such as Google glasses or Apple watches; webs of non-human interaction among intelligent machines connect appliances that 'talk' to one another to coordinate their functions; 'litbots' read and remember digital texts (McEneaney 2011). Initiatives such as the Hour of Code (https://hourofcode.com/us) suggest a future where children will need to learn computer literacies to program and think *with* machines. The term *socio-material literacies* captures the embodied nature of these interactions without privileging the human and suggests the extended reach that is enabled by machine–human–material integration through connected networks and augmented realities. In this model, our smartphones and tablets are extensions of bodies that we look through to see more, act through to reach more, and connect through to engage more machine/person assemblages. In the same way, bodies extend the reach of machines and provide human input into co-productions by initiating ideas and actions or providing power or programming.

Each model is an oversimplified and discursive construction that legitimatizes particular sets of relationships among materials, humans, and realities. Models and their associated supporting discourses converge and collide whenever a new technology emerges, evident in transformative technologies from the printing press to the smartphone (Luke 1989, 2007). Thus new technological practices through their novel mergings of machines, humans, and meanings make visible the ways that literacy models and discourses overlap and produce sites of contestation. Contestation incites discourse, that is, discourse recruits and generates more discourse (Foucault 1978) as models are circulated through efforts to keep an extant set of practices securely in place. But what would be visible if we expanded our perspective to recognize change as the typical state of things (Latour 2005)? What pedagogies could emerge if we stopped trying to catch and capture mobile technologies?

Theoretical Framework for Examining Literacy Learning Models

To examine how literacy discourses converge in children's action texts with mobile technologies, I draw on mediated discourse theory (Vygotsky 1935/1978; Wertsch 1991) and actor network theory (Latour 2005).

Mediated discourse theory provides the construct of nexus of practice (Scollon 2001) framework that reveals how children's play with digital media engages embodied expectations for technical skills in digital literacy or cultural practices in participatory literacies or human/machine assemblages in *socio-material literacies*.

I examine children's digital play as taps, swipes, and other small actions, situated in (1) interaction orders (Goffman 1983) such as student-with-teacher or player-against-player relationships, (2) historical bodies or engrained expectations for particular actions (i.e., habitus, Bourdieu 1977), and (3) discursive interpretations of co-players in peer culture and fan media cultures and teachers in school culture. Play is examined as both a literacy and a tactic (Wohlwend 2011), that is, social and semiotic practices that young children engage when they play together to create action texts such as animated films with digital puppetry apps on touchscreen tablets (Merchant 2015).

Actor network theory (Latour 2005) explains people and computers as actants that co-produce interaction, within flows that travel along constantly evolving networks. In this view, change is the constant; that is, we should expect continual change as the status quo. Rather than focusing tightly to identify a linear trajectory of development and measuring a child's growth as change over time, we should be noticing where people/thing assemblages are forced to be static. Thus, educational researchers should be cultivating a suspicion of immobility and looking at the stuck places in networks for evidence of institutions' or other actants' efforts to hold things in place. And in pushing learners toward a narrowed, common goal, what learning deviations (or rather innovations) are suppressed? For example, standardization works against the natural tendency of things toward variation. In educational systems governed by skills mastery discourse, huge investments of time and energy are expended to measure, sort, and keep everything securely the same. When co-actants (an iPad/game/players assemblage) meander away from a standard, what forces are mustered and what resources are expended toward redirecting learners back on track? What anchors the wandering trajectories of learning assemblages? Together mediated discourse theory and actor network theory support a nexus analysis approach for studying the trajectories of literacies, whether materialized on a page of print, in embodied play, or in digital animation, that can help illuminate how iPads function as paradoxically mobile and anchoring sites.

Methods

Nexus analysis, a version of mediated discourse analysis (MDA), (Scollon and Scollon 2004; Wohlwend 2011; Jones 2015) enables examination of technology-mediated interactions and their trajectories over time and space, microanalysis of tool-handling in digital literacies, interactional analysis of participatory literacies, and macroanalysis of literacies and augmented realities.

1. **Hand/Screen Actions and Nexus of Practice**: MDA makes visible a nexus of practice, identifying small high-frequency physical-mediated actions by hands with touchscreens that make up digital literacy practices. When literacy practices combine with valued ways of behaving at school, they become routine and expected as the appropriate way of pulling off a literate identity. Close analysis

of hands' handling of touchscreens locates the skills and expectations users bring to a moment of iPad play.

2. **Multiplayer and Multimodal Interaction**: MDA offers interactional analysis that explains children's collaborative production as movements among players, materials, meanings, and discourses. Close analysis of action-by-action turns within a multimodal context reveals moments of shifting participation and changing power relations. MDA locates how players wield meanings, modes, and actions within participatory literacies to negotiate, disrupt, or anchor their co-constructed shared texts or social spaces. In this article, MDA of children's composing on a digital puppetry app illustrates the conceptual and methodological tools that reveal complex flows of (1) touches, swipes, and other actions in digital literacy practices; (2) multimodal layers of colorful images, dialogue, sound effects, and movement in animated stories; and (3) negotiation and contestation among children around turn-taking and story ideas.
3. **More-than Human Assemblages and Trajectories**: MDA tracks trajectories across time scales and geographies to understand how transitory (con)texts enter into and flow from assemblages of iPad/user/environment in augmented realities. MDA locates timescales to understand a mediated action as a moment in a set of intersecting trajectories of historical bodies, interaction orders, and discourses of place. Any action, then, is a temporal and spatial location in an indeterminate cycle of prior events and meanings, which also carries histories that shape expectations for the present moment as well as anticipations for its future emanations.

In the following section, I use one MDA level of analysis to examine an example of iPad play and to interpret each vignette through the lens of one literacy model. The instances of technology play selected for the analysis are excerpted from classroom data in ongoing Literacy Playshop research that I have conducted in early childhood classrooms, working with 10 teachers and over 200 3–8-year-old children. Data sources included video of children's play and filmmaking activities, and children's toys, puppets, drawings, and films. Microanalysis enabled by video analysis software tracks hand actions during small group play with digital animation on iPads to identify literacy practices and peer culture relationships, while macroanalysis connects image, machine, and body interactions to educational theories and learning models that shift across time and space. The following example illustrates how close analysis of finger movements on touchscreens reveals literacy practices interpreted through a model of digital literacy.

Reading an E-Book, a Digital Literacy Illustration

Amy bent intently over the iPad, tapping through the pages of a personalizable e-book (i.e., JibJab Jr) featuring a cartoon character: a pizza chef with cutout of Amy's face. Using an integrated photo feature, Amy snapped a selfie with the iPad and the app inserted it into the main character. On each page, she chuckled as her personalized pizza chef moved humorously through the steps of mixing dough, adding toppings, and baking a pizza. She paused frequently to show the pages to her friends at the table. However after a few readings, she lost interest in the pizza book and moved on to more interactive apps that allowed her to create or change characters, backgrounds, music, or sequences of events.

The touchscreen interface of iPads and other mobile devices has dramatically increased accessibility of digital media. Young children playing with iPad apps engage in a range of digital tablet-handling practices, supported by non-print multimodal affordances. Researchers note that navigation that leverages the affordances of modes of image and touch facilitates digital literacy learning (Matthews and Seouw 2007). Touchscreens enable navigation through large simplified icons that allow children who do not yet recognize printed words to navigate screens using images. In addition, iPads are highly responsive, giving instantaneous feedback that makes the effect of a finger tap immediately obvious. Elsewhere I have suggested that touchscreens on mobile devices require knowledge of *Concepts Beyond Print*, an expanded set of conventions for interactive modes including touch, image, and speech[1] (Wohlwend 2017). In this framing, e-book reading is literacy practice made up of a set of mediated actions with touchscreens and buttons on an iPad which engage modes of image and touch. These mediated actions—gazing, clicking, tapping, swiping—coordinate body action and sensory modal information with the images visible on a glass screen. Furthermore, e-book reading often involves digital literacy practices that make use of other iPad features such as speech recognition controls, the embedded digital camera, or the spatial layout of the touchscreen (see Table 4.1).

Spatial layout is another mode with relevance for iPads. A top or bottom left corner is a frequent location for a back arrow that when tapped retrieves the previous screen. And when no arrow is visible, tapping the empty space may cause an arrow to appear. In other apps, icons may be located elsewhere (Kucirkova 2014). This means that while digital literacy develops a set of practices, it also develops a set of learner dispositions such as flexibility in problem-solving, an attitude of experimentation, and a willingness to persevere. In addition to discerning the meaning of an e-book's text and reactions of interactive features, children need critical literacy skills to distinguish between actual content, advertising, and in-app purchases.

An iPad's interface seems 'intuitive', contributing to a cultural model that constructs young children as 'digital natives' (Prensky 2001) or natural experts who seem to 'just know' how to use new techno-literacies with little adult help. The model is circulated by social media fascination with technological precociousness in 'iPhone Baby' viral videos that draw millions of views on YouTube. This model relies on an individualistic view of learning that overlooks the hours of immersive demonstrations as children closely observe older members of their families actively engaged in daily living activities. From a mediated discourse perspective, digital

[1]The notion of Concepts Beyond Print builds upon Clay's (1975) Concepts About Print for paper books and Merchant's (2005) Concepts About Screens for desktop computers.

Table 4.1 Key practices and mediated actions in a digital literacy model

E-book reading	• Tapping an icon to open e-book • Pressing a toggle button to increase volume on e-book • Tapping arrows to turn page • Tapping words to activate highlighting and read aloud features
Voice recording and recognition	• Talking to character, image, avatar with expectation of response (e.g., on-screen movement, action, verbal response including repetition of copied voice.) • Talking to other people synchronously or asynchronously (e.g., phone calls, recorded messages) • Talking to voice-recognition program (e.g., Siri)
Image uploading	• Tapping to take a selfie or other photo; tracing photo to create cutout • Tapping to import photo as personalizing content into e-book
Touchscreen navigating	• Swiping scroll bars to load more options • Tapping icons/words to launch an app • Swiping the screen to turn a page, return to a screen, or load the next photo • Pressing a button to go to the home screen with app menu to change apps • Tapping an icon (e.g., checkmark, 'x') to confirm and proceed or cancel an action or to close a page or application • Tapping arrow icons or lightly touching areas of screens where arrow icons are not visible but expected in order to open a new screen

literacy practices are learned in car seats, grocery carts, and parents' laps as children notice how people use mobile devices to shop, chat with friends, check Facebook, or share a video. These technology-mediated social practices signal a nexus of practice when enactments demonstrate a user's understanding and co-membership in performing insider practices valued by a particular group. A growing body of educational research shows that from infancy, young children learn imaginary play in families (Marsh et al. 2015a), and that touchscreens provide key mediators that support very young children's development in movie-making (Matthews 2006).

Multiplayer Collaboration with an Animation App, a Participatory Literacy Illustration

Heads together, three players hunch over an iPad as they intently create an animated video using the PuppetPals app (Polished Play), voicing and recording dialogue and animating a stock set of fairy tale characters in a castle scene: a princess, a knight, and a fairy godmother. The player in the center directs the action, announcing to the girl on her left, "You can be the princess and I'll be him [knight]," as a third girl looks on. The girls laugh as they quickly move their hands around the screen, each player manipulating a different character: sliding their fingers across the glass touchscreen, turning a princess upside down, spinning the knight in rapid circles, squeezing and spreading the images to resize their characters in quick transformations, now gigantic, now tiny. Now and then a player gestures in a

> directorial move that suggests where a particular character should move on the screen layout. As the filmmaking progresses and action picks up, their hands crowd together on the screen. Participation moves intersperse with animation moves as hands brush, nudge, and rest on top of one another's hand to gently alter the movement of someone else's character. Often these hand actions are nonverbal and subtle accompanying dialogue, sound effects, singing, laughter, and action. At other times, the action is more physical with elbows blocking another character competing for the same space and arms pushing intruding hands out of the way. "True love," sings the princess, and all three players laugh.

In the PuppetPals digital puppetry app, children select up to eight cartoon characters and either photos or drawings as background scenery. After pressing a red record button (which activates the iPad microphone and video screen capture within the selected background frame), they drag and drop characters on stage or off stage, positioning, rotating, and resizing characters with their fingers while simultaneously voicing dialogue or narrating story action. Pressing the red button again stops the recording and changes the button to a green triangle for immediate playback of their enacted story. Furthermore, this example of playful composing shows children actively exploring the meaning potentials of the modes that touchscreen tablets and interactive media such as apps offer. They do this while managing participation in a cramped space that keeps everyone at the table and that merges their ideas into a single, shared text. Mobile tablets support collective imagining, which can be contentious as well as collaborative. As children vie for physical space on the glossy surface of a 9.5-inch screen, they must also work through their disparate visions for the unfolding story. The result is collective imagining made from mediated actions, modes, and meanings:

1. actions: touches, swipes, and other embodied actions that make up digital literacy practices
2. modes: sensory aspects of context such as colorful images, dialogue, sound effects, and movement that enliven animated stories
3. meanings: directions and storylines negotiated and pooled into a shared pretense

Play is a leading example of a participatory literacy in which multiple players co-construct meanings to create, negotiate, enact, revise, and share an action text, while they also learn how to become an active cultural participant. Participatory literacies include ways of interpreting, making, sharing, and belonging in increasingly globally and digitally mediated cultures. Jenkins et al. (2006) define participatory cultures as open digital spaces where people congregate online to create and share.

> Participatory literacies reflect new ways of thinking about learning to read and write with technology that moves away from the model of an individual reading or typing print on a computer screen. Instead, participatory literacies reflect the principles of social media like Twitter, YouTube, or Facebook or video games and virtual worlds: global participation, multiplayer collaboration, and distributed knowledge. These principles enable participation in vast digital networks through posting, blogging, recording, remixing, uploading, and downloading. (Rowsell and Wohlwend 2017: 72)

When dramatic play combines with the portability and modal affordances of touchscreens on mobile devices, the potential for collaborative text-making grows. However, many educational apps fail to offer features that can realize the potential of digital literacy play. To evaluate how well mobile apps support fluid, collaborative, and meaningful production, we studied children's actual iPad play and identified several dimensions of participatory literacies, including multiplayer, productive, multimodal, multilinear, and connected (Rowsell and Wohlwend 2017).

1. **Multiplayer**: This dimension enables groups of co-players and teams who negotiate a shared play text or scenario as they cooperatively keep play going. Co-players decide who can play, who gets the next turn, who will play whom, and what the next action will be. Apps that enable co-playing are joint productions, with dynamic meanings that emerge in an action text that is a sequence of interactions, moves, and counter-moves. Unlike a computer mouse which accommodates one hand, the touchscreen interface on a tablet accommodates multiple hands, as long as the app can sort through the chaos of multiple simultaneous taps and slides sent by a jumble of players' hands moving around the touchscreen.
2. **Multilinear**: The open-ended dimension provides for multiple storylines, revising, or hypertext that allows divergent endings. Dramatic play is multilinear, with players' divergent ideas braided together in a shared text. When players disagree, play can break down as players decide which strands make sense to them and how ideas should be integrated into their shared pretense. In collaborations on apps, games and films unfold in an unpredictable sequence, with unexpected challenges as each player contributes moves (actions) and ideas (meanings) through their hand motions or manipulation of materials and space (modes). The immediacy and responsiveness of mobile devices combined with its facility for revision adds to this fluidity of story directions, encouraging DIY dispositions to follow meandering texts under construction (Buchholz 2015). Hypertext capability enables loops and alternate paths (as in the choose-your-own-adventure books, popular in the late twentieth century).
3. **Multimodal**: The dimension of multimodality expands a verbalized idea into an immersive pretend context through iPad features that enable multiple modes (sound, touch, image, music, spatial layout) and allow players to manipulate sound, images, live-action video, or animation. Multimodality recognizes that materials mean differently according to design logics, shaped by culture and histories (Kress 2004, 2010). Apps for iPads vary in modal complexity (Norris 2004) or amount and intensity of sensory experience and the degree to which these integrate to create an immersive engagement. This multimodality provides greater accessibility to literacy for learners when it alleviates the need to transduce or reduce reality to a single verbal mode such as print or speech, with benefits for children who are emergent literacy users or who are learning English as a new language. Multimodality opens action and image alternatives for conveying information that provides crucial support to very young literacy learners. For example, play allows young children to imagine a character's perspective

and 'walk around' inside the story, deepening comprehension (Rowe et al. 2003). In this way, apps that combine dramatic play with action texts in multiple modes open alternative pathways that scaffold meaning-making and participation.

4. **Productive**: The productive dimension supports players' production of original content as in digital paint programs, photography, filmmaking, or editing a text through editing, dubbing, remixing clips, images, or music. In order to learn the purposes, features, and identities associated with these social practices, players need to actually create and engage texts in a cultural context (Buckingham 2003; Burnett and Merchant 2013; Marsh et al. 2015b). Young children, particularly in low-income families, have few opportunities to make and share their own media and most often engage books and games that adults have produced for them (Rideout and Katz 2016). Productive experiences help children develop the critical realization that e-books, apps, and other digital texts are not magically given, but made by people, and thus motivated and malleable (Wohlwend et al. 2013).

To understand participatory literacies as a nexus of practice, each dimension can be analyzed for observable mediated actions, modes, and shared meaning:

- Multiplayer: mediated actions of two or more players touching the screen in collaborative filmmaking teams (blue coding)[2]
- Multilinear: changing meaning trajectories in revising characters, scenery, or changing storylines to create multi-linear strands with repetitive loops or alternate directions (green coding)
- Multimodal: shaping shared meanings and participation through
  - auditory modes by adding or manipulating voice, sound effects, music (orange coding)
  - visual modes by adding or manipulating print, image, color, screen layout (purple coding)
  - embodied and environmental modes by adding or manipulating gaze, posture, movement, spatial layout (yellow coding)
- Productive: creating an action text by operating digital equipment features to create and record text through camera framing, touchscreen navigation, iPad operation (black coding)

The boxes marked in color-coded bands in the video timeline in Fig. 4.1 show coded instances of multiplayer collaboration (rows 1–3), multilinearity (rows 4–5), multimodal complexity (rows 6–13), and technical production (rows 14–18).
The excerpt of about eight minutes of iPad play in Fig. 4.1 shows the modal density (overlapping codes) and the modal intensity (frequency of modes) as well as the overall complexity in these play practices where all these dimensions of participatory literacies overlap. In such instances, the small screens of iPads are sites of

[2]Color-coding used in video analysis software (To see color-based coding, see electronic version of this book with color version of Fig. 4.1).

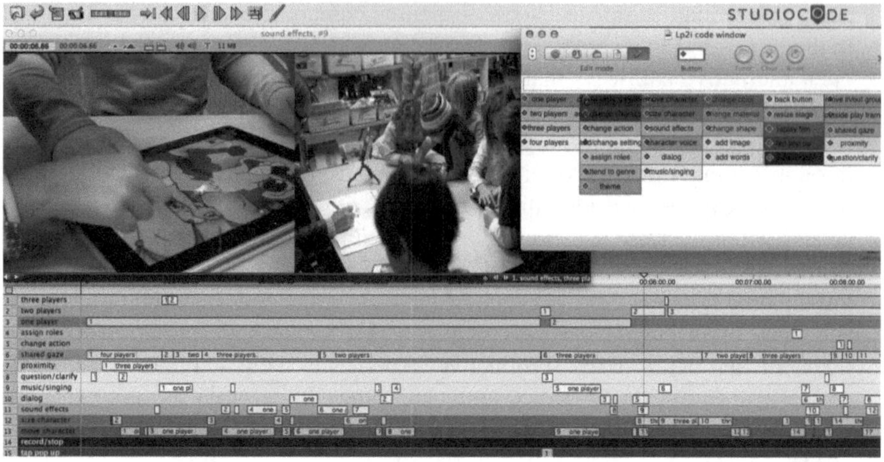

Fig. 4.1 Coded instances of multiplayer collaboration

intense negotiations as children make use of the narrative meanings of characters, storylines, but also their social meanings. In other play groups in this ongoing study, children incorporated photos of friends or classroom objects into their animated films. Like the personalization feature of the e-book app, the puppetry app's photography feature allowed children to create their own characters by taking a photo with the iPad and tracing around the image to create a digital cutout as puppet. In this way, meanings move among bodies, classroom space, and virtual text, blurring material/immaterial dimensions in ways that push multimodal explanations to go further.

Playing Pokémon Go, a Socio-Material Literacy Example

> A family of four young children crowd around a cell phone as they play the Pokémon Go app for the first time, setting up and learning to "swipe up" to capture a Pokémon. The two younger children struggle with seeing a Pokémon character superimposed on their phones' screens, "Wait, is this really real?" "I thought we were actually going to find them, like drive around and find them.," "He wasn't really—like—here". The oldest child explains that "It's kinda like he's invisible right there but then you can see him through the camera."

At the end of the video, the father, narrating for an imagined YouTube audience (realized in over 470,000 views), notes that the children while initially interested had 'more fun just playing outside' https://www.youtube.com/watch?v=BSdwP9J8Ag0. A quick perusal of YouTube reveals pages of similar walk-throughs, let's play playthrough demonstrations, and other fan videos for Pokémon Go, usually featuring adults narrating a screen capture of their game images. Clearly, players were fascinated by the mix of pretense and realities, reading and interacting with an animated character apparently an arm's length away.

Fleer (2014) introduced the concept of *flickering* to conceptualize the small and fluid moves children make between collective and individual imagining, in and out of imaginary scenarios, and between concrete objects and virtual representations on computer screens. Looking closely at collective and individual imagining makes visible how children flicker between concrete realities and collectively imagined spaces. Fleer uses the example of pretend fighting to illustrate how children remain physically present and aware of concrete consequences while carrying on an imagined fight.

However, other researchers (e.g., Lenz Taguchi 2014; Burnett and Merchant 2013) draw on new materialisms (Barad 2003; Latour 2005) to challenge sharp delineations between material and immaterial (Burnett et al. 2014), a move that seems particularly important for researching augmented realities. Where is the boundary between real and imaginary? Is the character imagined because it appears superimposed on a photographic image onscreen? Or is the screen image of a Pokémon always already just as physical as the grass that the Pokémon appears to stand on, the GPS and server that transmits it, the hand that swipes it, and the coding for haptics that read the speed and pressure of a finger touch, and so on. Each component is an actant that engages imagination and sensation, both initiator and responder at some point in the sequence of moments in the capture, so that intra-action among actants co-produces the 'capture'. A materialist lens allows examination of the assemblage of characters, bodies, natural and built environment, touchscreen images, game mechanics, and GPS as a flow that travels along networks where it intertwines with other flows of media, fandom, and commerce in the Pokémon Go phenomenon.

Understanding new technologies as assemblages and flows stretches dimensions of participatory literacies further if we begin to understand technologies as co-producers. Of course, a socio-material lens also expands and ruptures how we understand literacy practices in all sorts of contexts, including the most mundane engagements with a single sheet of paper (Thiel and Wohlwend 2017). How does the concept of assemblage differ from the concept of coordination in the already challenging convergence of dimensions in participatory literacies: managing a filmmaking team, negotiating roles and turns, teaching media production skills to peers, improvising to include friends or to keep play going, and combining multilinear stories with multiple potential directions? This complexity is magnified as more challenges appear in more-than-human interactions that consider machines not as tools but as co-producers: imagining with machines as co-actants while coordinating body actions to manipulate the digital in an unfolding, material text.

Perhaps one answer lies in moving away from cohesion and coordination as goals. In some Vygotskian interpretations, attention is focused and singular, grounding linear models of coordination and harmonious storymaking. Can a model of collaborative production incorporate the design logics of machines while embracing chaotic and temporary connections? Play could inform such a model. Children's play texts are transitory, their action trajectories shifting moment to moment within an emerging story moment to moment, adding and deleting characters in a fluid text, or building on one's own and other co-actants' actions.

Finally, it's important to keep children's lived experiences of digital play at the forefront. How different is Pokémon Go that catches virtual characters with a screenshot from an e-book personalized with a selfie shot? The content is pre-packaged and the interactions are largely limited to aiming the camera and swiping the screen. Children's reactions are telling: if they don't play after the novelty wears off, the game has little learning potential. Games and apps that have staying power allow players to learn and engage deeply through open-ended discovery, production of original content, and collaborative sharing that engage learners over time and space.

Literacy Models as Waves and Ripples

Table 4.2 summarizes this chapter's exploration of three learning models of mobile literacies and the components in each model's nexus of practice, including overarching assumptions about literacy texts, pedagogical models, literacy users, goals, and disparities as well as potential research questions, methods, and theories that align with each. The models in the chart are discursive approaches to understanding digital interactions, ways of interpreting changes in literacies. It is also important to note that the forms—e-book, app, or augmented realities—in this chapter are illustrative and suggest a particular model. However, each form could be combined

Table 4.2 Comparison of three models of technology-mediated literacy learning

	Digital literacy	Participatory literacies	Socio-material literacies
Literacy Practice Illustration	Reading E-book App: JibJab Jr.	Video Sharing Social Media: YouTube App: PuppetPals	Navigating Augmented Reality App: Pokémon Go
Theorization of Literacy Learning	Autonomous literacy Digital skills	Ideological multiliteracies Social practices (Street 1995; New London Group 1996)	(Im)Material Assemblages More-than-human intra-actions (Lenz Taguchi 2014)
Anticipated literacy user(s)	Single reader/writer	Teams of player/producers	Networks of machine/person co-actants
Literacy Goal	Knowledge Acquisition	Cultural representation	Integrated experience Extended reach
Disparity	Achievement gap	Participation gap	Disconnect/stasis
Research questions	What competencies are mastered?	Who is doing what with discourse?	Who–whats are becoming/doing/undoing?
Methods Theories	Standardized assessment Cognitive	Critical Discourse Analysis, Sociocultural	Actor network Post-human Nexus analysis Post-structural

into different assemblages that would support a different set of uses, actions, and goals if interactions were framed by a different model.

In this chapter, I have examined iPad action texts in three models of technology-mediated literacy, using mediated discourse as a tool to make practices visible for comparison. Constantly evolving technologies and expanding digital networks drive new practices that disrupt comfortably established theories of learning, in successive waves across time: first as Digital Literacy, then Participatory Literacies, and now Socio-Material Literacies. But these waves are also ripples that overlap one another, creating blurring and ambiguities that offer alternate explanations beyond dominant models and discourses.

Despite widespread availability of mobile technologies, early childhood education remains a digital desert, or perhaps an oasis, depending upon your discursive perspective. On one hand, visions of developmentally appropriate practice privilege 'natural' materials, creating oases in our classrooms from a daily barrage of popular media and glowing screens. On the other hand, a vision of young children as 'digital natives' and teachers as 'technology laggards' blames teachers for turning the early childhood education landscape into a widespread technology desert. In some ways, each model is a collective cultural imaginary (Medina and Wohlwend 2014) that circulates visions of childhood and legitimatizes the familiar and comfortable print-based literacy of our own childhoods while making screen-based mobile literacies off-limits for young children. However if we recognize that our imaginaries of childhood are dynamic and negotiated ideas, we can open up possibilities to look critically at these visions, question our assumptions, and reconsider ways of doing things.

References

Barad, Karen. 2003. Posthumanist performativity: Toward an understanding of how matter comes to matter. *Signs: Journal of Women in Culture and Society* 283:801–831.

Bourdieu, Pierre. 1977. *Outline of a theory of practice*. Cambridge: Cambridge University Press.

Buchholz, Beth A. 2015. Authoring time in the classroom: Multiage writers compose communities, relationships, and identities across timescales. Ph.D., Indiana University, Bloomington, IN.

Buckingham, David. 2003. *Media education: Literacy, learning, and contemporary culture*. Cambridge: Wiley-Blackwell.

Burnett, Cathy, and Guy Merchant. 2013. Learning literacies and new technologies: The current context and future possibilities. In *The Sage handbook of early childhood literacy*, 2nd ed, ed. Joanne Larson, and Jackie Marsh, 575–586. Los Angeles: Sage.

Burnett, Cathy, Guy Merchant, Kate Pahl, and Jennifer Rowsell. 2014. The immateriality of literacy: The significance of subjectivity to new literacies research. *Discourse: Studies in the Cultural Politics of Education* 351: 90–103.

Clay, Marie. 1975. *What did I write?*. Exeter, NH: Heinemann.

Fleer, Marilyn. 2014. The demands and motives afforded through digital play in early childhood activity settings. *Learning, Culture, and Social Interaction* 3 (3): 202–209. doi:http://dx.doi.org/10.1016/j.lcsi.2014.02.012.

Flewitt, Rosie. 2013. Multimodal perspectives on early childhood literacies. In *The Sage handbook of early childhood literacy*, ed. Joanne Larson, and Jackie Marsh, 295–310. Los Angeles: Sage.

Flewitt, Rosie, David Messer, and Natalia Kucirkova. 2015. New directions for early literacy in a digital age: The iPad. *Journal of Early Childhood Literacy* 15: 289–310.

Foucault, Michel. 1978. *The history of sexuality: An introduction*, vol. 1. New York: Random House.

Gee, James Paul. 1996. *Social linguistics and literacies: Ideology in discourses*, 2nd ed. London: RoutledgeFalmer.

Gee, James Paul. 2003. *Power up: What video games have to teach us about learning and literacy*. New York: Palgrave.

Goffman, Erving. 1983. The interaction order: American Sociological Association, 1982 presidential address. *American Sociological Review* 48: 1–17.

Guernsey, Lisa, Michael Levine, Cynthia Chiong, and Maggie Severns. 2012. *Pioneering literacy: In the digital wild west: Empowering parents and educators*. New York: New America Foundation and Joan Ganz Cooney Center.

Ito, Mizuko, Kris Gutiérrez, Sonia Livingstone, Bill Penuel, Jean Rhodes, Katie Salen, Julie Schor, Julian Sefton-Green, and S. Craig Watkins. 2013. *Connected learning: An agenda for research and design*. Irvine, CA: Digital Media and Learning Research Hub.

Ivanič, Roz. 2004. Discourses of writing and learning to write. *Language and Education* 18: 220–245.

Jenkins, Henry, Ravi Purushotma, Katherine Clinton, Alice J. Robison, and Margaret Weigel. 2006. *Confronting the challenges of participatory culture: Media education for the 21st Century*. Chicago: The MacArthur Foundation.

Jones, Rodney H. 2015. Discourse, cybernetics, and the entextualization of the self. In *Discourse and digital practices: Doing discourse analysis in the digital age*, ed. Rodney H. Jones, Alice Chik, and Christoph A. Hafner, 28–48. New York: Routledge.

Knobel, Michele, and Dana J. Wilber. 2009. Let's talk 2.0: Whether it's Web 2.0 or literacy 2.0, it's a whole new way of thinking. *Educational Leadership* 66: 20–24.

Kress, Gunther. 2004. Reading images: Multimodality, representation and the new media. *Information Design Journal* 12: 110–119. doi:10.1075/idjdd.12.2.03kre.

Kress, Gunther. 2010. *Multimodality: A social semiotic approach to contemporary communication*. Abingdon, UK: Routledge.

Kucirkova, Natalia. 2014, May 23. *Research blog: Touch in children's digital books*. Retrieved from http://www.booktrust.org.uk/news-and-blogs/blogs/booktrust/716.

Labbo, Linda. 2006. Understanding the role of classroom computers in the literacy development of young children: A semiotic perspective. *Journal of Reading Education* 31: 37–41.

Latour, Bruno. 2005. *Reassembling the social-an introduction to actor-network-theory*. Oxford: Oxford University Press.

Lenz-Taguchi, Hillevi. 2014. New materialism and play. In *Sage handbook of play and learning in early childhood*, ed. Liz Brooker, Mindy Blaise, and Susan Edwards, 79–90. London: Sage.

Luke, Carmen. 1989. *Pedagogy, printing, and Protestantism*. Albany, NY: State University of New York Press.

Luke, Carmen. 2007. As seen on TV or was that my phone? New media literacy. *Policy Futures in Education* 5: 50–58.

Marsh, Jackie, Peter Hannon, Margaret Lewis, and Louise Ritchie. 2015a. Young children's initiation into family literacy practices in the digital age. *Journal of Early Childhood Research*. doi:1476718X15582095.

Marsh, Jackie, L. Plowman, Dylan Yamada-Rice, J. C. Bishop, J. Lahmar, F. Scott, A. Davenport, S. Davis, K. French, M. Piras, S. Thornhill, P. Robinson, and P. Winter. 2015b. *Exploring play and creativity in pre-schoolers' use of apps: Final project report*. In *Technology and Play*. Retrieved from www.techandplay.org.

Matthews, John. 2006. Very young children's development in movie-making. *Mind, Culture, and Activity* 13: 130–156.

Matthews, John, and Seow, Peter Sen Kee. 2007. Electronic paint: Understanding children's representation through their interactions with digital paint. *Journal of Art and Design Education* 26: 251–263.

McEneaney, John E. 2011. Web 3.0, litbots, and TPWSGWTAU. *Journal of Adolescent and Adult Literacy* 54: 376–378. doi:10.1598/JAAL.54.5.8.

Medina, Carmen Liliana, and Karen E. Wohlwend. 2014. *Literacy, play, and globalization: Converging imaginaries in children's critical and cultural performances*. New York: Routledge.

Merchant, Guy. 2005. Barbie meets Bob the builder at the workstation: Learning to write on screen. In *Popular culture, new media and digital literacy in early childhood*, ed. J. Marsh, 183–200. New York: RoutledgeFalmer.

Merchant, Guy. 2015. Apps, adults, and young children: Researching digital literacy practices in context. In *Discourse and digital practices: Doing discourse analysis in the digital age*, ed. R. Jones, A. Chik, and C.A. Hafner, 144–157. New York: Routledge.

Mills, Kathy. 2016. *Literacy theories for the digital age: Social, critical, multimodal, spatial, material and sensory lenses*. Bristol: Multilingual Matters.

Needleman, Sarah E. 2016, July 16. 'Pokémon Go' craze raises safety issues: Days after smartphone app's launch, players shared tales of dangerous encounters. *Wall Street Journal*. Retrieved from http://www.wsj.com/articles/pokemon-go-craze-raises-safety-issues-1468365058.

New London Group. 1996. A pedagogy of multiliteracies: Designing social futures. *Harvard Educational Review* 66: 60–93.

Norris, Sigrid. 2004. *Analyzing multimodal interaction: A methodological framework*. London: Routledge.

Prensky, Marc. 2001. Digital natives, digital immigrants. *On the Horizon* 9: 1–2.

Rideout, Victoria J. 2013. *Zero to eight: Children's media use in America 2013*. San Francisco, CA.

Rideout, Victoria J., and Katz, Vikki S. 2016. Opportunity for all? Technology and learning in lower-income families. *A report of the families and media project*. New York, NY: Joan Ganz Cooney Center at Sesame Workshop.

Rowe, Deborah Wells, Fitch, Joanne Deal, and Bass, Alyson Smith. 2003. Toy stories as opportunities for reflection in writers' workshop. *Language Arts* 80: 363–374.

Rowe, Deborah Wells, Mary E. Miller, and Mark B. Pacheco. 2014. Preschoolers as digital designers: Composing dual language ebooks using touchscreen computer tablets. In *Handbook of research on digital tools for writing instruction in K-12 settings* ed. Rebecca S. Anderson and Clif Mims. Hershey, PA: IGI Global.

Rowsell, Jennifer, Mary G. Saudelli, Ruth M. Scott, and Andrea Bishop. 2013. iPads as placed resources: Forging community in online and offline spaces. *Language Arts* 90: 351–360.

Rowsell, Jennifer, and Karen E. Wohlwend. 2016. Free play or tight spaces? Mapping participatory literacies in apps. *The Reading Teacher*. doi:10.1002/trtr.1490.

Scollon, Ron. 2001. *Mediated discourse: The nexus of practice*. London: Routledge.

Scollon, Ron, and Suzanne W. Scollon. 2004. *Nexus analysis: Discourse and the emerging internet*. New York: Routledge.

Sefton-Green, Julian, Jackie Marsh, Ola Erstad, and Rosie Flewitt. 2016. Establishing a research agenda for the digital literacy practices of young children: A white paper for COST action IS1410. Retrieved from http://digilitey.eu/wp-content/uploads/2015/09/DigiLitEYWP.pdf.

Shuler, Carly. 2012. *iLearn II: An analysis of the education category on Apple's app store*. New York: Joan Ganz Cooney Center.

Street, Brian V. 1995. *Social literacies: Critical approaches to literary development*. Singapore: Pearson Education Asia.

Thiel, Jaye J., and Karen E. Wohlwend. 2016, December 1. *From spitballs to spinners: A posthuman approach to paper as a crucial material in literacy practice, pedagogy, and research.* Paper presented at the Literacy Research Association, Nashville, TN.

Vygotsky, Lev. 1935/1978. *Mind in society: The development of higher psychological processes*. Cambridge, MA: Harvard University Press.
Wertsch, James V. 1991. *Voices of the mind: A sociocultural approach to mediated action*. Cambridge, MA: Harvard University Press.
Wohlwend, Karen E. 2009. Early adopters: Playing new literacies and pretending new technologies in print-centric classrooms. *Journal of Early Childhood Literacy* 92: 119–143.
Wohlwend, Karen E. 2011. *Playing their way into literacies: Reading, writing, and belonging in the early childhood classroom*. New York: Teachers College Press.
Wohlwend, Karen E. 2017. Toddlers and touchscreens: Learning "concepts beyond print" with tablet technologies. In *Reclaiming early childhood literacies: Narratives of hope, power, and vision*, ed. R.J. Meyer, and K.F. Whitmore. Mahwah, NJ: Lawrence Erlbaum.
Wohlwend, Karen E., Beth A. Buchholz, Christy Wessel-Powell, Linda S. Coggin, and Nicholas E. Husbye. 2013. *Literacy playshop: New literacies, popular media, and play in the early childhood classroom*. New York: Teachers College Press.

Author Biography

Karen E. Wohlwend is Associate Professor of Literacy, Culture, and Language Education at Indiana University. She reconceptualises young children's play as an embodied literacy, produced through popular media and digital technologies in online spaces and classroom cultures. She is the author of *Playing Their Way into Literacies: Reading, Writing, and Belonging in the Early Childhood Classroom; Literacy Playshop: New Literacies, Popular Media, and Play in the Early Childhood Classroom*; and with colleague Carmen Medina *Play, and Globalization: Converging Imaginaries in Children's Critical and Cultural Performances*.

Chapter 5
Multimodal Layering: Students Learning with iPads in Primary School Classrooms

Alyson Simpson and Maureen Walsh

Scenario

Two boys sit at a computer screen watching a video of themselves working on iPads using the app GarageBand to create a recording of an advertisement that incorporates voice-over with a musical theme. One researcher stands behind the students filming their interaction with the computer screen and each other. A second researcher interviews them about the learning processes they went through to turn their original notes about fast foods from a brainstormed text on butchers' paper to a digital sound recording. The iPad video shows two boys sitting on a carpet working away from the rest of the class; their intent is to create an audio text that meets the criteria set by their teacher using different modes (such as print and sound in music and voice tone) to communicate a persuasive message. The video of the boys looking at themselves on the computer screen shows two boys explaining to two researchers a critique of their ability to collaboratively adopt the affordances of technology working with prescribed classroom limitations. In the shift between the private improvisation and the public reflection a semiotic reconfiguring of the GarageBand audio text occurs as a video recording, which enabled the students to re-examine their appreciation of how the use of the iPad app enriched the choices they had in creating their text.

A. Simpson (✉)
University of Sydney, Sydney, Australia
e-mail: alyson.simpson@sydney.edu.au

M. Walsh
Australian Catholic University and University of Sydney, Sydney, Australia
e-mail: maureen.walsh44@gmail.com

C. Burnett et al. (eds.), *The Case of the iPad*,
DOI 10.1007/978-981-10-4364-2_5

Introduction

The introductory scenario is an episode from a 2-year empirical study run in a Grade 5 classroom of 11–12-year-old boys in an urban primary school in NSW Australia, where all students had their own iPads. The students were about to sit a standardized national literacy test that would require demonstration of such text features as correct grammar, spelling and effective vocabulary choice when writing a persuasive text. Rather than just teach to the test, the classroom teacher took advantage of the iPad affordances to integrate support for students' development of linguistic knowledge with awareness of multimodal communication techniques. As the teacher had a master app through which student iPads could be controlled, work completed by students in isolation tucked away in a corner of the room could be harvested and displayed on the Interactive Whiteboard (IWB) at the swipe of a finger. Each time a text was repurposed in this way it became a public document which on one hand provided a stimulus for new learning to the whole group but also provided opportunities for individual students to reflect on their work. The uptake of iPads/tablets in schools worldwide has increased year-on-year but as yet there has been little research into the modal complexity offered by this learning device that takes into account the context in which learning takes place. While there is no doubt that mobile tablet technology brings access to new affordances, both the material and social nature of learning and literacy with these platforms needs problematizing in order to investigate implications for pedagogy.

The research discussed in this study defines an emerging theoretical concept—multimodal layering—as a way of investigating the complexity of cohesive meaning making when semiotic systems interact in a text which is then recontextualized in new semiotic configurations. The chapter foregrounds this concept to demonstrate the impact of socially situated and technologically mediated experiences of literacy on students' learning with iPads in the primary classroom. Although the one to one use of tablet technology suggests that learning might become highly individualized when using these devices, this study shows that the use of the touch pads provided collaborative opportunities for both public and private learning.

The research took a theoretical stance built on multimodal/semiotic theory informed by studies of twenty-first century learning and literacies. A methodological perspective was adopted that viewed videos, student 'think alouds', student print and digital work samples as data. Using qualitative analysis to interrogate modes or combinations of modes (spoken and written language, image, sound, movement, gesture) the study provides insight into students' learning with iPads. Our deliberations have led us to further explore the related issues of dynamic materiality and meta-awareness. We have defined dynamic materiality elsewhere as 'the way touch technology enables the constant shift between modes and texts through which students need to navigate to build cohesive layers of meaning' (Walsh and Simpson 2014: 102). The iPad platform is particularly generative in this regard. This chapter explores what multimodal layering is in relation to tablet use and how such layering is significant in providing rich learning opportunities for students. It concludes by arguing that the metaphor of multimodal layering helps to identify dynamic instances of semiotic and cognitive complexity.

Theoretical Perspective

The study is informed by complementary theoretical frameworks belonging to the semiotics of multimodality, (Kress and van Leeuwen 2001; Jewitt 2009; Kress 2010), and twenty-first century learning, (Wohlwend 2010; Groves 2012; Rowsell et al. 2013). The theory of multimodality has enabled researchers to explain and explore the way meaning is made both separately and simultaneously through modes of communication such as language, image, sound and gesture. It has been particularly significant in examining multiple literacy practices within digital frameworks. More recently, we have investigated the significance of touch as a mode for meaning making with use of tablets/iPads (Walsh and Simpson 2013, 2014; Simpson and Walsh 2014) and we have shown evidence of the dynamic learning processes that can occur in primary school students' interactions with multiple modes on screen while interacting with their teacher and peers in classroom tasks. Through our research, we have investigated the nature of the literacy demands made on students when multiple screens and modes are accessed through tablet use. Our findings have led us to consider the impact of multimodality with the use of digital technologies specifically.

For example, in examining the complex processes that can occur with the use of digital technologies, we have considered other metaphors that address the way meaning can be articulated between and across semiotic modes along with the nature of 'materiality/immateriality' (Leonardi et al. 2012; Burnett et al. 2014) of gesture and touch as we developed the concept of 'multimodal layering'. To explore this concept epistemologically, we now examine the different metaphors used to clarify how our theoretical perspective of multimodal layering contributes to the field.

Epistemological Metaphors

To investigate how researchers (including ourselves) represent concepts of multimodality, we first turn our attention to the implied connotations of terminology used in their research. Theorists have borrowed metaphors from a range of disciplines such as mathematics and science in order to make concrete their epistemology. Each one of these metaphors construes meaning with particular semiotic impact positioning the reader to comprehend abstraction through mental associations. We present a number of epistemological metaphors below noting how each one provides a particular perspective on the scenario shown earlier.

The term transduction, used in the fields of biology and physics, is used to describe a change in state in a one-to-one relationship of something recast into another form, whether it be genetic material or electrical energy, for example. In explaining the semiotics of multimodality, Kress states that transduction is the '...process of moving meaning-material from one mode to another' (Kress 2010: 125) so that meaning is represented in a different mode, as in a verbal narrative being represented visually. As Kress comments this is a common process that occurs in many different types of communication. So transduction is useful in understanding the re-articulation of meaning from one mode to another but it does not convey the complexity of meaning that can occur with the convergence of multiple modes. Similarly, Iedema's (2003) use of the term 'resemiotisation' describes the way meanings are transformed from one mode to another in different social contexts. This epistemological metaphor would only account for the part of the scenario where written text was realized as image such as when one student drew a cartoon on their butchers' paper notes to represent the overweight person described in statistics in the fast food fact sheet.

As another example, the term multiplicative references mathematical conceptualizations—when more than one mode occurs in a communicative event then the impact of the modes is increased in a compound effect. That is, in this metaphor the semiotic impact of individual modes does not simply add up, one to another. Rather the modes interact with each other so that the meaning is complicated through combined semiotic impact. Lemke exemplifies the term as 'the meaning resource capacity, of multimodal constructs is the logical product, in a multiplicative sense, of the capacities of the constituent semiotic resource systems' (Lemke 2002: 303). With this metaphor, the theorist provides an image of expansion, which binds elements together in relation to each other as meaning making boundaries shift. This epistemological metaphor would only account for parts of the scenario when video image and audio interact to create a complex text demanding multiple forms of decoding. For example, when the twin audio tracks from the video within the video need to be understood as relating to different recordings of the boys working on their iPads.

By contrast the term modal density references scientific conceptualisations—when more than one mode occurs in a communicative event then the impact of each mode increases relative to the others. That is, in this metaphor the semiotic impact of individual modes does not merely become more intense. Rather the modes interact with each other so that as a whole they take on more semiotic weight. Norris exemplifies the term as: 'Modal density refers to the intricate interplay of various modes of communication or the intensity of a certain mode that a social actor employs' (Norris 2004: 102). This is a metaphor that contracts attention inward to collect elements together one in relation to each other. This epistemological metaphor only draws attention to the scenario text as a bounded whole privileging perhaps image as the mode with most potent impact.

So, in order to take account of what we see as semiotic reconfiguring that is prompted as students shift constantly from private to public learning spaces, we need a term that allows for that complexity. While the above three terms provide insight into the characteristics and quality of semiotic interactions as texts we offer the concept of 'multimodal layering' to further explore these interactions taking into account the contexts in which they play out. This metaphor attempts to shift the focus of analysis to how semiotic interactions contribute to potential points of meaning making coherence. For example, in relation to the scenario at the beginning of this chapter, this epistemological metaphor accounts for how the audio of the GarageBand video is repurposed and becomes part of a new text as the researchers' prompt for the student's think aloud. That is, the new text reworked the modal configuration that the students had experienced to serve new purposes yet carried fossilized within its multimodal layering its own semiotic history.

We chose the term layering to reference geological conceptualisations, which encourage perception of landscape. We have selected this discursive viewpoint to take into account not just the isolated semiotic systems evoked through modes but also the ontological impact of the social context within which a text is interpolated and the meaning making events take place. For example, the boys' original handwritten notes on the disadvantages of fast food are used during the learning sequence to create a digital text combining spoken words and an audio track, which becomes an oral presentation to the class. There is simultaneously a transference of meaning across different modes as well as accretion of meaning from the start of the lesson to the end. To deal with this complex situation the boys need to deal with multiple forms of decoding and encoding to incorporate, understand and respond to the language of persuasion including appropriate speech tones and sound effects.

In proposing this concept, we acknowledge that various theorizations of modal complexity already exist. However, we see the need to expand these conceptualizations by investigating not just how modes interact at the textual level but also how modes interact at the contextual level, in this case the classroom, which leads to changing meaning making possibilities. This metaphor thus enables the researcher to attempt a semiotic analysis of the multimodal literacy demands within learning events that incorporate literacy in digital communication as individuals interact with text in private or public spaces (Walsh and Simpson 2014).

We have suggested that the multiplicative effects existing within the semiotic boundaries of a text alter when multimodal layering occurs as the text is repurposed in a new interaction and the learner is repositioned to respond to the reconfiguring of semiosis. For example, because of the interview context where the video data of the boys' work became a prompt for reflection, the students had to deal with an additional layering of modes as they discussed their learning across the different stages of the classroom tasks. Our data show that students' learning is enhanced when they have to deal with multiplicative effects experienced in new contexts.

We propose that what we traced during the classroom interactions using digital texts of various kinds reveals evidence of students creating complex meaningful connections as a result of enacting different literacy practices through sedimented layers of semiotic modes. This conceptualization of learning is similar to what Tierney et al. (2006) described as a 'complex layering of concepts' but it is also different as it takes account of the fluid and immaterial nature of meaning making prompted in reading and writing with iPads as well as its physicality. That is, rather

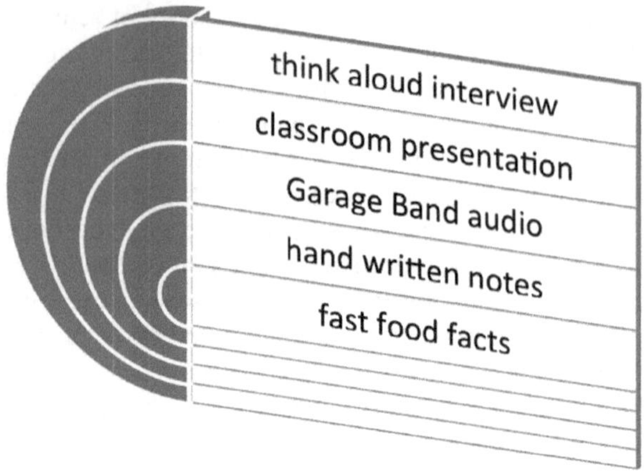

Fig. 5.1 An example of multimodal layering

than focusing merely on static texts and concepts we have incorporated data, which records social interaction in dynamic learning events. In this way, we can attend to the importance of attending to the 'here and now' including what Leander and Boldt (2013: 24) refer to as the 'sensations and movements of the body in the moment-by-moment unfolding or emergence of activity' as well as the pedagogy that enables the action. The semiotic history accumulating in the layers of learning summarized in our scenario, is illustrated in Fig. 5.1.

Figure 5.1 represents how the epistemological metaphor of multimodal layering accounts for the semiotic reconfiguring that occurred in the specific classroom experience summarized in the opening scenario. It indicates how reading (about fast food facts) informed writing (of a persuasive text) which was recorded with music, broadcast and reviewed. We explicate the process further by providing descriptive analysis (See Exemplars 1, 2, 3, 4, 5 and Coda) and extracting key themes that emerge to be explored in the discussion.

Methodology

Conceptualized as a small-scale qualitative, interpretive case study, the research is informed by qualitative methodology due to its focus on interaction in the social context of the classroom when iPad/tablets were used by primary school students in English/ Language Arts lessons. This kind of study is best explored in a case study, which allows the collection of rich data garnered from a variety of sources and through close observations over a period of time (Yin 2012) that captures the 'local specificity' (Dyson and Genishi 2005: 3) of a particular classroom. The study does not pretend to have high generalizability but can assert that it achieved useful findings, which will be relevant to teachers and teacher educators in showing the potential of multimodality to provide supportive scaffolds for meaning making.

The study was originally designed to investigate the nature and processes of digital and multimodal reading practices as experienced through touch pad technology. The specific research focus investigated how students' reading practices varied across digital and print forms of text in terms of modal complexity and student perceptions of literacy practices within the classroom learning context. As Jewitt (2009) has shown, multimodal analysis is a new and somewhat contested area of research. Several researchers (e.g. Kress et al. 2001; Flewitt et al. 2009; Crescenzi et al. 2014) have used varied approaches to transcribing and analysing multimodal data in order to represent the relationship between different modes and meaning making. Methods of analysis use images, graphics, diagrams and tables to represent the impact of modal interactions on semiotic exchange. Influenced by these researchers we have previously used diagrams and tables to examine the relationship between modes and students' learning responses and social interactions (Simpson and Walsh 2014). In this chapter, we are further testing the potential of such a framework focusing on the interaction of modal affordances in public and private learning spaces.

Participants in the ethics-approved study were twenty-eight Year 5 (aged 10–11 years) students in an urban independent school for boys in Sydney, NSW Australia. The study ran for three school terms, approximately 7 months. In the data collection phase, two researchers visited the participating class once a week during morning literacy sessions to observe the 28 students and their teacher. Our qualitative methodology prompted the collection and coding of different data sets in order to address our three focal points: 1. Literacy practices; 2. The modal affordances of literacy practices using iPads; and 3. The classroom context in terms of zones of interaction. This paper provides exemplars representing the three foci as viewed through a methodological perspective attending to mode and learning purpose. Data were collected as video recordings of students reading print and touch tablet texts, artefacts in the form of work samples created during lesson time, fieldnotes of whole class lesson observations and pair or individual student think alouds. Think alouds are a method of data collection, which prompt students to reflect orally on their learning either during or shortly after a lesson takes place. The spoken thoughts are recorded by the researcher and transcribed for analysis. The researchers found think alouds to be a particularly robust source of information especially when students observed videos of their own actions and explained the impact of modes on their learning. The way these data were collected provided additional insight into the complexity of students' learning helping the exploration of multimodal layering.

To illustrate student learning over time a sequence of learning activities, run over a number of days, has been selected for descriptive analysis. The end goal of the set of literacy tasks was for pairs of Grade 5 students to produce a persuasive text in the form of a radio advertisement about the dangers of junk food and to present this to the whole class. Throughout the sequence the teacher taught the students about the purpose, structure and language of persuasive texts by modelling successful texts and providing them with resources such as factual and persuasive texts about junk food in print and video forms. The students accessed these resources on their individual iPads as well as viewing them on the IWB during whole class discussion. Students were required to discriminate between opinion and fact through deconstructing texts and writing their own phrases and sentences. There was a constant shift between whole class work and individual/paired work with the texts on the students' iPads. By the end of the lesson sequence the students had planned and written their persuasive texts and produced them as radio ads using multimedia for recording and editing with GarageBand on their iPads.

Framework for Analysis

As this chapter concentrates on exploring the concept of multimodal layering in terms of private and public learning spaces, our data analysis mainly addresses the dual focus of the individual student/learner and the classroom as a social context. The video recordings of students working in the classroom were analyzed by modal affordances and zone of social interaction. To make this kind of analysis possible we devised a methodological template, or framework of analysis, which attends to individual modes as well as the meaning making opportunities created from interrelated modes employed to achieve literacy tasks.

The three focal points were included in the framework for analysis of student learning events and represent the decisions we made as researchers to attend to:

1. Literacy practices = the explicit literacy focus the teacher introduced in a learning event
2. Modal affordances = the interplay of semiotic systems including but not limited to digital platforms such as iPads
3. Zone of social interaction = the interconnections of private and/or public spaces where student attention was directed by the learning context

The three headings relate to our interest in examining how the design of classroom contexts can construct opportunities for students to engage in multimodal digital practices that improve their literacy capabilities and contribute to critical reflection on learning.

Exemplars with Descriptive Analysis

The exemplars were selected from the data corpus as they track one pair of students who collaborated on the creation of their persuasive text from beginning to the end. These students were the only pair to take part in the reflective interview process watching a video of themselves working on their iPads. Each exemplar provides a progressive snapshot across the learning sequence that demonstrates how the multimodal layering builds up. The exemplars illustrate the way we have used our framework to analyse the interrelationships between literacy learning demands and modal interactions that were negotiated as students moved between private and public learning spaces in the classroom to achieve the literacy tasks. In each example, we introduce the classroom learning context and juxtapose it with a summary of what occurred captured in table format. A short transcript extract of student language is included in each exemplar where relevant to demonstrate students' thought processes as they worked with the multimodal tasks. Included at the end of each exemplar is a comment about evidence of student learning. We demonstrate through this descriptive analysis how our concept of multimodal layering aptly captures the dynamic learning processes in which students were engaged. It should be noted that the distinction of 'zone of interaction' focus is viewed as more of a cline rather than either/or. After considering these snapshots of data capturing the social dimension within which the individuals act as learners, we will discuss the impact of multimodal layering on student learning.

Screenshot images for each Exemplar are included in Fig. 5.2 to show the shifting focus of attention from meaning making with 'isolated', private texts to intrapersonal meaning making with texts shared communally in public spaces. The images are positioned in Fig. 5.2, according to their semiotic reconfiguring in relation to Multimodal Layering.

Exemplar 1: Reading Phase

See Table 5.1.

In the reading phase of the sequence the boys read information to themselves. There was no discussion and no writing. The researchers did not interrupt the students' silent reading so we only have the images as verification of the individual, contemplative work they were doing. Our observations note students attended to and interpreted text elements, as they were required to discriminate between fact and opinion at an individual level of understanding. From the range of examples students read and viewed on paper and screen, they were given opportunities to identify how words, visual and also sound effects were used in persuasive texts compared with factual texts.

See image 1, Fig. 5.2 Screenshot of student reading fast food facts on iPads.

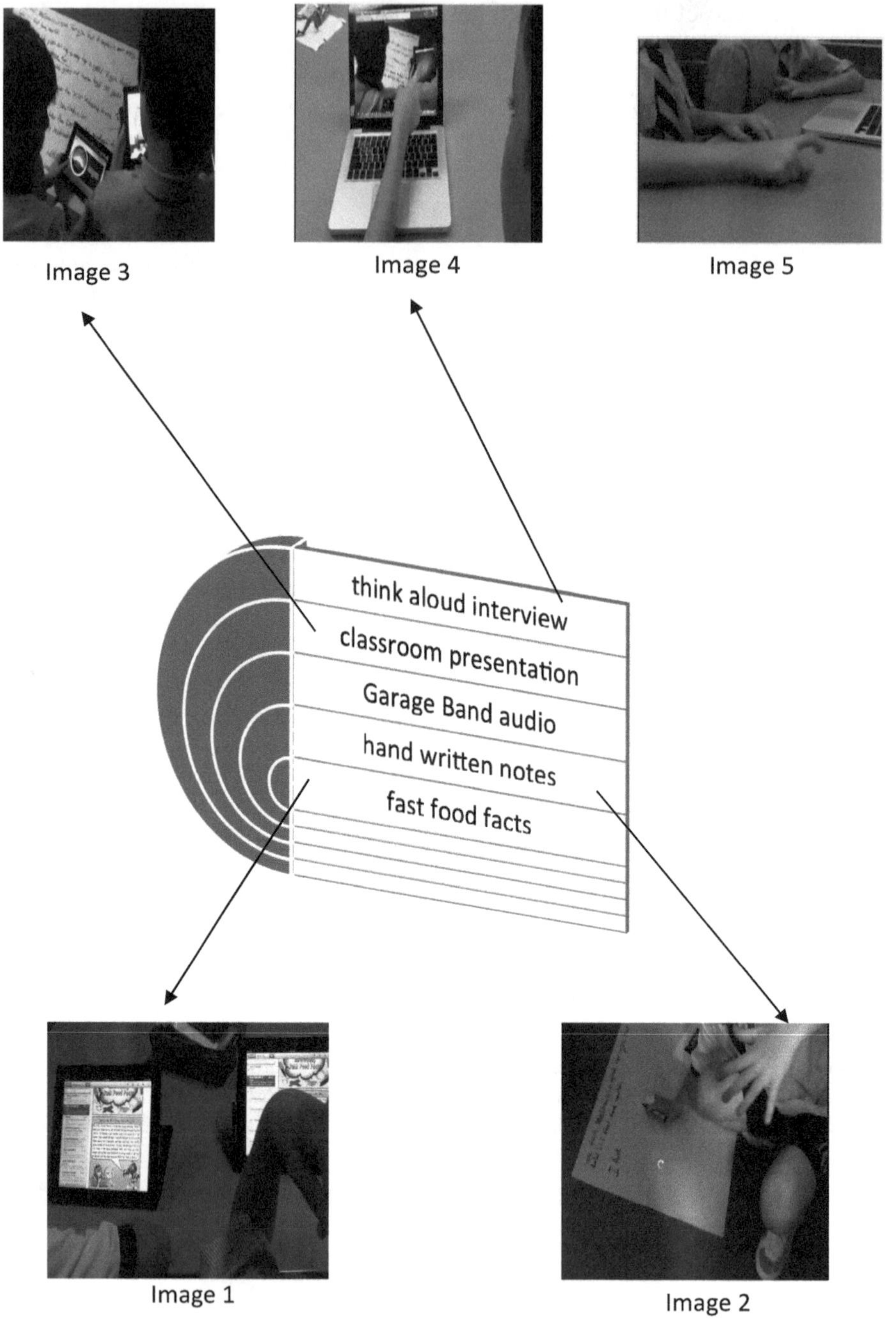

Fig. 5.2 Illustrated example of semiotic reconfiguring as multimodal layering

Table 5.1 Multimodal layering at reading phase

Literacy practices	Modal affordances	Zone of social interaction
Reading of factual and persuasive texts	Written, visual with audio mode backgrounded	Private and public shift in focus of attention Individual students read own screens then watch video of ad on IWB

Table 5.2 Multimodal layering at writing phase

Literacy practices	Modal affordances	Zone of social interaction
Writing persuasive expressions	Using written language from models read and viewed	Private and public shift in focus of attention Individual students brain storm ideas then digital post-its are shown on IWB Student pairs write on the paper collaboratively

Exemplar 2: Writing Phase

See Table 5.2.

During the writing phase of the sequence the boys reflected on their thinking as follows:

R Why did you start the sentence with I think?
S1 Oh because it is an opinion and then followed by a fact
R exactly
S1 We're writing I think McDonald's gives out too many toys a year

[S1 waves hand for emphasis]

See image 2, Fig. 5.2 Screenshot of hand written draft of radio ad on butchers' paper

Note the students' use of thinking verbs and nouns associated with the concept of persuasion as well as recognition of mode of communication. As indicated by the bold typeface, the students were using tone to emphasize their opinion. Students had attended to and interpreted the link between the generic models and applied them to their own practice. The language on individual post-it notes shared on the IWB showed the similarity of persuasive expressions students had chosen to record. The shared notes led to more complex examples of persuasive writing when students collaborated in pairs.

Exemplar 3: Talking and Listening Phase (Private)

See Table 5.3.

During the creation of the radio text the boys simultaneously created two texts—spoken and music—the overlapping lines indicate their shift of attention between purposeful choice of modes in the following transcript.

Table 5.3 Multimodal layering at talking and listening phase (private)

Literacy practices	Modal affordances	Zone of social interaction
Creating radio advertisement from written text	Heightened emphasis on audio mode foregrounded, e.g. voice tone, music based on written text accessed by touch on screen	Student pairs record radio ad on GarageBand

S1 [starts to read text from sheet on the floor] You think McDonald's is good for you but it represents… McDonald's gives out way too many toys a year, if you don't
S2 [navigates to music part of the app]
S1 have to OK? restart that
S2 I've discovered a little piano—[he works on creating a music theme and saves it]
S1 [resets S2 iPad GB to start recording]
S1 We need to say a line each, We have to say a line each
S2 [plays music theme from iPad]

See image 3, Fig. 5.2 Screen shot of GarageBand audio production

Note the way the students used language (e.g. 'I', 'We','need to','have to') to self direct themselves about the use of the modes as they were composing their GarageBand text. The students reinterpreted and reframed concepts from their original monomodal print text repurposing them through the use of synchronous semiotic modes and transforming them into a new multimodal text demonstrating cohesive construction of meaning.

Exemplar 4: Talking and Listening Phase (Public)

See Table 5.4.

At the end of the lesson when the teacher asked the students to listen to a radio ad one of their peers read aloud, the students were given a rubric to assess text features such as cohesive argument, facts with supporting evidence, persuasive language and emotive vocabulary. The short text extract from the transcript shows a student identifying the language he heard in the radio ad. Then it shows the teacher reminding the students about the kind of 'tone' they were aiming for in order to amplify their persuasive language through voice.

Table 5.4 Multimodal layering at talking and listening phase (public)

Literacy practices	Modal affordances	Zone of social interaction
Listening to texts to identify linguistic features	Major emphasis on audio	Public—students read persuasive text as radio ad to class audience

Teacher what was very impressive about that group's radio advert?
S1 instead of just saying McD is very bad for you he said this is why I agree McDonald's is.
Teacher Yes he does use those connective persuasive openers and those connecting phrases. Microphone to S2 please. What style is yours? dramatic group—Switch on to find out why the world is so bad (spoken in a dramatic voice)…

Note the way the teacher modelled the voice tone that he intended students to associate with a mode of communication for intended purpose and student reflection on grammar and tone. Students attended to and interpreted the modal elements used in the peer text discriminating the use of grammatical features and appropriate voice tone at an individual level of understanding prompted by an assessment rubric. They demonstrate well-developed textual awareness. It should also be noted that this transcript is evidence of how the facts that were read originally in the McDonald's prompt sheet in Exemplar 1 became layered into the new audio text created on the iPad.

Exemplar 5: Critical Reflection

See Table 5.5.

In the final example analyzed the video shows a pair of students watching a video of themselves on an iPad. Therefore, in image 4 the screen shows two layers of multimodal interaction from the researcher's perspective looking over the shoulder of the boys as they look over their own shoulders on the archived recording.

S1 So at the start L was lost and … [gestures with hand in front of iPad]
S2 So basically he was helping me [S2 points to himself using the iPad] to find what to do here, he's just helping me [S2 points at S1 in iPad video] and then we record using that [points at specific icon on the GB screen visible on the iPad] function, the microphone
S1 the audio recorder
S2 the audio and then we just read what we had on the script [S2 uses broad sweep of his hand across the image of the butchers' paper on the iPad] and record it [S2 gestures to the iPad he was using that shows him recording] and then add some music in at the start and at the end and yeh. That is what we did

Table 5.5 Multimodal layering at critical reflection phase

Literacy practices	Modal affordances	Zone of social interaction
Reviewing own work	Heightened emphasis on visual mode with audio, and written embedded	Private and public shift in focus of attention as student pair shares thoughts with researchers

S1 and to make it a bit more fun we added some pictures [S1 points at the little cartoon on the butchers' paper seen on the iPad]

See image 4, Fig. 5.2 Screenshot of students watching a video of themselves as they create their radio ad.

Note the use of verbs and nouns associated with the affordances of the tablet to achieve the literacy task as well as recognition of modes of communication. The viewing of a video of themselves enabled the students to provide a spoken reflection on their use of multimodal affordances. They demonstrated critical awareness of how they had deliberately chosen synchronous semiotic modes transforming them into multimodal texts for cohesive construction of meaning.

Coda

We present one more example of layering during the interview where one of the students spontaneously commented on the affordances of the iPad. This point is important as, unprompted, the student notes the difference between the physical action of writing on paper compared with the multiple actions available with a keyboard and tablet. Image 5 is a still image that captures his action of physically mimicking the action of writing as he states:

See image 5, Fig. 5.2 Screen shot during reflective interview

S1 Like I said it [the iPad] has more options so as he was saying it's, in a book you go write, write write (student uses similar gestures mimicking his peer's action and pretending to write on paper) where in an iPad you say will I add this in or maybe I'll leave that out and then I'll add that later (student imitates the gestures of working on a keyboard and tablet going from different movements, actions). It's just got more on it than in a book.

This comment reveals the student's understanding of how modes impacted on his learning. The physical actions accompanying his speech underline his realization of the relationship of embodied materiality on immaterial meaning making.

Summary

In our analysis of this sequence of private and public literacy events sketched with exemplars shifting through reading, writing, talking and listening and viewing and representing we found there was often a pattern of learning that was interwoven with activities in such a way that multimodal affordances became a support to students' meaning making practices (Rowsell et al. 2013). As we documented the constant to-ing and fro-ing between texts, devices and learners we observed what appeared to be instances of student insight into how the modal affordances of the iPad supported their learning. However, this intellectual exercise depends on the students being able to make complex conceptual connections that could be described as cognitively demanding. For example, at the same time we observed that accompanying these intellectual insights were instances of engagement conveyed through hand gestures (indicated in Exemplar 5) and tone of voice. These were evidence of affective responses that demonstrated the intensities of the students' involvement in their learning (Leander and Boldt 2013). We find that the term 'multimodal layering' best describes the outcome of these combined processes and actions as the different modes of learning became sedimented one over the other. The images and the transcript examples above demonstrate multimodal layering in action during the lesson sequence about persuasive text writing. The exemplars showed students engaged with texts at different metacognitive levels to make meaning as their focus was drawn from private contemplation to public sharing of texts. It is important to note that the conceptual understanding of students within modal layering was made possible by the way the teacher planned the learning tasks to provide a range of affordances in a range of interactive contexts.

Discussion

Our methodological framework of analysis enabled us to document students' learning through the successive stages of the classroom tasks. As shown in our data samples taken from observation, video clips and talk alouds, through our analytic framework we were able to examine the impact of multimodal layering on student learning. It appears to us that the methodology enabled us to identify how the use of the iPad in this learning context led to complex meaning making and affective engagement. Close examination of classroom interactions using a framework for analysis such as this demonstrates the dynamic interrelationships and interdependence of modes (e.g. touch, sound, image, spoken and written language) within pedagogical contexts (Leander and Boldt 2013). This approach allowed us to acknowledge the complexity of modal layering created in the collaborative learning activities made possible as student attention shifted from independent private to teacher directed public spaces (Simpson and Walsh 2014). Although it is not a delicate instrument with timing and actions monitored closely (Crescenzi et al. 2014), the contribution of the methodological 'framework of analysis' to multimodal studies is that it displays the interactions between meaning making events. We deliberately did not stage our data collection to monitor students moment-by-moment preferring rather to capture the learning schematic and view the conceptual traffic through a modal lens. What this approach revealed was the ways in which learners attend to and cope with modal complexity. Rather than presenting a finalized topography of the learning, the approach examines the individual layers of learning processes as they build one on another. Students were observed reading and creating texts using a variety of modes on screen and in print within different learning contexts in the classroom. The framework allowed us to attend to the interplay of these material and immaterial learning spaces. We propose that by slowing down the action we are able to identify phases of conceptual development for students working individually and with others. In our previous papers (Walsh and Simpson 2013, 2014; Simpson and Walsh 2014) we focused on touch. In this chapter we have taken a broader approach to see how the iPad supported multimodal literacy learning to occur across a range of modes.

Our findings in this study have addressed the question, what is the impact on complexity of conceptual understanding when different modes are layered into a learning context? We have shown that dynamic materiality influences the blurring of 'public' and 'private' learning spaces to create greater opportunities for individual as well as collaborative learning. The use of iPads in this classroom enabled the constant shift between modes through which students needed to navigate to build cohesive layers of meaning between reading and writing for literacy and learning tasks at school. This modal layering prompts students to reconfigure their existing mental schema as comprehension plays out as socially mediated cognition (Cain 2010). We claim that there is evidence of students developing meta-awareness through the processes they used when they were composing their radio ad text. Their talk is peppered with references to thought processes as well as the purposeful use of specific modes, as shown in a students' comment to the teacher:

S5 Well instead of just saying like McDonald's is very bad for you. He said like, (uses presentation voice) 'This is why I agree that McDonald's is very bad for you'.

Student think alouds provided us with verification or new interpretations of their learning. This one shows, for example the student's awareness of how persuasive rhetoric can be enhanced by changes in wording, emphasis and tone.

Further, if we go back to the quotation from one of the boys shown in the Coda we can see the physical, cognitive and affective engagement of this student as he evaluates their work and comments on the differences between writing on paper and creating on screen. He physically uses his hands to tap on the desk as he says 'in a book you go write, write write' emphasizing a dominant tone in his repetition of the word 'write' as he taps. In contrast when he describes the increased options of the iPad he uses a gentler persuasive vocal tone as he imitates the gestures of working on a keyboard: '… in an iPad you say will I add this in or maybe I'll leave that out and then I'll add that later'. His explanation and accompanying actions reveal the multimodal layers of learning he has experienced from the initial task of reading and creating a persuasive text to reflecting on the process and affordances of different modes.

For these students learning was an organic process, as they worked conceptually and emotively through progressive tasks located at the intersection of private and public spaces. The data exemplifies how the affordances of the iPad help to constitute dynamic learning/teaching events. Leander and Boldt (2013: 44) question whether a teacher can 'recognize differences, surprise, and unfolding that follow along paths that are not linear'. Our study has uncovered the layered nature of learning opportunities. We hope that our research can provide insights into the potential of multimodal environments, which could inform pedagogy and support student learning.

Conclusion

The iPad platform provided students with ways to explore modes, design, enhance and communicate their textual creations. The analysis of student data revealed the development of conceptual complexity growing in a cumulative fashion as the students moved from planning and creating a persuasive text to reflecting on their learning at the end of the process. By tracking from reading, through writing, talking and listening and onto representing and critiquing we were able to show how the modal demands were layered as texts were repurposed from context to context. We were also able to show that due to the semiotic processing required to deal with each new configuration of text, students became more aware of their meaning making choices. We suggest there was a symbiotic relationship between the digital and non-digital literacy practices supported through the iPad platform.

Results show students shifting across modes and dimensions of social complexity through dynamic multimodal meaning making practices. Our conclusion is that as the students in this class were making meaning in public and private learning spaces using iPads/tablets they needed the flexible ability to attend to, interpret and repurpose synchronous semiotic modes in what Bezemer and Kress called a 'chain of materialization processes' (Bezemer and Kress 2008: 172). Through the use of qualitative analysis, as read through the frame of multimodal theory, we have demonstrated how our working definition of multimodal layering enabled us to attend to the multiple demands made on student attention in terms of semiosis and cognition.

Human subject research protection: this study was reviewed and passed for ethics permission from the University of Sydney

References

Bezemer, Jeff, and Gunther Kress. 2008. Writing in multimodal texts: A social semiotic account of designs for learning. *Written Communication* 25 (2): 166–195.

Burnett, Cathy, Guy Merchant, Kate Pahl, and Jennifer Rowsell. 2014. The (im)materiality of literacy: The significance of subjectivity to new literacies research. *Discourse: Studies in the Cultural Politics of Education* 35 (1): 90–103.

Cain, Kate. 2010. Reading for meaning: The skills that support reading comprehension and its development. In *Interdisciplinary perspectives on learning to read: culture, cognition and pedagogy*, ed. Kathy Hall, Usha Goswami, Colin Harrison, Sue Ellis, and Janet Soler, 74–86. Abingdon: Routledge.

Crescenzi, Lucrezia, Carey Jewitt, and Sara Price. 2014. The role of touch in preschool children's learning using iPad versus paper interaction. *Australian Journal of Language and Literacy* 37 (2): 86–95.

Dyson, Anne Haas, and Celia Genishi. 2005. *On the case*. New York, NY: Teachers College Press.

Flewitt, Rosie, Regine Hampel, Mirjam Hauck, and Lesley Lancaster. 2009. What are multimodal data and transcription? In *The Routledge handbook of multimodal analysis*, ed. Carey Jewitt, 40–53. London and New York: Routledge.

Groves, Christine Edwards. 2012. Interactive creative technologies: Changing learning practices and pedagogies in the writing classroom. *Australian Journal of Language and Literacy* 35 (1): 99–113.

Iedema, Rick. 2003. Multimodality, resemiotization: Extending the analysis of discourse as a multisemiotic practice. *Visual Communication* 2: 29–57.

Jewitt, Carey. 2009. An introduction to multimodality. In *The Routledge handbook of multimodal analysis*, ed. Carey Jewitt, 14–27. London and New York: Routledge.

Kress, Gunther. 2010. *Multimodality. A social semiotic approach to contemporary communication*. London: Routledge.

Kress, Gunther, and Theo van Leeuwen. 2001. *Multimodal discourse. The modes and media of contemporary communication*. Edward Arnold: London.

Kress, Gunther, Carey Jewitt, Jon Ogbourn, and Charalampos Tsaterelis. 2001. *Multimodal teaching and learning: The rhetorics of the science classroom*. London and New York: Continuum.

Leander, Kevin, and Gail Boldt. 2013. Rereading "A pedagogy of multiliteracies": Bodies, texts, and emergence. *Journal of Literacy Research* 45 (1): 22–46.

Lemke, Jay L. 2002. Travels in hypermodality. *Visual Communication* 1 (3): 299–325.

Leonardi, Paul, M., Bonnie, A. Nardi, and James Kallinikos. 2012. *Materiality and organizing: In a technological world*. New York: Oxford University Press.

Norris, Sigrid. 2004. Multimodal discourse analysis: A conceptual framework. In *Discourse and technology: Multimodal discourse analysis*, eds. Philip, LeVine, and Ron Scollon, 101–115. Washington, D.C: Georgetown University Press.

Rowsell, Jennifer, Gunther Kress, Kate Pahl, and Brian Street. 2013. The social practice of multimodal reading: A new literacy studies-multimodal perspective on reading. In *Theoretical models and reading processes*, 6th ed, ed. Donna E. Alvermann, Norman J. Unrau, and Robert B. Ruddell, 1182–1207. Delaware: IRA Publication.

Simpson, Alyson, and Maureen Walsh. 2014. Pedagogic conceptualizations for touch pad technologies. *Australian Journal of Language and Literacy* 37 (2): 128–138.

Tierney, Robert J., Ernest Bond and Jane Bresler. 2006. Examining literate lives as students engage with multiple literacies. *Theory into Practice* (45) 4: 359–367.

Walsh, Maureen, and Alyson Simpson. 2013. Touching, tapping… thinking? Examining the dynamic materiality of touch pad devices for literacy learning. *Australian Journal of Language and Literacy* 36 (3): 148–157.

Walsh, Maureen, and Alyson Simpson. 2014. Exploring literacies through touch pad technologies: The dynamic materiality of modal interactions. *Australian Journal of Language and Literacy* 37 (2): 96–106.

Wohlwend, Karen. 2010. A is for Avatar: Young children in literacy 2.0 worlds and literacy 1.0 schools. *Language Arts* 88 (2): 144–152.

Yin, Robert K. 2012. *Applications of case study research*. Thousand Oaks, CA: Sage.

Author Biographies

Alyson Simpson is an Associate Professor in the Sydney School of Education and Social Work at the University of Sydney, Australia. Current research projects in higher education and primary schools include work on the role of children's literature in education, the power of dialogic learning and the impact of digital technology on reading practices and pedagogy. She has served as a consultant to state and national education bodies across all sectors. She is the author of *The use of children's literature in teaching: A study of politics and professionalism within teacher education.*

Maureen Walsh is Honorary Professor in the Sydney School of Education and Social Work at the University of Sydney and Adjunct Professor in the Faculty of Education and Arts at the Australian Catholic University (ACU). Previously Professor of Literacy Education at ACU, she was the recipient of two national awards for university teaching. Maureen has published nationally and internationally in areas of TESOL, children's literature, reading education and visual literacy. For several years her work has focused on the impact of digital communication on literacy education and she developed a theoretical framework around multimodal literacy in several publications.

Chapter 6
The New Digital Divide: Digital Technology Policies and Provision in Canada and Australia

Joanne O'Mara, Linda Laidlaw and Jill Blackmore

Introduction

As mobile touchscreen digital devices have quickly moved into a more prominent position in early years classrooms, the development of new policies to address the use of these devices has also occurred at a rapid pace. Merchant (2015) notes that it is now almost impossible to think of early years language and literacy teaching without thinking of technology as a part of it. This was not the case in early years settings before the iPad was released in 2010. As language and literacy researchers, we have been investigating how language and learning may be transformed through the usage of these devices (e.g. O'Mara and Laidlaw 2011; Laidlaw et al. 2014; Laidlaw et al. 2015).

Our chapter focuses on the findings from a policy analysis of texts addressing the provision and usage of mobile digital devices for the early years of primary/elementary education in education departments and schools in the state of Victoria in Australia and the province of Alberta in Canada. We embarked on this policy analysis as part of a larger project, *A Comparative Investigation of Pedagogical Possibilities of Digital Tools for Family and School Early Literacy Education*. In our comparative work in schools, we were attempting to theorize how language and learning may be transformed through the usage of mobile devices. As we considered 'what was happening' in classrooms, we saw that there were significant differences between how the mobile devices were provided and used, and that these differences were largely determined by

J. O'Mara (✉) · J. Blackmore
School of Education, Deakin University, 221 Burwood Highway, Burwood 3125, Victoria, Australia
e-mail: joanne.omara@deakin.edu.au

J. Blackmore
e-mail: jillian.blackmore@deakin.edu.au

L. Laidlaw
University of Alberta, Edmonton, Canada
e-mail: llaidlaw@ualberta.ca

C. Burnett et al. (eds.), *The Case of the iPad*,
DOI 10.1007/978-981-10-4364-2_6

state and provincial policies addressing their provision and use. This led us to compare the different ways that the state and provincial policies were influencing the approach to mobile devices between Alberta, Canada and Victoria, Australia.

As language and literacy educators, we recognize the socially constituted nature of understandings of children as learners. We framed our study drawing from Bacchi (2009), asking the question why this policy now, how is the policy problem defined and resolved, who benefits, and with what effects on practice and outcomes? We began our policy readings asking questions about how mobile devices might be promoted to enable students to record, create and produce texts in more interesting ways. We were surprised, however, that rather than engaging with the pedagogical affordances of mobile devices, these texts focused on risk management and what we describe as domesticating the devices.

We sourced the policy documents from a variety of sources: state/provincial department websites, and individual schools. Structurally, the chapter tracks how state/provincial mobile device policies have shifted and developed over the 4 years of our project, and how these policies have been taken up by a sample of schools and teachers in similar urban contexts in Alberta, Canada and Victoria, Australia. This chapter situates the policy analysis in terms of what these policies look like when they are enacted 'on the ground', particularly in terms of device provision. We provide examples of the ways policies are enacted and consider how these policies shape what is possible for teachers and schools to achieve.

The Rapid Shifts in the Technology Landscape of Schooling

Schools mediate and negotiate complex entangled environments of socio-geographic location, the demographics of increasingly diverse community and student populations, systemic and organizational environments, and policy environments. Together these entangled environments are at once enabling and disabling of innovation (Blackmore 2015). The enabling/disabling aspect of policy is particularly evident for digital technologies and is especially pertinent to language and literacy teaching and learning. In this section of the chapter, we review some of the general policy discourse discussions around information and communications technologies (ICT) and highlight some of the changes that are occurring/have occurred as a result of mobile devices being introduced into schools. While the policy discourse about twenty-first century learners has been circulating within Australian and Canadian systems as well as globally for a decade (Bellanca and Brandt 2010), something significantly different has been occurring more recently with regard to ICT.

Two earlier studies (Lankshear et al. 1997; Blackmore et al. 2003) argued that technology take-up required putting 'teachers first'. Early professional development meant it was more likely that teachers gained a sense of competency and confidence in using new technologies once in the classroom. At the same time, both reports indicated that while teachers focused on gaining technical competence, systems focused on the technical aspects and provision of computers and the pedagogical possibilities of new technologies had not been addressed. Selwyn (2014), noted that it was the techno-anxiety related to computers as well as the lack of technical support and inappropriate spaces—the 'fragility' and uncertainty around the use of the tools noted by Lankshear et al. (1997)—that discouraged use relative to the discursive policy hype and claims as to their potential.

In 2012 Laidlaw and O'Mara[1], found that the existing 'technology use' policies tended not to take into account mobile touchscreen devices, as the introduction of these devices, particularly into early years schooling settings was relatively new. Despite this policy gap, from 2012 to 2016 there was an enthusiastic take-up of mobile devices in elementary/primary school settings in Alberta, Canada and Victoria, Australia. While the take-up of affordances of 1:1 technology usage since the 1990s (e.g. laptop computers) has been slow despite considerable government and school investment, particularly in Victoria (Yelland et al. 2014), the rate of the wide-scale adoption of iPads in particular has been exponential. In many ways this was because iPads resolved some of the difficulties of confidence, fragility and the amount of time needed to keep the technology up and running identified by the earlier studies. The teachers we worked with generally felt confident with using mobile technologies. Teachers reported to us in interviews that iPads were robust, 'apart from screens', 'reliable' and 'rarely have glitches'. Most schools across the urban and suburban settings in Alberta and Victoria had reliable wireless networks. Additionally, the 'mobility' of the mobile devices meant that teachers found that they did not disrupt regular practices at home or at school, but fitted well into current approaches to and patterns of everyday communication between home and school. Indeed, iPads and Wi-Fi networking finally provide the potential promised in policy discourses and issues raised with regarding literacy and technology adoption by teachers and students in the Digital Rhetorics Project 20 years previously (Lankshear et al. 1997).

Policy and Centralized/Decentralized Systems

In Australia and Canada, the processes of policy production, circulation and reception reflect systemic, socio-demographic, historical and curricular contexts. Systemically, Australia has a federation of states with an increasingly centralized approach to education policy, exemplified in the National Curriculum Framework, the MySchool website providing comparative data on all schools and the National Assessment Program on Literacy and Numeracy (NAPLAN) test regime. Canada is more a loose confederation of provinces where education remains fully a provincial

[1]Laidlaw, O'Mara and Makovichuk, Literacy learning in playful spaces: Using multimodal strategies to develop narrative with young learners, Social Sciences and Humanities Research Council of Canada Insight Development Grant.

responsibility with regard to funding, and curriculum and policy are more decentralized. Provincial Canadian education systems have emerged out of contexts of distinct differences in relation to history, region, language (French and English), culture and religious distinctions (see Sumara et al. 2001), and rely on provincially based public education funding. In both countries state/provincial departments of education develop policy guidelines, although in Australia these are informed by federal frameworks and shaped by differential funding of public and private schools, with the states responsible for public schools and the federal government for the significant non-government sector constituting over 33% of all students. How those funds (other than those under federal jurisdiction in Australia) are allocated in both countries is a state/provincial or sectoral (non-government and government) matter. Both countries have overarching statements about the importance and role of schooling, such as the Melbourne Declaration in 2008 in which all Australian state governments optimistically stated:

> Rapid and continuing advances in information and communication technologies (ICT) are changing the ways people share, use, develop and process information and technology. In this digital age, young people need to be highly skilled in the use of ICT. While schools already employ these technologies in learning, there is a need to increase their effectiveness significantly over the next decade (MEECTYA 2008: 3).

In Australia, as in Canada, curriculum reforms have been occurring simultaneously but with provincial/state differences and cross-fertilization of ideas and strategies (2011). Both jurisdictions indicate deliberate moves toward more personalized, competency-based and inquiry-based curriculum, with an increased emphasis on integrated use of digital tools and texts. The shift from fixed computers in dedicated spaces, to computer pods, then shared computers in pods, to laptops and now mobile technologies has finally led to a convergence between the technological capacity with regard to connectivity, flexibility and mobility and educational philosophies underpinning contemporary theories of learning around learner-centred pedagogies and individualized learning (2010).

Testing and Technology

There is also the policy connection between standardized tests and technology. In Australia and Canada, mobile devices were initially generally promoted for the recognition of their affordances, such as portability, video and audio facilities, connecting to the Internet, multimodality and offering accessibility tools, rather than for their capacities to store text books and be aligned to any sort of 'common core' and testing, as is the case in many parts of the USA. In terms of standardized testing, currently in Alberta, the provincial achievement test is given in Grades 3, 6 and 9 and is under revision/reform to provide initial assessment information on student learning needs at the start of the school year. In high school, Grade 12 final exams have recently shifted from 50% of final grade to 30%, which is the reverse trend to Victoria where school-based assessment has reduced. In contrast, Australia has more recently shifted to national mandated standardized testing (NAPLAN) in 2000 and in 2008 that occurs once a year for Years 3, 5, 7 and 9. NAPLAN remains a highly controversial phenomenon, particularly with the publication of individual school test results on a public website, MySchool (Gorur 2013), causing some schools (and systems) to operate in 'emergency mode' in response to any perceived fall in NAPLAN scores (O'Mara 2014; Lingard et al. 2016). One of the 'unintended consequences' of such testing is that it will lead to further inequities in the Australian education system, where inequality between schools and students has increased (Lingard et al. 2016). Australia's schools are, therefore, driven centrally through these policy mechanisms, making them highly accountable and with great transparency. In Australia, the NAPLAN testing is being rolled out online from 2017. The online tests are designed to be accessed from a range of devices and machines. For schools, which are heavily reliant upon mobile devices, it can be assumed that these will be used for the tests, as these schools tend to have not investigated heavily in laptop or desktop computers.

'Take Up' of Mobile Devices

In both Australia and Canada there are high rates of ownership and usage rates of devices, with slightly higher rates in Australia. Statistics on mobile ownership are developed regularly by global marketing firms as part of their strategies for marketing various goods to consumers, often with detailed reports around consumer behaviour. Such reports cite statistics regarding how often, how many, how much, who (gender, age), and location, as well as further details on what is clicked, viewed and purchased (See, for instance, Chaffey 2016; Alcorn and Smith 2015). The German-based multinational telecom and marketing group, TNS, found in 2014 that 38.9% of Australians used an iPad or Android tablet and the rate in Canada was 32.6%. This take-up also is indicative of the wider discourse in both countries around device ownership: more = better. Both countries reflect a competitive stance in reporting in news media and technology publications—where ownership and 'up take' are presented as league tables, with statements such as, 'Australian comes in sixth'… and 'Australians are far more likely to own a smartphone than their cousins in the US', although in popular media reports are also likely to use terms like 'addiction' or 'mobile millennials' to disparage owners of devices, while noting exponential increases in use and ownership. The everyday use of mobile technologies in the home has educational implications in terms of what expertise and knowledge children, even in early years, bring to school and how teachers engage them in learning. Previously the 'digital divide' described by researchers such as Snyder (1998) and Blackmore et al. (2003), identified quality and access to up-to-date technologies in the school context contrasted with what was available in the familial context in disadvantaged communities, creating a digital divide in terms of home/school usage and knowledge.

Bring Your Own Device

While the penetration for mobile touchscreen devices is very similar between Canada and Australia and many children and parents have devices at home, there are very different policies and approaches to bringing your own device to school. Over the period of our study, Victoria was undergoing a seismic shift in the proliferation of 1:1 devices. While Victoria had been in the forefront in Australia in promoting computers in schools since the 1990s, this push has moved into the early primary school setting. While most technology related policies are state based, in 2008 the Labor Federal government provided a netbook to every student in Year 9 designed to bring about a 1:1 ratio of computers from Year 9–12 in all Australian schools. When this funding was discontinued after 4 years, schools and systems, in an effort to maintain and increase provision throughout the school system, introduced 'bring your own device' programs (BYOD). While this program began initially in the secondary sector, it firmly established the idea and policies of BYOD. With the desire of primary schools to also shift to 1:1 mobile devices many schools across sectors have introduced 'bring your own device' programs. The arguments to support this shift have centred on provision and cost, with students wanting to use and bring in their own devices and because there was already high rates of usage and ownership of the devices. Furthermore, personal devices already owned by students and families privatize the cost of initial device purchase, software purchasing and responsibility for updates, thus freeing up schools to allocate their funds elsewhere. As devices get older and go out of date, the cost of replacement also is shifted to the family.

In Alberta, the diversity of the uptake of devices is also related to the different ways that iPads or other digital devices come into schools. The expectation in policy and practice is that devices should be supplied by the school, rather than provided by parents. In general, schools have had limited amounts of money to spend on technology, which also limits numbers of devices that the school can buy. Edmonton schools have a 'site-based decision-making' funding model, also known as decentralized decision-making (Edmonton Public Schools 2015), which means that individual schools focus on particular spending priorities, such as funding a music specialist, or providing addition supports for inclusion, with relatively few schools choosing to emphasize technology in spending. Some schools may be able to access special initiatives funds through Alberta Education grants, but otherwise it is less common to see 1:1 programs. 'Bring your own device' programs have been less common in Alberta, with a considerable number of the policy documents we found in connection with students' own devices focusing on restrictions to use rather than making them compulsory. Such policies were evident even in secondary schooling where mobile phone ownership amongst young people is extremely high, similar to the Australian context.

While individual school policies vary, significant restrictions for BYOD are still common. One informant reported a situation where he, a secondary school biology teacher, wanted the students to take photographs to document their biology lab work. As students' personal mobile phones were easily accessible, he ignored the school policy restricting use of mobile phones, and allowed the students to use their phones to photograph their work. This action, however, was frowned upon by administration and resulted in a reprimand for the teacher (Teacher Interviews, Alberta). This example is in complete opposition to what is happening in Victoria, where the students now are frequently using their phones in school. We also did not find any policies in Edmonton that required elementary students to bring their own iPads to school, unlike the Australian policies. Even with more recent shifts in Alberta, policies to bring devices to school seem to aim to persuade parents of the value of BYOD and resemble 'marketing' statements (including links to special parent pricing), rather than school requirements.

Domesticating the Device

The ubiquitous use of mobile technologies also produces challenges for systems, schools, teachers and parents. In Australia, while the devices are most often owned by the students and their families, the schools nevertheless try to control the ways in which the devices are set up, used, operated, which apps are purchased and what can and cannot be done with the device in school time. The link in Australia between national agendas (testing) and technologies is also changing practices in schools. NAPLAN tests are commencing online rollout in 2017 to be completed in 2019. The Australian Curriculum, Assessment and Reporting Authority (ACARA) commissioned Pearson to complete a device effect study (Davis 2015) and have since worked with industry to create 'locked down' browser apps that disable the inbuilt features (such as auto-correct and text to speech) of the iPads so that students cannot draw upon these during the test. Because the testing is compulsory for all schools and students, we anticipate Australian schools will shift to demanding that devices brought to school will need to have the facility to run the 'NAP locked down browser app' (ACARA 2016) in order to fulfill ACARA's suitability requirements. The notion of the locked browser means that the 8-year olds in Year 3, having been using their devices freely at school, will have to modify their practices with the device during the test.

This 'domestication' of the mobile device will mean that in addition to the current training of young children in how to fill in multiple choice questions on tests, they will be learning to work on 'disabled' devices with reduced features. Additionally, older devices may no longer be compliant. Therefore, schools that have lower levels of wireless connectivity will be forced to upgrade, as will parents if there is BYOD. At the same time that the testing is moving to online with many students set to complete the tests on tablets, ironically, widespread tablet usage has been blamed for drops in writing skill test results in NAPLAN in 2016, with claims young people 'immersed in digital devices' are not developing writing skills (see, for example McDougall 2016). We also question the ways in which devices owned by families are controlled in these ways.

Affordances of iPads

In the Australian early primary school sector, the rapid increase of 1:1 devices has tended to be iPads or another brand of mobile touchscreen devices rather than computers. The ease with which mobile touchscreen devices can be used in the early years setting has hastened this move. Additionally, many of the arguments made for secondary school students (the devices were ubiquitous in secondary schools) are now true for early primary students. This quote from a teacher who used 'iPads in the Bush' with indigenous students sums up the affordances early years teachers often describe about usage:

> …very effective and versatile learning tool…Their portability allows them to be used in out-of-classroom activities and they are great for small group work and differentiated learning. (McLaren 2015: 12)

The push towards 1:1 computing in early primary school in Victoria has been highly successful, with a very strong uptake of these devices in schools, and increasing numbers of schools shifting to 1:1 mobile devices (i.e. an iPad for every child). The Department of Education and Early Childhood Development (DEECD) have been very enthusiastic about the affordances aspect of iPads in early schooling, engaging in a series of 1:1 trials as soon as the iPads were released, and publishing numerous resources. The term, 'iPads', rather than the more generic term, 'tablets' is promoted by the department in the usage of the term and documents on the website. Following this, there has been a rapid uptake in the use of iPads and shift to 1:1 across the years of schooling.

Mapping the Landscape of Provision

Due to the lack of government monitoring in both countries and the move to mobile technologies, it is difficult to determine the extent of technology provision per student, aside from schools with special government funding for 1:1 provision in Alberta in place in some high need schools. One key policy document is Alberta Education's *Learning and Technology Policy Framework* (2013). Additional documents are also available such as several reports and discussion documents, including *Bring Your Own Device: A Guide for Schools*, and *iPads: What are We Learning?* (Government of Alberta 2011). The *Learning and Technology Policy Framework*, 2013 builds on an earlier discussion document for educational reform, *Inspiring Education* (Government of Alberta 2010: 5), which argues that through the usage of their own devices, students will be 'engaged thinkers who use technology to learn, innovate, collaborate, communicate, and discover'. With a new government in place (a shift after forty years of leadership by the previous provincial party), the ongoing moves to curriculum reform have temporarily slowed, with immediate government priorities focused on curriculum updates and the development of 'expert working groups' to develop the new programs of study (Alberta Government 2016).

At the level of individual schools, we found selective interpretations of ministry of education documents to reflect school-based policies in Alberta. For example, two schools with significantly divergent policies on BYOD both cited portions of the *Learning and Technology Policy* framework to support their individual school approach, with one focusing on student-centred aspects of the framework (a school with an open BYOD guideline, where students are encouraged to bring devices), and the other (with restrictions more emphasized) focusing on 'effective use':

> The policy process is iterative and additive, made up of interpretations and translations, which are somewhat inflected by existing values and interests (teachers have a multiplicity of values and interests, personal and institutional), by context and history, and by necessity (Ball et al. 2012: 68).

In our detailed search of policies related to digital mobile devices on school websites in 2014 in Alberta and Victoria, we observed that in the creation of individual school policy in relation to digital devices, school administrators drew heavily from the Learning and Technology Policy Framework in Alberta, but individual school policy statements were quite varied, as noted earlier. In another example, one of the two public school boards, Edmonton Catholic Schools (ECS), has developed policy for all their schools based on a 'digital citizenship' approach (ECS 2012). The Alberta school BYOD policies reflected a significant range of acceptance of digital devices in school. In many schools, students are free to bring their own devices and be responsible for them, while other schools restrict student usage, including confiscating phones at the beginning of the day. The language used in a number of the policies was also sometimes outdated in terms of current technical developments (e.g. all hallways at one of the schools are to be 'ring-free' areas; mention of 'diskette' use in connection to bringing student materials to school). Although restricting or forbidding devices like iPads intended for educational purposes was uncommon, we noted that student personal smartphones were sometimes positioned differently, with phone usage not permitted in a number of schools, with statements that student mobile phones are to be handed into a teacher or the office, and 'locked up' over the school day. This approach appears to be less common than statements such as: 'Students are required to turn all electronic devices off during class, unless specific permission and parameters are given for their use by the classroom teacher' more common within the policy documents. At this time, Alberta public schools do not require students to fund their own devices, yet over the writing of this chapter we have noted recent shifts that we categorize as 'encouraging ownership', with a suburban school website referring to 'bring your own robust device' and encouraging participation in a district purchase plan for high school students (Grade 7–12), and a 'personal owned device' POD initiative active in a school district in another large Alberta city, with persuasive recommendations for K-4 Elementary students to purchase Apple iPads third or fourth generations, Android tablets, or Windows Surface devices:

> Schools with a POD initiative usually have enough devices for daily student sign out. [School district] has found that in POD schools over 90% of students bring their device on a daily basis.

However, parental provision of devices and such initiatives remain as 'suggestions' rather than 'expectations'.

In our desktop analysis, an Alberta sample of 35 elementary schools near the University of Alberta in an urban area in the city of Edmonton was undertaken. While the schools provided iPads, the uptake for mobile touchscreen devices in Alberta was more diverse overall. (Some schools also elected to spend their limited technology budget on cheaper Chromebook options.) School ownership of devices was extremely varied, from one or no iPads in some schools to specific programs having 1:1 provision. Since 2014, there have been ongoing shifts in Alberta with policy statements including phrases such as 'Students are encouraged to bring their own technology (laptops, netbooks, tablets) to school for classroom work', more frequently evident. However, some districts that were increasing pressure on families to provide technology and had stronger BYOD initiatives have also backed away from this after receiving opposition from their school communities.

School websites in Edmonton revealed that they were more focused on conveying 'information' than the Victorian websites, which tended to have a higher emphasis on marketing the school. In both Edmonton Public Schools and Edmonton Catholic Schools (both publicly funded districts) decisions about technology and public individual school web-design are often made at the level of individual schools, although both districts have centralized websites which provide access to secure and consistent school, classroom and student information. The highly competitive nature of the Victoria school systems, both public and private, has led to significant investment in school websites to market the school as well as publish school policies and activities.

A desktop analysis of policies on the websites of 35 Victorian elementary government schools in Burwood, a middle-class suburban area of Melbourne, and Warrnambool, a rural town in Victoria, was undertaken in 2014. Over half of the Burwood schools have a statement about their iPad program (51%) on their website and 31% in Warrnambool schools. Many of the Burwood schools were running 1:1 iPad programs with either school provision or BYOD with additional school provision for those students who do not own an iPad. This suggests that the policy environment in Victoria, where the marketization of schooling has been heightened since the 1990s, both within and between public and private sectors, and with an increasingly decentralized system of school self-management and reduced funding per student is significant. Australia generally has a high level of privatization of costs of education because of the large non-government sector; as well, parents appear to have a greater acceptance of bearing such costs. Parental willingness to bear the costs suggests that the social contract between individuals, their families and the state has changed in Victoria due to neoliberal reforms over two decades, with the individual and family taking greater responsibility for costs and is also reflected in the greater polarity between individuals and schools on PISA tests as educational inequality has increased (Lingard et al. 2015). Similar trends are occurring in a more ad hoc manner in Canada.

Digital Policies and Practices in School and at Home

In both countries, parents are not always enthusiastic about the speed of the perceived change or about the usage of the devices in school. In Victoria, we have noted a variety of ways schools have introduced mobile devices. Generally the approach is a whole school program that follows community consultation, although some schools take a more gradual introduction, one year at a time. This approach spreads out costs for parents with multiple children in the school. However, we are aware of one Victorian school that did not consult the community widely, and simply put the iPad on the supply list of items to be purchased by parents for the next school year. Even in schools where there has been a high level of consultation, parents often have mixed feelings about the introduction of the iPads and in some cases this has led to systematic and ongoing campaigns by groups of parents against the principal and school leadership, although these have not tended to be successful.

School provision for students who cannot afford devices varies across the schools in Victoria, and is an area of concern, as most methods seem to involve students without the devices being excluded or singled out in some way. Perhaps in response to problems experienced by schools, the Victorian Education Department published a document, *Planning for 1:1 Learning* (October 2014), that outlines all the steps that principals and school councils need to take to shift into 1:1 provision. This document states the rules and approaches to funding the iPad program, with a push towards parents funding the devices, named as 'co-contribution'. In Victoria, co-contribution is seen as the parents contributing the device, where the school is contributing the infrastructure to make the program possible. The planning document notes that, 'Consideration should be given to ensure students who are unable to participate in a BYOD program are not disadvantaged'. In some schools there are a small group of devices in the classroom for those who do not have one, and students are able to use these. Sometimes these students also complete their work on paper instead of on a device. Other schools have students sign the device in and out of the office every day, but the device is left at school and students have no access to the device outside of school time. We have not yet found an approach where a student might borrow the device for the entire term or school year. Some schools have fundraising to purchase devices for those who cannot afford them, or the local rotary club raises money to provide the devices.

However, one alternative way that schools pay for new digital devices is through parent and school fundraising. One of the most lucrative forms of fundraising, which many Alberta schools use, is what we have termed, *the casino model*. Alberta has a charitable gaming model used in connection to the operation of gambling casinos in the province. Schools and other organizations (e.g. non-profit child care centres, not-for-profit service organizations) can access charitable status, and then may apply for a gaming license where volunteers (parents or members of the school community) engage in tasks at the casino in return for a percentage of the casino's profits for that particular day (or night). Under the gaming regulations, these casino generated proceeds can only be used in specific ways, for example they cannot be used to pay for salary for teachers or for items that are deemed requirements for the operations of schools. Items and resources that are positioned as 'extras', however, are eligible expenses for spending the (often considerable) casino funds. This can include field trips, special school activities, paying for visiting artist workshops and additional physical education equipment, but very commonly schools will use casino funds to pay for updating and increasing the technology, such as purchasing class sets of iPads or a Chromebook cart.

This funding approach has several implications. Schools with an actively involved parent community who likely already have significant material resources are also more likely to be successful in applying for and operating 'casino nights' than schools in areas where parents are less affluent, new immigrants, working at jobs where they would be unable to take time off required to work a casino shift, or who take an ethical or religious stance against use of the proceeds of gambling. As well, it is in the interest of these schools to continue to have digital devices as positioned as 'extras' rather than as 'essential' learning resources. Several years ago, the Catholic Archbishop made a decision to ban casino fundraising for the public Catholic schools, based on victimization of those living in poverty due to gambling. However this seems to be a decision without a particular timeline, given the heavily reliance on the funds:

> Institutions such as schools that rely to a large degree on revenues from gambling cannot be expected to change this overnight. Time will be needed for transitioning away from casino revenues, and the exact timelines will be determined in consultation with administration officials. (The Catholic Archdiocese of Edmonton 2011)

When we were comparing the Victorian system of 'bringing your own device' and the Albertan system where parents work in casinos to raise funds for devices, we found both countries provided examples that were viewed as rather shocking in the other context. For an Australian, the casino work was seen as scandalous, and we receive gasps when we talk of this in Australia. For a Canadian, the parents having to provide so much of the equipment in a public school is equally scandalous, and our Canadian audiences have been shocked by our discussion. Consistent through both examples, however, is the conclusion that, although the education systems of both countries are very keen to have the latest technology in schools, they are not prepared to foot the bill.

Risk Management

One phenomenon we have noticed growing exponentially with device take-up is the growth of 'Acceptable Use Policies' on school websites. These statements of use and policy documents convey how new tools and existing literacy practices are being interpreted by administration and stakeholders in various jurisdictions. The acceptable use policies sometimes outline how the devices are provided and organized within the school. However, such policies also to an extent determine how the teachers might use devices in the classroom and what is expected of students. In Alberta, sometimes these were quick adaptations of older policies, redrafted 'on the run'. For example, in one elementary school, the school follows an 'acceptable use policy—technology' based on similar school district guidelines, and which, though acknowledging that students 'can access the network through Chromebooks, iPads or personal devices', appears to be adapted from a prior policy aimed at use of desktop computers. All students and their parents are required to sign an agreement indicating they 'understand and accept the expectations and consequences'. Devices are expected to be used for educational purposes, with the school having the rights of 'surveillance', that is 'the right to scan, view and delete files if necessary'. Curiously, within the school policy document, students are told to 'refrain from using personal diskettes from home' signalling past technology material, likely no longer in use at the school.

While students are encouraged to bring their personal devices, in the policy document it is clear this is not a regular occurrence for students, and there are no school guidelines aimed at care and organization of student devices, aside from policy statements limiting student use (e.g. instructions to turn off all electronic devices during class). In some classrooms particular students use a dedicated device (iPad or Chromebook) due to accessibility needs or disabilities. Technology use across the school is somewhat erratic, with some teachers using the Chromebooks or iPads for instruction more regularly and some teachers rarely choosing to use them for learning tasks.

Surveillance and Control

In earlier work (Laidlaw and O'Mara 2011), we noted the extent to which schools seemed to be concerned with surveillance and control of digital devices, the ways in which they were situated within the schools, and fears about the devices being lost and destroyed as well as fears in regards to negative influences on children. We referred to the practices that often result from such concerns as a 'domestication' of the devices. In the early primary setting, for example, there are a range of concerns articulated by parents, such as device related concerns: cost, fear of the devices being broken and concerns about whose responsibility it is to replace the device if broken (it is the parents'). As well, parents articulate teaching/skill-related concerns: the demise of handwriting, that the devices will replace teachers, or that teachers will fail to teach and simply send students to work on the iPad. Behind many of these concerns seems to be a sense of nostalgia for the adults' own childhood schooling practices, a fear of change, and deep concern for their own child's 'different' schooling.

In an environment of surveillance, it is difficult for teachers to recognize digital literacy practices as valued and valuable in contrast to traditional literacy practices in the early learning classroom. We found, in our analyses of current digital rules and policies, that this aspect has changed more recently, with both Victoria and Alberta taking much more comprehensive approaches to device usage. The Victorian Department of Education and Training *Safe and Responsible Use of Technology* policy published on their website (DET 2016) frames mobile device usage in schools in the context of:

> Teachers, students and parents are increasingly using digital technologies to teach, learn and communicate, challenging the traditional concept of a school. While advances in technology have created opportunities to engage students in the classroom in new and exciting ways they also present an opportunity to be both intentionally and unintentionally misused.

The guidelines take a much broader approach to technology, including the responsibility of schools to 'educate children and young people and address the underlying values (ethics) and responsible behaviours expected of them online and off'. The Department recommends that schools take a 'holistic approach' and 'teach Cybersafety education explicitly' (see DET 2016 online). To support this approach, DET has a series of suggested lessons and supported Cybersafety programs that have been rolled out in both primary and secondary schools and integrated into the curriculum. We have also observed a similar trend in Alberta. In particular, the Edmonton Catholic District (one of two publicly funded school districts in the city) has a strong emphasis on digital citizenship. This has shifted the framing for technology usage in the classroom towards an approach that communicates an approach supportive of students making 'mistakes' at school so teachers can provide explicit guidance. While some statements in the policy documents from both countries still emphasize external 'surveillance and control' of devices, we note significant shifts towards emphasis on safety and citizenship, placing increasing responsibility in the hands of students and their teachers.

Technological Shifts in Complex Entangled Environments: Implications for Practice

At the start of our inquiry into digital policies, we naïvely expected that we would find more similarity than disjuncture between our two contexts. After all, we have been observing teachers incorporating mobile touchscreen devices into their literacy teaching practices over the past few years, and in focusing on pedagogical matters, we could see many similarities, with differences that seemed fairly minor. Our work in this more policy-related investigation again reaffirms the importance of context—that the policies created in each jurisdiction are deeply connected to how technologies are situated and used in local schools. Policies and decisions at the level of provision that we had, until now, overlooked, are very significant and the emotional responses our audiences have expressed about the provision approaches—the widespread demand that parents purchase the devices in Victoria and the parents working voluntarily in the casinos in Alberta to raise money for the school technology budgets—point to deep differences between privatization and funding arrangements that are normalized in each location. The policy decisions around provision have larger impacts with regard to a new digital divide and teacher practice. For example in a school where 1:1 provision by parents is assumed, teachers are likely to be more compelled to use devices throughout the school day and to develop 'innovative' projects to showcase and thus justify parental expense. In a school where there may be only a few devices, or none, teachers may encounter more difficulty in developing their own familiarity with apps or innovative practice, in addition to challenges in connection to consistent and sustained student access.

What became evident through the policy analysis was how seemingly small differences often had larger unintended pedagogical consequences. Both Canada and Australia have shared in the rapidly emerging phenomena of mobile digital devices, and in both places this has created perturbations and interruptions while education systems respond, including their attempts to develop guidelines and 'instructions' for uptake and use, often 'catching up' to what was happening in practice. One line of continuity across both contexts is that the rate of change and introduction is rapid, although Victoria is experiencing widespread shifts in the outward appearance of what the classrooms look like, in response to the influx of devices. And, as we quoted from the state's Department of Education and Training earlier, the 'traditional concept of a school' is being challenged by technology, presumably from the connections both into and out from the school classrooms and also what constitutes an innovative learning environment (Blackmore et al. 2011). In Alberta, while the outward differences are not as consistently visible, teachers are actively participating in professional development sessions in connection to technology changes, and discussion of the implication of mobile devices for learning is prominent in local public media. With a recent significant change in government and their stated commitment to educational reforms, it is difficult to predict what the future will hold.

In several of the policy texts we examined, the rise of iPads and touchscreen technologies have been referred to as creating a paradigm shift. However we have not observed as yet, to the same extent, a fundamental change in the pedagogical approaches to the teaching of language and literacy. Most policies that assumed that with provision of the new technologies, pedagogical change will occur to inform teaching and learning. That is, the focus is still, at the policy level in systems and schools, on the technical, domesticating the devices, and risk management rather than a focus on the pedagogical. In particular, with regard to literacy learning, we have yet to see the valuing and usage of oral language more broadly, in ways that are made possible with more extensive usage and provision of these multimodal devices. In Australia we are also seeing the possibility of the devices being used to implement the national testing regime. One of the first images we noted and collected, early in the arrival of iPads into schools, was of the devices attached to the wall, and 'chained up' to mirror a conventional 'computer lab' structure, because the school did not know what to do with mobile devices. While the devices are now moving 'freely' in and out of classrooms, the next phase requires investing in teachers' pedagogical repertoires to use mobile technologies to enhance learning.

Acknowledgements The authors acknowledge the Social Sciences and Humanities Research Council of Canada for their support of the research described in this article, and in the project, *A comparative investigation of pedagogical possibilities of digital tools for family and school early literacy education.*

References

ACARA Australian Curriculum, Assessment and Reporting Authority. 2016. NAPLAN online: Technical requirements. http://www.nap.edu.au/online-assessment/naplan-online/technical-requirements. Accessed 1 Aug 2016.

Alberta Government. 2016. Alberta updating curriculum to better prepare students for future success. Press release, 15 June 2016. http://www.alberta.ca/release.cfm?xID=429254F30CF8B-FC56-7936-ADA544AE037D475C. Accessed 1 Aug 2016.

Alcorn, Nicola, and Jeremy Smith. 2015. Media consumption behaviours: Trends that will influence how you engage customers. http://www2.deloitte.com/au/en/pages/technology-media-and-telecommunications/articles/media-consumer-survey-2015. Accessed 15 Aug 2016.

Bacchi, Carol. 2009. *Analysing policy: What's the problem represented to be?*. French's Forest, AU: Pearson.

Ball, Stephen, Meg Maguire, and Annette Braun. 2012. *How schools do policy: Policy enactments in secondary schools*. London: Routledge.

Bellanca, James, and Ron Brandt (eds.). 2010. *21st century skills. Rethinking how students learn*. Bloomington, IN: Solution Tree Press.

Blackmore, Jill. 2015. *Mobile touch-screen devices and techno-literacies: Emergent policies and practices in Canada and Australia.* Symposium paper for the American Educational Research Association, Chicago, IL.

Blackmore, Jill, Lesley Hardcastle, Esmé Bamblett, and Janet Owens. 2003. *Effective use of information and communication technology (ICT) to enhance learning for disadvantaged school students.* Canberra: Commonwealth Department of Education, Science and Technology.

Blackmore, Jill, Debra Bateman, Mary Dixon, Anne Cloonan, J. Jill Loughlin, Joanne O'Mara, Kim Senior, and George Aranda. 2011. *Innovative learning environments research study.* Melbourne: OECD/Department of Education and Early Childhood Development.

Chaffey, Dave. 2016. Statistics on consumer mobile usage and adoption to inform your mobile marketing strategy mobile site design and app development. http://www.smartinsights.com/mobile-marketing/mobile-marketing-analytics/mobile-marketing-statistics. Accessed 15 Aug 2016.

Davis, Laurie Laughlin. 2015. Device effects in online assessment: A literature review for ACARA. Pearson study. http://nap.edu.au/docs/default-source/default-document-library/naplan-online-device-effect-study.pdf. Accessed 1 Sept 2016.

DET Department of Education and Training. Victoria. http://www.education.vic.gov.au/school/teachers/support/Pages/safeandresponsibleuse.aspx. Accessed 1 Sept 2016.

Edmonton Catholic Schools. 2012. Digital citizenship administrative policy. https://www.ecsd.net/ParentsStudents/ParentResources/Documents/137%20Digital%20Citizenship%20Policy.pdf. Accessed 5 July 2016.

Edmonton Public Schools. 2015. Fiscal oversight and accountability. https://www.epsb.ca/ourdistrict/policy/c/co-bp/. Accessed 15 Aug 2016.

Gorur, Radhika. 2013. My School, my market. *Discourse: Studies in the Cultural Politics of Education* 342: 214–230.

Government of Alberta. 2010. Inspiring action: Discussion paper. Edmonton, Alberta: Government of Alberta, Education.

Government of Alberta. 2011. iPads: What are we learning? Summary report of provincial gathering day—October 3, 2011, 1–23. Edmonton, Alberta: Government of Alberta, Education.

Laidlaw, Laidlaw, Joanne O'Mara, and Lee Makovichuk. 2014. With rest… and time… and a little hope: Moving into virtual worlds through multi literacy forms. In *International perspectives on teaching English in a globalised world*, ed. Andrew Goodwyn, Louann Reid, and Cal Durrant, 223–234. London, UK: Routledge.

Laidlaw, Linda, Joanne O'Mara, and Suzanna Har Wong. 2015. Daddy, look at the video I made on my iPad!: Reconceptualizing 'readiness' in the digital age. In *Rethinking readiness in early childhood education implications for policy and practice*, ed. Jeanne Marie Iorio, and Will Parnell, 65–77. Palgrave Macmillan.

Lankshear, Colin, Chris Bigum, Cal Durrant, Bill Green, Eileen Honan, Wendy Morgan, Joy Murray, Ilana Snyder, and Martin Wild. 1997. *Digital rhetorics: Literacies and technologies in education—Current practices and future directions*. Canberra: Department of Employment, Education and Youth Affairs.

Lingard, Bob, Greg Thompson, and Sam Sellar (eds.). 2016. *National testing in schools: An Australian assessment*. London: Routledge.

McDougall, Bruce. 2016. http://www.dailytelegraph.com.au/news/nsw/high-school-naplan-scores-decline-for-students-immersed-in-digital-devices/news-story/a408d0213a96875b77c3b25913fc2027. Accessed 5 Sept 2016.

McLaren, Dan. 2015. iPads in the bush. *Practically Primary* 20 (1): 3.

Merchant, Guy. 2015. Keep taking the tablets: iPads, story apps and early literacy. *Australian Journal of Language and Literacy* 381: 3–11.

Ministerial Council of Education, Employment and Training and Youth Affairs. 2008. *Melbourne declaration on the educational goals for young Australians.* Canberra.

O'Mara, Joanne. 2014. Closing the emergency facility: Moving schools from literacy triage to better literacy outcomes. *English Teaching: Practice and Critique*. Retrieved from: http://edlinked.soe.waikato.ac.nz/research/files/etpc/files/2014v13n1art1.pdf.

O'Mara, Joanne, and Linda Laidlaw. 2011. Living in the iworld: Two literacy researchers reflect on the changing texts and literacy practices of childhood. *English Teaching: Practice and Critique 10* (4): 149–159. Retrieved from: http://edlinked.soe.waikato.ac.nz/research/journal/view.php?article=trueandid=754andp=1.

Selwyn, Neil. 2014. *Distrusting educational technology: Critical questions for changing times*. London: Routledge.

Snyder, Ilana. 1998. *Page to screen: Taking literacy into the electronic era*. New York: Routledge.

Sumara, Dennis, Brent Davis, and Linda Laidlaw. 2001. Canadian identity and curriculum theory: An ecological, postmodern perspective. *Canadian Journal of Education/Revue canadienne de l'education* 26 (2): 144–163.

The Catholic Archdiocese of Edmonton. 2011. Gambling: FAQs. http://caedm.ca/AboutUs/PoliciesProcedures/GamblingFAQs.aspx. Accessed 1 Aug 2016.

Yelland, Nicola, Caja Gilbert, and Nicolle Turner. 2014. iPlay, iLearn, iGrow: Using iPads in a play-based kindergarten program. *Every Child* 20 (3).

Author Biographies

Joanne O'Mara is an Associate Professor in the Faculty of Arts and Education, Deakin University, Melbourne, Australia. Her research and scholarship focuses on emergent literacies and new textual practices; digital games; drama pedagogy; and the spatial, social and temporal dimensions of teachers' work. O'Mara's current research program includes her collaboration on the investigator on a SSHRG IDG project, *A Comparative Investigation of Pedagogical Possibilities of Digital Tools for Family and School Early Literacy Education*, led by Linda Laidlaw. She won the Faculty of Arts and Education Mid Career Researcher Award in 2015. A hallmark of her research program has been the focus on establishment of ongoing strategic partnerships with inbuilt benefits to all parties, working in collaboration with key education authorities, professional associations, schools, teachers and students.

Linda Laidlaw is a professor in literacy education at the University of Alberta, Edmonton, Alberta, Canada. She works as a literacy researcher and teaches courses in undergraduate and graduate language and literacy education, research methods, and curriculum studies. Her current research focuses on digital literacies and multimodal practice for young learners. In collaboration with Joanne O'Mara and Jill Blackmore she has been engaged in a Social Sciences and Humanities Research Council of Canada (SSHRC) funded research project exploring the use of mobile touchscreen devices and other digital tools in literacy education.

Jill Blackmore is Alfred Deakin Professor in the Faculty of Arts and Education, Deakin University, former Director of the Centre for Research in Educational Futures and Innovation and Fellow of the Academy of Social Sciences Australia. Her research interests include, from a feminist perspective, globalisation, education policy and governance; international and intercultural education; educational restructuring, leadership and organisational change; spatial redesign and innovative pedagogies; teachers' and academics' work, all with a focus on equity. Recent higher education research has focused on disengagement with and lack of diversity in leadership, international education and graduate employability. Her research has focused in particular on the re/constitution of the social relations of gender in and through education in the early twenty-first century.

Chapter 7
Slate-Enabled Literacy Practices in a Futureschool@Singapore Classroom

Siew Hiang Sally Ng

The pace of change is so quick now, if our people don't have the skills and we don't have the infrastructure, we're out of the game (Channel News Asia. 2016. Singapore needs to stay ahead while pursuing smart nation vision. http://www.channelnewsasia.com/news/singapore/singapore-needs-to-stay/2688112.html).
Dr. Vivian Balakrishnan, Minister-in-Charge of the Smart Nation Programme Office, Singapore

Mobile and Twenty-First Century Literacies

In recent years, there has been a growing volume of research examining how young people's in-school and out-of-school techno-literacy practices have impacted their lives and learning (boyd 2008, 2014; Chinnery 2006; Ito et al. 2010; Jenkins 2006; Merchant 2009; Pegrum 2014; Warschauer 2006, 2011). This body of work, which is mostly ethnographic in nature, shows that new media technologies such as social networking sites and online digital games which can be accessed via portable devices, has changed how youth socialize, and learn both in and out of school.

Some researchers (Backer 2010; Cochrane and Bateman 2010; Chinnery 2006; Merchant 2012; Kolb 2008; Parry 2011; Pachler et al. 2010; Pegrum, 2014) describe the way people used mobile devices, such as iPads, tablets, smartphones, to go about everyday activities, as *mobile practices* or *mobile literacies*. In particular, in the context of mobile learning, I find Pegrum's categorization of mobile literacies very useful. Pegrum suggested that literacies can be mobile in three different ways:

When the *device* is mobile (e.g. a portable device supported by wireless platform)
When the *learner* is mobile (e.g. the learner can move around the class or learn 'on the go')

S.H.S. Ng (✉)
Singapore Ministry of Education, Singapore, Malaysia
e-mail: elanteach@gmail.com

C. Burnett et al. (eds.), *The Case of the iPad*,
DOI 10.1007/978-981-10-4364-2_7

When the *learning experience* is mobile (e.g. through geo-tagged learning, augmented reality).

Research in this area of mobile literacies underlines the imperative to equip young people with sophisticated new literacies previously not addressed by print and non-mobile practices (Mills 2016). The Future WorkForce Skill 2020 report (The University of Phoenix Research Institute 2011) provided a list of the literacies associated with the changing technological landscape, and urged policymakers to provide school experiences that expose students to the full range of literacies as a national priority. These literacies are often referred to as *twenty-first century literacies* or *twenty-first century competencies*. Burnett, et al. (2014) in the book, *New Literacies Around the Globe*, summarized the twenty-first century literacy frameworks of a number of countries. Generally, in the various frameworks, twenty-first century literacies comprise a set of skills and dispositions, such as digital literacy, critical thinking, creativity and self-directed or collaborative learning competencies. These new literacies are often seen as necessary for one to thrive in the "new world order" (Baguley et al. 2010)—characterized as a highly networked, mobile and globalized organization of capital, production, management, labour and market (Castells 2009, 2010).

Like the twenty-first century frameworks of other countries, the Singapore twenty-first century competencies (21CC) framework (Fig. 7.1) makes explicit the

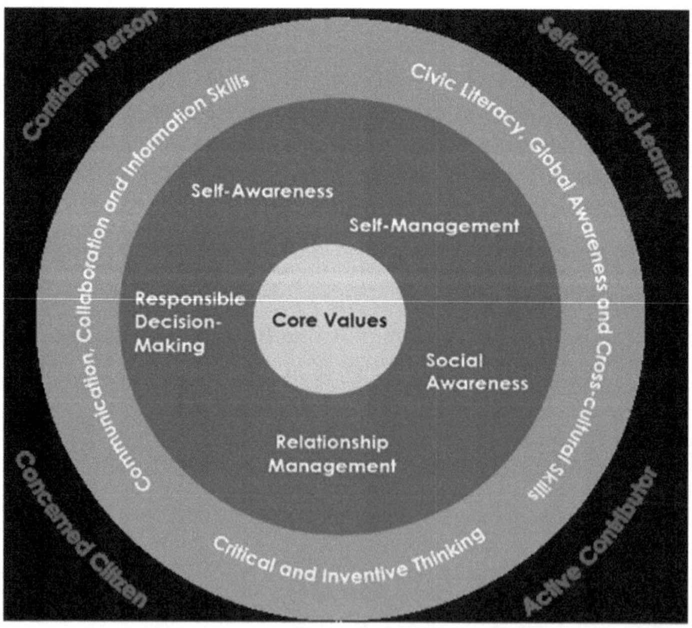

Fig. 7.1 MOE Singapore 21CC framework. *Source* Ministry of Education, Singapore (2015b). https://www.moe.gov.sg/education/education-system/21st-century-competencies

same literacies, although the digital dimension is given less emphasis. This is because Ministry of Education, Singapore (MOE) has thus far been integrating the use of technology into everyday teaching and learning, rather than teaching it separately. There are internal policy documents that make explicit the type of digital know-how, such as the use of mobile devices and cloud-based technologies, which students need to be exposed to, in order to support the achievement of the various domains in the 'outer ring of the framework [that] represents the emerging 21CC necessary for the globalized world we live in' (Ministry of Education, Singapore 2015a). These digital literacy outcomes are also aligned to the ICT Masterplans in Education.

One central feature of 21CC as defined by the MOE, is that it is value centric. It is the ministry's belief that 'knowledge and skills must be underpinned by values' (Ministry of Education, Singapore 2015a). In Singapore schools, explicit teaching of how these values (Respect, Responsibility, Resilience, Integrity, Care, Harmony) manifest in the digital sphere is done through cyber wellness lessons (which can be considered Singapore's version of digital citizenship education), as part of the citizenship and character education syllabus.

Researching the Mobile Literacies 'Ecosystem'

The study reported on in this chapter is situated in the field of New Literacy Studies, which maintains that literacy practices should be understood as actual instances of what people do with literacy, situated within a socio-cultural context. In other words, it provides a situated representation of a classroom rather than a generalized state of all classrooms across the Singapore system. My research adopts a micro-ethnographic approach (Green and Bloome 1997) to provide a thick description of literacy in a FutureSchool classroom. Such schools serve as pathfinders for the Singapore education system in the search for ways to leverage the 'Infocomm-integrated lifestyle' of students for teaching and learning (Ministry of Education, Singapore 2012). This candid situated representation aims to highlight various processes and agents at work in the FutureSchool@Singapore classroom ecology, with the explicit intention of giving a glimpse of the alignment and gaps between the nation's plan and actual implementation in a school.

In adopting an ecological approach to understand in-school techno-literacy practices, I take the view that the instructional context is part of the larger school *ecosystem* of Singapore. The question 'What's going on in the classroom' needs then to be considered within the context of the national agenda for education—that is the distinct entitlements and obligations of the school, as well as the concerns of frontline educators. At the same time, it is important to acknowledge that school plays a significant part in students' lives, it is where values, attitudes and dispositions are shaped, and this influence continues into their adult lives. The view of the ecosystem is an amalgamation of information evident in various national and school level documents collected, informal interviews conducted with the teacher participant, and global discussions about Singapore and her education system. This understanding of the socio-cultural context of the research site is pivotal in analyzing and interpreting the technology literacy practices in the Future School classroom. In what follows, I give a brief overview of the different layers of this ecosystem, focusing first on the National Level and then on the school level before focusing on the classroom.

National Level

The Singapore government's intention is to make the country a smart nation by developing a clear digital strategy with the vision to transform Singapore into an intelligent nation by 2015. In order to actualize this plan, nationwide efforts to lay the high-speed optical fibre network in all geographical locations have been successful. When my research was conducted, the government had already managed to wire up most homes, buildings, non-building access points, and all schools to catalyze the development of ICT-enabled mobile business transactions, digital services and of course, learning. In other words, the Singapore mobile learning ecosystem is not merely confined within the four walls of school. It has the capability to enable anytime, anywhere learning, making mobile literacies an inseparable part of schooling for all Singaporean students a reality.

The ICT Masterplans in Education could be seen as MOE's interpretation of its role in the country's larger national Masterplan. MOE launched its fourth ICT Masterplan in Education (mp4) in 2015 (Fig. 7.2).

School Level

In the following paragraphs, I describe the mobile learning infrastructure of the FutureSchool my research is located in, so as to provide the background needed to understand the literacy practices found in my research. I term the school *Tech High* for easy reference.

Tech High is a secondary school, catering for 13–16-year olds, with an approximate school population of 1200. It features a fully wireless networked system and a one-to-one computing environment. At the time of the research, not many Singapore schools boasted a one-to-one computing environment, but Tech High was one of the pioneer FutureSchools which function as trailblazers for the system in the development of teaching and learning. This means that the organization and curriculum structures in Tech High are intended to serve as a possible model for other schools within the system to emulate, as the system presses on in the ICT Masterplan in Education journey. As part of this, each student from Tech High has a personal tablet computer which the teachers and students refer to as a slate. The class of students in this study used a Windows powered Slate PC, which

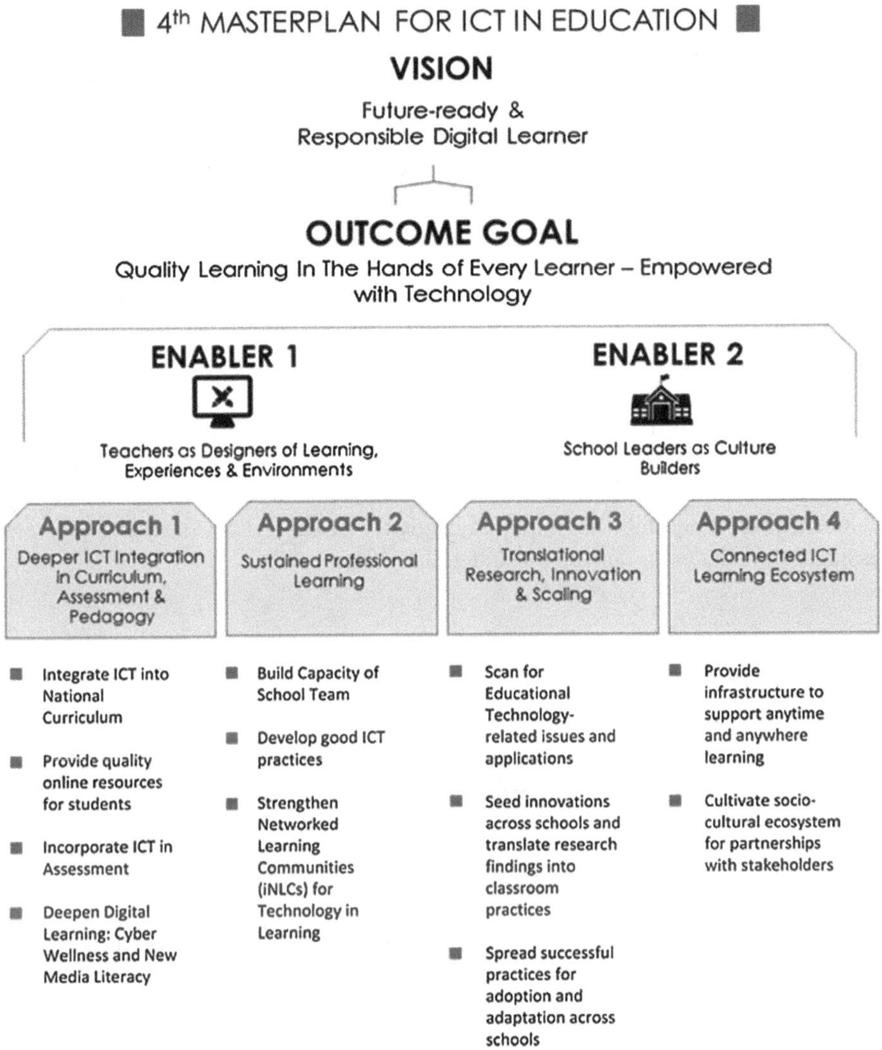

Fig. 7.2 MOE 4th Masterplan for ICT in education. *Source* Ministry of Education, Singapore (2015a, b)

was comprised of a touchscreen tablet, a detachable keyboard and a stylus. These slates were purchased under a co-payment model, jointly funded by parents and school.

I learned through interviews with teachers and students that the slates were pre-installed with learning applications. Some of these were co-developed by the school and industry partners they worked with. An example of this is the unique Virtual Global Learning Faculty (VGLF) which enabled teachers to remotely monitor the students' screens, share screens, students to submit assignments, chat within a closed network, etc. In addition, the students were given cloud storage space, access to the school management system and a suite of Microsoft Office applications and Google web-based productivity tools. The school provided technical training on the use of the slates, the various applications installed and simple troubleshooting for new students. In addition, the school also had its own in-house technicians to resolve more difficult technical problems or do repairs.

Interviews also revealed that *all* the students in the class in which my research was based also owned a smartphone. This is not surprising, given that the average Singaporean possesses at least 3.3 connected devices, one of the highest in the world, based on the findings of *The Consumer Barometer* (Low 2014). The students informed me that they were allowed to tap on the wi-fi network provided by the school via their smartphone since many of them used their personal smartphones to support their learning.

Finally, in order to ensure that the investment in the mobile ICT learning infrastructure is appropriately utilized, Tech High had a number of staff designated to look into various aspects of ICT use for teaching and learning, a chief technology architect in learning and three subject heads for ICT, such as infrastructure, professional development, curriculum integration, etc.

A Classroom Micro-ethnographic Approach

The school appointed Mr Xu[1] the key teacher participant in my research. He was the form teacher and English Language teacher of a secondary one class comprising of forty students. At the time of the research, the students were aged between 13 and 14 years. In order to achieve my research aim—to provide a thick description of the literacy practices in this Tech High classroom, I adopted a micro-ethnographic approach (Green and Bloome 1997). Classroom ethnography provides a principled means of capturing and describing everyday school life. It foregrounds the daily life of classrooms, and views teachers and students as active agents who shape and are shaped by the culture of the classroom context which they are part of. In addition, it seeks to understand the classroom activities and significance of classroom activities from an emic (insider) perspective, rather than an etic (outsider) perspective.

In the case of my research, the focus was to study a *slice* of classroom life where teachers and students go about teaching and learning using the slates, in order to answer the following research questions:

1. What are the slate-mediated literacy practices found in the classroom?
2. What are the competencies students gained from these practices?

Classroom observations which spanned two school terms, retrospective interviews and focus group discussions were carried out to answer these research

[1]In order that participants remain anonymous I have used fictional names throughout.

questions. The data were systematically analyzed using Computer-Assisted Qualitative Data Analysis Software (CAQDAS) to extract literacy events and themes which shed light on how the slates were used to support (or not to support) the learning of twenty-first century competencies. I used Engeström's (1999, 2001) revised version of Activity Theory to perform a content analysis of the segment of the lesson transcript identified as a literacy event. Each activity system could therefore be viewed as a micro-system of the larger ecosystem of the study; that is, the Singapore education system.

In this chapter, I have chosen to present two of the literacy events found, which revolved around a digital writing task which all classes in the cohort had to do (a digital pre-writing event and a teacher/peer-assessment event); the key findings also draw from other events identified in my research. I will discuss, in particular, how the key teacher participant and students made sense of a slate-enabled curriculum and how that related to the timed individual pen-and-paper assessment that was mandatory at the time.

Literacy Event 1: Pre-writing

This event shows the pre-writing stage of a digital process-writing task. According to the teacher, Mr Xu, the task was positioned as a formative assessment. The students could choose one out of four narrative essay writing questions. The questions of the digital process-writing task were similar to the individualized pen-and-paper task that students would encounter in their examination. The differences in this digital process-writing task were that students could use their slate to write and had more time to plan, draft and work with other students to complete their essay. Based on the analysis, there were two activity units at work in this literacy event (Activity System 1.1 and 1.2).

Activity System 1.1—Developing a Coherent Content

See Table 7.1.

The *object* which the students had to produce for the activity was a writing plan on a template which the teacher Mr Xu had earlier emailed to the students, which would reveal if the *goal* was met. Mr Xu had chosen to mediate this activity with the use of MS OneNote, which was one of the pre-installed programs in the students' slates. Extract 1 shows Mr Xu explaining to me (S) his choice of tool.

Table 7.1 Summary table of codes for Activity System 1.1

Codes	Details
Goal	Develop coherent content for a narrative essay
Objects	Writing plan
Subjects	Students
Tools	MS OneNote, networked one-to-one slate
Rules/norms	Timed piece; use the digital template provided by the teacher
Community	Teacher, Google Search, previous lesson resources
Division of labour	Individual

Extract 1

Xu: Actually I want to use Google Docs but decided to try this (OneNote) instead because it allows me to put it in draft 1 and draft 2 very neatly. It is better than Google Docs that way you see.

S: Google Docs has that versioning thing.

Xu: But you can see (pointing out the individual tabs in the OneNote document where he labelled plan, draft and final)

S: As if it is a physical file?

Xu: Yeah correct I wanted to try out. I was struggling between the two. Coz Google is already set up, but I thought I will try (OneNote) and see what happens.

S: They seem quite comfortable with OneNote. They have training before?

Xu: Yes.

Extract 1 reveals that Mr Xu's choice of tool was influenced by the commonly understood formulaic linear structure of the process-writing strategy (Flower and Hayes 1981). His rationalization of the choice of MS OneNote over Google Docs, that it allowed him 'to put it in draft 1 and draft 2 very neatly', reinforced this claim. It was clear that Mr Xu was aware of the technical affordances of the two ICT platforms. After careful deliberation and 'struggling' between the two, he decided to experiment with the use of MS OneNote because to 'see' the different drafts, as the semblance of a paper-based file appeared important to him. In doing so, Mr Xu superimposed paper-based writing practices over this digital writing task.

Extract 2 shows that the students seemed aware that doing their writing plan on paper would fulfil the learning goal of the task just as well, while Extracts 3 and 4 show Mr Xu constantly making reference to how the slate-enabled task is not much different from the pen-and-paper task. Clearly, Mr Xu was attempting to reconcile traditional print-based school literacy practices with the digitally enhanced learning environment, by using the slate as a 'better pencil' (Baron 2009).

Extract 2

Xu: (Raine noticed that Sut's OneNote template was empty) Hey, what happen to you? Two minutes left you know. How? show me what you have

Sut: (showed Xu the piece of paper she did her planning) I will transfer now.

Extract 3

Xu: That's why I ask you to spend 15 min to plan. But let's say next week, I give you 50 min to write the timed piece the story how much time should you devote to planning?

Tracy: 5 min

Xu: Ok about 5 min to have a very good idea how your plot will be structured and then you would start writing.

Extract 4

Chris: Mr Xu can we like search Google? Can we like search Google like get interesting ideas we need to know to write the story?

Xu: (pause) Yes. The thing is class work you want to surf the net to look for things go ahead. I will not stop you. But you know this is not going to be allowed ok during your timed piece and mid-year examination. So, you might want to simulate that situation.

Ash: Can we all do the same story plan like the one we did for story-telling?Xu: Go ahead you can all do the same story.

Extract 4 also shows a student asking Mr Xu if she could 'Google' for new ideas, and another asking if she could simply reuse an old idea which was previously discussed in class. Mr Xu's response seemed to indicate that creativity is less important than keeping time and being able to operate within the rules of examination. While Mr Xu did not encourage the use of internet, although he did acknowledge it as a learning resource. In fact, a number of students were already using the internet before the exchange in Extract 4. When the class heard that Mr Xu did not prevent them from using it, more of them went on Google to search for ideas. This is an example of how the slate-enabled classroom context provided room for greater student agency in learning. Students could take a more proactive approach in their learning, despite the teacher's pedagogical intent. However, not all students displayed similar self-directed learning behaviour by harnessing the slate; others continued to depend on the teacher as a main learning resource as is evident in Extract 5.

Extract 5

Nav: Can I say dilapidated or must I say deserted?
Xu: I leave it to you. What is the effect you are going for?
Nav: Like I want to say there is no one there?
Xu: Which one do you think would be a better word?
Nav: Deserted?
Xu: Exactly. Dilapidated is about the condition of the place. Deserted is that kind of atmosphere you are trying to create. Different things ok? Very good at least it shows that you are starting to think about the choice of words.

The question that the student asked in Extract 5 could have been answered by doing an internet search. Nav knew how to conduct such a search as I had seen her do that many times. However, Mr Xu did not direct her to use it as a learning resource. Mr Xu's response in an informal interview about the use of Internet in class could provide insights as to why he did not do so. He mentioned that he preferred his students to ask him questions so that he could know what they knew and he could detect misconceptions. If the students used the Internet to learn, he would not be able to do these informal formative assessments.

Activity System 1.2—Sharing Digital Writing Plan

See Table 7.2.

The purpose of digitizing the writing plan was to pave the way for the next stage of the digital process-writing task where teacher and students could provide online comments and feedback to each other (Event 2). To do so, the students had to upload the writing plan they did in Activity 1.1 to their MS SkyDrive cloud-based accounts and then share it with Mr Xu and their classmates. However, they encountered many technical issues. When Mr Xu tried to articulate the peer comment structure, he was

Table 7.2 Summary table of codes for Activity System 1.2

Codes	Details
Goal	Share digital writing plan to MS SkyDrive (cloud storage) for teachers and peers to access and comment on
Objects	Solve technical issues of sharing the digital writing plan
Subjects	Teachers and Students
Tools	MS OneNote, MS SkyDrive, Email, networked one-to-one slate
Rules/norms	(No rules coded)
Community	Students, teacher, Google Search, online help
Division of labour	Collaborative

unsuccessful in translating the structure into technical instructions for the students. Activity 1.2 involved the teachers and students engaging in the technical problem-solving process of how to share the digital writing plan. In Extract 6, a role reversal occurred where the teacher was the 'subject' or learner when he asked the students how they resolved the technical issue.

Extract 6

Xu: (X walked to group 5 to talk to them) What is that you all do. Why is it that you can?

Kelly: I put it into my notebook. I just drag it.

Xu: How?

(Kelly demonstrated and then Xu showed the class what Kelly showed him)

The students looked to others or to other resources in the community to help them when they knew Mr Xu might not know how to resolve their technical issues. I noted three students attempting to troubleshoot by accessing the online help available in MS OneNote, while another student googled *how to share OneNote to SkyDrive* and clicked on a YouTube video which showed her how to do it. When the students were successful, they would show their classmate how to do it. Even though the class was rather noisy, most of the students were on-task. The students were proactively seeking and offering help to one another, persevering to resolve the technical issue collaboratively, instead of approaching Mr Xu. They were, in fact, engaging in informal peer mentorship (Jenkins 2006).

One of the students in the class, Kelly, was technologically savvy. She often offered help to her peers and sometimes to Mr Xu too. At an informal interview with Mr Xu, he mentioned that he thought Kelly was "too vocal". Extract 7 shows Kelly offering a piece of advice and Mr Xu rejecting her offer to help.

Extract 7

Shirley: My SkyDrive is not working

Xu: Why is your SkyDrive not working?

Kelly: Then you save it to MLG (the school portal)

Xu: No, no it will be too difficult then. If you know how to share it to SkyDrive, can you do it now.

(the students who knew how to share to MS SkyDrive started teaching their classmates)

Kelly's suggestion to Shirley to save her document in another cloud storage could solve the problem. However, Mr Xu dismissed the suggestion and I saw Shirley attempting to resolve her technical issue independently by logging out of the wireless network and logging on again. It appeared to work.

The class continued to face a number of technical issues but by the end of the event, Mr Xu decided not to pursue these issues. Only ten out of the class of forty students successfully shared their MS OneNote with Mr Xu and their classmates. That is, the *object* and *goal* of the activity were not met. Thus, most of the students did not manage to get teacher or peer feedback for their writing plan.

Literacy Event 2: Teacher/Peer Assessment

Literacy Event 2 occurred after Event 1. It revealed how Mr Xu and his students resolved the technical issue of sharing the writing plan so that they could give teacher and peer feedback to one another. Mr Xu, realizing that his initial foray into MS OneNote did not go well, asked the students to transfer their writing plan to Google Docs so as to avoid the issues of uploading an offline document to an online storage. However, he still insisted on the linear presentation of the draft and instructed the students not to edit directly over their drafts using Google Docs. He wanted them to copy-and-paste the writing plan using the header *plan* and their initial draft under the *header draft 1*, and their improved composition under the header *final copy*.

The primary activity in this event involved students giving online peer feedback to each other both during and after curriculum hours. When describing this activity, I also present another smaller activity embedded within the primary activity, which occurred among a group of students. As one of the students, Kelly, played a significant role in the two activities of this event, she will be referred to a number of times. Kelly was the same student Mr Xu considered earlier to be too vocal. Based on my interview with her on her out-of-school techno-literacy practices, she was clearly a digital resident (White and Le Cornu 2011) who harnessed varied social media such as blogs, Facebook, and Instagram to pursue her personal interests and connect with friends.

Activity System 2.1—Peer Assessment

See Table 7.3.

The 'Object' of Activity 2.1 was an improved version of the students' initial writing based on online peer feedback guided by a set of rubrics given by Mr Xu. The *goal* of the activity was for students to understand their areas of improvement through teacher and peer review.

Table 7.3 Summary table of codes for Activity System 2.1

Codes	Details
Goal	Improvement in composition writing
Objects	Improved composition based on peer feedback
Subjects	Students
Tools	Google Docs, networked one-to-one slate
Rules/norms	Word limit, Linear drafts, Rubrics
Community	Students, teacher, Google Search
Division of labour	Pair work

The timestamps on the Google Docs comments show that the students continued to give and reply to each other's comments outside of curriculum hours. This is an example of how the networked one-to-one slate was harnessed to enable mobile and collaborative learning which transcends the temporal and spatial boundaries of school. For each draft, Mr Xu expected the students to give focused comments on one criterion of the rubrics, but students did not always keep to the structured peer feedback format. Extract 8 shows Kelly's overall comment to one of her peers' drafts.

Extract 8
Good storyline!:) Mm I think you might need to check your grammar! You have made some careless mistakes but it is a good story! When you have direct speech ("blah blah," he said), you must make sure 'he said' or whoever said it is just behind the speech. Not on the next line.

> E.g. "Hello I am grape," Mrs Grape said.
> Do not write as
> "Hello I am grape."
> Mrs Grape said.
> Understand?:) Okay that's all! Good job! *applause*

Kelly's comments were clearly informal, punctuated with online language features such as emoticons and visual sound effects (*applause*). During my interviews with Kelly, she said it would be "weird" if she gave comments the same way Mr Xu did, as she was not the teacher. When I spoke with Mr Xu, he said that he would have preferred the student to keep to formal language even when commenting, but 'it was a losing battle'.

It appeared that Mr Xu had also fought a losing battle in getting Kelly (and some other students) to use Google Docs in the linear way he wanted them to. Kelly told me that she edited over the initial drafts and the comments given by her peers were deleted as she had addressed them and the comments could easily be traced using the revision history function. She said that Mr Xu's instructions to copy-and-paste the composition below the previous draft 'did not make sense' to her.

Extract 9
Where are your other drafts? Kelly, you have to share you work with others so that they can give you feedback too.

You have a flair for writing no doubt and creative in many ways. But that can also work against you. Interesting how you have chosen to write this story in the first perspective, not entirely wrong but one would be expecting the third perspective. The dialogues were very natural and that is good. I like how you developed the whole idea of losing and finding courage again. Well done.

Extract 9 shows that Mr Xu recognized Kelly's creativity in writing, but was concerned that it might not be appreciated under test conditions, and he brought this to her attention by suggesting that creativity 'can also work against' her. During an informal interview with Mr Xu, he used the term 'risky' to describe students' attempts to write differently as 'you don't know how the marker will take it'.

I have identified a smaller activity system, interwoven in this class-level activity, that involved Kelly and classmates who sat near her (*subjects*). Based on Mr Xu's comment in Extract 9, he was probably unaware of this smaller activity. Kelly had woven the names and stories of her favourite pop band, One Direction, into her composition. During the lesson, Kelly was discussing with her group mates, who also liked One Direction (*community*), how she could incorporate ideas of the band into her composition (*object*). It seemed that on top of *the goal* of improving her draft, she was also trying to write an essay which would be personally meaningful. In class, I saw Kelly and her classmates sharing screens, looking at what seemed like a blog of One Direction (*tool*). After class that day (approximately 9.30–9.45 pm), I observed a synchronous online chat in Google Docs (*tool*) between Kelly and two of her classmates about ideas in her composition. Neither of the two classmates were the designated peer which Mr Xu had allocated to comment on Kelly's draft. The designated peer had earlier made some comments on Kelly's Google Doc during class time and did not add further comments after class. I did not always understand the synchronous online chat between Kelly and her two classmates as they used a number of acronyms and codes which were mutually intelligible between them. For example, 'LPRz!', which I later found out from Kelly meant 'Liam Payne Rocks!' (Liam Payne is one of the One Direction band members), and '2XC4U' which meant too sexy for you. I asked Kelly why they did that and she said 'for fun'. Then, she added that she 'didn't want him (referring to Mr Xu) to know everything' that they were talking about. Based on the last modified time stamp, I noted that Kelly continued to work on her composition up to

12.08 am the next day. Kelly's final composition and Mr Xu's comments (Extract 9) clearly showed that that she had successfully reached the *goal* the teacher had set for her. It also showed that Kelly had reached the *goal* she had set for herself for the activity.

Warschauer (2011) found that a networked one-to-one computing environment served as a way to scaffold learning, that allowed students to engage in active knowledge building and increased opportunities for students to tap into the 'four Cs: content, community, construction and composition' (p. 30) for learning. These findings were evident in Kelly's use of the device. She drew ideas from the One Direction blog and discussed with her friends ways to incorporate them in her composition. Warschauer also reported that students tend to write more when composing digitally. This was also observed in Mr Xu's class and he seemed to view it as a negative rather than positive outcome of writing digitally.

Extract 10

Xu: Do you know Google Docs can do word count for you also?
Lin Lin: Can meh? I don't know leh.
Xu: You just go Tool Word Count (Demonstrate)
Lin Lin: Hey, Ouyang, got Word Count in Google Doc!
Xu: Why do you have to do in Word (asking Lin Lin and Ouyang)
Lin Lin: I we didn't know
Xu: Nevermind now you know. We are we are exploring. So, why don't all do directly over there.
Ouyang: Look! 698!
Xu: No no you have to select then do word count
Lin Lin: My essay is 638 already.
Xu: Can you end it quickly?
Lin Lin: I also don't know. I just keep writing writing writing
Xu: I know but you must learn to end as well.

Extract 10 showed Mr Xu advising students to use the word count function to monitor how much they had written and to be cognisant of the word limit. Mr Xu had transferred this "rule" for paper-based writing to digital writing. During the interview with Mr Xu, he mentioned that the students typed a lot faster than they wrote and thus 'tend[ed] to over-write', and he was concerned that they would not be able to complete their composition in the examination. Such evidence of the washback effect of pen-and-paper assessment (Alderson and Wall 1993) recurs in nearly all of the literacy events in this study.

Literacy Practices and Outcomes

As evident from Events 1 and 2, the teacher's approach to simply superimpose the print-based process-writing practices on a digital and mobile learning environment met with unexpected challenges. They serve as good examples to illustrate the need to recognize that giving each student a networked slate is different from giving them a 'better pencil' (Baron 2009) to learn the same way.

In spite of the print-centric and 'performative pedagogy' (Hogan 2010) of the wider educational environment, Mr Xu's experimental approach to the use of the slate in his teaching seemed to have unintentionally created some room to allow for students to engage in self-directed and collaborative learning, fostering new media literacies like 'transmedia navigation' and 'multitasking' (Jenkins 2006). In Event 1, some students actively sought out resources in their environment and engaged in trial and error technical troubleshooting, and in Event 2, some students did what made sense to them by editing over their Google Docs composition instead of having three distinct versions. These students probably learnt such digital literacies when engaging in out-of-school digital literacy practices. As the students in this classroom were provided with the same digital resources (such as the slates, internet access and cloud-computing options) available to them in their out-of-school environment, they were able to transfer their out-of-school digital literacy practices into the school context easily.

Another reason which encouraged the transference of out-of-school practices into the school context may be Mr Xu's implicit (rather than explicit) discouragement from bringing out-of-school digital literacy practices into his classroom. The implicit discouragement did not deter some students from pushing the boundaries to bridge their in-school and out-of-school digital literacy practices. They also encouraged or taught their peers to do the same in the process. This finding is consistent with Mills' (2007, 2010) study, that a teacher's ability to resist employing coercive power (Carspecken 1996) can increase or decrease students' agency and social space for learning. By providing some leeway and flexibility in interpreting the rules and structure he set up and the use of ICT in his classroom, Mr Xu inadvertently encouraged the mobility of digital literacy practices from the students' out-of-school space to their in-school space. While Mr Xu appeared uncomfortable during instances of role reversal where the students led the learning instead of him, this move towards a more equal teacher and student learning partnership is a prerequisite for effective new pedagogies to nurture twenty-first century competencies (Fullan and Langworthy 2014).

The mobile learning ecology in this twenty-first century classroom and the presence of digital residents (White and Le Cornu 2011) among the students played a huge part in increasing student agency and shaping the formal literacy practices in this classroom. The environment provided these students with an avenue to actively appropriate their out-of-school techno-literacy practices for the school context. These students function as catalysts of new literacy practices and nudge all members in the ecology to push the boundaries of learning with ICT and foster the learning of twenty-first century competency (21CC).

The mobile learning ecology in this twenty-first century classroom and the presence of digital residents (White and Le Cornu 2011) among the students played a huge part in increasing student agency and shaping the formal literacy practices in this classroom. The environment provided these students with an avenue to actively appropriate their out-of-school techno-literacy practices for the school context. These students function as catalysts of new literacy practices and nudge all members in the ecology to push the boundaries of learning with ICT and foster the learning of twenty-first century competency (21CC).

Conclusion

In this chapter, I have provided a window into a Singapore one-to-one slate-enabled classroom by showing two literacy events at work. In doing this, I have provided glimpses of noteworthy attempts to align the nation's plan with actual implementation. The key literacy practices identified in the two literacy events presented in this chapter are similar to other literacy events in my research (Ng 2015). In particular, three sorts of literacy practices emerged as common themes across the literacy events studied:

(1) "Old wine in new wineskins". In the attempt to make sense of the conflicting demands of preparing students for traditional pen-and-paper assessment and nurturing twenty-first century competencies, the resulting teaching practices observed were 'old wine in new wineskins'. Interviews with my key teacher participants and his colleagues revealed that the pressure of performative pedagogy, which culminates in unauthentic individual pen-and-paper assessments, plays a major part in preventing them from embracing the learning possibilities that the networked one-to-one slate-enabled environment can offer. This creates a gap between the policy and implementation.

(2) Students as co-shapers of literacy practices. Besides the two literacy events presented in this chapter, it was observed that the one-to-one slate-enabled environment empowered some students to be active agents of their in-school techno-literacy practices. This impacted on the eventual literacy outcomes. On the other hand, the teacher was observed to have a challenging time managing such active student agency. Professional development to equip teachers to handle such active participation by students is necessary.

(3) Learning experiences were not mobile. Using Pegrum's (2014) categorization of mobile literacies, referred to in the beginning of this chapter, the literacy events showed that both the device and the learners were mobile in this classroom. However it was also clear that the learning experience was yet to go mobile. There was still much untapped potential in terms of mobile learning in

this classroom. In other words, the school and parents had not maximized the returns from their investment.

These prevailing themes reveal areas of disconnect between policy, professional development, investment and implementation. It is imperative for MOE to work on these areas as the entire system pushes forth its mp4 journey to enable anytime, anywhere learning. Developing twenty-first century mobile learning goes beyond putting in place policies and providing a pervasive networked one-to-one mobile computing environment. It also requires on-going systemic study of classroom literacy practices, as frontline educators and students are equally important in moulding literacy practices. Findings from such studies shed light on the actions required to align planned and actual in-school literacies and cannot be sidelined.

References

Alderson, J.Charles, and Dianne Wall. 1993. Does washback exist? *Applied Linguistics* 14: 115–129.

Backer, Elisa. 2010. Using smartphones and Facebook in a major assessment: The student experience. *EJournal of Business Education and Scholarship of Teaching* 4:19–31. http://www.ejbest.org/upload/eJBEST_Backer_2010_4(1).pdf. Accessed 13 June 2016.

Baguley, Margaret, Darren L. Pullen, and Megan Short. 2010. Multiliteracies and the new world order. In *Multiliteracies and technology enhanced education: Social practice and the global classroom*, ed. Darren L. Pullen, and David R. Cole, 1–17. NY: Information Science Reference.

Baron, Dennis. 2009. *A better pencil: Reader, writer, and the digital revolution*. Oxford: Oxford University Press.

boyd, danah. 2008. Why youth (heart) social network sites: The role of networked publics in teenage social life. In *Youth, identity and digital media,* ed. David Buckingham, 119–142. Cambridge, MA: The MIT Press.

boyd, danah. 2014. *It's complicated: The social lives of networked teens.* http://www.danah.org/books/ItsComplicated.pdf. Accessed 13 June 2016.

Burnett, Cathy, Julia Davis, Guy Merchant, and Jennifer Rowsell. 2014. *New literacies around the globe: Policy and pedagogy*. Hoboken: Taylor and Francis.

Carspecken, Phil. 1996. *Critical ethnography in educational research: A theoretical and practical guide*. NY: Routledge.

Castells, Manuel. 2009. *The rise of the network society*. Malden, MA: Wiley-Blackwell.

Castells, Manuel. 2010. *End of millennium*. Malden, MA: Wiley-Blackwell.

Channel News Asia. 2016. Singapore needs to stay ahead while pursuing smart nation vision. http://www.channelnewsasia.com/news/singapore/singapore-needs-to-stay/2688112.html. Accessed 13 June 2016.

Chinnery, George M. 2006. Going to the MALL: Mobile assisted language learning. Language Learning & Technology 10:9–16. http://llt.msu.edu/vol10num1/pdf/emerging.pdf. Accessed 13 June 2016.

Cochrane, Thomas, and Bateman, Roger. 2010. Smartphones give you wings: Pedagogical affordances of mobile web 2.0. Australasian Journal of Educational Technology 26:1–14. http://www.ascilite.org.au/ajet/ajet26/cochrane.pdf. Accessed 13 June 2016.

Engeström, Yrjö, and Reijo Miettinen. 1999. *Perspectives on activity theory*. NY: Cambridge University Press.

Engeström, Yrjö. 2001. Expansive learning at work: Toward an activity theoretical reconceptualization. *Journal of Education and Work* 14: 133–156.

Flower, Linda, and John R. Hayes. 1981. A cognitive process theory of writing. *College Composition and Communication* 32: 365–387.

Fullan, Michael, and Langworthy, Maria. 2014. The rich seam: How new pedagogies find deep learning. http://www.michaelfullan.ca/wpcontent/uploads/2014/01/3897.Rich_Seam_web.pdf. Accessed 13 June 2016.

Green, Judith, and Bloome, David. 1997. Ethnography and ethnographers of and in education: A situated perspective. In *Handbook of research on teaching literacy through communicative and visual arts*, ed. James Flood, Shirley Brice Health, and Diane Lapp, 181–202. NY: Simon & Schuster Macmillan.

Hogan, David. 2010. *Current and future pedagogies in Singapore—Presentation at TE21 Summit.* http://www.nie.edu.sg/files/Current_and_Future_Pedagogies_in_Singapore-final.pdf. Accessed 13 June 2016.

Infocomm Development Authority of Singapore. (n.d.). *iN2015 vision.* http://www.ida.gov.sg/Infocomm-Landscape/iN2015-Masterplan. Accessed 13 June 2016.

Ito, Mizuko, Baumer, Sonja, Bittanti, Matteo, boyd, danah, Cody, Rachel, Herr Stephenson, Becky, Horst, Heather A., Lange, Patricia G., Mahendran, Dilan, Martinez, Katynka Z, Pascoe, C. J., Perkel, Dan, Robinson, Laura, Sims, Christo, and Tripp, Lisa. 2010. *Hanging out, messing around, geeking out*. London: MIT Press.

Jenkins, Henry. 2006. *Convergence culture: Where old and new media collide*. NY: New York University Press.

Kolb, Liz. 2008. *Toys to tools: Connecting student cell phones to education*. Eugene, OR: ISTE.

Low, Aloysius. 2014. Singapore has the highest smartphone adoption rate in the world. http://www.cnet.com/uk/news/singapore-has-the-highest-smartphone-adoption-in-the-world/ Accessed 13 June 2016.

Merchant, Guy. 2009. Virtual worlds in real-life classrooms. In *Digital literacies: Social learning and classroom practices*, ed. Victoria Carrington, and Muriel Robinson, 95–112. London: SAGE Publications.

Merchant, Guy. 2012. Mobile practices in everyday life: Popular digital technologies and schooling revisited. *British Journal of Educational Technology* 43: 770–782.

Mills, Kathy A. 2007. "Have you seen Lord of the Rings?" Power, pedagogy and discourses in a multiliteracies classroom. *Journal of Language, Identity and Education* 6: 221–241.

Mills, Kathy A. 2010. "Filming in progress": New spaces for multimodal designing. *Linguistics and Education* 21: 14–28.

Mills, Kathy. 2016. *Literacy theories for the digital age: Social, critical, multimodal, spatial, material and sensory lenses*. Bristol: Multilingual Matters.

Ministry of Education, Singapore. 2012. Media Release: Factsheet on Futureschool@Singapore programme. https://www.moe.gov.sg/media/press/files/2012/11/annex-1-factsheet-on-futureschools.pdf. Accessed 13 June 2016.

Ministry of Education, Singapore. 2015a. 21st century competencies. https://www.moe.gov.sg/education/education-system/21st-century-competencies. Accessed 13 June 2016.

Ministry of Education, Singapore. 2015b. 4th masterplan for ICT in education. http://ictconnection.moe.edu.sg/masterplan-4/overview. Accessed 13 June 2016.

Ng, Siew Hiang Sally. 2015. *Decoding ICT-mediated literacy practices in a networked one-to-one computing classroom in Singapore*. UK: Lancaster University.

Pachler, Norbert, Ben Bachmair, and John Cook. 2010. *Mobile learning: Structures, agency, practices*. NY: Springer.

Parry, David. 2011. Mobile perspectives: On teaching mobile literacy. EDUCAUSE Review 46. http://net.educause.edu/ir/library/pdf/ERM1120.pdf. Accessed 13 June 2016.

Pegrum, Mark. 2014. *Mobile learning: Languages, literacies and cultures*. UK: Palgrave Macmillan.

The University of Phoneix Research Institute. 2011. Future Work Skills 2020. http://www.iftf.org/uploads/media/SR-1382A_UPRI_future_work_skills_sm.pdf. Accessed 13 June 2016.

Warschauer, Mark. 2006. *Laptops and literacy: Learning in the wireless classroom.* NY: Teachers College Press.

Warschauer, Mark. 2011. *Learning in the cloud.* NY: Teacher College Press.

White, David S., and Le Cornu, Alison. 2011. Visitors and Residents: A new typology for online engagement. http://firstmonday.org/article/view/3171/3049. Accessed 13 June 2016.

Chapter 8
Apps and Autodidacts: Wayfaring and Emplaced Thinking on iPads

Jennifer Rowsell, Fernando Maues, Sharon Moukperian and Chrystal Colquhoun

Introduction

As scholars concerned with what children and teenagers think about and pay attention to, we believe that literacy policy and pedagogy need to make a decisive shift away from existing models of reading and writing to account more for the consequential nature of tablets as influential pedagogical objects. However much international policy promotes 'twenty-first century' or 'future-forward' skills and competencies, educators are still left with fairly anachronistic orientations to reading, writing, speaking and listening (Burnett et al. 2014). Admittedly there is research showing that tablet-based reading is hybrid and nonlinear (Kress 2010; Walsh and Simpson 2013) and there is research that examines the nature and properties of haptic reading (Mangen 2008; Simpson et al. 2013). However, arguing that iPad engagements are web-like and woven together through threads of movements and lines in a manner that resembles Tim Ingold's ontological framings of the environment and patterns in nature *is* new. In research reported in this chapter, we observed young people using iPads for a wide variety of tasks that entailed such traditional literacy activities as word searches and letter sorting and as open and free as playing *Minecraft* and researching how to fine-tune designs in *Minecraft*.

In this chapter we present data from a research study that took place in an after-school tutoring program in the Niagara area. Having served families for over 25 years, the tutoring centre works with families in the Niagara community and the

J. Rowsell (✉) · S. Moukperian · C. Colquhoun
Brock University, St. Catharines, Canada
e-mail: jrowsell@brocku.ca

S. Moukperian
e-mail: smoukperian@brocku.ca

F. Maues
Universidade Federal do Para, Belém, Brazil
e-mail: fernando@fernandomaues.com

C. Burnett et al. (eds.), *The Case of the iPad*,
DOI 10.1007/978-981-10-4364-2_8

reported research focuses on a smaller cohort of children and teenagers who were tutored on iPads. Tutor participants and the research team documented how iPad literacy practices differed from more traditional literacy practices during tutoring sessions. A consistent pattern in our findings has been how much young people engage in autodidactic practices that are hybrid and web like. The chapter is divided into four sections: the first section connects Ingold's ontological approach to meaning making with what we witnessed during the research; the second section presents the research background and context; the third and fourth sections present Cole and his passion for autodidactic practices and designing in digital worlds. In these sections we apply Ingold's environmental, anthropological framings of social practices to theorize iPad thinking and epistemologies and to explore how Cole's hybrid, rhizomatic and web-like navigations point to reframings of literacy practices that are valued by younger people.

Applying Ingold's Ontology

Tim Ingold approaches social practices and objects that surround practices from an anthropological, environmental perspective. Ingold focuses on material worlds and materialities but not necessarily for their physical properties, but instead for their lived, embodied, somatic properties. Such work acknowledges the processes of people working within their contexts through objects, practices, spatial features, and the idiosyncratic nature of human beings. Ingold talks about how materials have dynamic properties on their own, not to mention when they are combined with other, live materials. In this way, objects "act back" (Ingold 2010: 94). Using a building or living in a building as a metaphor, he says, 'a real house is always a work in progress' (2010: 94). Inhabitants can 'steer' a home in the right direction, but they cannot completely control its properties. So, we argue that an iPad as an object has many properties, beyond simply being multimodal, active objects, they flow, meander, and exist in a web-like form that follows the materials. There is something particularly generative about Ingold's ontology when applied to readers we observed over the course of the reported research.

Ingold theorizes how humans exist with materials—following their lines—charting their ways of becoming through material flows—and we attempt to do precisely this as we explore the story of one young man, Cole (pseudonym), and his iPad. Cole is a teenager who has been coming to the tutoring centre for seven years. Cole finds school learning boring and unmotivating, yet he can spends hours online watching Ted Talks, YouTube videos, and reading wide-ranging texts on his iPad. He is a self-proclaimed autodidactic and he is the sole case study that we foreground in this chapter.

To explore Cole's story, we harness Ingold's theorizing of objects as made up of living, agentive materials to Cole's fascination with texts on the Internet and we argue his practices are a form of wayfaring. Cole assiduously and enthusiastically works his way through texts—curating—digesting—producing texts—then curating again and these movements are felt and embodied in powerful ways. As Ingold

(2010) maintains, 'it is about becoming rather than being' (p. 99). When Cole gathers information there is a momentum and fearless creativity (Sheridan and Rowsell 2010) about it that is unmistakably a state of becoming.

Tutoring by Design: An iPad-Driven Tutoring Research Study

The reported research took place over 10 months in an after-school tutoring program one night a week (devoted solely to the research) with a cohort of 40 children. There were a range of ages involved from children, adolescents to teenage research participants who used iPads and completed multimodal knowledge work for their literacy tutoring. The project, *Tutoring by Design: Twenty-First Century Approaches to Literacy Tutoring* involved a team of researchers (Chrystal Colquhoun, Fernando Maues, Sharon Moukperian, and Jennifer Rowsell) who observed teacher education students at Brock University who took part in the research by tutoring children, adolescents and teenagers on iPads on the designated evening. Each researcher sat beside or near tutors as they worked with tutees and we filmed their interactions and took detailed fieldnotes. Research questions that framed the study were: How do tutees practice/enact multimodality? What reading and writing practices emerged? What is the role of the iPad and its shape/format/materialities in shifting reading and writing practices? After every evening, the research team debriefed about what was observed and we mapped out patterns and recurring strands. The research design comprised a researcher blog for fieldnotes, interviews with all tutees and tutors, detailed fieldnotes, and 20 hours of video-recordings of iPad engagements. Fernando joined the research team in October of the school year and he was included in the research ethics board approval alongside Chrystal Colquhoun, a Masters student, and Sharon Moukperian, a PhD student. As researchers, we documented practices, problem-solving and thinking processes enacted during tutoring sessions and in our fieldnotes we noted the particular nature of acting and thinking through iPads, but we also visualized the process. Focusing on different apps, games, and ibooks (Rowsell 2014), tutees worked closely with tutors on digital texts that they use significantly outside of school and also documented practices, problem-solving, thinking processes enacted over the course of tutoring sessions.

Context

Before showcasing Cole's story, it is important to contextualize the tutoring centre and its surrounding community to give the research a richer back story (Flewitt 2011). There is a cluster of cities in close proximity to the tutoring centre that can best be described as blue-collar towns. These cities share demographics with long-standing White working-class families and more recent immigrants who have immigrated to Canada. We do not want to put a deficit lens on our research contexts and prefer our work to sit alongside researchers who represent social class with a sensitive touch (Collier 2014; Hicks 2002; Jones and Vagle 2013). Falling back on such careful research, we have tried to sensitively frame social class in a manner that Code (2000) describes as 'responsible inquiry that entails an effort to be 'true to' the everyday practices of knowing' (p. 217). The communities where our research took place are White, blue-collar towns with some unemployment over the years, primarily due to the collapse of the automotive industry and a lack of other employment opportunities. Children and teenagers involved in our research were from this population.

The tutoring centre was established 25 years ago. The original intent was to offer reading assessments, interventions and tutoring services. The model of teacher education students in a concurrent and consecutive teacher education program tutoring children, adolescents, and teenagers in the community remains intact. Over the years, the tutoring centre has moved away from a psychological approach to literacy to more of a balanced literacy approach. As of September 2014, the centre adopted a digital, multimodal approach for some tutoring clients (particularly those who were interested) and they used iPads with different reading programs such as *Reading A to Z* to tutor as well as more than 40 different literacy apps. The tutoring centre works on reading strategies and skills as well as writing, word study, numeracy, and oral language. The tutoring program runs every evening of the week during the school year from September until early June.

Data Analyses

For data analysis, we followed an inductive process by reviewing blog posts, video data, interview transcripts and identifying recurring themes and patterns across the case studies. Cole stood out to us as the strongest, most compelling example of autodidactic practices and we wanted to devote the chapter to his story in an effort to underscore what took place when he curated information. As a prominent code within our data, autodidactic actions such as referring to a source or finding a source on the iPad or using an app like *Minecraft* and then moving to another web text represented varied repertoires of autodidactic practices that were enacted. To theorize these different types of autodidactic approaches to topics, we applied Ingold's work in social anthropology on how humans make meaning. We found his language of description and conceptual framing of life particularly helpful in mapping out how Cole made meaning because terms like wayfaring, emplacement, and meshwork captured the hybrid and rhizomatic way that Cole moved through multimodal forms of information.

Unpacking Autodidacticism and Its Wayfaring Properties

Wenger (1998) claims that 'knowing is defined only in the context of specific practices' (p. 142). Cole comes to know and demonstrate knowledge by moving across different types of texts to think and learn and he frequently engages in practices that are spontaneous and that require on-demand information that he seeks out. Often learning happens through a process of apprenticeship (Rogoff 2003) either by a person or informational text where Cole will either ask an authority or find an authoritative text. Ingold (2010) talks about a 'logic of inversion' that happens when intersecting pathways of people, materials, resources, ideas and energies constitute a classroom. If we think about learning in these terms and through these concepts learning becomes unmoored from more formalized framings of learning that are linear and unidirectional and learning then becomes more spontaneous, fluid and self-directed. This is the type of learning that we witnessed daily in the tutoring centre over the course of the 2014–2015 academic year.

Applying Ingold's ontology to our research, what we documented during tutoring sessions were movements and meanderings across visuals, moving images, sound-based texts like podcasts when tutees used a variety of apps, websites, and social media to play and think. Relating this textual travel to the work of Ingold, Cole exhibited what could be described as wayfaring and we think of printed texts as emplacing people more than digital texts. Ingold (2008) defines emplacement as follows: 'there would be no places were it not for the comings and goings of human beings and other organisms to and from them, from and to places elsewhere' (p. 1808). We are clearly adapting Ingold's sense of emplacement and using it slightly differently as Ingold centrally talks about emplacement as a form of enclosing. To us, books pin down a reader more and they do not allow for as much transport as digital texts. In fact, Ingold actually refers to this in a chapter: 'Travel through cyberspace resembles transport. Experienced users, however, tell me that, as they 'surf' the net, they seem more like a mesh than a net' (Ingold 2000: 38). Ingold goes on to say that surfing the net is more like wayfaring. Cole is definitively an experienced web user who is not emplaced in his journeying through web-based texts, but rather a wayfarer who follows the flow of information in digital worlds.

There was a freedom to the type of tutoring that happened in the tutoring centre where tutors start each hour looking at a text the tutee is interested in and then they discuss what drives this interest. Another descriptive phrase that we applied to the practices and processes we witnessed was *sliding across* or *flowing in and out of* several different types of texts. There are losses and gains in this type of spontaneous textual engagement—a loss being sustained reading of one text and a gain being a variety of sensorial, somatic engagements. Jennifer noted that tutees followed rhizomatic patterns to reading and thinking where they read or slid across many different genres of texts to gather information, create designs or write compositions based on their readings.

Over the 10 months, there was a wayfaring with tutees moving to and from a text to gather information. Cole is particularly proficient at journeying and following the flow of information about a wide range of topics—from energy to herpetology to swords—in order to understand a given topic. Within Ingold's ontological framing of meaning making, he talks about meshwork where intersecting paths of life and experience are knotted together at varied moments to constitute a place and state of mind. Cole gathers information from different sites, apps, and sources and they intersect into a meshwork of knowledge that he can extemporize about when prompted (he often liked to talk about what he has learned). At the beginning of tutoring sessions, various tutors encouraged Cole to share his meshwork and we feature this prompting and its implications later in the chapter.

Within his conceptual framing, Ingold (2010) also talks about threads of movements and wayfaring as periodic movements that constitute place. Within our research, wayfaring happened when research participants brought together, merged, and melded knowledge acquired over a series of texts that they read, engaged with and sled across texts and that meshed together into a designed product such as a gaming world or a PowerPoint or a written narrative or a visual composition. Wayfaring works so well with how we conceptualize our research and attendant research questions because, based on Ingold's definition of wayfaring as knowledge integrated with a meshwork of movements from place to place, the knowledge that we saw tutees enact showed a culling of information, curated from a wide range of texts and apps, applying senses and thinking processes, making, doing, and designing things. In this way, autodidactic practices became a form of wayfaring as a meshwork of textual genres merged and melded into another entity. Ingold (2007) writes that 'wayfaring is neither placeless nor place-bound but place making' (p. 101). Repeatedly, Cole *made places* by cobbling together knowledge that he gathered from a variety of sources, authorities, and modalities. At times these authorities were Ted Talks or YouTube talks and at other times he read information in books or on websites. This kind of self-directed learning or knowledge wayfaring was on prominent display as Cole researched topics on iPads during our tutoring research. Ingold (2007) describes the wayfarer as 'one who participates from within, in the very process of the world's continual coming into being and who, in laying a trail of life, contributes to its weave and texture' (p. 81). Based on observations of Cole's pathway into content on iPads, he had a fluency of thought when he meandered across multiple genres of information. Ingold (2015) claims that wayfarers leave traces of themselves as 'any enduring mark left in or on a solid surface by continuous movement' (p. 43). Cole left markers of self through his many compositions that he created over the course of his research and these markings were frequently visuals but not always. Ingold speaks of every somewhere being on the way to somewhere else, and as we watched tutees work across hybrid types of texts from apps to websites to Word documents to social media, there was a logic behind the movement as an intent but at the same time a spontaneity and experimentation with the process. The goal was often design-driven, but the final product was fairly spontaneous and curiosity-driven.

Focal Case Study: The Case of Cole and His Tablet

Cole was fourteen at the time of the research and he has many diverse interests. On his individualized education plan it stipulates that Cole should use a laptop or iPad as an assistive technology to complete his schoolwork. At the beginning of the research Cole was reading at a grade 4 level. From the beginning of the research, Cole's Mum gave us some wise advice, 'find a subject that peaks his interest and he cooperates and will find different ways to seek out information'. Some of Cole's interests include *Minecraft*, cadets, reading and playing on his iPad, making up his own stories, and he is interested in specific topics such as metal-work, energy, and biology. Cole has attended the tutoring centre for many years and has had many different tutors over time. Consistently, Cole exhibited interest and excitement when he could talk about his autodidactic research—often outside of school work. All four of us have worked with Cole and we have experienced his love of information and curating facts. Cole is upfront and ebullient about his aptitude for information gathering and research skills:

> I do research and projects on my iPad – anything that crosses my mind I research. For instance, today I looked up – what is energy? Everything is energy, but on the website that I was on, it said that energy is an object that is everything. The cosmos is another word for everything and the world. Our planet is an asteroid – everything has its own energy. Cole, March 10th, 2015

We have witnessed Cole's wayfaring and the more at ease he felt with each of us, the more he enjoys extemporizing on a given topic.

Journeying Through Cole's Castle of Mind

Returning to Ingold's ontology, Ingold talks about the comings and goings of people and Cole's traveling involved not only moving about across a myriad of texts online and offline, but also a sorting of facts, design, and thoughts in his head. Sharon spoke with Cole at length about his 'Castle of the Mind' (a phrase that Cole invented to describe the patterns of his mind) and in one of her fieldnotes, she outlined it in detail:

> During the time I worked with Cole, we would focus on two things at the same time. First, we would talk about an assignment he needed to complete for school, and second, his thought process around that assignment. Most students at his grade level would just talk about what the assignment required; however, I was able to ask Cole how he thought about the assignment and what strategies or process he would use to make connections. Cole's response was that he worked with words, and these words would lead to ideas. He had just finished reading three novels, one for recreation and two for school: *Ghost, Lock Down,* and *Acceleration.* We discussed learning strengths that he had, which involved seeing patterns in the main characters' behaviours and story plot in these novels. When asked how he did this, he said he would pick up on the similarities in attitudes, life events, or circumstances between novels. In particular, words drew his attention and then the ideas around what was

> similar between characters or plots would emerge. In the instance of the three novels, Cole identified, 'pain, alone, and inflict pain' as key words. Next, a discussion ensued where he justified with examples from the literature his observations. I asked him how he was able to make the connections between the key words and the insight into the characters, and his response led into a dialogue about Cole's Castle of the Mind. Sharon Moukperian, March 2015.

When we met about this specific fieldnote entry, Sharon elaborated on what Cole means by, in his words, 'a Castle of the Mind'. He described his mind like a castle with many doors and behind each door there is knowledge about a specific topic. The doors or ideas do not connect on their own. Sharon asked him to explain how the information behind the doors connected with other doors with information. This is where Cole described his ability to use patterns or similarities. Sharon asked if that allowed him to connect information behind other doors in his mind if that information was similar. Cole thought about it and said yes he believed that is how it worked. Each week the conversation was expanded on this metaphor of the castle and knowledge being compartmentalized behind doors. Observing Cole as he talked about his thinking allowed Sharon to make a list of repeated behaviours (i.e. strategies) that Cole could use to move along the corridors. The strategies became the corridors connecting the doors in this castle of the mind.

During the dialogue that Cole and Sharon had, a question was asked about his first two semesters at high school and which semester was more engaging for him. In one semester he had science, history and math. The other semester had English, physical education and computers. Since Cole is more of a tactile, haptic, and visual learner, he struggled with academic skills such as the mechanics of reading and writing, so Sharon assumed that he would prefer the semester with more hands-on activities. Cole's response surprised her. In fact, he found the semester with hands-on activities was dull and repetitive. His reason was there were no ideas that engaged him. For Cole, there is something more generative about challenging subjects that engage him. Sharon noticed that there was a strong affect and embodiment to his reactions when he discussed science. We believe that a strong source of this embodiment comes from his wayfaring process whereby Cole generates ideas, sorts them and connects them to different corridors that lead to doors in the Castle of his Mind.

Cole's Wayfaring Ways

Wayfaring, according to Ingold (2015), involves 'labyrinthine movements' (p. 133) that are attentional and not intentional. 'Attentional movements' imply an unpredictability that is more in-the-moment and on-demand than 'intentional' movements. Sharon has had the most experience with Cole when he recounted how he sought out information. Cole came in for his first tutoring session and did not believe he needed to continue with tutoring as a high school student. However, instead of following the usual introductory process, Sharon asked Cole to describe his hobbies. Cole responded to this request by providing a mini-lecture on one topic of interest—manufacturing swords. During this tutoring session, the tutor and researcher observed Cole's thought process and listed the steps he used. The debrief engaged Cole's attention and interest in understanding more about himself as an autodidact (See Fig. 8.1):

> Today's lesson was originally planned to have Cole complete the client reading interest survey, the San Diego word assessment, a language experience story, and a word game. Due to Cole's age, interests, and years of experience at the tutoring centre, we decided to scratch our planned lesson after discussing it with Sharon. One challenge that we experienced today with Cole was that we do not know him very well yet. We learned that he tunes out when he is not interested in something or if it seems like it might be boring (*Romeo and Juliet* for example). Throughout the session the researcher noted that Cole acquired information in five steps:
>
> 1. He gave us a general overview before going into specific details especially when prompted with questions like What is…
> 2. He listed the terms that related to the subject (swords).
> 3. He defined those terms once he noticed that we did not know them.
> 4. He provided us with examples through creating a visual drawing.
> 5. He explained the reasoning behind the visual.
> 6. Then, he moved into other texts to extend and nuance his knowledge. February, 2015.

Throughout Cole's lesson about swords we observed that he has a wide range of vocabulary knowledge, and that he comprehends vocabulary if it relates to his

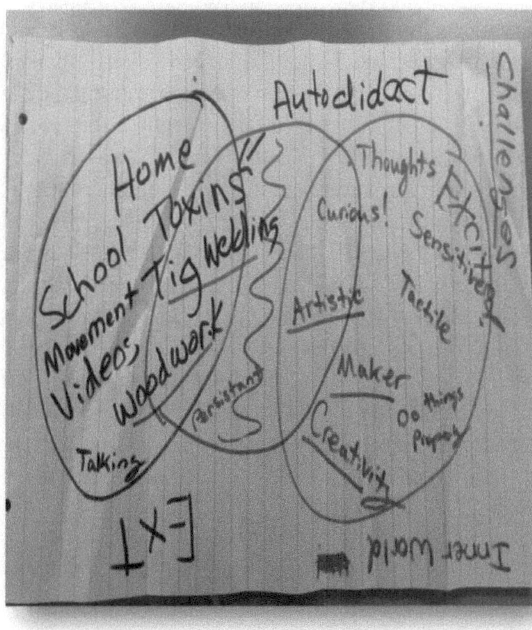

Fig. 8.1 Reflecting on his wayfaring autodidactic practices

interests. Swords are present in his *Minecraft* worlds and they are tied in with his interest in weaponry that connects, albeit distantly, with his cadet training.

When Cole discusses school, his associations tend to be about feeling bored and apathetic and he does not have a happy relationship with schooling. Cole has been on an individualized program for some time and despite being so well-versed on a range of topics, he has struggled with literacy. We did not recognize Cole's description of his schooling self/learner in a more formal space. Instead we saw him as a voracious information seeker. For instance, in the above fieldnote excerpt, Cole modelled how he thinks about a topic of interest and the process he follows. Cole begins thinking about a topic by entering a search for a YouTube information video related to the concept of swords. Cole confirmed that online texts allow him to access knowledge using a combination of visuals and words since he is a visual thinker and works from pictures to words. He uses an iPad and Google to provide independent access to information he needs in a format that aligns more with the way that he thinks. Cole talks about having a number of texts open at the same time and how he has a hybrid way of following them. He uses the same approach with Sharon when she is unable to understand his drawings and explanations.

After Cole finished using the iPad to create meanings for Sharon, she asked him if he understood what had happened during his explanation of sword manufacturing. At this point, Sharon, Cole and the tutor debriefed about Cole's thinking process using diagrams to visualize Cole's thinking and learning behaviour.

During the debriefing, Cole was told that he uses autodidactic practices, and he wanted to understand what that meant. He was asked to describe things that he did that he could observe (e.g. using TIG welding to make a sword, or looking up information about toxins on an iPad). The left circle in Fig. 8.1 represents these concrete observable behaviours. However, Sharon asked how these behaviours happen and did they happen with prompting? Cole described personal attributes that he possessed. In Fig. 8.1 the right circle represents these abstract attributes. Sharon observed that Cole did not stop when he was explaining his ideas about swords when his audience still did not understand. He was persistent and found another way to expand his explanation. This persistence made a connection between the concrete observable behaviours represented in one circle and the abstract personal attributes that triggered those external behaviours in another circle. The centre circle of the Venn diagram represents new knowledge or meaning and how his autodidactic learning style involves both external resources and internal, naturalized wayfaring habits of the mind. The use of the iPad allows him to persist because he can independently research information on a specific topic and curate them across web-based texts. In Ingold's terms, he can follow hybrid or rhizomatic pathways to develop a meshwork as a way of finding a place and anchoring an understanding.

Clashes Between Linear Schooling Models and Rhizomatic Wayfaring Models

Cole speaks freely about how his self-directed learning/autodidact habits contradict schooling models of learning that seem more linear to him. Cole's Mum talks openly about how schooling has not been particularly kind to Cole. It is clear to us that Cole is a reader and communicator, but for some reason, this does not transfer over to school and we could not quite piece it together. Sharon believes that it is the linearity of schooled approaches to reading and writing that demotivates Cole.

Cole's autodidactic approach to learning is not limited by his thinking processes, but instead by the mediums through which content is presented and the degree of open and free knowledge work that he is allowed to do. In school, Cole finds that he is 'not heard or seen' in ways that he would like. He finds formal teaching hard to follow because it is so word-based and so teacher-led. On one particular evening when Sharon observed Cole's tutoring session, she noted the hybrid nature of his thinking process:

> Tonight, Cole told me about: 1. 'zombie slug' and he is looking for a bacteria that invades a host and takes over...I think like the Walking Dead idea but in a nonfiction, real life scenario. 2. Working with liquid metal to convert it to a gas, liquid or solid. 3. Some kind of 'ray gun' or synthesizing machine. I wanted to work with Cole to organize his thoughts a bit more into a pattern. I know that Cole loves cadets – order, the military, discipline, etc. I wonder if there is a way to connect his hybrid way of thinking with his cadets? April, 2015.

The curiosity that he displays in his tutoring sessions is not replicated at school. Part of it may be due to the fact that Cole likes people to listen to him as he extemporizes about topics and facts which is more difficult at school when there are more students to navigate and listen to. Cole finds aspects of school learning more challenging because he needs to focus on one topic for longer periods of time than he prefers and learning is more linear.

From Autodidacticism to Design Work

Like many others, Cole is a *Minecraft* enthusiast. Some of his drive for autodidacticism comes from his design work that he fixates on in *Minecraft*. During a few tutoring sessions, Cole recounted how he does 'background research for *Minecraft* designs' (17 March 2015). During the session, Chrystal, Fernando and Jennifer sat outside of the cubicle where Peter (pseudonym for his tutor) and Cole worked together. Peter had been tutoring Cole for a year and they had a natural rapport that showed through when we observed them. During this particular session, Cole and Peter analyzed different spaces/environments that Cole has created on *Minecraft*. Peter was keen to focus on Cole's writing skills for this session, so he engaged in stimulated recall with Cole by asking him questions as Cole navigated through a particular village that he built in *Minecraft*. The village is Medieval and Cole completed a significant amount of research on all aspects of Medieval life as he designed the world. Cole went into a lot of detail when explaining aspects of his world from its topography, buildings and structures, natural resources (including crops), living beings, and tools that he uses (see Fig. 8.2). When Peter asked him if he had any inspiration from any real-world sources he said that everything is original and created 'from his mind'. To help start off categorizing his world, Peter asked him to think about the crops, climate, societal structure and buildings. They started off with his world which they referred to as the 'Village'. Peter decided to encourage Cole to write down his thoughts about his designs in *Minecraft* and he asked him to map out his design process through a Venn diagram. It was observed that when Peter asked Cole to pause the game and to start filling in the Venn diagram he was hesitant—this could have been for a few reasons. To begin with, Cole was invested in what he was doing and he did not want to be distracted. Second, Cole seems hesitant with writing. On our research blog, Peter noted the following:

> I constantly noticed throughout the session that when he was writing he would pause and wait for my feedback to help him correctly spell out the word. Cole spells words phonetically (for example 'church' was spelt 'cherch' or 'houses' was spelt 'hoases'), and throughout the session he had a harder time with vowel blends. This session I did most of the writing as I saw Cole was becoming frustrated (and shy), and for next session, I am going to give Cole the option of working with a word processor or writing on paper and have Cole do more of the writing.
>
> Near the end of the session I asked Cole to highlight unique features of his Village that we wouldn't expect to find in other places around the world (or in history). He said that everything we would find in the world and he was particularly interested in Medieval Times (which next week we will start to learn about Medieval cities and note the similarities and differences). We started reading about different types of buildings although we didn't have a lot of time for this. When we were finished with the session Cole said he sees himself as a 'little scientist' and started explaining to me about how he is really intrigued about energy, particularly energy in stones. Cole frequently referenced Albert Einstein's theory of energy and he wants to find out how to harness the energy from stones to usable energy. March, 2015.

The Venn diagram allowed Cole to step back and categorize wayfaring knowledge that he picked up and emplaced when he designed the Medieval world in *Minecraft*.

Peter understood the rhythm of Cole's work and he shaped tutoring lessons around his preferences, which Peter described as: (1) talk/catching up; (2) some reading and/or writing; (3) game play (*Minecraft* or something else); (4) extend game play with other related texts on the web; and (5) writing prompts based on research. Often, when it came to work on *Minecraft*, the research that Cole completed led to design work of some kind or another.

There were several other instances when Jennifer observed Cole demonstrating what he had learned online about topics when he designed an impromptu text such as the PowerPoint in Fig. 8.3. For example, after speaking with his tutors about herpetology, he wanted to create a PowerPoint on the topic.

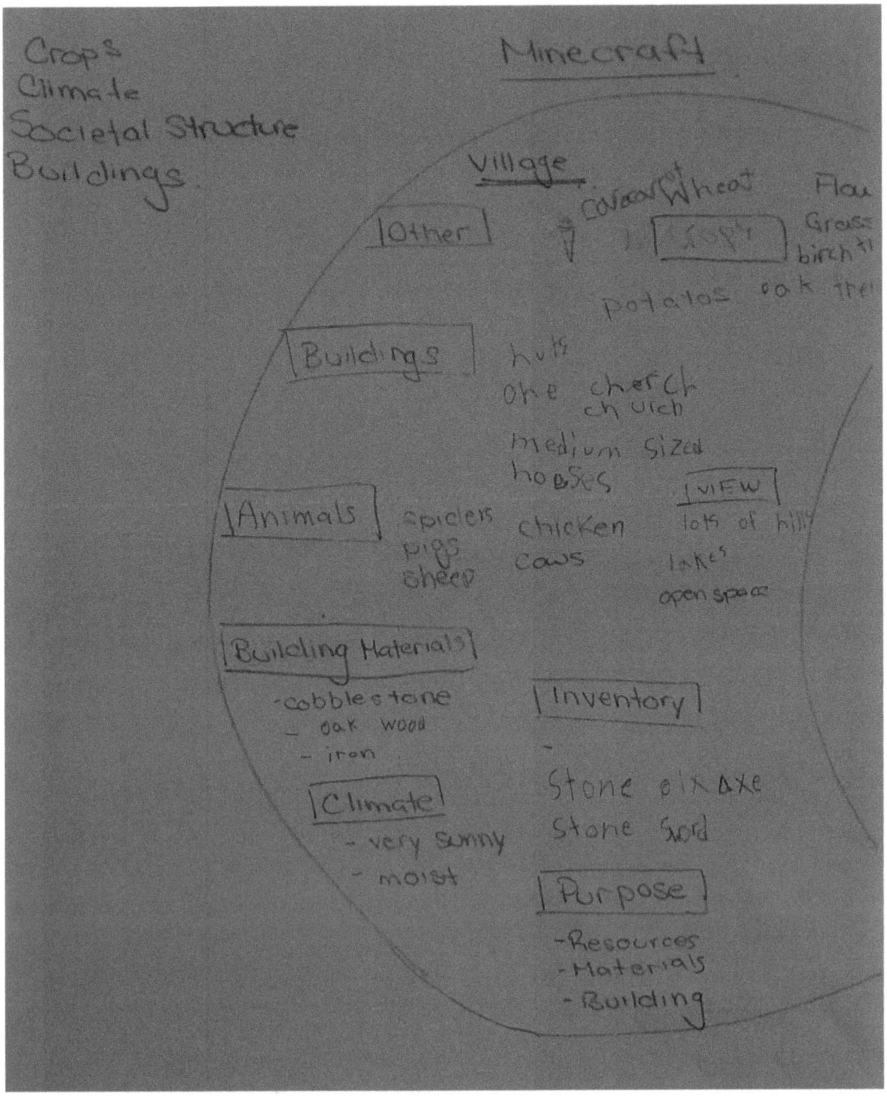

Fig. 8.2 Venn diagram of *Minecraft* village

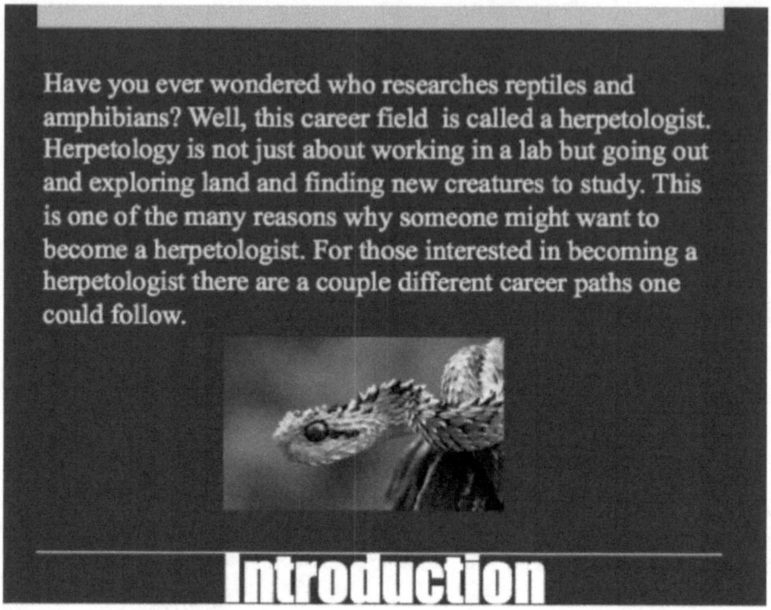

Fig. 8.3 Researching for designs

Apps as Autodidacts

Although all apps cannot be created equal (Rowsell and Wohlwend 2016), Cole liked to use different apps as part of his autodidactic approach. A specific app that he gravitated to is the *Exploratorium* app that explores a wide range of topics such as colour, sound, electricity and heat. Cole often uses this app as a catalyst to curating different types of information as seen in the following fieldnote:

> We started off with the original tutoring plan but then switched gears as I observed reading was a bit difficult specifically the pronunciation of words and concentrating due to Cole's cold and flu, therefore I did most of the reading this session and we had a lot of conversation about different topics.
>
> We started off with the app *Exploratorium Sound Uncovered*, which caught Cole's attention last session. Within the app there are a lot of modules that you can work through to explore sound. We started off on the first module but as we were moving through, Cole wasn't interested in some of them and therefore wanted to skip them. I asked him why he enjoys some modules more than others but he wasn't really sure. While moving through some of the more interesting modules, Cole and I shared reading alternating paragraphs. In the modules he was interested in he was inclined to read and participate in the activities outlined in the app.

> While reading the app Cole made a lot of connections to other topics having a lot of good questions surrounding the topic of sound—in particular when we got to the part about echolocation in humans. Cole had knowledge about echolocation in animals but has never heard about humans being capable and therefore we researched more about echolocation on Wikipedia. While exploring the Wikipedia page, since there is a lot of text information I noticed Cole scrolling through looking mainly at the pictures. Therefore, I helped direct his attention to the headings to see if we could narrow down our search reading the text and looking at the diagrams for more information.
>
> After a bit of research we took a quick break. After coming back from the break, Cole asked if there was one month where there were more birthdays which then we switched our focus and started researching trends in birthdays. This topic didn't show up in the first half of our session, so I am unaware of why he had this question although we looked into it since he was interested in the question. Similar to the Wikipedia page, on the website there were both text and graphs which Cole was more inclined to read the graphics. February, 2015

Jennifer observed this specific tutoring session and noted how organic the whole process was, from the app—to a discussion about echolocation—to finding more information about it—to correcting assumptions about it—to creating something about echolocation. In this moment, the app spoke to both Cole's visual sensibilities as much as it satiated his love of facts and information, especially in the area of science. It is clear that the app led naturally into a longer discussion about echolocation which led to trends in birthdays and so on and so forth. With Cole, you never knew where you would end up in his wayfaring for knowledge.

Following Wayfarers

In undertaking this research we sought to describe what happens when tutors teach through iPads with a fidelity to their affordances. By that we mean we wanted to know how modes impact thinking, accounting for combined modes and modes in isolation. In the spirit of wayfaring, we wanted to know about the properties and processes of iPad reading and composing. Initially, we were aware that iPads naturally invite a more hybrid reading path and that tutees tend to read shorter texts and that there is a closer relationship between reading and writing. There were other serendipitous findings such as young people who do not like iPads or young people who only liked image-based apps or exclusively played spatial games. But, we kept returning to our fascination with Cole and his Castle of the Mind.

The thing about Cole that continues to intrigue us is how committed he is to information. In dealing with issues that bother him like school, Cole turns to facts. One of the most natural ways for Cole to cope with being a teenager is to turn to facts and information and share what he finds out with anyone who will listen. There is a rhythm to his wayfaring that intrigues us and it looks a bit like this:

(1) Start with talk by asking questions (e.g., how are swords made?)

⇒ (2) Brainstorm terms

⇓

(3) Trial and error with terms (i.e., sometimes Cole is wrong about terms and we check the term on the iPad)

⇒ (4) CO-PRODUCE VISUAL WITH COLE (create meta-thinking drawings while Jennifer creates visuals of information with Cole)

⇓

⇒ (5) Cole explains reasoning behind the visual

⇒ (6) Cole moves onto other texts to continue his wayfaring on his own

It is probably true that this pattern can be replicated at school. It is probably also true that Cole does not always have to learn and think in this way. It is perhaps even true that there is nothing especially profound in what we uncover in this article. But, to us, the key finding is the agentive, meandering nature of Cole's passion and search for information. Cole has to put his mark on facts—even if his mark is not, strictly speaking, correct—it is the searching, finding and reconstituting that drives him. If we are wise as researchers we listen to young men like Cole and document their meanderings, emplacement and wayfaring as knowledge markings. Cole is not alone; there are many other Coles listening to Ted Talks and adding to their growing repository of facts, and if we are not patient listeners then we will never change our mindsets about the sophisticated repertoires that hide in the shadows of schooling.

References

Burnett, Cathy, Julia Davies, Guy Merchant, and Jennifer Rowsell (eds.). 2014. *New literacies around the globe: Policy and pedagogy*. London: Routledge.

Code, Lorraine. 2000. Naming, naturalizing, normalizing: 'The child' as fact and artefact. In *Toward a feminist developmental psychology*, ed. Patricia H. Miller and Ellin Kofsky Scholnick, 215–237. New York, NY: Routledge.

Collier, Diane. 2014. 'I'm just trying to be tough, okay?': Masculine performances of everyday practices. *Journal of Early Childhood Literacy* 15: 203–226.

Flewitt, Rosie. 2011. Bringing ethnography to a multimodal investigation of early literacy in a digital age. *Qualitative Research* 11 (3): 293–310.

Hicks, Deborah. 2002. *Reading lives: Working-class children and literacy and learning*. New York, NY: Teachers College Press.
Ingold, Tim. 2000. Against space: Place, movement, and knowledge. In *Boundless worlds: An anthropological approach to movement*, ed. P. Wynn Kirby, 29–43. New York and Oxford: Berghahn Books.
Ingold, Tim. 2007. *Lines: A brief history*. Abingdon, Oxon: Routledge.
Ingold, Tim. 2008. Bindings against boundaries: Entanglements of life in an open world. *Environment and Planning* 40 (8): 1796–1810.
Ingold, Tim. 2010. The textility of making. *Cambridge Journal of Economics* 34: 91–102.
Ingold, Tim. 2015. *The life of lines*. London: Routledge.
Jones, Stephanie, and Mark Vagle. 2013. Living contradictions and working for change: Toward a theory of social class-sensitive pedagogy. *Educational Researcher* 42: 129–141.
Kress, Gunther. 2010. *Multimodality: A social semiotic approach to contemporary communication*. London: Routledge.
Mangen, Anne. 2008. Hypertext fiction reading: Haptic and immersion. *Journal of Research in Reading* 31 (4): 240–262.
Rogoff, Barbara. 2003. *The cultural nature of human development*. Cambridge: Cambridge University Press.
Rowsell, Jennifer. 2014. Toward a phenomenology of contemporary reading. *The Australian Journal of Literacy and Language* 37 (2): 117–127.
Rowsell, Jennifer, and Karen E. Wohlwend. 2016. Free play or tight spaces? Mapping participatory literacies in apps. *The Reading Teacher* 70 (2): 197–205.
Sheridan, Mary P., and Jennifer Rowsell. 2010. *Design literacies: Learning and innovation in the digital age*. London: Routledge.
Simpson, Alyson, Maureen Walsh, and Jennifer Rowsell. 2013. The digital reading path: Researching modes and multidirectionality with iPads. *Literacy* 47 (3): 123–130.
Walsh, Maureen and Alyson Simpson. 2013. Touching, tapping ... thinking? Examining the dynamic materiality of touch pad devices for literacy learning. *Australian Journal of Language and Literacy* 36(3): 148–157.
Wenger, Etienne. 1998. *Communities of practice: Learning, meaning, and identity*. Cambridge, UK: Cambridge University Press.

Author Biographies

Jennifer Rowsell is Professor and Canada Research Chair at Brock University's Faculty of Education. Her research interests include: research in schools and communities doing multimodal, arts and media work with young people; exploring how children and youth think and interact through technologies, videogames and immersive environments; and, longitudinal work in homes connecting artefacts and material worlds to literacy practices and identity mediation. Her latest books are *The Routledge Handbook of Literacy Studies*, co-edited with Kate Pahl, and *Literacy Lives in Transcultural Times*, co-edited with R. Zaidi.

Fernando Maues is Literature Professor at Universidade Federal do Para in Brazil. Dr. Maues teaches various levels of Portuguese Literature and Literature Teaching Training. His research interests include Medieval and Renaissance Literature and he has published books like *A prosa doutrinaria na corte de Avis* and *O Palmeirim de Inglaterra de Francisco de Moraes* to investigate in English teacher education. He also directs a program on vernacular language practices in low-income schools in the city of Belem, Brazil.

Sharon Moukperian is a Ph.D. candidate in Education and is supporting students with learning disabilities and ADHD as a Learning Disabilities Specialist in a university environment. She teaches undergraduate courses in Literacy and Reading Development and she tutors students in the Brock University Learning Lab. Her Ph.D. research examines ways that embodied emotional memories affect reading and literacy development.

Chrystal Colquhoun is a Master of Education candidate at Brock University. Her research explores preservice teacher attitudes on technology, digital literacy and ways in which iPads and apps impact literacy development in children with reading difficulties.

Chapter 9
Game 2 Engage: Using iPads to Mediate and Develop Social Relationships in College Learning

Jamie Caine, Julia Davies and Bronwyn T. Williams

Preamble *The setting is a college in the north of England; it's a bleak day and as the two visitors make their way up the steep incline and past McDonald's, the boisterous voices carry chaotically in the blustery wind. The kids are confident and lively, easily carrying their college stuff in fashionable bags. Coming in closer to the college the building is impressive; a strikingly tall iconic multi-storey complex with a spanking-new clean construction situated close to the city's major transport links—buses, trains and trams. Some kids arrive on bicycles—as is the fashion, and in twos and threes the ultra cool clandestinely inhale deeply on cigarettes. Following the long walk leading to the main entrance, the students are faced with a set of barriers; they have to swipe their student cards to access the rest of the building. Proceeding on from these prominent security measures, is a steep set of steps that lead to a noticeably long atrium area overseen by balconies, then further stairs to a canteen area, a lift and corridors to first floor curriculum areas of the College. These teens are 'coming of age', waiting for afternoon classes for re-takes of exams failed at school; for university entrance courses; for professional training in hairdressing, engineering, media ... As the visitors, two researchers enter the vestibule, they become aware of a more muted gathering; they are protectively ushered by two women, caring and attentive, checking off names in notebooks, looking in student bags—a very different melange than the 'youth presence' hanging and geeking out elsewhere.*

J. Caine
Sheffield Hallam University, Sheffield, UK
e-mail: J.Caine@shu.ac.uk

J. Davies (✉)
The University of Sheffield, Sheffield, UK
e-mail: j.a.davies@sheffield.ac.uk

B.T. Williams
University of Louisville, Louisville, USA
e-mail: bronwyn.williams@louisville.edu

C. Burnett et al. (eds.), *The Case of the iPad*,
DOI 10.1007/978-981-10-4364-2_9

This chapter is the story of how the two researchers got to know the students inside the vestibule; of how their teacher brought together students from a media course to work with them and how iPads mediated relationships between individual and across groups of students, giving rise to a range of encounters that facilitated learning in diverse ways. The chapter is authored by the two researchers (Bronwyn and Julia), and the teacher practitioner (Jamie), now himself a university academic. We use the first-person plural to narrate our chapter.

Introduction

This study is based on a UK Further Education (FE) setting, a sector which traditionally is associated with the vocational provision, and with helping students 'catch up' on traditional 16+ qualifications. In England, FE has traditionally supported students deemed to have failed to acquire 'minimal' qualifications at General Certificate of Secondary Education (GCSE) level in conventional schooling. Thus, FE tutors have helped prepare students for GCSEs and also provided a range of basic and additional GCSE programmes to suit the interests of a variety of students of all ages. FE colleges have also often offered subjects that are more diverse than those which schools can conventionally offer, such as additional modern languages, sociology or psychology, for example. In some areas of the UK colleges provide most post-16 education, whereas, in others, the college route is much less conventional. In recent years, FE has been forced to diversify its offerings due to governmental constraints (Simmons and Thompson 2008) and now finds itself delivering various educational routes including pre-GCSE, vocational training and Foundation Degrees. It is with the pre-GCSE provision that this project locates itself. Some of the most vulnerable students' work within this curriculum area and their vulnerabilities can, as we show, either be helped or exacerbated by college life.

Marsh and Bearne (2007: 133) talk about the sometimes 'uncomfortable spaces' that emerge in educational settings where there are discernible gaps in access; where exclusion is a process within communities, so that students may not share the same social spaces; may not have the same cultural power as others; and where individual identities are also in process. In all communities, pedagogical practices can both reinforce or challenge those processes of exclusion as learning happens.

We feel that the project described in this chapter suggests ways forward for all students; we suggest that sometimes the assumptions made about learners and about how those needs are best met, need to be challenged. In this chapter, we show how drawing on students' funds of knowledge and channelling those to 'deepen their understandings and broaden their perspectives on their own and others' lives' (Moll et al. 1992: 90) can build bridges across relationships as well as help students learn. We also examine how the technology of iPads worked to mediate the relationships in this educational setting, including effects we did not expect, on relationships between students and between students and some members of staff. In addition, we show how students can mentor each other and where transformations can take place within the student body. This was a 'strategic intervention' (Leander and Sheehy 2004), where two quite distinct groups of students worked together and using iPads were able to build meaningful relationships, that promoted a more equitable experience for everyone involved.

The Project Participants

The project was led by Jamie, the College Practitioner, while the two university researchers collected primary research data through observation and playing an active role in the practitioner-led workshops. The three of us are now situated in three different universities and are reflecting back on this project of some years ago, in 2013.

Importantly, the project brought two distinct sets of students together; vocational 'Digital Media students' studying at levels 2 and 3 which could be used as university entry qualifications; studying BTEC (Business Technology and Education Council) courses and so-called 'Practical Skills students' (Entry Level 1–3, pre-GSCE—General Certificate in Secondary Education), hoping to gain entry to other courses at the college in years to come. This second group of students were being taught basic 'life skills', such as cookery, shopping, and even learning to travel by bus from home to college and back, through accompanied travel schemes.

The Digital Media students were confident in using technology both socially and academically; many had strong preferences for gaming technology. All these students carried mobile phones. The Practical Skills students had varying access to technology, but several carried phones with them and occasionally revealed skills of playing Minecraft; others did not possess such items. The Practical Skills of students were often very dependent on staff; support for them included Learning Support Assistants (LSAs) who assisted them not only during class time but also during leisure time around the college. The main focus of the LSAs' role was to provide additional support to students alongside assisting the teacher in the hands on delivery of classroom activities. Although in some cases students had severe physical difficulties and learning needs we reveal through this chapter, how gaming technologies including the iPad facilitated their learning, independence, identity building, self-empowerment and relationship building. These seemed to challenge the way LSAs perceived the Practical Skills students and positively affected their relationships with them.

Jamie had, in previous years at the college, noticed how support arrangements for Practical Skills students could, counter-intuitively, mediate against their abilities to successfully integrate with other students. It was not simply that the courses they followed separated them, but also that they arrived separately on buses, were required to stay in college at breaks and whose comings and goings from the classrooms were closely monitored. Set against the other students, who came and went when they pleased—aside from checking into register when they arrived; who wandered in groups to college or travelled together on public transport, and who enjoyed frequenting and selecting from fast food outlets close to and within the college. Close monitoring of the Practical Skills students meant that other youth gave them a wide margin; so friendships remained insular and reified differences, casting an invisibility cloak over any similarities. Thus, bringing together two groups of students from either side of this institutionally constructed ability fence was to mark the bringing together of two distinct social communities too. This was something that Jamie aimed to do, by bringing Digital Media students to the classroom, sharing their expertise in media and hoping to draw out friendships at the same time. Research on motivation emphasizes the critical role relationships can play in developing and sustaining internal motivations (Deci and Ryan 2000; Sheldon 2015). Individuals who perceive that their actions are valued by others demonstrate more persistence in achieving their goals, as well as more satisfaction during and after the process (Norton et al. 2012; Wilson 2011). Of course, the Digital Media students learned too from the Practical Skills students, who despite many seemingly obvious barriers to their learning, including visual difficulties, autism, literacy de-coding problems and physical challenges, did have funds of knowledge they could share. The Digital Media Students obviously also not a homogeneous group, had diverse challenges of their own, and as might be expected, learned much through this project.

Fancy Spaces for Learning

Subject to a multimillion pound development within the last decade, the college boasted modern facilities and developed bespoke areas for specific curricula. This included a custom designed aircraft simulation for aviation courses, tools and equipment for construction courses, state-of-the-art hairdressing facilities and a comprehensive suite for catering and hospitality. However, from a student perspective looking beyond the fancy architecture and facilities for learning, the social spaces created for students only facilitated congregation in atrium areas through the provision of occasional recreational facilities.

Students who had opted for subjects requiring sophisticated machinery etc., thus enjoyed the bounty of the college's facilities (ironically developing *their* 'practical skills'); support for the Practical Skills students meanwhile, existed in a different kind of expensive bubble, one with specialist teachers and support workers, and as mentioned, this support ironically disabled them in other ways, separating them from others and robbed them of independence and any sense of cool or kudos.

Jamie felt that allowing these Practical Skills students access to new technologies, to facilitate greater socialization with other students and to use cool stuff in class, would help effect a more socially integrated student culture within the college. The aim was fundamentally, to dissolve the social isolation of Practical Skills students. Hence the aptly named 'Game 2 Engage' project was born.

Making IT Personal (MITP)

'Game 2 Engage' developed through previous college initiatives, but principally grew out of a European Social Fund venture 'Making IT Personal' (MITP Digital 2017). MITP aimed to tackle digital exclusion by empowering citizens in South Yorkshire to mentor their friends, family and colleagues in utilizing basic IT. This model was rolled out within the College to the Digital Media students who mentored their family members to make use of IT. Two, from many success stories, stood out from the MITP activity amongst the Digital Media group—itself as mentioned above, like all groups a heterogeneous mix of individuals, with diverse dis/advantages in life. The first, a mentoring experience that involved a student utilizing gaming technology to develop the social skills and cognitive capacity of his severely autistic sister. The second, a level 3 student who excelled in providing diverse examples of helping his family to learn and apply IT; this second student himself severely disabled after contracting meningitis as a child, had overcome extreme challenges in his own learning and was hence in the Digital Media group. Later, we explore the intricacies involved in the relationships formed with this particular Digital Media student and the Practical Skills students. However, it was the first example that Jamie and the Project Sponsor within the College reflected and agreed that we should facilitate an in-house project whereby the Digital Media Students will befriend and mentor the Practical Skills students through a common medium, gaming technology. The intention to aid social engagement, therefore, was envisaged to grow through mentorship initially and friendship ultimately.

Preparing the Digital Media Students and the Launch Event

Before communicating the project goals to the students, the 'buy in' from the specialist teachers of the Practical Skills students was needed. In principle, they agreed with the project aims but Jamie had an initial concern to develop the Digital Media students' awareness of issues that might arise when working with students who have complex physical, emotional and learning needs. Jamie hence set up and ran a training workshop for the Digital Media students to provide them with knowledge relevant to working with the Practical Skills students and to set and manage their expectations.

Following the workshop, a project launch event brought both sets of students together to initially introduce them to each other and to help them begin developing relationships. This workshop was based on a bespoke blog tool developed at The Rix Research and Media centre, which '… explores and develops ways of using new technologies to transform the lives of people with learning disabilities'. The blog tool allows students to introduce themselves to others on a private site; it was ideal in helping students explore the theme 'About Us', facilitating students to work

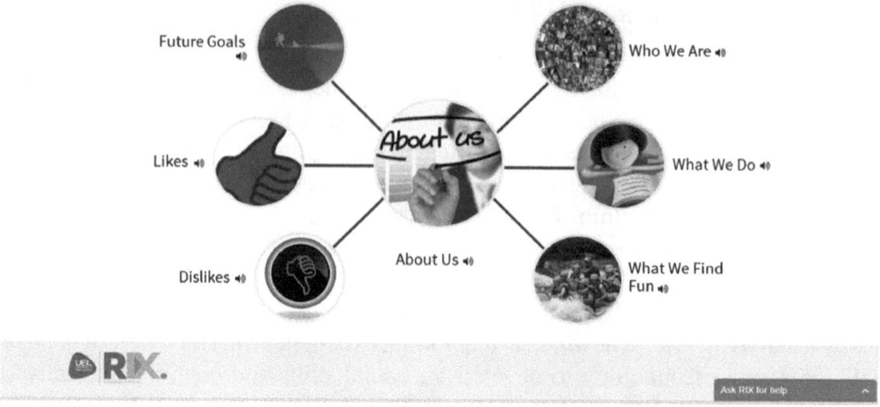

Fig. 9.1 The Rix blog tool. With permission from Rix Research and Media

together and populate content based on: Who we are, What we do; Likes; Dislikes; What we find fun; Future goals (Fig. 9.1).

During the launch event, the Digital Media students worked with the Practical Skills students, talking to them about their interests and preferences and helping them upload their responses using the blog tool. The event allowed students to mix and exchange personal information—but with the emphasis on Practical Skills students telling the Digital media students about themselves; the LSAs sat close to the Practical Skills students,' monitoring' the interactions. Physical proximity between the support workers and Practical Skills students meant that Digital Media students sometimes hovered awkwardly on the edges of intimate huddles; in other groups, the Digital Media students seemed to 'take over' the technology slightly to the side of the Practical Skills students. But slowly as the day progressed, the task gradually took over and conversations became more lively; the LSAs discernibly and literally moved back leaving space for the young to interact together.

To the surprise of the staff, close to the end of the day, the students seemed to relax and engaged in what might be termed a spontaneous 'show and tell' session. One of the students mimed to her favourite pop song; another danced and others joined in; there was an impressive demonstration of break dancing, but the pinnacle was probably the emotional outburst from one Practical Skills student, Lucia, who stood up and loudly proclaimed:

> …all I want to say now is that I've got some new friends now, I felt like nobody likes me or respects me the way that I am and I thank you a lot for being there for me today, thank you very much

This was a direct response from Lucia, whose major and complex learning difficulties had so far prevented her from being able to read or write beyond the preliminaries of her name; her phrasing echoed familiar schooled discourses of friendship and gratitude. Nevertheless, the spontaneity and the bravery of her words, disclosing her feelings so openly, surprised us all.

The applause that ensued came from both staff and students but it was clear there remained much to be done since during the lunch break on this day, the Digital Media students followed their usual protocol and went out to buy food; while the Practical Skills students were closely supervised inside and ate the lunch provided. But the groundwork was laid.

Technology: Combining the Mundane and the Exotic

An interesting aspect of the way technology is still used in many educational institutions, is the way it is almost revered, kept preciously in separate almost sanitized spaces, away from the pen and paper literacy practices of the mundane classroom world. The practices of digital literacy and 'traditional' literacy remained determinedly separate. Hence at the beginning of every lesson, two student monitors were required to ritualistically collect the iPads from the staffroom where they were kept in a filing cabinet under lock and key. The students liked to be picked for this task, taking the responsibility seriously and being trusted not to get lost, ferrying the merchandise safely back to the class. The iPads as precious cargo were solemnly handed over to students, pristine in their stylish, branded boxes, some even still with the tissue paper wrapped around them, lovingly replaced at the end of each lesson. The status conferred on the objects by institutional structures (Miller 2009) became a significant factor in shaping how the students perceived and interacted with the tablets. These items, originally intended by Jamie to be kept by students and taken home, were nevertheless kept on college premises 'in case students did not take care of them'. This seemed unlikely to be the case since the students often even used the iPads while they were still in their boxes; it was only after some weeks of lessons that they began to use them in the mobile manner which their design affords. For the students, these were highly precious objects, revered and honoured; and we noted how differently both the Digital Media and the Practical Skills students were in their handling of their own personal gadgets, confidently, almost casually pulling them in and out of pockets, consulting them; these were quotidian objects of identity and taken for granted.

This exoticization of the precious objects made them seem almost alien classroom tools; they did not seem like the easy mobile objects described, for example by Merchant (2015) in the early years' classroom, or children's easy acceptance of using technologies in the primary school (Burnett 2015). Despite the desire to invest in home practices and transfer them to college, it seemed that the institution's policy over the care of resources conspired against the normalizing of what was happening. This certainly acted as a barrier to the empowerment of students.

All students had their own college log-in address that allowed them to get online and access their media accounts. These were 'unfriendly' codes, generated by the college system and comprising letters and numbers in odd combinations; of course for students with limited literacy skills this was a major hurdle and logging on sometimes took almost half an hour. What's more, the 'touch' interface of the tablet also became an issue at such moments. While, on the one hand, a strength of the iPad interface was that it allowed students who had limited literacy skills to touch and swipe in order to manipulate images, words, and applications, at the same time, as anyone who has used a touchscreen knows, getting the tablets to respond to a touch requires a combination of precise accuracy and pressure that was a further challenge for some of the students who also had issues with fine motor dexterity or vision. Mastering the art of the right kind of touch was a steep, and often frustrating, learning curve for some of the Practical Skills students as well as a reminder that every form of literacy technology will have unintended consequences with a particular audience. The LSAs would help by noting down the log-in codes on paper in the same little books they carried with them all day—books which held the students' emergency phone numbers, travel arrangements and so on, now had log-on details. These were books the students never held or consulted; even the Digital Media students could not assist since the numbers were all inaccessible to them too. Everything was organized with the best interest of the Practical Skills students in mind; but the LSAs were the custodians of students' access online and therefore the students were disempowered. The anticipated freedom of the Internet was hard to win and students became demoralized and frequently angry at how long it took to get things sorted out before they could begin using them in class. It is also the case, however, that some of the students persisted in trying to master their log-in codes. When, after close to six months, Manj logged on by herself one day, and made a point of announcing that she had done so, it was a clear moment of accomplishment for her. The timeline of this achievement, however, reinforces how the introduction of digital technologies in such a context requires both patience and a long view of what constitutes progress.

Two students would often seek refuge while waiting for things to get going; learning using the mobile phones they brought with them daily, independently from each other they began playing on *Minecraft*,[1] taking time from the lesson to build up their cities or to demolish things. Researchers, Julia and Bronwyn, noticed how these activities were at first surreptitiously executed; but later the two became comrades. They exchanged eye contact with each other and after a while gravitated to sit together for short periods, looking over each other's shoulders to see what each was doing. Not much was said, but occasionally they could be seen exchanging phones, allowing the other to execute actions on their games, and then returning the devices after a while. It was clear in these mainly silent manoeuvres, that a relationship was accumulating; they were sharing unspoken understandings and enjoying each other's company. The project was working—the Practical Skills students were interacting together, learning from each other and building on expertise they had brought in from home. But this was a peripheral activity; and it was a patient waiting game that Jamie played for this kind of conduct to slowly drip feed into the mainstream activities of the class.

---

[1]*Minecraft* was emerging as a game at that time and the two were early UK adopters.

When Julia and Bronwyn chatted to the two *Minecraft* students about what they were doing, the two realised their behaviour was not against the rules, that this was allowed! The private and surreptitious engagements became more openly collaborative; they more and more exchanged tactics, showing each other how to do things and learn together. The contrast with how these two used their mobile phones, against the boxed up iPads was notable. Not for them the barrier of encoded access to their tools; their games were always on and these students were savvy and connected, relaxed in their participation with online gaming. Later these students used *Minecraft* on their iPads—so that the digital tool represented a tangible link between home tools and college practices.

Learning Support Staff and Tandem Learning

A valuable asset in the lives of the Practical Skills students were the support staff; they were ever patient, knowledgeable about the students' lives, were skilled in defusing the many 'difficult' social situations that could suddenly arise, and threw themselves into the 'digital treasure hunt' that was arranged in the local shopping mall. They would always seize the opportunity to help out in any way they could.

From the outset, however, the LSAs were bemused by the activities that happened in the classroom. They were baffled as to why iPads should be used when pen and paper seemed (to them), easier. They felt somewhat usurped by the presence of the Digital Media students. They told the researchers that they were not so keen on technology and they liked the more practical lessons, taking students to the shops, baking, and going on trips. The focus of Jamie's project on less directly tangible concepts, such as relationships, social groups, and self-representation, were not only part of the familiar curriculum, and were also potentially less easy to control. The assistants' training did not include the kind of curriculum that was the focus of Game 2 Engage, and so it took a while for them to figure out how they could fit into the work taking place in Jamie's classroom. The assistants also confided that at home they rarely had access to computers and that even the TV remote control was not usually available to them—being operated by their children or husbands. The responses of the assistants were a reminder that, while our focus as the project began was on issues of disability, other identity positions, particularly with the intersections of age, gender, and class, were always present and often interacting in ways that we had not anticipated. As time went on, however, while Jamie explained tasks to the class, showing them apps, asking them to populate a range of sites with personal and social information, taking pictures, making comments, they learned alongside and became more confident. They continued to take notes for themselves on paper, and in this way using both traditional and digital tools, they became adept. They started to surf, helping students find pictures they wanted to use in their work; found answers to questions and alongside the Practical Skills students learned in tandem. As they engaged with the technology their ongoing relationships in working with the students re-emerged as a strength in the classroom, as they integrated existing strategies for working with the students into the various digital media projects.

Negotiating Identities

The idea of involving Digital Media students was that they would be able to support and mentor Practical Skills students in the same way that had happened on the MITP project. Usually, the Practical Skills students would arrive first, having always been marshalled in punctually, lacking the more free and casual privileged rights of the others. The Digital Media students seemed to possess a certain cachet in the classroom, which seemed to emanate from their seeming confidence, carefully styled clothes and other 'accoutrements'; they might, for example have with them a takeaway coffee from the refectory; they might noticeably receive alerts on their phones; they seemed connected to the world beyond that which the Practical Skills students inhabited. Yet this seemed to change over time; the more the students mixed, and sometimes this happened outside the class, the more the differences between them fell back. This was accelerated through some 'digital social' lunchtime sessions organized by Jamie, where gaming consoles, iPads and laptops were used to play games. One of the standout activities involved the Xbox360 *Dance Central* game. This sparked a collective happiness and brought about a true social between both sets of students. In addition to this, the 'Digital Champions' initiative also helped facilitate overcoming the differences. This placed the Digital Media students as gurus supporting staff and students with any personal IT and media related problems. The Practical Skills students felt comfortable enough to drop in from time to time.

The classes became noisier, there was more chat and Digital Media students leaned more closely in and the LSAs sometimes congregated together leaving the younger learners to get on with things together. As they talked about the carefully designed tasks, played games together and discovered they had interests in common (music, shopping, sport, films), they gradually blended as a group.

As mentioned above, one of the Digital Media Students (Lance) had contracted meningitis at five years old. This had resulted in severe physical impairments; his speech was very difficult to understand and he had a support worker who was able to interpret and re-articulate his words. In the past, he had used a computer to articulate his words but he now rejected this, telling Julia, 'it's like being an android. It's a barrier'. Lance was in a wheelchair and also had problems holding objects. Lance was very intelligent and was a highflier in the Digital Media class and although, having been successful in the MITP, he had been keen to work on Game 2 Engage. However, this was not an easy situation; his presence as a severely disabled student was seen by some of the Practical Skills students as very confusing; they would refuse his help and would refuse to try and understand what he was saying. Lance sometimes resisted using his interpreter seeing his presence as an amplification of his disabilities, 'I don't like it', he told Julia, 'it makes me look ridiculous … People should just try harder to understand me'. It was problematic over several sessions with Practical Skills students resisting the help and support of Lance, who having been rejected would turn to work on his own and on one occasion leaving early.

The breakthrough for Lance came when Manj needed to have her photo taken in order to upload it to a profile page. Lance patiently took her photo multiple times, waiting each time while Manj evaluated the images and finally agreed to use one of them. After this, she took a photo of Lance and selected it for her 'friend' page. This was an exchange of images as the main mode of communication and so again, we use this as an example to show a levelling of the playing field through the use of technologies. The technology mediated the friendship in this way and Lance was drawn a little closer into the group. Manj had managed this situation and in this case, a Digital Media student had been supported by a Practical Skills student.

Learning at the Mall

Well known to all the students is a large shopping mall a few miles away, a tram-ride from the college. From the outset, Jamie had wanted to get the students away from the college taking the iPads with them. He liked the idea that the students would be able to use mobile devices to help them locate things in the environment and use them to record what they were doing as they went. Whilst many of the students did have access to their own devices, many did not and this was an opportunity for them to experience a trip where they could use devices in the way they had seen others do so. He also wanted the students to 'get away' from college. This was a much anticipated outing with a complex risk analysis to be done ahead of time, parental permissions and the schedule needed to sync with students' timetables.

The day began with students congregating in McDonald's. There had been an arrangement with the manager that we could exclusively use downstairs where there was good wi-fi. The students bought drinks and set themselves up around tables using their iPads to log details as requested by Jamie and to take photos of items for the treasure trail. They were excited; some acted cool while others talked about how they hardly ever went to the mall; some talked about how boring it would be—but with a careful nonchalance that betrayed otherwise. We travelled by tram, looking out of the windows as if for the first time at the city passing by. They needed to notice things, record them by taking photos and store them in an application folder. The students were competitive, excited to spot things first, but helping each other keep in sync. Only Jamie knew the answers and some questions were obscure, requiring careful observation skills; we were all in the same position, learning together, travelling together, drawn to and unified by the iPads that the Practical Skills students held at all times.

At the mall there was more to do; a treasure hunt which involved locating objects, using their first letters to spell out a word, and then with the solution, even going to the mall's concierge to give the secret password that they had uncovered. Each student received a shopping voucher that they spent immediately, before travelling back to college, again on the tram.

The structure of the day facilitated opportunities for socializing in spaces that the Practical Skills students would normally only go to with their families; in this trip they were there as teenagers, with other teenagers, hanging out at fast food places and at the Mall. They used their digital tools in everyday ways, taking photos, looking stuff up and noting things down. Importantly they were the custodians of the information; they held the iPads, they recorded the quiz answers, they were empowered. The quiz was difficult; students had to work together and all were on an equal footing; the Digital Media students knew as little or as much as the Practical Skills students and were frustrated when the answers did not come easily.

The pedagogical skills Jamie exemplified included staff learning, social learning and learning about the environment they share. Students were given 'real-world' problems to investigate at the mall but also had to resolve difficult social issues in the classroom. They needed to navigate the boundaries across the divisions amongst the student body, as well as those where college technology was 'othered' in comparison to home technologies. The lessons had a connectedness to the world they lived in, where they felt they could bring in home tools and knowledge into the learning spaces. This coming together of students and digital tools allowed them to explore some of the social barriers that whilst unarticulated, nevertheless worked as effectively as the barrier cards when they entered the college.

We argue that whilst we saw the effectiveness of this project, as a standalone enterprise it could not independently empower students and create a college-wide integrated community. The project reflected the first steps in this endeavour and we would argue that for such a project to enjoy success and bring about lasting change, these kinds of practice need to be integrated into the educational institution's modus operandi.

Conclusions

In this chapter we identified a problem caused by institutional structuring, that Jamie sought to address by drawing on students' funds of knowledge and helping them engage socially with others through literacy work. From this we would draw out some principles that we think would be helpful in replicating and developing this kind of project further:

Meaningful Engagement: One notable focus of the Game 2 Engage project was the emphasis on meaningful engagement for the Practical Skills students. While other parts of their curriculum did indeed offer important skills for negotiating daily life, Game 2 Engage emphasized the importance of offering the students a technology and space through which they could express their ideas and negotiate relationships. Not only does perceiving of a task as meaningful increase motivation, but such a perception also can have a significant effect on an individual sense of agency, particularly in the context of literacy practices (Wenger 1998; Eodice et al. 2017; Williams 2017). Unfortunately, too often digital technology projects begin with the selection of a technology or software, and then try to incorporate it into student learning and life. The success of Game 2 Engage came, in part, from Jamie's clear goal, from the beginning, of trying to find a way to strengthen bonds of community and social belonging for students. He turned to the technology, with the goal already in mind.

Reciprocity and Collaborative Learning: In bringing together the Practical Skills students and Digital Media students, there was an emphasis from the beginning that they could, and would, be learning from each other. There was not a sense that one group was being asked to come in and 'take care' of the other. Instead, Jamie's approach to the project reflected the concept of 'hospitality' in an educational setting (Haswell and Haswell 2016). Haswell and Haswell propose that hospitality, in its more traditional sense, is a disposition in which, in contrast to a one-sided teaching and learning relationship, emphasizes that reciprocity is not only possibility, it is expected. Both sides are expected to be open to learning, and to teaching, not in an expectation of unlimited good feeling, with an expectation that people and ideas will be welcomed and considered, even when that may entail some risk. The Game 2 Engage project illustrates how technology can mediate relationships by helping to create an environment in which hospitality is possible. In this case, the digital technologies created a new landscape for interacting and a new means of interacting between the Digital Media and Practical Skills students. What's more, the tablets helped reset the cultural context in a way that, instead of further separating the students, refocused the means and methods of learning and collaboration. Finally, we, as teachers and researchers, all worked to try to create for the students an environment and expectation of reciprocity and collaboration—both between students and between the students and us—that was crucial to the context of this project.

Unintended Consequences: The introduction of any new literacy technology will result in unintended consequences. Such unanticipated challenges may be, as we noted in examples above, struggles with technology interfaces or software, or concerns of power and identity, or issues of institutional systems and rules. Regardless of the reason, the objects that we bring into any context will shape the behaviour, at the same time that culture and experience will shape the uses of the objects (Miller 2009) New technologies change the landscape, both in the embodied classroom and in digital domains. While it is impossible to plan for specific unanticipated challenges, it is possible to build flexibility into a classroom and a project. Adjusting classroom plans, and leaving time for such adjustments, is the most obvious form of flexibility. There are, however, other ways to build flexibility into a project. For example, leaving time for conversations among participants that can address concerns or problems that arise, or taking time to reflect on an unintended consequence in terms of the overall project. The initial response to an unanticipated problem might be to see how to 'fix' things and eliminate what hasn't been planned for. Yet, to step back and rethink what has happened may, in fact, lead to the understanding that the unintended consequences, rather than a problem, are an opportunity.

Time and Patience: The speed of digital technology often leads to rhetoric and expectations that introducing it into any classroom setting will produce faster and more efficient results. Certainly, the discourse in the culture at large, promoted by technology corporations, reflects this bias as well. Yet, in a project in which the building of relationships as well as agency was the goal, it is important not to fall into a trap of expecting quick results. Indeed, because new technologies take time to learn and incorporate into daily practices, there is actually the need for more patience, for a longer timeline, in a project such as this one. Someone coming into the Game 2 Engage classroom early in the project, and seeing the combination of tentativeness and frustration that marked some of the early attempts to use the tablet, might have had doubts about the efficacy of the undertaking. Six months later, however, a routine of daily practices had developed in which students, who almost all had, in some measure, more facility in using the tablets, could be seen logging on, manipulating images, browsing the internet, and creating their own texts that would represent their own idea. Technology is not magic. Yet, as in the case of Game 2 Engage, it can prove to be disruptively productive and genuinely empowering.

Student Centred Technology Enhanced Learning: Throughout this project, we have experienced how a student-centred approach can be enhanced by technology. Carl Rogers, who is considered amongst the founding members for the client-centred approach in psychology; influenced education to adopt student centred practices (Matheson 2015). Drawing upon Rogers (1961), (Motschnig-Pitrik and Standl 2012) emphasise three of the conditions that are imperative for significant learning to occur within a student centred approach:

- Realness, transparency,
- Acceptance, unconditional positive regard,
- Understanding, empathy.

We were able to foster and enhance these conditions by allowing the technology to become a platform that facilitated expression for both sets of students. The tasks designed by Jamie facilitated transparency from both sets of students and through this they were able to find commonalities amongst each other. These commonalities seemed to begin to erode the structured inequalities that had become institutionalised. Through student testimonies given by the Digital Media students we came to the understanding that they had developed an unconditional positive regard which developed sincerity along with understanding and empathy; thus positively contributing to building relationships. This form of student centred learning was unique because it wasn't just between student and teacher it was co-created; Jamie creating the environment and the Digital Media students enacting a humanist approach in their mentoring and befriending of the Practical Skills students.

The Rix blog tool was supported by the iPad's operating system in a way that enabled the students to create, edit and save digital artefacts all from the one device. Each Practical Skills student would create their own artefact and as a result, become influenced by student centred technology enhanced learning. It is clear that the role of technology in this project was not only key to learning but also in facilitating the development of relationships between both sets of students.

Afterword

As we, Bronwyn and Julia, left the building for the last time at the end of the project, we noticed that while the students waited by the main door for their separately organised transport, the Learning Support Staff notebooks were less in evidence and the Practical Skills students were nodding towards friends as they passed to go home. It would have been even better if they had been waiting outside with the cool kids, or if the cool kids hung out indoors—but small steps towards this had been made.

The Game 2 Engage project later received the accolade of a Further Education Innovation Award demonstrating leadership in innovation.

References

Burnett, Cathy. 2015. Being together in classrooms at the interface of the physical and virtual: implications for collaboration in on/off-screen sites. *Learning, Media and Technology*, 1–24.

Deci, Edward. L. and Ryan, Richard. M. 2000. The 'what' and 'why' of goal pursuits: Human needs and the self-determination of behaviour. *Psychological Inquiry* 11: 227–268.

Eodice, Michele, Anne E. Geller, and Neal Lerner. 2017. *The meaningful writing project: Learning, teaching, and writing in higher education*. Logan, UT: Utah State University Press.

Haswell, Richard, and Janis Haswell. 2016. *Hospitality and authoring: An essay for the English profession*. Logan, UT: Utah State University Press.

Leander, Kevin, and Margaret Sheehy. 2004. *Spatializing literacy research and practice (New literacies and digital epistemologies)*. New York: Peter Lang.

Matheson, David. 2015. *An introduction to the study of education*, 4th ed. New York: Routledge.

Merchant, Guy. 2015. Keep taking the tablets: iPads, story apps and early literacy. *Australian Journal of Language and Literacy* 38 (1): 3–11.

Marsh, Jackie. and Bearne, Eve. 2007. Uncomfortable Spaces, In *Literacy and Social Inclusion: Closing the Gap*, ed. Marsh, Jackie. and Bearne, Eve.

Miller, Daniel. 2009. *Stuff.* London: Polity.

MITP Digital 2020. 2017. Digital 2020. Digital participation. http://www.digital2020.org.uk/participation/dots. Accessed April 2017.

Moll, Luis, C., Amanti, Cathy, Neff, Deborah, and Gonzalez, Norma. 1992. Funds of knowledge for teaching: Using a qualitative approach to connect homes and classrooms. *Theory into Practice* 31: 132–141.

Motschnig-Pitrik, Renate, and Bernahard Standl. 2012. Person-centered technology enhanced learning: Dimensions of added value. *Computers in Human Behavior* 29: 401–409.

Norton, Michael, Daniel Mochon, and Dan Ariely. 2012. The IKEA effect: When labor leads to love. *Journal of Consumer Psychology* 22: 453–460.

Rogers, Carl. 1961. *On becoming a person: A therapist's view of psychotherapy*. Boston: Houghton Mifflin Company.

Rowsell, Jennifer and Pahl, Kate. 2014. *The Routledge handbook of literacy studies*. London and New York: Routledge.

Simmons, Robin and Thompson, Ron. 2008. Creativity and performativity: The case. *British Educational Research Journal,* 601–618.

Sheldon, Kennon, M. and Schuler, Julia. 2015. Agency and its discontents: A two-process perspective on basic psychological needs and motives. *APA Handbook of Personality and Social Psychology* 4: 167–187.

Wenger, Etienne. 1998. *Communities of practice: Learning, meaning, and identity*. Cambridge: Cambridge University Press.

Williams, Bronwyn. T. 2017. *Literacy practices and composing identities: Perceptions of agency*. London: Routledge.

Wilson, Timothy, D. 2011. *Redirect: The surprising new science of psychological change*. New York: Little Brown.

Author Biographies

Jamie Caine is a Senior Lecturer and Course Leader at Sheffield Hallam University. He has a track record of developing staff with technology enhanced learning and has recently developed standards for student feedback via screen cast technology. Jamie has a diverse teaching background covering information systems, web development, entrepreneurship and IT infrastructure. He is currently reading for a PhD in Enterprise and Business Architecture.

Julia Davies is a Senior Lecturer and Faculty Director of Technology Enhanced Learning at The University of Sheffield. Julia teaches and researches in the field of digital text making practices and is interested in the interface between our uses of technology in everyday life and in academic contexts. She co-edited *New Literacies around the Globe: Policy and Pedagogy* and *Virtual Literacies: Interactive Spaces for Children and Young People*; she co-authored *Web 2.0 for Schools: Learning and Social Participation*. Recent work on Facebook includes, 'Facebook Narratives' in *The Routledge Handbook of Literacy Studies* (Rowsell and Pahl 2014).

Bronwyn T. Williams is a Professor of English and Director of the University Writing Center at the University of Louisville. He writes and teaches on issues of literacy, identity, digital media, and popular culture. His books include *Shimmering Literacies: Popular Culture and Reading and Writing Online,New Media Literacies and Participatory Popular Culture Across Borders* (with Amy Zenger), and *Identity Papers: Literacy and Power in Higher Education*. His current project is the forthcoming book, *Literacy Practices and Composing Identities: Perceptions of Agency* (Routledge), to be published in 2017.

Chapter 10
The Affordances of Touchscreen Tablets and Digital Cameras as Tools for Young Children's Multimodal, Multilingual Composing

Deborah Wells Rowe and Mary E. Miller

We live in a globalizing world. People, information, and goods travel across national borders with increasing speed and frequency. While the economic and political impacts of transnational flows are often discussed, the flow of people to new locations also provides new kinds of opportunities and challenges for education. In the US schools, where we work, global trends are played out daily in the increasingly multicultural and multilingual composition of classrooms. Our local school district serves students speaking 139 different languages who hail from many more nations. Schools and teachers find themselves in need of ways of learning about and publicly valuing the cultural perspectives and experiences of a rapidly changing student population. At the same time, teachers need strategies that encourage multilingual learners to use their heritage languages as support for learning English, the mandated language of instruction. Teachers are also challenged with helping students make connections between school subject matter, their transnational experiences, and their current experiences in the U.S. communities where they live.

In this chapter, we describe two related studies exploring the use of touchscreen tablets and digital cameras as a means for creating a "third space" (Gutierrez et al. 1999), where intercultural sharing and multilingual composing was invited and valued as part of classroom literacy events. Specifically, in both of the studies discussed here, we invited students to use digital cameras and tablets to take photos at school, home, and in their communities, and then to use these images in the classroom for composing multimodal, multilingual eBooks. In Study 1, we collaboratively conducted design-based research across two school years. We developed eBook composing activities for 4-year old, emergent bilinguals enrolled in publicly funded prekindergarten classrooms in our mid-size U.S. city. In Study 2,

D.W. Rowe (✉) · M.E. Miller
Peabody College, Vanderbilt University, Nashville, USA
e-mail: deborah.rowe@Vanderbilt.Edu

M.E. Miller
e-mail: mary.e.miller@Vanderbilt.Edu

C. Burnett et al. (eds.), *The Case of the iPad*,
DOI 10.1007/978-981-10-4364-2_10

Miller built on these experiences to design eBook activities for multilingual second graders enrolled in the same school district.

We focus here on three facets of student composing easily accomplished using digital technologies: (1) composing with photographs, (2) composing with oral recordings, and (3) publicly sharing student work by connecting to the classroom's digital projector. We explore how digital tablets, book-composing apps, and digital cameras afforded teachers and children new opportunities for *multimodal* composing beyond those available in traditional page-based activities. Given that our overarching goal was to create third space activities that disrupted the English-dominant ideologies of school literacy activities and invited students' personal and cultural experiences into the classroom, we also explore the affordances of digital tools for *multilingual* composing and *multidirectional sharing of cultural experiences.*

Theoretical Frame

Our research explores how digital tools can be used to support the learning of children who are emergent or developing writers and who are also emergent bilinguals. As such, our work is framed by research and theory related to translanguaging, third space environments, emergent writing, and digital literacies. We briefly address the key ideas derived from these perspectives guiding our design of eBook activities.

There is converging evidence (García and Kleifgen 2010) showing that supporting children's use of their heritage languages is positively related to long-term academic achievement when learning a new language. Translanguaging theory (García and Kleifgen 2010) suggests that hybrid language practices are the norm for bilinguals (Palmer and Martínez 2016) who purposefully and flexibly alternate among and combine their languages to communicate (Hopewell 2013). From this perspective, languages are always in contact and complement each other as resources for communication (Canagarajah 2013). While US schools often fail to use children's heritage languages to support learning, there is growing evidence that translanguaging practices such as translation can heighten students' metalinguistic awareness and reading comprehension (Orelanna and Reynolds 2008; Jiménez et al. 2015). Students' beliefs about the utility of their heritage language play an important role in how, when, and how effectively they transfer literacy skills across their two languages (Jiménez et al. 1996). Our research is further framed by the work of Moll and colleagues (Moll et al. 2001; González et al. 2009) highlighting the importance of linking school literacy activities to the social and cultural funds of knowledge students and their families form at home and in their communities. Together, this work has encouraged us to adopt a translingual orientation that capitalizes on the strengths of emergent bilinguals by providing them opportunities for using both their languages to communicate and learn in school.

Research and theory describing features of third space environments have been foundational to our thinking about ways of promoting translanguaging in English-dominant schools. Third space can be thought of as a kind of a borderland region bringing together texts, contexts, relationships, identities, and material spaces from a variety of Discourse (Gee 1999) communities (Wilson 2000; Moje et al. 2004). Both hybridity and challenges to dominant practices are defining characteristics of third space. The richness of third space environments for learning occurs as students draw from the resources of existing spaces and Discourses, but imaginatively rework them to create hybridized practices that transform the ideologies from which they were formed (Dyson 1999; Wilson 2000). Because third space environments challenge recognized boundaries such as those between English and students' heritage languages or between school and home knowledge, they are often constructed as "counterspaces" of resistance to dominant practices and ideologies (Soja 1996). From a third space perspective, difference is seen as a major resource for learning rather than as a deficit to be overcome (Gutierrez 2000; Kress1997), and third space interactions are expected to propel learning and promote cultural and educational change (Gutierrez et al. 1997). In the present studies, third space theory has challenged us to design for creative hybridization of English and heritage languages and page- and screen-based composing. It has also encouraged us to create more permeable boundaries between home and school that encourage the multidirectional travel of information, interests, texts, tools, and, people.

Emergent literacy perspectives and constructivist views of written language learning (Harste et al. 1984; Yaden et al. 2000) also have shaped our design of eBook activities. Research shows that, beginning in early childhood and continuing into the elementary years, children construct increasingly sophisticated hypotheses about print through participation in authentic writing events where they record their own messages (e.g., Rowe and Wilson 2015; Dyson 2003). Young emergent bilinguals are simultaneously learning about writing in both their languages (Soltero-González and Butvilofsky 2016). These perspectives have encouraged us to design eBook activities where students are invited to use their emergent understandings about writing and speaking to compose messages in both their languages even if the resulting text or oral performance is not fully conventional. Adults accept and value children's emergent writing, provide scaffolded instruction, and create opportunities for sharing eBooks with audiences of peers, teachers, and family members (Cambourne 2009; Short et al. 1996).

Finally, our work builds on research showing that young children are capable of using tablets and composing apps to produce multimodal products integrating photos, drawings, writing, and voice recordings (e.g., Lynch and Redpath 2014; Wohlwend 2013). While digital tools can provide new opportunities for composing (New London Group 1996), their affordances are not fixed. From a sociocultural perspective, it is not just individuals' perceptions and the physical features of a tool that shape its affordances, but also the cultural, historical, and institutional setting in which it is used (Carr 2000; Greeno 1994; Wertsch 1991). The affordances of digital tools are collaboratively constructed and continually negotiated as part of the social practices of the child's Discourse community. These perspectives have encouraged us to view digital tablets, apps, and cameras as placed resources (Kennewell 2001; Rowsell et al. 2013) and to examine how children in our studies perceived the affordances of these tools within the designed context of eBook composing activities.

Study 1: The Prekindergarten eBook Project

Research Context

Study 1 was conducted by Rowe and Miller as a two-year, design-based research study (Cobb et al. 2003; Cobb, Jackson, and Dunlap, in press) in which we iteratively refined our understandings of ways tablets, composing apps, and digital cameras could be used to support multimodal, multilingual composing for children who were emergent bilinguals and emergent writers. Each year we worked with children enrolled in one prekindergarten classroom (Year 1, n = 19; Year 2, n = 18). All children, but one, spoke a language other than English at home, and most were just learning to use English for academic purposes. Each year, 4 or 5 heritage languages were represented in the classroom including Spanish, Kurdish, Nepali, Karen, Arabic, and Burmese. Spanish–English emergent bilinguals comprised 60% and 83% of students in Years 1 and 2, respectively, with other languages represented by 1–3 speakers. Though the school welcomed children's heritage languages in informal interactions and provided translators for parent communications, by state law, English was the primary language used for instruction. In our study, Rowe and Ms. Camden, the classroom teacher, used some Spanish words, phrases, and sentences to communicate with Spanish-speaking children, while Miller often held instructional conversations in Spanish. No adult speakers of other languages were present in the classroom.

Our goal in Study 1 was to disrupt patterns of English-only instruction by designing curricular activities where children's heritage languages were valued as resources for learning. To do so, we needed to develop strategies for supporting students whose languages we did not speak, as well as those with whom some members of our team could communicate bilingually. This multilingual context encouraged us to invite children and their families to contribute culturally and linguistically relevant content to be used in school literacy events.

Digital Tools and eBook Composing Routines

For eBook composing, we invited children to use touchscreen tablets (iPads) equipped with apps that included *Book Creator* (Red Jumper Studio 2013, 2014), an app used to produce multipage, digital books, and *Drawing Pad* (Murtha

Designs Inc. 2012, 2014), a digital drawing app. On each eBook page, children could insert digital drawings or photos taken at school with the tablet's built-in camera. Beginning at midyear, we also invited children to take home kid-friendly digital cameras to photograph home and community events they wanted to write about when cameras were returned to school. Home photos were uploaded to the iPad's photo library, and were available for eBook composing. In addition to images, children used their fingers to write directly on the screen. Figure 10.1 shows an eBook page Sasha composed using a photo of the swimming pool at her apartment complex. She used invented spelling to produce handwritten bilingual texts (*DWAR* for "water" and *AW* for "agua"). Some children also produced emergent writing using the tablet's digital keyboard. We invited children to read their written messages and then to add English and heritage language oral narrations using the iPad's voice recording tool. To support multilingual composing, we purposefully chose a book making app capable of including multiple sound recordings on each digital page. As seen in Fig. 10.1, Sasha orally recorded her message in English and Spanish, creating the two sound icons seen at the bottom of the page. Once her book was complete, adults added typed transcriptions of her oral messages (enclosed in quotation marks) to preserve them when paper copies of eBooks were shared with families.

eBook composing activities were offered as a choice during the learning centers period 2–3 days per week across the school year. To demonstrate eBook composing, Ms. Camden composed and shared an eBook using pictures taken at school, with accompanying text and bilingual (Year 1: English/Spanish) or multilingual (Year 2: all children's languages) oral recordings.

Fig. 10.1 A prekindergartener's home photo eBook page

At the eBook center, researchers typically launched composing sessions by inviting children to use the iPad to draw a picture, take photos in the classroom, or select home photos from the photo library. Children, peers, and adults engaged in extended conversations as they browsed through the library of child-produced drawings, classroom photos, or home photos. Next, children used the bookmaking app to insert a photo on the digital page, write a message, and record an oral narration. We encouraged children to record a second oral narration in their other language to create multilingual books. Children had opportunities to read child- and teacher-produced eBooks in the classroom library several days per week. About once a week, at group time, Ms. Camden used the classroom projector and speakers to display children's eBooks on a large screen. This provided an opportunity for publicly celebrating children's emergent writing and use of both their languages, and for sharing information about home photos.

The Affordances of Digital Tools

Composing with photos. Putting iPads and digital cameras in young children's hands afforded them with opportunities to explore ways of visually representing important parts of their lives at school and home. Because these tools were sturdy and portable, they traveled with children to familiar spaces and children used them to take photos reflecting their interests. In the classroom, children spent considerable time moving about, and using the iPad's built-in camera to view peers' and teachers' activities on the tablet's big screen. Along the way, they snapped photos of familiar people, objects, and activities. For example, children used iPads to take photos of peers and teachers reading books, painting, and building with blocks. They photographed objects such as art products drying on the easel, partially completed puzzles, and friends' new tennis shoes.

Similarly, when children took digital cameras home, they moved about their homes and communities taking photos of friends and family members, meaningful objects, and community activities. Analyses of the 911 home photos taken by children and their families in Year 1 showed that about half of children's photos pictured friends and family members, with the remaining photos focused on objects or places in their homes and community. Children most frequently took pictures of toys, foods prepared for family meals, and the artwork, photos, and religious objects displayed in their homes. Their photographs also prominently featured popular culture, media, and technology. Children snapped photos of *Spiderman* bedspreads, took television screenshots of *Dora the Explorer* cartoons, and photographed their parents' cell phones. Children took photos in the car on the way to church, at a community center where a Chin National Day celebration was in progress, and at a Chinese restaurant favored by one student. Photos showed family activities such as a father cooking on an outdoor grill, children playing with a pet chick, and brothers and sisters riding scooters.

Our analyses of eBook events showed the ease of producing, browsing, and composing with digital photos afforded opportunities for communication that were especially important for young children learning to write and learning English as a new language. Children's classroom and home photos provided an important focal point for conversation. When browsing photos on the tablet's screen, children and adults used well-developed skills for interpreting images along with their emerging oral language skills to create shared common ground (Tomasello 2008) for communication and composing. Classroom photos provided immediately available images of people, places, and events known to all participants. Both adults and children pointed to parts of photos as a means of communicating. Conversation about the photos provided deeply contextualized opportunities for children to notice and comprehend the language used by adults. Children practiced English vocabulary they were learning at school and adults provided 'timely responses' (Goldin-Meadow 2014) that extended children's English productions. Adults valued children's heritage languages by inviting them to record dual language narrations and by asking children to teach them words related to the photos.

Equally important, the two-way travel of photos between home and school provided a means for children and families to contribute instructional content that was relevant to children's personal and cultural experiences. Through viewing and talking about children's home photos, teachers and peers learned about children's lives outside of school. Emergent bilinguals had opportunities to take up roles as experts when interpreting the content of the photos for a classroom audience. Home photos sparked the interest of both peers and adults, providing occasions for extended conversations and personally meaningful topics for multimodal composing.

Composing with oral recordings. Opportunities to add voice recordings as part of children's multimodal compositions were particularly important to our goal of encouraging children to use their well-developed heritage language skills to expand the messages they were constructing as emergent writers and emergent speakers of English. We conjectured that the voice recording tool would afford emergent writers with opportunities to record oral messages that were more developed than those they represented in emergent writing. We also conjectured that the tool would afford emergent bilinguals with opportunities to compose heritage language narrations that expanded the meanings expressed in English. Further, we conjectured that adult invitations to use tablets for multilingual composing would afford opportunities for both adults and children to demonstrate the importance and value of children's developing bilingual skills, and create a welcoming third space where translanguaging was viewed as a resource for learning and communicating in the classroom.

Our analyses of children's use of the tablet's sound recording tool showed that adding voice recordings to the page was less familiar to children than composing with photos, drawing, and print. While initially children needed assistance operating the sound recording tool, by spring, they added oral narrations to their eBooks with less help. Some children used the sound recording tool to read their written messages exactly as written. Other children orally expanded the written message or used voice recording as an opportunity to say something not signaled in writing. Overall, children's oral messages were syntactically more complex than their written messages. Analyses of a sample of beginning- and end-of-year eBooks from Year 1 showed that 65% of written message were single words naming objects and people depicted in the images, 22.5% were phrases, and 12.5% were sentences. When these patterns were compared to children's oral messages, we found that children tended to use more complex structures in their oral recordings with 40% of oral messages composed as single words, 10% as phrases, and 50% as sentences.

Our request that children make dual language oral recordings also required more scaffolding than we initially expected. In Year 1, we worked with Ms. Camden to record a Spanish/English eBook as a demonstration of the types of dual language products we hoped children would compose. Because members of our team spoke Spanish, adults were able to demonstrate how children could translate their English messages into Spanish, and vice versa. Initially, some children seemed perplexed by our request for dual language recordings and were unable or unwilling to produce heritage language recordings. However, by the end-of-Year 1, all Spanish/English emergent bilinguals were actively recording in both their languages, with many children independently requesting opportunities to add heritage language recordings. We were mostly unsuccessful, however, in encouraging speakers of languages other than Spanish to record in their heritage languages, ending the year with only one dual language book in Nepali and English.

To address this problem, in Year 2, we redesigned eBook activities to include multilingual demonstration books containing oral recordings of all languages spoken in the class. We invited parents and community members to record oral translations in all the children's heritage languages, and added a page with translators' photos and names to recognize the important ways familiar adults used their bilingual abilities. Additionally, near the beginning of Year 2, we engaged each child in a composing session where we demonstrated oral recordings in all children's heritage languages, with special emphasis on the purposes of dual language texts for multilingual audiences.

In response to these design changes, all Year 2 children recorded dual language texts, regardless of the heritage language spoken at home. However, despite a comparable number of adult invitations, Spanish/English emergent bilinguals chose to come to the eBook center almost twice as often as children speaking other languages. The average number of eBook Sessions per child was 4.4 for Spanish/English speakers while children speaking other languages participated in an average of 2.6 eBook composing events. Additionally, when participating in eBook composing, Spanish-speaking children more often included both their languages in their texts. The 11 Spanish–English bilinguals composed dual language recordings in 62% of their eBooks, while the six speakers of other languages created dual language recordings in 38% of their eBooks.

Interpreting these patterns, it is clear that the affordances of digital tools are not fixed, but instead are constructed in relation to the sociocultural contexts in which the tools are located. Though all children used the same digital tablets for composing in Years 1 and 2, they constructed the affordances of the tablet's sound recording tool differently. Our analyses suggest that the ways children took up invitations to compose dual language recordings were shaped by their personal experiences and language capabilities, the languages spoken by peers, the language ideologies shaping school instruction, and the designed and implicit ideologies embedded in eBook composing activities. Children's responses to design changes in Year 2, showed that the emergent bilingual prekindergarteners in our study were more likely to see digital tablets as tools for learning and communicating in both their languages when: (1) school composing invitations were coupled with multilingual demonstrations, (2) bilingual adults participated as sponsors of dual language composing, and (3) when the social purposes for composing dual language texts for bilingual audiences were emphasized.

Projecting eBooks for public sharing. A third feature of digital tablets shaping children's eBook composing was connectivity with a projector and speakers to enlarge and make eBooks visible/audible for a large group audience. Touchscreen tablets not only afforded child authors with opportunities for digital composing, but also for public sharing of completed eBooks. Given our interest in creating a third space environment where official instruction welcomed multilingual communication and composing, we designed weekly opportunities for children to share some of their eBooks with the whole class. In these large group meetings, Ms. Camden explicitly praised children's use of both their languages. Once children began to compose in many different languages in Year 2, these large group sessions provided opportunities for speakers of minority languages to hear their own heritage languages featured alongside Spanish and English—the languages spoken by the majority of their peers.

Our analyses identified two noteworthy child reactions to these public sharing sessions. First, children expressed excitement at hearing their heritage languages spoken aloud for the group when the books were shared, and in the process, often made public home-to-school connections. Large group sessions were typically conducted by the classroom teacher who sat facing the group as she directed the activity. When child authors came to the front of the group to share their eBooks on the large screen, they shared the teacher's powerful role and their expertise as emergent bilinguals and emergent authors was publicly validated.

In Year 2, we more consciously used these large group share sessions as a means of publicly bringing minority languages into the official space of the classroom. When some speakers of minority languages were initially reluctant to record dual language translations of their books, we asked community translators and parents to add heritage language translations to the children's books. Playing the adult translator's heritage language voice recordings during large group eBook sharing elicited strong emotional responses and public declarations of linguistic expertise. For example, the first time a book with Karen/English voice recordings was shared at group time, Shway, the child author, loudly proclaimed that the female voice of the community translator was her mother. When Miller shared that the oral translation was provided by another woman who also spoke Karen, Shway adjusted her claim insisting that the speaker was 'my mother's friend.' For Shway, hearing Karen spoken in the school context signaled close personal connections to family. Throughout the year, as peers read Shway's book and tapped the icons for the Karen narrations, they also commented, 'That's Shway's mother's friend.' Our analyses showed that public sharing of eBooks provided an authentic audience for all the languages spoken by children and their families, even when the majority of the class did not speak the child's heritage language. This public context provided a forum for the teacher and children to discuss the purpose for including different languages in eBooks and afforded opportunities for all members of the class to form shared understandings of children's personal and family connections to heritage languages.

In a second response, children sometimes reacted to hearing unfamiliar languages with laughter or by imitating the tone or rhythm of the speech with nonsense language play. While it is likely that children's responses were playful reactions to the sound patterns of other languages, we were concerned that minority language speakers would feel disrespected by their peers. The teacher and researchers responded to this unanticipated reaction by quieting the language play and positively recognizing the power of different language sounds as ways of communicating. While the willingness of speakers of all languages to compose dual language eBooks suggests that the design of Year 2 activities provided a positive space for intercultural sharing and translanguaging, we also concluded that future iterations of eBook activities should include explicit supports for building more inclusive language attitudes.

Study 2: The Second Grade eBook Project

In a second study, Miller built on these experiences to design eBook composing activities for a group of second graders. This study used similar digital tools and apps and the same general framework for eBook composing. As in Study 1, photos taken by children at school and at home continued to serve as visual anchors for eBook content and conversations. Similarly, invitations to use the tablet's digital audio recorder to create multilingual book narrations anchored children's translanguaging practices during eBook composing. However, in Study 2, eBook activities were redesigned to: (1) explicitly promote positive attitudes and develop shared norms around translanguaging in the classroom, (2) provide increased support for translanguaging by all students with special considerations for minority language speakers, (3) provide more opportunities for sharing eBooks with multilingual audiences at school and home, and (4) expand family engagement in eBook composing.

Research Context

Study 2 was conducted in the same school district as Study 1 by Miller, in collaboration with one second grade teacher, Ms. Trenton. Miller and Ms. Trenton were the primary adult participants working with 18 emergent bilingual second graders in a yearlong study. All of the children in Ms. Trenton's second grade literacy class spoke languages other than English at home. Seventeen children spoke Spanish and one spoke Somali and Arabic at home. Additionally, one child who was not a study participant spoke Arabic. As in Study 1, Miller communicated with Spanish-speaking children in Spanish during classroom composing activities, and encouraged and supported the Somali and Arabic speakers to share in their heritage languages. Ms. Trenton did not speak any languages other than English, but she routinely invited students to teach her words in their languages and practiced speaking Spanish, Somali, and Arabic during classroom literacy instruction.

Age differences between Study 1 and Study 2 participants created different kinds of opportunities for composing. The second grade students were further along in their writing development than our prekindergarten participants, and 94% of their eBooks (n = 48) included writing. Moreover, the second graders more frequently wrote in more than one language, with 51% of the eBooks containing dual language text. Lastly, students in Study 2 took opportunities to revise their compositions. Our prekindergarten participants in Study 1 composed one eBook per session, and eBooks usually included a few pages with an image, a written label, and voice recordings. Second grade participants often composed and revised the same eBook across more than one session with peers and adults offering suggestions about what color to make a page, which images to include, how to write words in English and/or heritage languages, and which languages to orally record.

Digital Tools and eBook Composing Routines

In Study 2, we (Miller and Ms. Trenton) invited children to compose eBooks at school using Samsung Galaxy tablets and the *Book Creator* app. Students worked individually and in small groups to compose eBooks at the classroom writing center two or three times a week. As in Study 1, photos were the launching point for composing. During initial composing sessions, students explored the tablet's functions, and we demonstrated key features such as typing, drawing, writing, voice recording, taking photos, deleting content, changing icon size, and changing content color. We also established the expectation that students compose eBooks in more than one language and explicitly invited and supported students' translanguaging during conversation, oral recording, and writing. Given Study 1 findings of the importance of whole group sharing for validating children's bilingual skills and providing multilingual audiences for children's eBooks, we increased the frequency of whole group eBook sharing to two or three times a week. Families also provided their email addresses if they wanted an electronic copy of their family's eBook.

As a way to model the multilingual eBook expectation, Ms. Trenton composed a teacher eBook featuring personal photos and multilingual voice recordings. To publicly value students' heritage language abilities, she invited the children, rather than community translators, to record the multilingual translations in her demonstration book. This design change normalized the practice of seeking assistance from bilingual peers and of incorporating languages the authors did not personally speak into eBooks.

Building on Study 1 findings, we continued to engage family and community members as co-photographers and translators, but also designed expanded opportunities for them to contribute heritage language written and oral messages to eBooks. First, in addition to the five Vtech cameras that were sent home with consented students on a rotating weekly basis, children also had opportunities to take home two *Dragon Touch* tablets to compose eBooks with their families. Family members included their heritage languages in print and were invited to record themselves reading the print. As a result, families composed 13% of the eBooks outside of school. When students returned the tablets to school, we invited them to individually read the home-composed eBooks with us at the writing center. Second, we sent home a journal with the cameras and tablets, inviting family members to use their heritage languages to write descriptions of photos taken at home and in the community. Children subsequently used these multilingual journal entries to support writing in their heritage language and English when composing eBooks in the classroom. These design decisions were especially important for children who were the only speakers of a heritage language in the class. Composing eBooks at home allowed family members to provide children with heritage language support as well as bilingual audiences for their dual language books.

The Affordances of Digital Tools

Composing with photos. Sending home cameras and tablets made it possible for students' lives outside of school to travel inside the classroom walls and become part of literacy learning. We designed both studies around home photos so we could learn about students' cultural knowledge and practices and make them visible in the classroom space.

Similar to our prekindergarten participants, second graders in Study 2 took photos of their families and friends engaged in a variety of activities such as eating at a restaurant, playing at a park, and celebrating a birthday. Moreover, many photos were object-oriented and featured pets, toys, houses, technology, and soccer balls. They also enjoyed using a feature of the Vtech cameras to add stamps to their photos, and 27% of eBooks included stamped photos. As seen in Fig. 10.2, Daniela selected a photo of her pet birds for the eBook page. She added an animal-themed frame and bird stamp to her photo to coordinate with her photo subject.

Fig. 10.2 A second graders' home photo eBook page

Overall, as in Study 1, we found that students and their families used digital composing tools in ways that showcased their daily lives and facilitated the two-way travel of ideas and practices between home and school. However, analyses also showed that changes in instructional design promoted a more complex circulation of ideas from home to school and within the community of digital composers in the classroom. In Study 2, children had more frequent opportunities to take home digital cameras and view their peers' photos. As a consequence, students started taking photos in ways similar to their peers. During school composing events, students observed others' photo composing practices and then tried out similar practices the next time they took home a camera or tablet. For example, Berto took photos of his television screen during a *Pokémon* show so he could compose an eBook about his favorite *Pokémon* characters. Each eBook page featured a screen image along with writing and audio recordings about a *Pokémon* character. Many of Berto's peers wanted to show they liked *Pokémon*, and the next week they also took photos at home depicting *Pokémon* characters. Moreover, other students took up Berto's practice of taking photos of screens to show something they liked and, overall, 13% of eBooks included screen images. Students took photos of screens depicting movies, television shows, and video games, and they labeled and described the digital content in their eBooks. When students presented their eBooks to the whole group, their peers called out connections to the featured shows or games.

The complex circulation of digital composing practices and tools between peer, family, and classroom spaces was also visible in Abdi's efforts to make a book about his baby brother the week he was born. Since Abdi was not assigned to take home the school digital camera that week, he used a peer-developed composing practice of taking photos of cell phone screens. Specifically, he used his own cell phone to take a photo of his new baby brother, brought his phone to school, asked Ms. Trenton for permission to use the phone in class, and then used the tablet to take a photo of his phone screen featuring his brother's photo. Although tablets, cameras, and cell phones made the mobility of ideas and practices possible, these analyses show that participants collaboratively constructed the affordances of digital tools for composing through interactions with peers, teachers, and family members.

Composing with oral recordings. One of the principle goals of both studies was promoting student and family translanguaging in the classroom. Oral recordings in eBooks provided a way for participants to describe their writing and images in their heritage languages as well as English. Even when adult family members or children could not write in a student's heritage language, they could still represent the language in an eBook by orally recording a message. In Study 1, we found that children needed support to orally record in their heritage languages, and all children recorded in their heritage languages only in Year 2 after we included multiple demonstrations of all children's heritage languages in eBooks. Building on these findings, in Study 2, we offered more intensive and intentional supports for translanguaging across all children's languages. As described earlier, when composing her first demonstration book at school, Ms. Trenton solicited children's help in adding oral translations in their heritage languages. When tablets were sent home, children and families were invited to use the voice recording tool to compose oral narrations in their heritage languages.

Analyses showed that while children and families collaboratively took photos and composed written messages, only children's voices were recorded in eBooks narrations. In some of these recordings, however, the sounds of students' homes and family members were audible in the background. For example, Abdi's home-composed eBook included a recording where the listener could hear Abdi's dad speaking in Somali on his cell phone. When Abdi presented his book to the class, it was the first time that most of his peers had heard someone speaking fluently in Somali. Angel, a Spanish–English bilingual, was curious about what Abdi's dad was saying. Since Abdi was the only Somali speaker in his class, the tablet provided a way for Abdi's heritage language and his family's voices to be included in the classroom.

The Somali oral recording began a process of building awareness of others' heritage languages and engaging students in creating a new kind of multilingual space in the classroom. While children and adults in Study 1 were becoming aware of others' heritage languages, in Study 2, children and adults were explicitly trying to learn their peers' languages and compose with them. Ms. Trenton and I intentionally took up roles as language learners, inviting children to teach us words and short phrases in their heritage languages so we could create oral recordings for our eBooks. Children enjoyed coaching us as emergent speakers of Somali, Spanish, and Arabic. Children also asked their peers to teach them words in languages they did not speak at home. Some second graders orally recorded messages in their peers' heritage languages. Ten percent of eBooks featured peers supporting each other to include more than two languages. For example, Daniela's eBook page (Fig. 10.2) featured oral recordings with Somali, Spanish, and English. Daniela, a Spanish–English bilingual, wrote sentences in Spanish and English to label her pet birds, while working with Ms. Trenton. Daniela taught Ms. Trenton the Spanish word for birds, *pájaros*, and she coached Ms. Trenton to read her Spanish text for an oral recording. On her second day of composing, Daniela shared the writing center table with Abdi, and I worked with both children simultaneously on their home photo eBooks. Daniela decided to include Somali in her book, and asked Abdi to teach her the word for birds. Daniela and I both practised saying the Somali word with Abdi's support, and I recorded it in Somali in Daniela's eBook. Oral recordings afforded opportunities for children and adults to practice speaking new languages, to include those languages in classroom literacy activities, and to value others' heritage languages.

By the end of the year, students looked to their peers as their language teachers, and they valued eBooks with multiple languages. Several children commented during individual interviews that they wished they had included more languages in their eBooks all year long. Overall, Study 2 children almost always included dual language recordings on each eBook page. Of the 264 oral recordings included in eBooks, 133 were in children's heritage languages and 131 were in English. The tablet's voice recording feature made it possible for children to represent their heritage languages in an English-dominant environment.

Projecting eBooks for public sharing. We learned in Study 1 that sharing students' eBooks on the large screen publicly showcased their heritage languages and home photos for the class. During these sharing sessions, eBooks had a highly visible and valuable place in the literacy curriculum. Analyses of Study 2 data showed that the majority of second graders chose to present their eBooks to the whole class using the classroom projector. Ms. Trenton, as the classroom teacher, projected lesson materials, books, and websites on a daily basis. When students had opportunities to project their eBooks, they were aware of taking up roles as authors and presenters, like their teacher. Yet students perceived sharing personal photos and oral recordings on the large screen as a higher risk activity than sharing paper and pencil classwork. For this reason, Ms. Trenton was the first person in the class to share a personal eBook for which students had provided the multilingual translations. She demonstrated how to read and describe the eBook and accept questions from the audience. As Ms. Trenton presented her eBook to the class, students were initially shy about hearing their recorded voices, particularly listening to their heritage languages. Students giggled, one student buried her face in her hands, and Abdi briefly went into the hall.

In the prekindergarten study, some children had responded similarly to hearing unfamiliar languages in the classroom, and we learned that we needed to build norms around large screen sharing. In Study 2, we intentionally worked with students to establish norms that included listening without talking, raising hands to ask the author questions, and respecting each other's languages. Ms. Trenton emphasized that it was important not to laugh at others' languages, and instead to learn from them.

Our analyses showed these norms for respecting class members' languages were especially important to students, and they often repeated the norm during eBook sharing and composing sessions. For example, after Daniela recorded in Somali in the eBook featured in Fig. 10.2, Abdi told her she had said the word correctly. He continued by saying it did not matter whether she said it right or not because it was a rule that we do not laugh at our peers' language. Daniela quickly affirmed his statement. Children relied on this norm to support taking risks as language learners and sharers. Consequently, by the end of the year, 60% of eBooks had been presented on the large screen.

In interviews, several students commented that they were afraid to share initially, but became more confident after positive sharing experiences. For example, Angel was one of the first children to share a home photo eBook on the large screen, and he was reluctant to stand in front of the class. Each page featured an image and writing in English and Spanish. Angel read both languages, and some Spanish–English bilingual students read quietly with him. Students in the audience made connections to Angel's photos of the trampoline and tool shed in his backyard. Berto announced that he and Angel were neighbors, and they liked to jump on the trampoline together. Ms. Trenton learned that Angel had broken his arm at the beginning of the school year by falling off his trampoline. One student asked who used the tools in the shed, and Angel responded that his dad used them because he built houses. Angel's response prompted several students to call out, 'my dad too.' Subsequent presentations followed a similar pattern of reading the eBook and interacting with the audience about the contents.

Overall, large screen sharing provided an opportunity for peers and teachers to learn about, connect with, and place value on the linguistic and cultural knowledge represented in eBooks. Participants' perceptions of the tools' affordances were collaboratively shaped and reshaped by the social interactions and ideological framings built over time in the local context of eBook composing and sharing events.

Discussion

Our overarching goal in these studies was to design composing activities, within an English-dominant school environment, where all children's language capabilities could be used for communication and learning, where emergent forms of talk, writing, and composing were valued, and where multimodal, multilingual texts were the expected product. Translanguaging theory (e.g., Canagarajah 2013; García and Kleifgen 2010) encouraged us to challenge monolingual school practices through the design of instructional activities that provided authentic reasons for emergent bilinguals to use both their languages. Emergent literacy theory (e.g., Harste et al. 1984) encouraged us to engage young children in using their emerging skills in writing, speech, drawing, and photography to compose their own texts, even if the result was not entirely conventional. Digital literacies research with young children (e.g., Lynch and Redpath 2014) encouraged us to put touchscreen tablets and digital cameras in young children's hands and to support their multimodal composing. Third space theory (e.g., Soja 1996; Gutierrez 2000) encouraged us to promote creative hybridization across spaces (home and school), Discourse communities (peers, teacher and students, families), languages (English and heritage languages), literacy practices (emergent and conventional), semiotic modes (photography, drawing, writing, oral narration), and production modes (page and screen).

Soja (1996) has argued that third space is produced by a process of "critical thirding" (p. 5) through which people selectively draw from opposing categories to create hybridized practices that transform the ideologies and practices from which they were formed (Dyson 1999; Wilson 2000). In this way, spaces are restructured and new alternatives are created for what counts as knowledge and as representations of knowledge. Our analyses showed critical thirding at work in Study 2 eBook activities as students, their families, and teachers selected and combined resources from a complex circulation of interests, cultural experiences, languages and composing practices. While we initially imagined each child composing with his/her heritage language and English, in the more developed third space environment of Study 2, participants drew on the collective pool of language resources to compose multilingual eBooks, to serve as expert language teachers, and to act as learners of words and phrases in new languages. In this environment, teachers became learners, and learners became teachers. Home composing practices such as taking screen shots of favorite media figures were taken up in peer culture, and then recontextualized as school practices for eBook composing. Oral recordings, like Abdi's father's Somali conversation, were created at home as part of family-produced eBooks but traveled back to school to circulate in the classroom as resources for bilingual composing and meaning-making, and as a cultural and linguistic resource influencing the practices and attitudes of speakers of other languages. Hybrid practices occurred across modes and tools, as well. In Study 1, we initially imagined children would use the tablet's sound recording tool to translate and read written messages aloud. While this did occur, the openness of eBook activities allowed children to use the voice recording tool to produce on-screen dramatic play performances or expanded story telling events which displayed new kinds of hybridized relations between images, language, and print. As tools and texts circulated from home to school, children invented new kinds of connections between the page and screen, as when children used their family's bilingual journal entries to support their on-screen composing of bilingual print and oral recordings.

It is difficult to imagine how these kinds of composing activities could have occurred without the digital technologies of touchscreen tablets and kid-friendly digital cameras. As small, mobile devices, cameras and touchscreen tablets physically traveled with students around their classrooms, to their homes and communities, and back to the classroom, affording opportunities for multidirectional travel of images and cultural content between home and school. When photos were loaded into touchscreen tablets, the large screen became the focal point for conversation—a shared visual field—where adults and children with differing language capabilities could use multilingual and gestural forms of communication to support meaning-making. Composing apps made it easy for students to combine images, writing, and voice recordings. The tablet's built-in sound recording tool afforded opportunities for children and families to use their bilingual skills to make voice recordings in both their languages. Tablets were easily transported to spaces where peers, family members, and community translators could assist with translations to create bilingual and multilingual texts.

Despite the influential role of digital tools, a simple view that equates their affordances with their physical properties is incomplete. As we learned over time, the affordances of digital technologies for eBook composing were not determined only by the physical characteristics of the tools. As Hammond (2010) suggests: "The essence of an affordance is that it 'points both ways' to the object and to the organism. An affordance is an emergent property of an object." (p. 206). While the physical properties of touchscreen tablets and apps remained the same, the perceived opportunities for action were shaped by learners' histories, skills, and identity narratives and the cultural, historical, and institutional settings in which we used them (Carr 2000; Greeno 1994; Wertsch 1991). In our eBook studies, children, teachers, and families collaboratively constructed and continually negotiated the affordances of touchscreen tablets and digital cameras as they moved across increasingly permeable boundaries between home and school.

Overall, we are encouraged by the potentials of digital tools for supporting multimodal, multilingual composing in classrooms that encourage, demonstrate, and publicly value children's developing bi/multilingual language and literacy skills. In the future, we look forward to lower cost tablets that will travel with children between home and school on an even more frequent basis and the possibilities for including families' linguistic and cultural resources that such tools could afford. However, we conclude with a reminder. Digital tools hold only part of the potential for designing new opportunities for literacy learning. The rest lies in the ideological and interactive practices of the classrooms, homes, and communities where they are placed.

References

Cambourne, Brian. 2009. Revisiting the concept of "natural learning". In *Changing literacies for changing times. An historical perspective on the future of reading research, public policy, and classroom practices*, eds. James V. Hoffman and Yetta Goodman. New York: Routledge.

Canagarajah, A.S. 2013. Negotiating translinguial literacy: An enactment. *Research in the Teaching of English* 48: 40–67.

Carr, Margaret. 2000. Technological affordance, social practice, and learning narratives in an early childhood setting. *International Journal of Technology and Design Education* 10 (1): 61–79.

Cobb, Paul, Jere Confrey, Andrea diSessa, Richard Lehrer, and Leona Schauble. 2003. Design experiments in educational research. *Educational Researcher* 32 (1): 9–13.

Cobb, Paul, Kara Jackson, and Charlotte Dunlap. in press. Conducting design studies to investigate and support mathematics students' and teachers' learning. In *Handbook of research on mathematics teaching and learning,* ed. J. Cai. Reston. VA: National Council of Teachers of Mathematics.

Dyson, Anne. 1999. Transforming transfer: Unruly children, contrary texts, and the persistence of the pedagogical order. *Review of Research in Education* 24: 141–171.

Dyson, Anne. 2003. *The brothers and sisters learn to write. Popular literacies and school cultures.* New York: Teachers College Press.

García, Ofelia, and Jo Anne Kleifgen. 2010. *Educating emergent bilinguals. Policies, programs, and practices for English language learners.* New York: Teachers College Press.

Gee, James Paul. 1999. *An introduction to discourse analysis. Theory and method.* London: Routledge.

Goldin-Meadow, Susan. 2014. How gesture helps children learn language. In *Interaction: Studies in honor of Eve. V. Clark,* eds. I. Arnon, M. Casillas, C. Kurumada and B. Estigarribia. Amsterdam: John Benjamins Company.

González, Norma, Luis C. Moll, and Cathy Amanti (eds.). 2009. *Funds of knowledge. Theorizing practice in households, communities, and classrooms.* New York: Routledge.

Greeno, J. 1994. Gibson's affordances. *Psychological Review* 101 (2): 336–342.

Gutierrez, Kris. 2000. Teaching and learning in the 21st century. *English Education* 32 (4): 290–298.

Gutierrez, Kris, Patricia Baquedano-Lopez, Hector Alvarez, and Ming Ming Chiu. 1999. Building a culture of collaboration through hybrid language practices. *Theory Into Practice* 38 (2): 87–93.

Gutierrez, Kris, Patricia Baquedano-Lopez, and Myrna G. Turner. 1997. Putting language back into language arts: When the radical middle meets the third space. *Language Arts* 74 (5): 368–378.

Hammond, Michael. 2010. What is an affordance and can it help us understand the use of ICT in education? *Education Information Technology* 15: 205–217.

Harste, Jerome C., Virginia. A. Woodward, and Carolyn. L. Burke. 1984. *Language stories and literacy lessons.* Portsmouth, NH: Heinemann.

Hopewell, Susan. 2013. Strengthening Bi-literacy through translanguaging pedagogies. In *62nd yearbook of the Literacy Research Association,* eds. Pamela J. Dunston, Susan King Fullerton, C.C. Bates, Pamela M. Stecker, Mikel W. Cole, Anna H. Hall, Danielle Herro and Kathy N. Headley, 234–247. Altamonte Springs, FL: Literacy Research Association.

Jiménez, Robert T., Samuel David, V.J. Keenan Fagan, Mark B. Risko, Lisa Pray Pacheco, and Mark Gonzales. 2015. Using translation to drive conceptual development for students becoming literate in English as an additional language. *Research in the Teaching of English* 49 (3): 248–271.

Jiménez, Robert T., G.E. García, and P. David Pearson. 1996. The reading strategies of bilingual Latina/o students who are successful English readers: Opportunities and obstacles. *Reading Research Quarterly* 31 (1): 90–112.

Kennewell, Steve. 2001. Using affordances and constraints to evaluate the use of information and communications technology in teaching and learning. *Journal of Information Technology for Teacher Educatioin* 10 (1 & 2): 101–116.

Kress, Gunther. 1997. *Before writing: Rethinking the paths to literacy.* London: Routledge.

Lynch, Julianne, and Terri Redpath. 2014. "Smart" technologies in early years literacy education: A meta-narrative of paradigmatic tensions in iPad use in an Australian preparatory classroom. *Journal of Early Childhood Literacy* 14 (2): 147–174.

Moje, Elizabeth B., Kathryn M. Ciechanowski, Katherine Kramer, Lindsay Ellis, Rosario Carrillo, and Tehani Collazo. 2004. Working toward third space in content area literacy: An examination of everyday funds of knowledge and Discourse. *Reading Research Quarterly* 39 (1): 38–70.

Moll, Luis C., Ruth Saez, and Joel Dworin. 2001. Exploring biliteracy: Two student case examples of writing as social practice. *The Elementary School Journal* 101 (4): 435–449.

New London Group. 1996. A pedagogy of multiliteracies: Designing social futures. *Harvard Educational Review* 66 (1): 60–92.

Orelanna, Marjorie F., and J. Reynolds. 2008. Cultural modeling: Leveraging bilingual skills for school paraphrasing tasks. *Reading Research Quarterly* 43: 48–65.

Palmer, Deborah K., and Ramón Antonio Martínez. 2016. Developing biliteracy: What do teachers *really* need to know about language. *Language Arts* 93 (5): 379–385.

Rowe, Deborah Wells, and Sandra Wilson. 2015. The development of a descriptive measure of early childhood writing: Results from the Write Start! Writing Assessment. *Journal of Literacy Research* 47 (2): 245–292. doi:10.1177/1086296X15619723.

Rowsell, Jennifer, Mary Gene Saudelli, Rugh Mcquirter Scott, and Andrea Bishop. 2013. iPads as placed resources: Forging community in online and offline spaces. *Language Arts* 90 (5): 351–360.

Short, Kathy G., J.C. Harste, and C.L. Burke. 1996. *Creating classroom for authors and inquirers*, 2nd ed. Portsmouth, NH: Heinemann.

Soja, Edward W. 1996. *Thirdspace. Journeys to Los Angeles and other real-and-imagined places*. Malden, MA: Blackwell Publishers.

Soltero-González, Lucinda, and Sandra Butvilofsky. 2016. The early Spanish and English writing development of simultaneous bilingual preschoolers. *Journal of Early Childhood Literacy* 16 (4): 473–497.

Tomasello, Michael. 2008. *Origins of human communication*. Cambridge, MA: MIT Press.

Wertsch, James V. 1991. *Voices of the mind. A sociocultural approach to mediated action*. Cambridge, MA: Harvard University Press.

Wilson, Anita. 2000. There is no escape from third-space theory. Borderland Discourse and the in-between literacies of prisons. In *Situated literacies. Reading and writing in context*, eds. David Barton, Mary Hamilton and Roz Ivanic, 45–69. London: Routledge.

Wohlwend, Karen. 2013. *Literacy playshop. New literacies, popular media, and play in the early childhood classroom*. New York: Teachers College Press.

Yaden, David, Jr., Deborah W. Rowe, and L. MacGillivray. 2000. Emergent literacy: A matter (polyphony) of perspectives. In *Handbook of reading research*, eds. Michael Kamil, Peter B. Mosenthal, P. David Pearson and Rebecca Barr, 425–454. Mahwah, NJ: Erlbaum.

Author Biographies

Deborah Wells Rowe is professor of early childhood education at Peabody College, Vanderbilt University. Her research focuses on how preschool and primary grades children learn to write. Recently, she has developed a descriptive measure of preschool writing and conducted research exploring young emergent bilinguals' use of iPads and digital cameras to create multimodal, multilingual eBooks. She is the author of a book, *Preschoolers as Authors: Literacy Learning in the Social World of the Classroom*, and numerous research articles. She has received the International Literacy Association's Dina Feitelson Research Award and serves as co-editor of the *Journal of Early Childhood Literacy*.

Mary E. Miller is a Ph.D. candidate at Peabody College, Vanderbilt University. Her work has been published in *Voices from the Middle*, *The Reading Teacher*, and *Journal of Early Childhood Literacy*. She works with emergent bilingual students in early childhood and elementary school classrooms, and her research examines how students' multilingual, family e-book composing supports bilingual literacy development and home to school connections. Her scholarly interests also include preparing teachers to educate culturally and linguistically diverse learners, while building on students' heritage languages and cultural experiences.

Chapter 11
Personalized Story-Making on the iPad: Opportunities for Developing the Self and Building Closeness with Others

Natalia Kucirkova and Mona Sakr

Introduction

This chapter presents case study data from a detailed observation of a 5 year-old girl and her father as they used an interactive iPad app designed to enable users to create multimedia personalized stories. Kucirkova and colleagues (2013, 2015, 2016) have studied multimedia personalized stories (MPS for short hereafter) extensively in previous work and Sakr (2012), Sakr and Kucirkova (forthcoming) have explored how digital devices may contribute to our sense of self and interactions between children and adults in the home. In this chapter, we explore further our shared interest in multimodal literacies and sociocultural theories of the self.

In line with other chapters in this book, we explore how the iPad, a specific semiotic resource, affords meaning in a particular context with a focus on the embodied and material experience of the child. Our analytic lens conceptualizes the self as a distributed self; that is, a self that is not a stable and solid entity, but rather a reflection of a dynamic and fragmentary sense of being. Sociocultural theories suggest that the self is actively constructed and re-made through networks of interactions with others and with the material world. In accepting this premise, we suggest that a self can be constructed differently depending on the people and semiotic resources available in a given situation. In this study, the semiotic resources available were a story-making app downloaded on an iPad, and the features of this app were experienced by a 5 year-old girl and her father.

We begin this chapter with a selected overview of the key points from Bruner's (1994, 2001) and Lemke's (2000, 2002) theories related to the notion of self. This is

N. Kucirkova (✉)
Institute of Education, University College London, London, UK
e-mail: n.kucirkova@ucl.ac.uk

M. Sakr
Middlesex University, London, UK
e-mail: M.Sakr@mdx.ac.uk

C. Burnett et al. (eds.), *The Case of the iPad*,
DOI 10.1007/978-981-10-4364-2_11

followed by an overview of our methodological orientation, which focused on multimodal interaction analysis, and the details of how this study was conducted. Our findings constitute four ways in which we saw personalization features shaping the child's sense of self and the exchanges she shared with her father. In the discussion at the end of the chapter, we consider the implications of these findings for early childhood, along with the limitations of the study and suggestions for future research in this area.

Multimedia Personalized Stories

There is a well-documented increase in the use of digital interactive media by young children in many Western countries (for a documentation of these trends see, e.g., Ofcom 2015-2016 for the UK or the 2011 and 2013 Common Sense Media reports in the USA). Interactive media such as iPads offer many programmes ('apps'), which provide children with a multitude of new ways to explore, practice and experience their identity. Kucirkova (forthcoming) argues that apps, which have personalization options, are particularly popular among young children and have the potential to influence their representation and experience of self. This is because personalized apps offer children a number of options to portray their faces (e.g., by inserting a selfie using the front-facing camera into a blank space or into a template), to add their own drawings, audio-recordings or texts. Some apps leave the extent of personalization up to the child (for example the story-making app *Our Story* has no templates), while other apps (for example *Toontastic*) have a standard 'story arc template' beginning with a setup, conflict, challenge, climax and resolution. A recent addition to the range of personalizable apps are interactive multimedia story-apps, that is apps which allow the child to individualize specific elements of a given story. The app used in this study is *Mr Glue Stories*, which offers children a library of stories to choose from, of varying levels of reading difficulty. When the user chooses a story to read and engage with, they are prompted at different points during reading the story, to name characters in the story, to decide on props that appear in the narrative, and to create audio and visual illustrations to accompany the story.

Sociocultural Theories of the Self

From some sociocultural perspectives, the self does not exist as a single or stable entity. Instead, our sense of self is constructed and gradually built up in everyday interactions with others, through ever-becoming events and practices. In Bruner's theory of constructivism, the self is not fixed, but described as emerging through dialogue with others. Bruner (1990, 1994, 2001) argues that our sense of self is most visibly and prominently constructed through the stories we tell others. Stories have a narrative structure with a beginning, middle and end, with a purpose and moral; through these features they can offer a structure to our experiences, feelings and thoughts. This helps with our own understanding of who we are and how we feel about our lives and the world around us. However, it also implies that the self can have many different forms and purposes, because there are different stories we share with different audiences and because stories take on different forms depending on the context and the resources available within a context. If we take it as our premise that self is distributed in 'action, in projects, in practice' (Bruner 1990: 117), then in addition to the features of the narratives we construct, we need to consider the wider action, project or practice in which this narrative takes place.

Lemke's exploration of the self considers how the self is brought together through texts despite its existence across multiple timescales. Lemke does not focus on narratives as Bruner does but instead, foregrounds the role of texts, which, he believes, are a way of collecting together the disparate self across time and place (Lemke 2000). A text can be in Lemke's model a paper-based text as in a book but also a multimedia artefact as in a digital story. Through texts, the self remains coherent across ever-changing configurations of objects, people and environments.

When we think about story-making on the iPad, both Bruner and Lemke's understanding of the self and how it is constructed will apply. Digital story-making offers an opportunity for users to collect the disparate self together through the production of narrative and the creation of a textual artefact. From a social semiotic perspective, as outlined by van Leeuwen (2005), the semiotic resources that are used in the story-making will shape how meaning is made, and we can posit that this will in turn influence the sense of self that emerges through the activity. Semiotic resources are the 'actions, artefacts and activities' (van Leeuwen 2005: 2) that are involved in meaning-making. In the study we present in this chapter, the semiotic resources on offer include the specific app used for the iPad story-making, and the personalization features built into this app, which are of particular interest to us. We are interested in how such features impact on the sense of self that is created and/or projected through the activity of parent-child story-making.

Closeness Through Collaborative Story-Making

As well as our interest in how MPS can shape the child's sense of self, we are interested in how the intersubjective exchanges between the child and parent might involve different personalization features in digital story-making. In theorizing the relationship between the child and the parent, we conceptualize the shared affect between the child and parent as something that is constantly changing and in dialogue with the environment and a specific activity occurring in this environment. We are particularly influenced by Stern's (2000, 2004) theory of 'moments of meeting'. These are moments in which children and parents experience heightened levels of attunement to one another: a 'mutual knowing of what is in the other's mind' (Stern et al. 1998, p. 4). Although Stern's theory was originally developed as a psychoanalytical tool, we are interested in using the 'moments of meeting' framework as a means of operationalizing the idea of parent–child closeness as it unfolds. Moments of meeting are visible through the behaviours of the child and the parent, and are often accompanied by a physical closeness and connection. Examples would include moments in play when both parties break into spontaneous laughter, or when a child takes the hand of the parent in order to give them the confidence to do something that they might otherwise be too fearful to do. Such moments are not decontextualized traits of a relationship but important in child–parent relationships and greatly enhance the overall quality of family interactions (Stern 1998). As such, Stern's theory can enrich the sociocultural perspectives we discussed in the previous section.

In previous work (Sakr and Kucirkova 2017) we have examined how moments of meeting are fostered in child-parent collaborative art-making and how the involvement of different semiotic resources in art-making can differently shape when these moments arise and what behaviours they comprise. For example, we found that when engaged in collaborative digital photography, a child and her father were likely to experience moments of meeting that were about their shared desire and attempts to capture on camera fleeting occurrences in the external environment. On the other hand, when using crayons and paper, moments of meeting were more likely to arise through the adults' demonstration of particular drawing techniques and the child's interest in copying these techniques. This finding relates to previous literature on the dynamics between children and adults when they engage in acts of digital creativity. Carter-Ching et al. (2006) studied children and adults using digital photography in the preschool and primary classroom and found that during such activities, teachers were likely to relinquish their authorship and were more likely to assume the role of co-investigator alongside the children in the class, thereby fostering higher levels of closeness and connection.

Again, when we consider a social semiotic perspective on how MPS shape child–adult interaction, we are encouraged to consider the particular semiotic resources that are involved and how these feature in the network of the interaction. The particular story-making app that this study looked at, *Mr Glue Stories*, involves different types of personalization, which occur in various modes (audio, visual, written) and have distinct relationships with the overall narrative that is being constructed. A micro-analysis of the interaction can help to elucidate how particular personalization features feed into the interaction between the child and the parent, including into moments of meeting.

Methodology

Our methodological approach stemmed from Lemke's (2001) assertion that semiotic artefacts play a fundamental role in the creation of a sense of identity, and that meaning-making acts that contribute to a sense of identity traverse time and space. We intended to identify moments of meaning-making that contributed to a sense of identity for a young child, and to investigate how these moments occurred in the different spaces of an interaction. More specifically, we were interested in the meaning-making that would occur in the physical interactions between a child and father, and the meaning making that would involve the digital tool of the iPad story-making and all of the constraints and potentials that this tool comprised. As a means for investigating meaning-making and how it is shaped within the spaces of an interaction, we applied a multimodal lens. Multimodality is a theoretical and methodological perspective that highlights how children's meaning-making occurs through multiple modes of communication in specific social and material contexts. With its focus on the importance of social influences, multimodality has its origins in Halliday's (1978) social semiotics, later elaborated by Kress and van Leeuwen (1996, 2001). As a theoretical and methodological framework, multimodality highlights the role that modes other than speech play in every interaction. These modes include gaze, gesture, movement, touch, physical manipulation, body orientation and posture.

Method

Observation

A 5-year-old child and her father were observed using the app *Mr Glue Stories* together in the home of the child's grandparents. The observation occurred on a weekday evening and was conducted by the child's aunt (second author of this paper). Prior to this observation, the child had had one experience with the app, while the father had not previously used the app. They were invited to play with the app together; no additional instructions were given. The observation was one of a series of observations conducted to explore the child's interactions with different story-making apps and different members of the extended family. In this chapter, we focus on just one observation in order to focus in detail on a particular instance when the child's sense of self and/or the child–parent interaction is brought to the fore. The observation lasted for 23 minutes and 5 seconds and ended when the child and the parent decided together that they wanted to do something else. The researcher videoing the interaction was not involved in the interaction except when the child or parent directly engaged with her. As the child's aunt, the interaction was more relaxed than if the recording had been conducted by a stranger, but the closeness between the observed and the observer also entailed a higher level of participation than might otherwise have occurred.

Analysis

Since our interest was in the interaction as it unfolded and how the child's sense of self visibly manifested during the activity, we took the approach of multimodal interaction analysis (Jewitt 2009; Jewitt et al. 2016; Norris 2011, 2012).

In multimodal interaction analysis, several modes, along with speech, are taken as meaningful and indicative of the underlying relationship dynamics on which the interaction is based. For example, in Sakr et al. (2016), multimodal interaction analysis was applied to observations of children as they explored the history of a local site of interest using iPads. The analysis elucidated aspects of the children's emotional engagement in their history learning and how this was mediated by the physical-digital activity as it occurred. The first stage of multimodal interaction analysis is a multimodal transcription of the video data, which demonstrates how different modes are drawn into the interaction and how they work together to achieve various communicative purposes. The transcript consisted of detailed notes of the behaviour of the child and the father against time stamps, as well as a concurrent description of the speech, special sound effects and pre-recorded messages displayed by the *Mr Glue Stories* app during the interaction. By focusing on the multiple modes of communication and interaction, we have developed insights into the child's engagement with the personalization features and how this manifested in her use of language, social interaction with her father using bodily gestures and sociolinguistic aspects such as laughter.

The transcript enabled us to identify moments that we wished to analyze in a higher level of detail. Since our focus was on the potential of personalization features to shape a child's sense of self and child–parent interactions, we looked for instances of interaction in which personalization features of the app were engaged with. Such moments included the use of the audio recording and drawing tools, or the naming of the characters in the story, or the selection of props that would appear in the story. Four such moments were identified across the observation. In Table 11.1, we have briefly described what each of these moments involved. For clarity, we only focus on the personalization moment here, not on the earlier stage of multimodal transcription.

Table 11.1 Personalization moments

Time stamp (in minutes and seconds)	Personalization moment (a short description of the app's personalization feature in use)
07:51	The child chooses the name of the main character to be 'daddy'. Dad, when reading the story, puts emphasis on his name as the main character in the story
10:02	The child and parent discuss the cultural and ethnic origin of child's friend (Hannah) NB: this moment was not analyzed in more detail in this study
11:15	The child creates a drawing to accompany an event in the story. Dad comments on the creature and pretends to be scared
12:22	The child draws a 'Stegosaurus' and discusses with dad why it's not a T-Rex, focusing on the app's drawing tools.
14:52	The child chooses the name for the second character 'Hannah' (the name of her friend). Dad mentions Hannah with an added emphasis when reading the story

At this point, our analysis returned to the research questions guiding the study and the theoretical frameworks that were outlined earlier in the chapter. Through iterative and collaborative viewing and discussion, we decided on four themes that constitute aspects of the interaction that personalization appears to offer. These aspects of the interaction relate in turn to the construction of the child's sense of self and the child's interaction with her father. In the findings below, we present these four themes. We briefly explain each theme, then illustrate it with a vignette from the data, and then discuss in relation to the theoretical perspectives we offered at the beginning of the chapter.

Findings

Personalization Empowers the Child to Have an Emotive Effect on the Immediate Audience

Through personalization features, such as the capacity to create illustrative drawings or make audio recordings relating to action taking place in the story displayed in *Mr Glue Stories*, the child produced semiotic artefacts that individually had an immediate impact on her father. In the example below, she creates a drawing that is designed to scare her father and in response he pretends to be afraid.

> The child is painting with her finger on the screen while her father continues to read the story. In the story, the main character, called 'daddy' (a name chosen by the child) is scared by a piece of paper with a drawing on it. Following this part of the story, there is a moment of shared eye contact between the father and the child and they laugh together. The child asks the father what she should draw.
>
> Father: I don't know, draw something on the paper that's gonna scare daddy!
>
> (The father taps on the ipad and chooses a colour) That colour!
>
> The child starts drawing with her finger, using the colour chosen by the father.
>
> Father: This is supposed to scare me, remember?
>
> The child eagerly distributes the yellow colour across the screen. There is a big splash of the colour across the entire iPad screen.)
>
> Child: Yeah. I'm trying, I'm just trying my best
>
> The father pretends that he is scared and gasps in fear as he looks at the picture. The child smiles. The father gasps in fear again.
>
> Father: No, don't draw anymore I can't take it!
>
> Father tickles the child on her tummy, as if trying to prevent her from drawing on the iPad, they both giggle. Then, the girl continues to draw, smiling.

In this moment, the child is empowered as an author of the story and experiments with choices that impact on those around her. Her sense of self is strengthened through these explorations since her involvement in the narrative enables her to understand her potential to shape the responses of others. In particular, two personalization features enable her to do this. Firstly, in naming the character in the story, she is shaping how the narrative relates to the immediate situation and relationships around her. Second, she is invited to create a drawing that has narrative importance, since this drawing is described in the story as scaring the main character. In making 'daddy' the protagonist in her story, she implicates her father in every decision that she takes in crafting the story. For example, her subsequent decision about what to draw is based on what will scare her father and she repeatedly gauges his affective reaction to what she is drawing. His verbal and physical responses offer momentum to her decision-making about what to draw and how to draw it.

The vignette comprises multiple signs of attunement between the child and father, including the moment of shared eye contact and laughter in response to the story, and the close physical affection involved in the father's response to the child's drawing. These multimodal features of the visual, physical and verbal mode are indicative of a positive engagement and enjoyment of the session. The device and the activity relating to it bring the child and the father together both on a verbal and physical level. This contributes to the learning potential of the session, with the child closely paying attention to the story and her father's response. It illustrates that, despite the frequently cited concern that technologies might disrupt or negatively affect parent–child interaction (see for example Ingram 2016 in *Daily Mail*), this is not always the case. Quite the opposite- the digital story has brought the parent and child together and constituted a point of joint attention and shared joy. This is similar to observations made by Goodwin (2000, 2007) about the bodily participation frameworks that emerge between two people when they engage with the same material artefact, and move their gaze back and forth between the other person and the artefact. Furthermore, the sense of closeness in this part of the observation stems from the inversion of typical child–parent power dynamics. In this instance, it is the child who has the power to frighten the adult and the father plays with this role reversal through his exaggerated performance of fear. This is a typical strategy used by adults in play therapy with children in order to build closeness (Cohen 2001).

Personalization Enables the Child to Reflect on Self-Competencies

In assuming responsibility for the creation of some of the elements in the story, the child is encouraged to reflect on what she can achieve with and without help. Since the story invites her to create drawings and audio recordings, which in turn demonstrate and respond to her comprehension of the complex plot, she becomes more aware through the personalization features of what she is capable of. In the example below, which follows on from the interaction described in the previous section, she is attempting to draw a Tyrannosaurus Rex, but her father mistakenly thinks that she is drawing a Stegosaurus. She reflects on what she was trying to do versus the effect she has actually achieved and explicitly points to how the properties of the iPad have impacted on her drawing.

> Father: It's a Stegosaurus! I knew you were gonna draw a Stegosaurus!
>
> Monika: Why? Are you scared? (Monika looks at him but continues drawing)
>
> Father: It's supposed to be a Stegosaurus, it's got the spikes. Is it a Stegosaurus?
>
> Monika: (continues to draw) No! It's a T-rex! I tried to do smaller ones but it didn't work… (points at the iPad screen)
>
> Father: Anyway…it's a good scary-looking dinosaur. Good job.

Although the father is mistaken in thinking that his daughter has drawn a Stegosaurus, his interpretation of the drawing relates to previous experiences they have shared together. This is a good example of how texts can exist across multiple timescales as described by Lemke (2002), and draw together experiences that have occurred at different points in an individual's life. As well as strengthening the sense of self, as described by Lemke, we see in this example how this has the potential to build closeness between individuals since they can remember together past experiences that they have shared and bring these into the current interaction.

When the child reflects on what she was trying to do, she implies that the iPad has constrained her actions. This might also explain why she does not feel offended by her father's mistaken assumption about what she is drawing. She attributes his misunderstanding at least partly to the iPad. This is interesting since it shows the child making sense of her competencies not just in relation to herself and the skills she possesses, but as part of a network of material factors – in this case, the material tools that she is using in the drawing. She commented on her drawing addressing her father, although the words she said were a reflection of an inner dialogue she must have had before uttering them. Indeed, on a metacognitive level, child's reasoning in this short episode is remarkable: she connects to the father's inner world as well as to the actual drawing she produced and the app's affordances. Her drawing reflects her aesthetic preference and internal standards or schema for what a Stegosaurus should look like. Her speech reflects her understanding of the story meaning and the sociocultural expectations connected to it (i.e. what is considered scary).

Personalization Offers a Chance for the Child to Celebrate Important Relationships

Through the app, the child has the chance to design aspects of the characters in the story, including changing the main characters' names. She uses this opportunity to celebrate important relationships in her life, with people that are both present and absent. In the previous two sections, we already noted that she changed the name of the main character in the story to 'daddy' and in the following example, we see how this simple change impacted on the parent–child experience of the story together.

> As the father reads the story, he places a slight emphasis on each changed name as it appears in the text. The child listens in delight, with her hands placed loosely along her body with the iPad resting on her knees. Every time the father says 'daddy' when reading the story, the girl smiles. The child starts to explain what is happening to Mona, who is quietly filming a couple of metres away.
>
> Child: He [the father] keeps on saying daddy because he typed in daddy. Who's doing it? Because daddy and me (Child points to her chest) and then it keeps on saying daddy, daddy, now it's saying 'Daddy shouts out for Hannah'! (The girl explains eagerly and loudly, turning her head from side to side, speaking to the camera, to Mona and to the father at the same time.) Daddy did this, daddy did that, daddy did this, daddy did that! (Child moves her arms quickly back and forth, then slumps back into the sofa, pretending to be exhausted)

This episode shows an orchestration of bodily and verbal resources to achieve a connection between the child and her father and the researcher. The child moves in space with big gestures, calling for attention from the father and the observer/researcher. She manipulates the volume of her voice to convey her excitement and attempts to elicit the same response in her family members—which she achieves with her laughter and funny dance moves. In a sociocultural perspective on the self, the self only exists in relation to others. As Bruner (1994, 2001) argued, narratives are important in developing a sense of self because they allow us to position ourselves in relation to others and make sense of the relationships that are important in our lives. This is clearly demonstrated in the part of the observation described above, when the child is enjoying hearing about her father in the story, and engaging with him on two levels—as the person supporting her in the immediate circumstances and as a character in the story that she had selected. Bruner (1994, 2001) suggests that each narrative exists on two landscapes—an action landscape and a character landscape. In the latter, narrative offers an opportunity to make sense of the motives, intentions and desires of others. Through naming the character 'daddy', the child is grappling with her own father's inner mind and world. In naming the main character in the story after her father, the child emphasises the importance of this relationship to her; the act establishes and comments on their closeness. In the following section, we see how as a character, the father is brought into contact with other important relationships that the child enjoys in her everyday life.

Personalization Can Connect Different Parts of a Child's Life

As mentioned in the previous section, personalization allows a child to celebrate their relationships with various people in their lives, not just those who are immediately present. In evoking their memory of other important individuals in their lives and those who are immediately present in the same narrative, the parent and child are intertwining different parts of their life. In the last vignette, the child uses the story as a way to bring together her father and her best friend at school, Hannah. Through the story, her father and Hannah interact as best friends. The child finds this extremely funny, as the following extract shows.

Father: (reading the story)'It was a very funny thing but when daddy needed a friend, Hannah turned up.'

The child interrupts the story and explains again to Mona why this is funny while giggling.

Child: And Hannah isn't even, isn't his friend…she is my friend!

She smiles and hugs herself, giggling.

The father continues reading the story text on the screen, the child listens eagerly.

Father: 'I'm pleased to see you, said daddy gratefully.'

The child repeats this loudly and laughs. The father and Mona laugh as well.

Monika: I put in Hannah and Hannah isn't even daddy's friend!

Father: Now I'm on an adventure with your friend! And I'm getting rescued by a five-year-old!

In this example, the child is playing with different social contexts in her life and making them interact in ways that they would not do normally. She finds this fictitious and unusual combination funny, suggesting that she has an explicit recognition of the differences between the imagined and real world and the different types of relationship that are important to her. The father is brought closer to the child's world through the imagined interaction between him and the child's school friend. He plays witness to the child gathering together different parts of herself, and the different positioning of herself in relation to others. From Lemke's (2000) perspective, the app mediates the father's understanding of the child's sense of self as it is distributed across multiple sites and timescales.

Discussion

We have suggested four ways in which personalization features in iPad story-making can facilitate the development of a child's sense of self and their closeness with others. Personalization positions the child as an author who can experiment with their effect on others in the immediate surroundings, and reflect on their competencies, as they are shaped by the immediate physical–digital environment. Personalization also offers the opportunity for the child to celebrate and play with important relationships in their life, making sense of themselves in relation to others and social contexts that they inhabit as part of their everyday life.

Story-making on the iPad with the *Mr Glue Stories* app appeared to offer a powerful platform for the child's construction and exploration of self. Lemke's (2001) work discusses the importance of semiotic artefacts in our sense of identity.

More than 15 years ago, he argued that our sense of identity is increasingly manifested in the context of a 'traversal culture' (p. 579). Traversals are movements of meaning-making across times and spaces. In an age of 'digital remix' (Lankshear and Knobel 2006), we fluidly traverse physical interactions and digital text-making. We carry meanings across these spaces, playing out our identity on multiple stages, each characterized by their own semiotic conventions. The child and father in our observation are engaged in a particular type of traversal. They move between the physical interaction they share and the story they create through the iPad app. For example, they shape a 'daddy' that exists on the iPad while simultaneously constructing a sense of identity for the 'daddy' that continues to exist beyond the creation of the story. Lemke suggested that traversals have the potential to challenge the ideological influence of mass-distribution media outlets; at the same time, he suggested that in a traversal culture, those with power would create 'semiotic packages' that constrain the creativity of our traversals and control how we move between times and spaces of meaning-making. The feature of personalization in the context of iPad story-making can be read in either way. On the one hand, we can think about personalization as destabilizing the intentions of the designers of the 'Mr Glue' app, since the users can exercise choice in the semiotic artefact they are engaging with. On the other hand, personalization encourages the user to enmesh their identity more fully in the parameters that the designers of the app have predetermined. For example, the story that features in the observation presented here is one essentially of 'good' and 'evil'. This narrative structure can be understood as a message about how the world works. By making 'daddy' the protagonist—the good character—the child and parent are more invested in the good/evil dichotomy. Thus, rather than diluting the influence of the app designers, the traversals between physical and digital interaction potentially heighten the impact of the structures imposed by those with the power to design and disseminate digital tools.

Shifting identities and power relations have been observed with non-digital resources before. For example, Grainger et al. (2005) observed children's writing and authoring of their own stories in a series of case studies in UK primary schools. They concluded that the personal voice experienced through story-making enables children to experience different parts of self: 'through telling personal tales children can voice their emotional, imaginative and interpersonal awareness which can motivate them to use language for intrinsic means, not external schemes, and investigate their identity in the process' (p.125). This quote resonates with Bruner (1994: 43), who conceptualized written and oral narratives as key building blocks for one's coherent sense of self because self 'is storied, or narrative, in structure'. Writing in itself is an activity which connects an individual focus to a wider shared narrative. It raises audience awareness and gives writing a shared, collective purpose. In other words, children's experience of writing enables them to connect their individual story to a wider shared narrative. This is what Grainger et al. (2005) described as an almost universal human desire, because 'when we are engaged in communication we need a response or some kind of feedback, whether from our own inner voices or from another human being to reassure us that we are having some impact on the world' (p. 56).

The *Mr Glue Stories* app connects the reading and writing process and the individual and shared identity through an interesting, so far little researched, approach: the child is not writing the entire story from scratch, nor is she inventing the story narrative. Rather, the app provides a template, a coherent, funny story the child only needs to customize with a few story elements. The choice of the story characters is up to the child and is a choice that any child can easily make. The story-writing is thus largely facilitated by the app. In Bruner's language, the app provides a convenient scaffold for the child's entry into the story-making world. As such, the use of *Mr Glue Stories* serves a dual aim: it fosters the child's writer identity and it also enables her to bridge the individual and shared story-worlds. In this particular instance, it enabled the child to be on an equal footing with her father in terms of a shared feeling of fun and humour.

Although we have examined personalization as it occurs in the context of iPad story-making, we are not suggesting that personalization is an entirely digital or tablet-based phenomenon. The personalization of stories can also occur in paper-based media or in oral storytelling. Children can, for example choose a name for the main character when they write a story on paper or when they perform a story in a school drama. However, iPad story-making is special in the extent to which it makes this opportunity possible with different types and levels of personalization. The personalization occurs seamlessly and is represented through multimedia elements (in sounds, pictures and text). The multiple modes available through iPad story-making make the personalization richer, but the frequency of personalization within iPad story-making is also important. iPad personalized story-making has therefore the potential to support children to explore their own experiences of the world, to develop a stronger sense of self, and to facilitate closeness with others. Furthermore, effective use of iPad story-making in the home can support children and parents to find out more about one another and strengthen their relationship.

Our conclusions are limited in that they are based on a single observation, which related to one child–parent relationship. When observed at different times, this child and parent may have interacted in different ways with the personalization features on offer. These will not necessarily occur in every interaction involving iPad story-making; other child–parent dyads may have interacted differently. In addition, other MPS apps will present distinct personalization opportunities and we presented only the key four possibilities of personalization features relevant to our data. However, our findings do show some of the ways in which personalization features can play a role in children's sense of self and their relationships with others. We therefore see our study and the findings we have reported here as an invitation to investigate further the potentials of personalization features in iPad story-making in relation to children's sense of self and their intersubjective exchanges with others, particularly adults in the home context. Future studies will change components of the sociocultural context and observe how this shapes the interaction differently—including changing the participants involved in the study and the app that is used.

A longitudinal perspective would also support further research in this area, since it would be interesting to see how the child and parents' interactions with the app change and shift over time as they become increasingly familiar with the personalization features on offer.

References

Bruner, Jerome. 1994. The 'remembered' self. In *The remembering self: Construction and accuracy in the self-narrative*, ed. Ulric Neisser, and Robyn Fivush, 41–54. Cambridge: Cambridge University Press.

Bruner, Jerome. 2001. Self-making and world-making. In *Narrative and identity: Studies in autobiography, self, and culture*, ed. Jens Brockmeier, and Donald Carbaugh, 25–39. Amsterdam: John Benjamins.

Bruner, Jerome. 1990. *Acts of meaning*. Cambridge, MA: Harvard University Press.

Common Sense Media, Zero to Eight: Children's Media Use in America 2011, Available from: https://www.commonsensemedia.org/research/zero-to-eight-childrens-media-use-in-america

Common Sense Media, Zero to Eight: Children's Media Use in America 2013, Available online from: https://www.commonsensemedia.org/research/zero-to-eight-childrens-media-use-in-america-2013

Ching, Carter, Wang Cynthia, Christine Xiao, Mei-Li Shih, and Yore Kedem. 2006. Digital photography and journals in a kindergarten-first-grade classroom: Toward meaningful technology integration in early childhood education. *Early Education and Development* 17 (3): 347–371.

Cohen, Lawrence. 2001. *Playful Parenting*. New York: Ballantine Books.

Goodwin, Charles. 2000. Action and embodiment within situated human interaction. *Journal of Pragmatics* 32 (10): 1489–1522.

Goodwin, Charles. 2007. Participation, stance and affect in the organization of activities. *Discourse & Society* 18 (1): 53–73.

Grainger, Teresa, Kathy Goouch, and Andrew Lambirth. 2005. *Creativity and writing: Developing voice and verve in the classroom*. London: Psychology Press.

Halliday, Michael. 1978. *Language as social semiotic*. London: Arnold.

Ingram, Lauren. 2016. Expert claims overuse technology parents never saying no reason children getting bored struggling school. In Daily Mail, Available from: http://www.dailymail.co.uk/femail/article-3607869/Are-spoiling-child-Expert-claims-overuse-technology-parents-never-saying-no-reason-children-getting-bored-struggling-school.html

Kress, Gunther, and Theo van Leeuwen. 1996. *Reading Images: The Grammar of Visual Design*, (2nd ed). London: RoutledgeFalmer.

Kress, Gunther, and Theo van Leeuwen. 2001. *Multimodal Discourse: The Modes and Media of Contemporary Communication*. London: Edward Arnold.

Kucirkova, Natalia, David Messer, Kieron Sheehy, and Rosie Flewitt. 2013. Sharing personalised stories on iPads: a close look at one parent–child interaction. *Literacy* 47 (3): 115–122.

Kucirkova, Natalia, Kieron Sheehy, and David Messer. 2015. A Vygotskian perspective on parent–child talk during iPad story sharing. *Journal of Research in Reading* 38 (4): 428–441.

Kucirkova, Natalia. 2016. Personalisation: A theoretical possibility to reinvigorate children's interest in storybook reading and facilitate greater book diversity. *Contemporary Issues in Early Childhood* 17 (3): 304–316.

Kucirkova, Natalia. (forthcoming). *Digital Personalisation in Early Childhood: An overview of digital personalization and how it impacts on early childhood.* London: Bloomsbury.

Lankshear, Colin, and Michele Knobel. 2006. Blogging as participation: The active sociality of a new literacy. *American Educational Research Association, San Francisco, CA* 11: 3–13.

Lemke, Jay. 2000. Across the scales of time: Artifacts, activities, and meanings in ecosocial systems. *Mind, culture, and activity* 7 (4): 273–290.

Lemke, Jay. 2001. Discursive technologies and the social organization of meaning. *Folia Linguistica* 35 (1–2): 79–96.

Lemke, Jay. 2002. Language development and identity: Multiple timescales in the social ecology of learning. In *Language acquisition and language socialization*, ed. Claire Kramsch, 68–87. Continuum: London.

Norris, Sigrid. 2011. Three hierarchical positions of deictic gesture in relation to spoken language: a multimodal interaction analysis. *Visual Communication* 10 (2): 129–147.

Norris, Sigrid. 2012. Multimodal Interaction Analysis. *The Encyclopedia of Applied Linguistics.*

Ofcom. 2015. Communications Market Report, Available from: https://www.ofcom.org.uk/research-and-data

Ofcom. 2016. Adults' Media Use and Attitudes Report, Available from: https://www.ofcom.org.uk/research-and-data

Sakr, Mona. 2012. 'Wrighting'the self: new technologies and textual subjectivities. *Learning, Media and Technology* 37 (1): 119–123.

Sakr, Mona and Natalia Kucirkova. (2017). Parent-child moments of meeting in art-making with collage, iPad, Tuxpaint and crayons. *International Journal of Education and the Arts.*

Stern, Daniel, Louis Sander, Jeremy Nahum, Alexandra Harrison, Karlen Lyons-Ruth, Alec Morgan, and Edward Tronick. 1998. Non-interpretive mechanisms in psychoanalytic therapy: The 'something more' than interpretation. *International Journal of Psychoanalysis* 79 (5): 903–921.

Stern, Daniel. 2000. *Interpersonal world of the infant: A view from psychoanalysis and development psychology.* London: Basic books.

Stern, Daniel. 2004. *The Present Moment in Psychotherapy and Everyday Life (Norton Series on Interpersonal Neurobiology).* London: WW Norton & Company.

Van Leeuwen, Theo. 2005. *Introducing social semiotics.* Abingdon: Routledge.

Author Biographies

Natalia Kucirkova is a Senior Lecturer in Early Years and Childhood Studies at University College London. Her research concerns innovative ways of supporting shared book reading, digital literacy and the role of personalisation in early years. Her publications have appeared in *First Language, Computers & Education, Cambridge Journal of Education, Communication Disorders Quarterly* and *Learning, Media & Technology.*

Mona Sakr is a Senior Lecturer in Education and Early Childhood at Middlesex University. She publishes on the play and creativity of young children and how this is changing in a digital age. She is currently researching collaborative creativity between children and adults, and how this is shaped by the use of mobile digital technologies.

Chapter 12
Children's Engagement with iPads in Early Years Classrooms: Exploring Peer Cultures and Transforming Practices

Karen Daniels

Introduction: Touchscreen Devices and Schooled Literacies

The use of touchscreen devices in early education settings has become increasingly commonplace and educators have been quick to explore the educational possibilities of iPad apps (Merchant 2012). The presence and use of iPads in early education settings may in turn influence the practices that take place there (Merchant 2014). It is clear that many children bring their experiences of using digital devices in the home to the classroom (see, for example Levy 2009), and hence such engagement with digital devices may be a significant feature of their funds of knowledge (Moll et al. 1992). But the funds of knowledge that children bring from home are not always related closely to the pedagogical goals of the school. This is particularly notable in early literacy education, where for some children the print literacy goals of school may differ significantly from the literacy practices familiar in the home. Herein lies a tension between new technologies, their role in the classroom, and the nature of early literacy as conceptualized in statutory curricula where literacy is broadly seen as a set of pre-determined skills to be acquired (Street 1995, 2003). Curriculum guidelines in England, for example suggest that such skills are predominantly related to those required to access print literacies, and may involve such skills as letter formation and the learning of grapheme-phoneme correspondences (see DFE 2014: 11).

Wolfe and Flewitt (2010) point out how access to digital technologies, when supported by adults, has the potential to facilitate children's metacognitive strategies. Where this is the case, children appear to engage more confidently with digital tools in the classroom. Marsh et al. (2015) noted how apps in the home have the potential to foster play and creativity in a wide range of ways subject to the child's preferences. But such access to digital tools, mediated by adults or otherwise, is not

K. Daniels (✉)
Sheffield Hallam University, Charles Street, Sheffield, UK
e-mail: k.daniels@shu.ac.uk

C. Burnett et al. (eds.), *The Case of the iPad*,
DOI 10.1007/978-981-10-4364-2_12

guaranteed for all children. Hence debates around young children's language socialization in the home and its relationship with the mastery of print literacies in school (for example, Heath 1983) are further compounded. Indeed the ways in which we conceptualize literacy, and the ways in which we see the relationship between print and digital literacy, are influencing the types of early literacy learning experiences to which children have access in classrooms. Burnett (2010) distinguished between two types of study related to technology and literacy: those which focus on technology as a 'deliverer of literacy', that aim to provide insights into the ways that specific programmes support print literacies; and those that look at how digital technologies shape meaning making, possibly generating novel ways of making meaning. It is this second set of open-ended studies in which I situate this chapter.

Apps, Literacy Goals and Expanding Communicative Repertoires

Children are far from passive recipients of schooled literacies. The work of Dyson (2003, 2008) draws our attention to the ways in which children innovate with literacy practices in order to turn them to something that is of significance to them. Kress shows us how learning and development are intimately connected to the types of meaning making tools available, and a child's increasing mastery of such tools (Kress 2010). This lens of interpretation of young children's meaning making activity gives due recognition to the multiplicity of modes and media that children draw upon in order to make meaning. Furthermore it provides a view of literacy learning that is inextricably tied to a child's expanding repertoire for making meaning and participation. Wohlwend (2015), for example, illustrates how it is children's playful engagement with the world that is significant to their resources for meaning making, and explores how such engagement shapes their worlds and impacts on their participation in peer cultures. In earlier writing (Daniels 2014, 2016), I drew on the work of Corsaro (2005) in order to look closely at young children's peer cultures in early years settings focusing on how these spontaneously emerge in and through children's playful activity. I noted the ways in which such activity is intricately related to early literacy development and the possibilities provided by the environment. Playful engagement with available material resources in the immediate environment, be it with pieces of card, bits of tape, character puppets, or touchscreen devices, is central to children's educational experiences as it gives rise to their participation within, and production of, local novel practices. In Daniels (2017), I observed how children's collaborative interactions around iPad apps prompted the expansion of children's semiotic repertoires for meaning making and conferred children's cultural agency. In this way, apps often enhanced children's learning and play experiences and gave rise to participation in peer cultures. In this chapter, I examine and contrast the ways in which children interact around a range of apps, two of which are designed specifically to support early print literacy development.

When considering the relationship between touchscreen devices and early literacy, texts are accessed or created using a very different set of skills to those associated with the tools of early literacy more commonly found within early years' settings. The skills, rules and routines for the use of books, pens, pencils and crayons are firmly established and have been seen to be in an orchestrated relationship with children's semiotic repertoires for meaning making (Rowe 2003). Such repertoires are also influenced by the ways in which such tools of literacy are presented in the classroom (see for example, Bomer 2003). The presence of the touchscreen device in classrooms, albeit less widely established as a tool of early literacy, is nonetheless significant to the practices that are taking place there. In this chapter, I argue that traditional practices and routines associated with print literacy development may be 'mapped' onto the design and intended use of apps in ways that fall short of the potential of the technology to support young children's learning.

It is clear that established practices shape the ways that technologies are taken-up in educational settings (See Burnett 2014; Ng, Chap. 7). It is also recognized that the physicality and interactive features of touchscreen devices shape the communicative practices that emerge around them (Merchant 2014). Walsh and Simpson (2014) for example, draw attention to how the communicative tools of gesture and touch are significant to meanings made using touchscreens devices. Similarly, Kucirkova et al. (2014) note how the materiality of touchscreen devices shapes the interactions that take place around them. Kress (1997) reminds us that young children have a predilection for drawing on visual, kinaesthetic and gestural modes and so it is not surprising that children quickly integrate these modes into their activity. Norris (2011) terms modes such as gesture and movement, or movement and handling of objects to serve the purpose of communication, as *visual modes*, pointing out that very often it is gesture that is the salient mode in such orchestrations. When observing a group of toddlers and a practitioner in an early years setting, Merchant (2014) identified the role that the hands and the body played in the interactions. Merchant noticed how patterns of movement and touch were orchestrated as adults and children interacted together with and around a range of iPad apps and from such observations developed a typology of hand movements which typically occur. These include: stabilizing movements, where a child uses hands and/ or knees to hold/support the iPad; control movements, for example, precision tapping and swiping; and deictic movements, which refer to pointing, or including gestures directing attention to the screen. Merchant's typology provides a useful frame to explore how gesture and touch merge with other communicative resources in young children's repertoires that take place around touchscreen devices. Children's communicative repertoires therefore are mediated by the affordances of the material resources in the classroom, and the iPad has the potential to mediate a set of cultural resources for communication. When examining children's meaning making then, it is significant to consider not only the ways in which children's experiences and histories come to the fore, but to seek to understand how these interplay with the available tools in the classroom and the part that these play in shaping the semiotic repertoires and the orchestrations of communicative repertoires that emerge.

With these considerations in mind, I draw on four episodes which I use as illustrative examples to explore varied relationships between apps, pedagogical goals and practices and children's repertoires for meaning making. I begin by outlining the episodes and then discuss how far children's engagement seemed aligned with the pedagogical aims associated with apps used. Next, I explore other ways in which children improvised with apps and consider the implications of this in relation to children's creation of and participation in peer cultures.

The Study, Data Collection, Selection and Analysis

The episodes presented in this chapter are extracted from a year-long ethnographic research study where I examined 4–5 year-old children's emerging literacy practices throughout their first year of compulsory schooling. Data collection involved field notes which were used as the basis of narrative accounts of what was taking place in the classroom. Episodes of self-initiated activity were filmed using a small hand-held camera in order to facilitate closer examination of children's communicative repertoires.

Over the course of the year, 254 min of footage were collected across 159 episodes. Twenty-nine of these episodes involved activity with iPads. The footage was gathered during times during the day when children had access to continuous provision. 'Continuous provision' is the term used in England to describe the practice of giving children time and space to explore the classroom environment and its resources freely, and to follow their own interests and lines of enquiry. The provision of resources for free access is a key principle of what is referred to as 'the enabling environment' in England's statutory curriculum for children from birth to five (DFE 2014). In the setting that was the focus for this study, the class teacher had selected a range of apps and installed these onto four iPads; children often selected from these apps freely. The iPads were a regular feature of this provision and were readily taken-up by the children.

The apps examined in this chapter include *Hairy Letters* © by Nessy Learning Limited, abc *Pocket phonics Letter Sounds and Writing* © by Apps in my pocket Ltd., (c), *Toca Robot Lab* by Toca Boca © and *Lego Story Maker* © by Lego. Table. 12.1 lists each app, gives a brief summary of the activity it promotes and identifies the app producer's aim as specified by the app producer in relevant publicity materials.

It is worth noting that while *Hairy Letters*, *Pocket Phonics* and *Lego Story Maker* were all marketed as apps to support various aspects of literacy development, *Toca Robot Lab* was marketed as a game app that promotes creativity. It enables the children to build a robot and guide the robot through a subterranean maze, and there are choices in the designing of the robot in the initial stages of the

Table 12.1 Apps and producer's aims

Name of app	Produced by	Producer's stated aim for the app	What the children have to do
Hairy Letters	*Nessy Learning Limited*	Learning letter sounds and names	Interact with animations and trace letter shapes with fingers. Build simple words
Pocket phonics Letter Sounds and Writing	*Apps in my pocket*	App for learning phonics as it would be in school. Uses same methods as specified in the National Curriculum for England (DFE 2013)	Trace and say letter names and sounds. Follow the arrows
Toca Robot Lab	*Toca Boca*	Design a robot with materials and tools. Promotes creativity	Select body parts for a robot. Steer robot through a maze to the shipping unit, following the arrows
Lego Story Maker	*Lego*	Fun and promotes design and creativity	Select scene, characters and accessories in order to make a multimodal story. Sounds can be added

game. I have included an episode in which children played with this app, partly because it proved very popular with the children, but also because playing it involved some of the haptic skills that children require in order to operate the iPad, and because its use was illustrative of the kinds of playful interaction which children brought to the apps.

In the transcriptions of each episode that follow I draw on Merchant's (2014) typology of hand movements which includes stabilizing movements, control movements, and deictic movements. I also draw on Taylor's (2014) work in transcribing children's multimodal activity, noting the semiotic modes of gesture, gaze, eye contact and speech, and describing what happens on the screen in orchestration with children's movements. I record the app as a participant in the interaction as I suggest that the materiality of the device and the multimodal affordances of the apps help shape children's interactions. Permission for filming was granted by the parents and the head teacher at the school. Negotiated ongoing assent (Flewitt 2005) was acknowledged as I observed the children.

Episode 1: Letter Formation—Lucy Traces Letters

This first episode shows Lucy tracing letters. On this occasion the iPads are placed on a table by the practitioner. I notice that usually the iPads are on the carpet area of the classroom. Lucy is clearly familiar with a range of letter formation and phonic apps and she quickly selects *Hairy Letters* ©, carries out an activity, hits the home button and then selects a different app. She uses both hands to operate the iPad and the apps. Lucy points with her right forefinger (deictic movement) and her head is bent low as she looks intently at the image of a letter 'd' on the screen. At the starting point of the 'd' is a spider, indicating where to touch the screen and begin tracing the letter.

Lucy	Touches spider (precision tapping).
	Begins to guide spider in an anticlockwise motion around the curve of the 'd' (control movement/swiping).
	Drags spider up the ascending rise of the d, then back down. Raises her finger away from screen.
App	Spider looks up from the screen.
App	Makes a 'tinkling of bells' sound.
	Large spider appears at the foreground of the screen, holding a 'well done' sign.
Lucy	Watches the spider intently.
	Looks up and across the table.
	Moves hair from her face and looks down again.
	Presses home button with her left hand (control movement).
	Selects a new app.

In this extract Lucy seemed well-practised in using the app and the haptic skills needed to draw the letters or select graphemes, dragging and dropping these at points on the screen. In the case of the spider's feedback, Lucy watched this intently, but then used the home button to select a different app. Lucy did seem to be enjoying this activity; she was focused and working with precision and intent. The simple repetition provided by this particular app and the option of being able to switch between functions freely seemed appealing to her, but she appeared to move from app to app frequently, so the activity did not promote sustained involvement.

Episode 2: Paul Explores a Phonics App

Paul is sitting on the floor in the carpeted area. The iPad is resting on a low table in front of him. I notice he is gazing intently at the screen, and is keeping very still. His hands are extended outwards, fingers splayed, just over, but not resting on the iPad. He presses the home button with his left hand, and an array of letters appear. I notice that the teacher has pre-selected the letters 'a', 'p', 's' and 't' for the children to select from. Clearly, this is to reinforce the first letters that are commonly taught to children in phonics lessons. Paul touches the 'a' with his left forefinger. A picture of an ant appears on the screen. Below the ant image, from left to right, the grapheme 'a', the word 'ant', and a second 'a', this time printed in dots, presumably for tracing, appear.

Paul	Pauses and looks at the ant, then hits the home button again.
App	The array of letters appear 'a, p, s, t.'.
Paul	Selects the 'p'.

App An image of a penguin, standing by a large icicle, appears.
Paul Hands are both still hovering over the iPad and he taps the penguin with his left forefinger (precision tapping). He taps again.
App The penguin takes a few steps to the side, then begins to peck repeatedly at the large icicle. As it does so, the app says 'p-p-p-p-p-p-p-p-p…'.
Paul As this action starts, Paul quickly moves his hands away, so they are hovering, ready paused, above the iPad.
App The ice cracks and falls. The penguin in triumph jumps up and down, flaps its wings and says 'p-p-p-penguin'.
Paul Presses the home button again, and selects 't'.

Here Paul was clearly intent on watching the short animations on the iPad screen, and his gaze was held throughout. Like Lucy, he quickly moved from one sequence to another, and was confident in operating the app. His hands, held out over the app throughout the episode in readiness, appeared to show his anticipation of what might happen. This stage of the app was fairly limited in the response it required, other than watching the film sequence.

What was notable throughout the study was that the apps related to phonics or letter formation, such as those accessed here by Lucy and Paul, were very often played individually and very rarely drawn on as resources around which to collaboratively interact. It may be that such apps support the consolidation of pedagogical literacy goals, and it was clear that children were using the necessary haptic skills needed to operate a touchscreen device, but as we move to the next two episodes, what happens when children collaboratively interact around apps is perhaps much more complex and, one could argue, provides a much richer play and learning experience.

Episode 3: Blaise and Harry Steering the Robot

In episode 3, Blaise and Harry are sitting in the carpet area side-by-side. Blaise is stabilizing the iPad using his knees and at times his left and/or right hand is placed on one side of the iPad. The backdrop to the app is the subterranean maze through which the robot needs to be guided. The user is required to propel the robot through the maze, following large white arrows. In order to keep the robot moving, and to prevent it from falling down deeper into the maze, it must be kept moving from left to right, right to left, or vertically, with swift and precise swiping movements (Fig. 12.1).

Blaise 'Watch it! Watch!…… Watch this….'
Harry Looks over and leans closer to the screen, clasping hands together.
Blaise Guiding the robot from left to right across the screen, using his forefinger to make swiping movements (control movements).
Drags the robot to the right of the screen ignoring the direction suggested by the arrows.

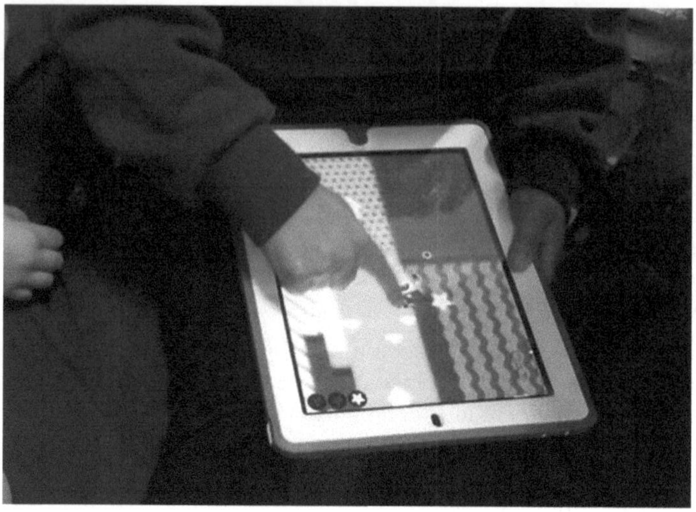

Fig. 12.1 Blaise and Harry steer the robot

	Uses both left and right hand forefingers alternately in order to propel the robot more quickly (using quick swiping control movements).
App	Robot is moving along, swaying from side to side as Harry propels it with his. Fingers.
Harry	Looking at screen. '….And then he'll be trapped!'
Blaise	Positions the robot over a long vertical drop in the maze and then pulls both hands back, away from the screen.
Blaise	'Arrrrghhh!
App	Robot falls vertically deeper into the maze and lands at the bottom.
Harry	'Oh!' Leans closer into the screen. 'Ah!' Looks at Blaise.
Blaise	Begins to guide robot back up the maze using left and right hand swiping movement with forefinger (control movement). 'I like that bit!'
Harry	'Can I have a go now?'
Blaise	'Watch it! Watch it!… After I have completed this mission.'

Here Blaise demonstrated his confidence in the use of haptic skills required to operate this app, and I noticed that he used predominantly swiping control movements. Blaise was clearly confident enough to complete the mission. So confident that he playfully thwarted this in order to watch the robot fall back down into the maze in order to entertain Harry. He also tried to speed up the action by using alternate left and right hands to swipe the robot upwards. Blaise's comment of 'completing a mission' illustrates how he is drawing on his experiences of computer games and Harry's comment 'And then he'll be trapped!' appears to illustrate an awareness of the plot lines and events typical of certain types of computer games. It was important to Blaise that Harry watched and was entertained. Harry's gaze was fixed on Blaise's operation of the app. The dramatic pulling away of his hands from the scene punctuated the tumble of the robot. Harry was suitably surprised.

Episode 4: Amalia, Abida and Sarah Play Lego Friends ©

Amalia, Abida and Sarah are gathered around the iPad, sitting on cushions in a carpeted area of the classroom. Amalia selects the app *Lego Friends Story Maker* © and sits, legs crossed, stabilizing the iPad by balancing it on her knees. Abida is facing her and Sara is sitting to her right hand side. All eyes are on the screen. I have noticed that this is a popular app with the children, and that they have favourite Lego Friends characters that they spot and name as they appear on the screen.

Amalia is pointing to the screen with her right forefinger. She touches the screen and an array of possible story settings appear at the bottom of the page. She moves her hand back, and her fingers are poised in the air just above the iPad. She remains still for a moment, then with a quick tap, selects a city landscape from the array which then fills the whole screen of the iPad.

Amaila	Poises her finger over the scenes again at the bottom of the page and selects the country scene.
Abida	'Lets go to… 'Ach!' Let's go to Martin's farm'…
Amalia	Moves finger over to beach setting and taps. 'A beach there…' Moves her hair back with left hand. Right hand is still poised over the iPad.
Amalia	Lifts both hands in air and twists from side to side, waving hands. Singing 'Yes—let's go to the beach'… Moves hair from eyes. Looks and smiles at Abida. 'Ye-ah'. Hovers her finger over the screen.
Abida	Smiles and watches Amalia.
App	A beach scene has appeared on the screen, and an array of characters appear at the bottom of the screen.
Amalia	Finger hovers over characters and she taps one.
App	Selected character moves to the middle of the screen.
Abida	'Yea!… Barbie girl.'
Amalia	'Ahh! Euwww!' taps figure again—and selects different accessories for the character from a new menu that has appeared below.

App	A microphone appears in the middle of the screen, below the character.
Amalia	'Oh what's that?'
Abida	Points to screen then quickly withdraws hand– 'Put a stamp on!'
App	The word 'Action' appears on the screen.
Amalia	Pulls her hands away from the screen.
App	Microphone icon flashes.
Abida	Presses microphone icon.
App	A green arrow appears.
Lucy	Leans in and shouts 'Hello!'
Amalia	Taps the icon again, and a pause sign appears.
Abida & Amalia	Pause and watch, smiling.
Abida	Taps the screen again (precision tapping).
App	Microphone appears.
Abida	Leans forward 'He-ll-ooooo'. Both girls are looking at screen and smiling.
App	Screen countdown; 5-4-3-2-1 ACTION—microphone re-appears.
Abida	'Hell ooooo!'
Amalia	Taps 'play' icon.
App	Plays recording of Abida's voice.
	All three girls lean back away from iPad, look to each other and laugh.
Abida	'That's my voice'...
Amali	Singing and twisting from side to side 'Hello! da da da da'.

Lego Friends was particularly popular with Amalia, Abida and Sarah, and it offered a number of options that the girls could choose from. Amalia held the iPad, operating the device throughout. Her decisions were guided though by others, such as by Abida's pointing and her request to, 'Put a stamp on'. Initially, Amalia selected cityscape, then Abida suggested a countryside scene—the reference to Martin's farm here is a popular local area for families to visit. Clearly the country scene has triggered memories of this and it offered a familiar setting for the play setting they were constructing together. Amalia chose the beach and asserted this as a good choice by singing, 'Yea-lets go to the beach!' raising her arms and twisting from side to side as though dancing. It seemed from this episode that the girls were gaining confidence in the use of this app, but that some of its functions were beyond them, and at times they seemed surprised by what was happening and Amalia experimentally tapped the scene to see what might happen. This unpredictability appeared to add to the enjoyment of their activity. In what seemed to be a series of intuitive responses, the girls worked out that the microphone icon and the countdown on the screen was an opportunity to record sounds, seemingly deducing this together. Amalia's question, 'Oh What's that?', as the microphone icon appeared, and the countdown and the microphone flashes, were interpreted by Abida who leant forward saying, 'hello'. A sequence of experimental tapping then led to the iPad playing the recording. As the girls heard the voice, Amalia leant back in mock surprise, the other girls leant back and they all laughed.

Discussion: Apps in the Classroom and Print Literacy Goals

Children's interactions with and around iPads in education settings may be interpreted to some degree in relation to the pedagogical goals that are part of everyday classroom life as education policy is realized in practice. Similarly, interpretation of what is taking place will be guided by what we perceive the educational potential of apps to be. Clearly, educational goals which aim to promote children's print literacy skills have been taken into account by the teacher when considering the selection of apps for use in this classroom. For example, the *Hairy Letters* app aims to support accurate orientation in letter formation and recognition of grapheme-phoneme correspondences. It is designed to use animation in order to prompt very particular responses, for example, the spider's 'well done' sign. The app indicates the starting point for the formation of each letter, and where the finger should make contact with the screen. As the child starts to trace the letter, the app quickly prompts the child, indicating if the letter is being formed correctly or incorrectly. The app's invitation to repeat the action encourages repeated practice.

Such an approach is similar to more traditional 'handwriting' instruction where the goal is to develop a child's correctly orientated, swift and fluent formation of letters. Lucy's tracing of letters with her extended fingertip is interesting as it appears to map traditional letter formation activities onto the potential of touch-screen devices. In many ways it sits in parallel with more traditional print-based literacy instruction where the repeated tracing of letters, either in the air, on the palm of the hand, or in a tray of sand, is a recognizable practice for young literacy learners. When looked at closely however, it is not clear how far the motor skills required to form print characters are similar to the control movements required to trace over a grapheme on a touchscreen device with a stylus or an extended fingertip, but what is clear is how the multimodal affordances of the app appear to have been utilized by app designers in the service of the discrete goals of print literacies and traditional practices associated with handwriting. The sustained touch required by the fingertip to draw a letter on a touchscreen, however, differs from the haptic skills or control movements needed to operate a touchscreen device, for example precision tapping and swiping (as identified in Merchant's typology).

Looking closely at Paul's activity as he interacts with the phonic app, again the multimodality of the app is used to service established goals of print literacies, focusing this time on the graphemes and their corresponding phonemes. Again, it is not clear how far a multimodal animation of a penguin relates to the process of reading. Phonics as a prime approach in the teaching of reading focuses on decoding words by learning individual phoneme-grapheme correspondences and synthesizing them in the order that they occur in the word. Again, the repetition of isolated skills is the approach to literacy learning here. What was noticeable in episodes 1 and 2 above was that the children did appear to be moving around the apps much more frequently, from and to the home button. Lucy continually re-selected different letters to trace and then moved quite quickly from app to app. During my study, I frequently observed such rapid shifts when children used apps with limited or closed content. It is inconclusive whether the app's intended pedagogical goals are realized through such activity and it is not the aim of this chapter to make or refute such an assertion. What was notable was that apps that were linked to traditional print literacy goals were often taken-up individually by children and there was very often much less collaboration or communication with other children as they used them. As we saw in *Lucy Traces Letters*, when apps were linked to specific goals, they were more likely to be placed on a table top and this in itself limited opportunities for small gatherings of children to assemble.

Apps, Operational Skills Associated with Touchscreen Devices, and Expanding Repertoires for Meaning Making

Pedagogical goals associated with print literacies are only part of what might be realized when children interact around digital devices. In the episodes above, it often appeared that, when engaging with apps with linear or closed content, children seemed to work quietly and individually, and shifted quite quickly from one app another. In other episodes, where the content of apps was not linked to specific and discrete literacy skills, or was more open ended, children did appear to access them differently. Collaborative interaction around such apps offered an opportunity for creative engagement as the children learned to control them, explore their possibilities, and infuse such activity with meanings significant to their lives and interests. In this way, the apps became a site for engagement amongst peers where friendships, relationships and shared interests emerged (see also, Daniels 2017). The ways in which children collectively transformed the apps were generated through and by the range of semiotic resources they drew upon during the episodes. The use of deictic, control and stabilizing movements (Merchant 2014) and their orchestration with other semiotic resources provided children with new opportunities to explore and extend communicative repertoires. *Toco Robot Lab*, for example as with other game apps accessed by the children, provided opportunities for repeated practise of haptic movements such as swiping or precision tapping. Any imprecise haptic movements when playing *Toco Robot Lab* would cause the robot to crash into the walls and fall down deeper into the subterranean maze. As we have seen with Blaise, this feature became an opportunity to playfully subvert the object of the game app.

If we apply Merchant's typology we can see how the deictic movements that take place prior to or following a control movement were interpreted by the children and as such they quickly became shared anticipated events. For example, a commonly occurring orchestration in the third and fourth episodes was when the children leant back and threw their hands away from the app into the air, either to express exasperation with or to revel in a response by the app. This often signalled a shift in gaze from the app to the other children, and was often followed by smiling, singing or other reciprocal or playful gestures. While Amalia and Blaise were the ones operating the apps, they responded to the gestures, pointing and suggestions of other children. In this way, the iPads, and the orchestrations of meanings stimulated by them and by the children, became shared cultural resources that stimulated children's peer cultures, and friendships.

The placing of the iPads again seemed to come strongly into play here. Pedagogical goals come with particular sets of practices and tools. Table tops are as strongly associated with early literacy in schools as are individual pieces of writing and individual texts to be read. As we saw with Lucy in Episode 1, table top activities are often used for individual activities. The classroom carpet however can be seen as a more flexible place, offering children a place where they could come and go, move around, or just gather. This fluidity of movement appeared to create a flexible space for children's interests, concerns and histories to emerge and to prompt novel interpretations and usage of the apps.

Shared Cultural Resources, Emerging Peer Cultures and the Significance of the Material Environment

This chapter began by considering how apps are used as educational tools and, as such, are often designed to meet existing literacy goals. When apps are mapped onto traditional literacy practices in an attempt to utilize their interactive features to support print literacy goals, we can often miss seeing their potential in children's early learning and play. At present, in England's statutory curriculum for children aged 0–5 (DFE 2014) there is very little guidance on the use of touchscreen devices in the early years setting. This may partly explain why the focus on print literacy appears to be driving what is selected for use. Many of the apps accessed in this early years setting were designed to support forms of knowledge which are written into the statutory curriculum, for example the literacy activities above and other apps related to shape and number recognition. Such apps often involved short activities with pre-determined pathways that were repeatable; traditional approaches to learning skills through repeated practice are embedded within the technology. Embedding goals in this way shapes the ways that children interact with the technology and each other in powerful ways. Apps can provide repetitive and relatively passive activity where there is little opportunity for novel activity and where the potential of the multimodality of the app merely replicates goals associated with earlier forms of knowledge. Where apps are aligned with traditional pedagogical goals and practices associated with print literacies, children's responses may be limited and the learning potential of touchscreen devices overlooked.

However, pedagogical goals are only a part of what is, or might be realized as children collaboratively and creatively take-up apps. In the episodes presented above we can see how apps can be a site for children's collaborative participation, where their friendships, interests and meaning making practices emerge. Given the opportunity, the children in these episodes readily drew on their cultural experiences, resources and communicative repertoires and used these to transform apps into things of significance to them. I noted how children's histories, experiences and repertoires often collectively transformed the apps in unpredictable ways, and at times activity appeared to arise more by accident than intention, as the moment-by-moment unfolding of activity took place.

The kinds of practices and repertoires described here can be seen as offering children new ways of being in the world. Corsaro (2005) illustrated how children drew from the adult world and transformed this to something of significance to them. Such childhood cultures in turn transform the adult world. When seen in this way children are cultural agents active in the process of cultural renewal. Observing and taking note of young children's interactions around touchscreen devices provides a fascinating illustration of this process. The multimodal and material affordances of such devices clearly offer new ways of communicating, and interactions around touchscreen devices further expand children's communicative repertoires. Children's activity with touchscreen devices often results in the transformation of the apps from linear correct/incorrect activities into experiences with a multiplicity of meanings and choices (see also Daniels 2017). As children interact with and around apps, the novel communicative repertoires that emerge are quickly taken-up by other children as they play together. Such collaborative interaction and novel orchestrations of communicative repertoires offer possibilities for participating and being in the classroom. These novel ways of participating are generative of children's peer cultures. As we saw in the episodes above, positive play experiences were taking place for the group of children in this study. Such activity, prompted in part by the app, by its multimodal animations, and in part by the touchscreen device's presence and shape, provided children with the opportunity to try out a broader set of meaning making practices that linked to, or became part of, their shared cultural experiences. When learning and development are seen as being intimately related to developing semiotic resources for making meaning and working with the materials to hand, the learning potential of iPads and apps clearly comes into focus.

The episodes in this chapter also raise broader questions in relation to the enabling environment and the significance of material resources to children's participation in peer cultures. The material resources to which children have access, be they pens, pencils, bits of paper or iPads and apps, both shape and are shaped by children's meaning making activity. When this shaping is a collaborative endeavour, novel communicative repertoires and peer cultures that facilitate children's participation emerge, and this offers children new ways of being in the world. Time and space need therefore to be seen as significant resources. Children need the space and time to gather around, to physically move in and out of activities and interactions, and to connect materials around them with their interests and concerns. Participation in peer cultures is facilitated and shaped by space, time and the opportunity for children to bring their lives and experiences to the classroom and to collaboratively explore the possibilities of the social and cultural resources to hand.

References

Burnett, Cathy. 2010. Technology and literacy in early childhood educational settings: A review of research. *Journal of Early Childhood Literacy* 10 (3): 247–270.

Burnett, Cathy. 2014. Investigating pupils' interactions around digital texts: A spatial perspective on the 'classroom-ness' of digital literacy practices in schools. *Educational Review* 66 (2): 192–209.

Bomer, Randy. 2003. Things that make kids smart: A Vygotskian perspective on concrete tool use in primary literacy classrooms. *Journal of Early Childhood Literacy* 3 (3): 223–247.

Corsaro, William. 2005. *The Sociology of Childhood*. Thousand Oaks: Pine Forge Press.

Daniels, Karen. 2014. Cultural agents creating Texts: A collaborative space adventure'. *Literacy* 48 (2): 103–111.

Daniels, Karen. 2016. Exploring enabling literacy environments: Young children's spatial and material encounters in early years classrooms. *English in Education* 50 (1): 12–34.

Daniels, Karen. 2017. Young children in an education context: Apps, cultural agency and expanding communicative repertoires. In *Apps, Technology and Young Learners*, ed. Garry Falloon, and Natalia Kucirkova, 280–290. London: Routledge.

DFE. 2013. National curriculum in England: English programmes of study. https://www.gov.uk/government/publications/national-curriculum-in-england-english-programmes-of-study. Accessed December 2016.

DFE. 2014. Statutory Framework for the Early Years Foundation Stage. Setting the standards for learning, development and care for children from birth to five. https://www.gov.uk/government/uploads/system/uploads/attachment_data/file/335504/EYFS_framework_from_1_September_2014__with_clarification_note.pdf Accessed December 2016.

Dyson, Anne Haas. 2003. Welcome to the Jam: Popular culture, school literacy, and the making of childhoods. *Harvard Educational Review* 73: 328–361.

Dyson, Anne Haas. 2008. The Pine Cone wars: Studying writing in a community of children. *Language Arts* 85 (4): 305–315.

Flewitt, Rosie. 2005. Conducting research with young children: Some ethical considerations. *Early Child Development and Care* 175 (6): 553–565.

Heath, Shirley Brice. 1983. *Ways with Words: Language, Life and Work in Communities and Classrooms*. Cambridge: Cambridge University Press.

Kress, Gunther. 1997. *Before Writing: Rethinking the Paths to Literacy*. New York: Routledge.

Kress, Gunther. 2010. *Multimodality*. A social semiotic approach to contemporary communication. London: Routledge.

Kucirkova, Natalia, David Messer, Kieran Sheehy, and Rosie Flewitt. 2014. Parent-child narrative accompanying a personalized iPad story. *Literacy* 47 (3): 115–122.

Levy, Rachael. 2009. You have to understand words… but not read them', young children becoming readers in a digital age. *Journal of Research in Reading* 32 (1): 75–91.

Marsh, Jackie, Lydia Plowman, Dylan Yamada-Rice, Julia Bishop, Jamal Lahmar, Fiona Scott, Andrew Davenport, Simon Davis, Katie French, Maddalena Piras, Sally Thornhill, Peter Robinson and Peter Winter. 2015. Exploring Play and Creativity in Pre-Schoolers' Use of Apps: Final Project Report. www.techandplay.org. Accessed December 15, 2016.

Merchant, Guy. 2012. Mobile practices in everyday life: Popular digital literacies and schools revisited. *British Journal of Educational Technology* 43 (5): 770–782.

Merchant, Guy. 2014. Keep taking the tablets, iPads, story apps and early literacy. *Australian Journal of Language and Literacy* 38 (1): 3–11.

Moll, Luis, C., Cathy Amanti, Deborah Neff, and Norma Gonzalez. 1992. Funds of knowledge for teaching: Using a qualitative approach to connect homes and classrooms. *Theory into Practice* 31 (2): 132–141.

Norris, Sigrid. 2011. The hierarchical positions of deictic gesture I relation to spoken language: A multimodal interaction analysis. *Visual Communication* 10 (2): 128–147.

Rowe, Deborah Wells. 2003. The nature of young children's authoring. In *Handbook of Early Childhood Literacy*, ed. Nigel Hall, Joanne Larson, and Jackie Marsh, 258–270. London: Sage.

Street, Brian. 1995. *Social Literacies*. London: Longman.

Street, Brian. 2003. What's "new" in New Literacy Studies? *Critical approaches to literacy in theory and practice in Current Issues in Comparative Education* 5 (2): 77–91.

Taylor, Roberta. 2014. Meaning between, in and around words, gestures and postures—Multimodal meaning-making in children's classroom discourse. *Language and Education* 28 (5): 401–420.

Walsh, Maureen and Alyson Simpson. 2014. Exploring literacies through touch pad technologies: The dynamic materiality of modal interactions. *Australian Journal of Language and Literacy* 37(2): 96–105.

Wohlwend, Karen. 2015. Making, remaking and reimagining the everyday: Play, creativity and popular media. In *Routledge handbook of Literacy Studies*, ed. Jennifer Rowsell, and Kate Pahl, 548–560. London: Routledge.

Wolfe, Sylvia, and Rosie Flewitt. 2010. New technologies new multimodal literacy practices and young children's metacognitive development. *Cambridge journal of education* 40 (4): 387–399.

Author Biography

Karen Daniels is a Senior Lecturer in Primary English at Sheffield Hallam University. She leads the development of provision for English in teacher education courses and her recent research focuses on emergent and affective dimensions of young children's literacy practices. Her publications include chapters for various edited volumes as well as articles for *English and Education*, *Literacy*, *Teacher Development*, *Education 3–13* and *Early Years in Education*.

Chapter 13
Collaborative and Dialogic Meaning-Making: How Children Engage and Immerse in the Storyworld of a Mobile Game

Fiona Maine

Introduction

In this chapter I argue that we can learn much about the complexity of children's literacy practices by investigating their engagement and immersion in the digital storyworld of a mobile game. By analysing the language that the children use as they play together, insights are given into how they collaborate with each other, but also how they position themselves as game players and how they respond to the narrative aspects of a game. Drawing on reader response theories (Benton 1992; Iser 1980; Rosenblatt 1994; Sipe 2008), and theories about dialogic learning (Alexander 2008; Mercer 2000, 2005; Wegerif 2011) as frameworks for exploring the children's encounters, an analysis is enabled that looks beyond the technology of the mobile device into the dialogic interactions that exist between games/texts and players/readers, and the transactions that support the meaning-making process.

The chapter employs a sociocultural framework, which Black and Reich (2013) describe as ideal for exploring the detail of children's engagement in virtual worlds. This perspective considers meaning to be created individually and between people, and literacy events to be influenced by their contexts and shaped by the prior knowledge and experiences of those involved. Focus on these features is the foundation of sociolinguistic and sociocultural discourse analysis approaches (Gee 2008; Gee and Green 1998; Mercer 2005; Mercer and Littleton 2007), as they examine language and interactions within their cultural context, often focusing on communicative situations, events and acts (Hymes 1972). Importantly, these approaches include qualitative and observational studies of how individuals use language to shape meanings (Mercer 2010).

F. Maine (✉)
University of Cambridge, Cambridge, UK
e-mail: flm27@cam.ac.uk

C. Burnett et al. (eds.), *The Case of the iPad*,
DOI 10.1007/978-981-10-4364-2_13

Particularly useful framing is provided by Gee (2015) who proposes a unified discourse analysis methodology. Stemming from an earlier sociolinguistic foundation (Gee 2008; Gee and Green 1998), he describes 'interactive, response-based, turn-taking conversations as the fundamental form of human communication and action in and with the world' (Gee 2015: 117). For Gee, this conversation extends beyond oral and written communication and he turns to gameplay as a 'communicational form' (p. 1). Beavis (2013: 58) too argues that games represent important examples of how, 'literacy is reconfigured and redesigned in digital times, and of the intersections between textual experience, meaning-making and the socially situated nature of play'. I argue that regarding digital gameplay as a current and relevant mode of literacy is an essential part of examining children's twenty-first-century textual experiences.

Playing or Reading

The issue of whether we play or read digital games has been argued before (see for example, Beavis 2013; Mackey 2007; Mukherjee 2015). Burnett and Merchant (2014) argue that binaries are not helpful in understanding our engagement with digital worlds, and instead suggest that we should embrace complexity and consider the affordances of examining different literacy practices across modes. If we are able to move to assume that there are parallels in the making of meaning from a variety of textual modes, though each mode might afford enrichment through different means, then we can enhance our concept of what it is to be literate and extend our repertoire of teaching for children who encounter a multitude of textual experiences on a daily basis. Whether engaging with a mobile narrative game is more 'playing' or 'reading' is then secondary to the consideration of the fluid movement between discussing video-watching to game playing to finding, for example, recipes for cooking. Their engagement with 'the world around the game', or paratexts (Beavis 2013, p. 66), meant that the children in the study regularly watched walk-throughs of games, or fan videos (*Minecraft* and *Stampy* videos on *YouTube* were mentioned by most children). For them, this was part of the game experience not extra to it, and their collaborations in game worlds easily and fluidly included these paratextual experiences.

In the after-school sessions the eight children played together in pairs, with their gameplay and talk captured through video and audio recording. Additionally, they were invited to make notes in their own notebooks, where they could add any reflections or drawing that they were moved to include. At the end of each session, we discussed their responses to the game, and wider opinions about gaming in general. As a sociocultural study, thus some contextual understanding of the players was gained, in order to better understand the schematic understandings (intertextual, domain-specific and general) that the children were bringing to the text (Anderson and Pearson 1984; Cairney 1990; Douglas and Hargadon 2000). The recording of the gameplay allowed for an analysis of the language that the children were using as an indication of the collaborative meanings that they were making and how they interacted together (Mercer 2005; Mercer and Littleton 2007). Appropriate ethical processes were followed: informed consent for recording was sought and all children are given pseudonyms in this chapter.

The game that the children played was *Monument Valley* (ustwo 2015), a simple narrative mobile game that involves players moving a princess, Ida, around a magical, geometrically challenging, Escher-like world (see Fig. 13.1). In the game, Ida encounters crows who squawk at her, sometimes blocking her path and a friendly four-block figure called Totem who assists her by reaching places she cannot go alone. Along the way, she occasionally meets a ghost-like figure who berates her, but also gives clues about her quest, and the backstory which informs it. The website describes the game as 'an illusory adventure of impossible architecture and forgiveness' (ustwo 2015).

Fig. 13.1 Ida and a crow in the world of *Monument Valley*

As the vehicle for a project exploring children's collaborative meaning-making and their immersion in a storyworld, *Monument Valley* was ideal. There is a sense of narrative in the game, but there is little exposition and much ambiguity, prompting discussions about motives and causes. Who needs to be forgiven, and why, is only gradually revealed and even then the story is open to interpretation. The game has 'ongoing learning', 'intuitive knowledge' and 'incremental' principles (Gee 2007) in its design that enable players to overcome increasingly complex problems as the game progresses, thus it is rewarding and challenging. It offers opportunities for critical thinking and creative problem-solving, highlighting the different gaming orientations that players have as they move through different scenes and, as the game calls them, 'chapters'.

The transcripts of the recordings were coded to explore the children's comments about their immersion in the storyworld, their engagement in the strategic play of the game and how they negotiated this together. Initially this meant open coding before analysing the relationships and patterns for more detailed thematic coding. However, this was not a formal grounded theory approach (Glaser and Strauss 1967) as pre-existing literature around engagement with narratives informed the categorisations. Urquhart (2013: 39) usefully describes 'middle-range' coding, which may draw on literature and a 'constant comparison' of data themselves for coding purposes. Consequently, this 'theory-seeking' approach (Bassey 1999: 62) also acknowledges the existing expectations of the researcher as a sociocultural agent informed by her interpretations of reader response theory and considerations of children's dialogic engagement with text.

Additionally, and in line with the sociocultural discourse analysis approach taken by Mercer (2005), simple word frequencies within the transcribed gameplay were analysed, exploring evidence of critical and creative problem-solving and possibility thinking (Craft 2000), goal-oriented language and words associated with game action. Caution was taken here as language indicators are only potential and cannot be assumed to have consistent meaning out of context (Maine 2015; Mercer 2005). However, they provided an interesting starting point for the analysis of the approaches that the children were taking.

Immersion in the Storyworld

Thematic coding of the session transcripts highlighted that when the children's talk turned to the storyworld of *Monument Valley*, their comments were either 'about' the game from a more removed stance as they tried to make sense of it and work out its goals, or comments that positioned them 'within' the storyworld of the game. Mackey (2007: 141) describes different diegetic levels as the distinction between looking 'through' or 'at' the story, linking to Rosenblatt's (1994) description of the 'lived-through experience' as immersion in the diegetic world. In Sipe's (2008) work exploring children's responses to picturebooks, he describes the lived-through experience as 'transparent response' in which children enter the 'secondary world' (Benton 1992) or storyworld on different levels. He found that a transparent response might be very simple, expressing emotion or making a sound effect, and this is certainly true of one pairing, Fred and Michael, as although they said little about the game, Michael often made sound effects and squawked back at the crows, or sang a 'la la la' song when he was confident in the movement of the character Ida.

Sipe recognised that a transparent response might be more complex though, and involve either talking to characters directly or assuming their voices. These latter levels of transparent response were very typical of another pair of children, Saba and Molly. As they played the game and their levels of excitement rose, they regularly talked quickly and directly to Ida, urging her to 'Come on!' or 'Wait!' Saba particularly, assumed Ida's voice, for example declaring, 'I'm the queen of the rainbow birds!' Deeper analysis of Saba's responses showed, however, that often, as she talked to the characters she seemed to assume an authority or 'directing' role within the storyworld. This was especially true of her responses to the crow figures that occasionally block Ida's way, 'You see, I helped you. Now you are smart', and, 'Come on, little crow boy!' she declared as she manipulated the geometry of the game to move a crow character. Her enjoyment in this role was highly evident, 'This is fun. I like it. I like making the crows do stuff, [adopting 'bad guy' tone of voice]… so then you are a little minion… I'll help you!' Rather than just assuming the persona of a character within the game, Saba seemed to insert herself into the diegetic world as an omnipotent presence, reflective perhaps of the player view in the game which hovers over the action. Furthermore, her omnipotent stance highlighted that being a 'player' was in itself a role she was taking. She positioned herself outside, above and within the game with fluidity, 'flickering' (Fleer 2014) between the real and virtual world, even within one utterance, as she described her enjoyment to her player partner, Molly, then spoke directly to characters in the game.

Word frequency analysis of the transcribed sessions highlighted that the most common word used by the children in any of the pairings was 'we'. In-depth analysis of incidences of the word revealed that children used 'we' not just to talk about themselves, the players, and their collaboration, but also included the key character, Ida.

In positioning themselves within the game, the children seemed to become its collaborators as they invested in the storyworld and their responses to Ida's side-kick, Totem, illustrated their desire to connect with the characters. Essentially, Totem is just a tower of four yellow blocks (see Fig. 13.2) and his role is to support Ida's movements, as by climbing on top, she can reach further. Saba and Molly, however, had an immediate affective response, squealing when he disappeared underwater, with Molly crying, 'Totem… Totem… Totem where are you?' and Saba saying, 'Maybe we will find him again… I'm sorry Molly', stepping out of her omnipotent role and back into her friend role. When Totem re-emerged later in the game they both shouted out with joy, much to the annoyance of the other children who complained that the girls were giving away 'spoilers'.

Fig. 13.2 Totem in the world of *Monument Valley*

In one of the post-session reflections, Molly described her feelings towards Totem:

FM So tell me a little bit about Totem and why did you respond to Totem in that way? Molly?
Molly Because he was cute.
FM So you've decided he is a 'he'. What made him cute?
Molly Because he had a big eye.

For Molly, Totem was personified by the inclusion of a moving eye on the top block of his tower-like figure. When he first appeared in the game, Molly said, 'I'm drawing Totem. He doesn't even have eyes. Wait. Oh I want to draw the circles on him. They're like eyes', and it is interesting that she used this personifying feature to explain her attachment in the discussion with me later. In another pairing,

Wes too seemed attached to Totem. His notebook contained profiles of all the characters, and he wrote, 'Totem is an amazing friend and would never let [Ida] down. He is my favourite character and he is so amazing… He is a really loveable character'. His partner Stephen wrote less, but also noted that Totem, 'was the best of friends', and both talked fondly of him in the post-session discussions, when Stephen described how he 'helped' Ida. Rather than just describing Totem's 'cute' features then, Wes and Stephen assigned him human qualities of friendship and loyalty.

These examples demonstrate more than Sipe's transparent responses of speaking in role or making spontaneous sound effects, and are closer to Iser's (1980) notion of 'entanglement' as they illustrate how the children became 'hooked' into the storyworld or secondary world (Benton 1992). Douglas and Hargadon (2000) describe complete immersion in a narrative text as being supported by the schematic expectations of a genre being met, allowing readers to exist within the storyworld and their attention not to be drawn to its structures or frame. In narrative mobile games, drawing on expectations about specific narrative genres from other modes is a reasonable approach to meaning-making. So, in an adventure quest story, that the main hero might have a sidekick or pet is a generic norm. On an intertextual level, even Totem's name echoes similar characters: Toto or Tonto. Whilst these might not be cultural links that the children made, their schematic expectations led them to imbue the figures with certain characteristics they expected from a sidekick—hence Wes's description of Totem being loyal, and Stephen's adoption of a narrative voice in declaring him, 'the best of friends'. At this point, the children were moving beyond transparent response into 'investment in the storyworld'. They were embellishing the simple game characters with personalities and motives, and assuming the character goals as their own. Their dialogic engagement led them to respond to Totem affectively and the game in turn responded by positioning Totem as a character that could 'help' Ida, not through agency, but through being a convenient bridge or tower on which she could stand.

Engagement with the Strategic Play of the Game

In addition to their description of immersion in narrative text, Douglas and Hargadon (2000) describe engagement as more of a critical and strategic stance and argue its pleasures come from 'a perspective outside the text' (p. 154) and through calling on schematic knowledge from many sources. To enter into a dialogic interaction with the storyworld of the game then also means responding to its design, working out the game goals and accepting its rules and logic, drawing on existing domain-specific knowledge in addition to schemas related to narrative text: to talk 'about' the text. For example, in *Monument Valley*, a key to success is to manipulate buildings so that their geometry reveals new pathways, creating impossible buildings akin to Escher's designs (see for example *Relativity*, 1953). This can be achieved through dragging buildings around until they line up. By chance the children in the project had completed a topic on Escher in the term before, and the connection was first noticed by Fred, 'It's the impossible triangle!' he declared in the first session. Later, when Wes noticed that each chapter of the game was represented on the side of a building he questioned whether there are only four chapters in the game. When told that there were ten chapters, he exclaimed, 'It's an infinity building!' Escher, impossible triangles, and infinity buildings were mentioned by all the pairs of children at several points throughout their gameplay. The following extract from Anna and Kirsty illustrates their strategic connection to this theme. They had just started Chapter IV which gives the introduction, 'Water Palace: In which Ida discovers new ways to walk' (ustwo 2015):

Anna	Maybe she could be upside down
Kirsty	Yeah
Anna	Okay—maybe she can walk without gravity. That would mean she can walk on every single place. Left, right, up, down
Kirsty	Look there's a bird… Maybe it can turn up to there…
Anna	And then maybe go to there… Oh my god it's like an optical illusion! So it's like the way you see it you think it's a path, but actually it wouldn't be able to be, because this [gestures] is like on the side. It looks like it's going there but actually it isn't.
Kirsty	Yeah—maybe it's a *new way to walk*, so maybe it will help.
Anna	She's going to the house! Of course '*new ways to walk*' she can walk on the side!
Kirsty	A little bit like Escher!

The children were not just drawing on their schematic knowledge of Escher's work here. Their experience as gamers enabled them to draw on domain-specific knowledge which led them to accept the physics of the *Monument Valley*. They were learning about the game design and the learning principles of the game gradually revealed the game goals to them (Gee 2007). The extract is also an illustration of the approach that Anna and Kirsty took to their strategic engagement in the storyworld and shows them as critical and creative dialogic readers (Maine 2015). They demonstrated possibility thinking (Craft 2000) through the use of language such as 'maybe', 'might' and 'could' and more critical reasoning through the use of 'because', 'but' and 'so' (underlined in the extract) (Maine 2014, 2015; Mercer 2000; Soter et al. 2008). They were able to reflect on the clue in the chapter introduction and were clearly pleased that they had been able to interpret it. For Anna and Kirsty, the aesthetic enjoyment of their encounter with Monument Valley seemed to be linked to their strategic gameplay and their ability to pull on their existing schematic knowledge: intertextual (drawing on art works), domain-specific (knowing that the physics of the virtual world might be different) and more general knowledge about the world (understanding gravity).

Wes and Stephen too seemed to enjoy the intertextual connections that they made as they encountered new scenarios and characters. They both recorded their observations in their notebooks and used their knowledge of narratives to support their interpretations of the story. This was true of their discussions about the role of the crows in the game. Initially the crows block Ida's way and squawk at her aggressively, however as the game progressed and they started to engage more with Ida, the boys discussed their motives:

Stephen	Oh look now there are crows walking around.
Wes	The crows are walking.
Stephen	Let's see what they do. Let's just see what they do. Okay they are crows. They are foes. Crows are foes.
Wes	They are blocking our way.
Stephen	Block our path. Maybe they are like guards.
Wes	Maybe at the end we'll find like the boss of the crows. The crows have the same power as us though: they can walk on walls.

The role of the crows offers a good example of Wes and Stephen's approach. Like Anna and Kirsty, the boys were critical and creative in their problem-solving, but this was more connected to the mystery of the story. They drew on their domain-specific knowledge of games to identify that there might be enemies in the game (with a nicely connected rhyme about foes from Stephen), but also examined the crows' purpose and how they might fit into the big picture of the story, using knowledge of stories and quests (to identify 'guards' and the 'boss of the crows'). The pair maintained this interest in the larger story and later Wes wrote, 'I'm sure the crows aren't bad anymore, but are just defending themselves', showing how the meaning of the story was evolving for him as more was revealed.

Not all the children took this creative problem-solving approach, however. Initial analysis of the transcripts showed Fred and Michael were far less inclined to use the language of critical or creative problem-solving as detailed about, but far more likely to use 'game action' words such as 'go', 'wait', 'look', 'turn', or 'stop'. In a quantitative analysis of the words used by the children, there was a negative correlation between words associated with critical and creative thinking and these game action words, showing they were unlikely to occur in the same sessions. Fred and Michael were goal oriented, so much so in fact that they spent much time checking to see how far other children had got in the game, to check they were not 'behind'. They talked far less than the other children, with their discussion limited to instructions to each other, or imperatives for game action. As a result they did not talk about the storyworld at all, nor the characters and their motivations. They made few notes in their books: their aim was to finish, and to achieve the goals set by the game.

Collaboration or Competition

Collaborating on an iPad is a physical challenge. The tablet is designed to respond to a single touch, and more than one finger on the screen means that the iPad is unresponsive or reacts unpredictably. As Fred exclaimed at one point in frustration, 'It just doesn't work when we have got two hands!' Playing a mobile game together means that players have to take it in turns to have physical control of the tablet, and the pairs were interesting in their approach to this. Close analysis of the video and transcripts showed that the children had different techniques for physically gaining control of the game. Anna and Kirsty were easily the most collaborative pair and their most frequent 'playing together' coded phrase was 'Do you want to try…?' which they both used throughout. It is interesting to note that they also had the highest incidences of problem-solving language, as their tentative or provisional language (for example, 'maybe', 'might' and 'perhaps') also served a negotiating function to enable social harmony (Barnes and Todd 1995; Lyle 1993; Maine 2015; Maybin 1994). The extract in the previous section from Anna and Kirsty's discussion about 'new ways of walking' demonstrates how they were responsive in building on each other's ideas, using co-constructive talk (Maine 2014, 2015; Rojas-Drummond et al. 2006) to negotiate meanings. Their collaboration with each other is shown through their agreements, and whilst Mercer and colleagues (see for example, Mercer 2000; Mercer and Littleton 2007) might dismiss this as cumulative talk, this agreement formed part of their negotiated meaning-making and successful collaboration.

Wes and Stephen also collaborated well together. They regularly told each other, 'it's your turn', although noticeable when coding their sessions was Stephen's pattern of suggesting, 'Let me just check…', as he pulled the tablet towards himself. Fred used a similar technique, he repeatedly said, 'Let me just think…' as he claimed the iPad from Michael. Fred's actions also had the impact of slowing the action down, and close inspection of his language highlights that he often referred to 'having a look around', suggesting that the drive for rushing quickly through the game might have been an orientation for Michael, for whom competition seemed more key than collaboration. At one point, after successfully navigating a section of the game, Michael declared, 'We win! High five!' Not only did he seem to be in competition with the other players, he was in competition with the game itself, eager to 'beat the system' which he viewed as set up to hinder his progress. On another occasion when Fred was ill, Michael chose to play the game alone, and in conversation about this, he reflected that he was happier doing so.

Analysis of the interactions of Saba and Molly offers some interesting insights into their collaboration. Molly actually had the most effective strategy for gaining and keeping control of the iPad. Watching the videos of her gameplay closely shows how she kept a fast-talking monologue which described her actions almost as a commentary:

> Molly: Oh oh oh, there's a moon! Okay wait, oh oh it's… look, oh my, look at this. Another turning building. What a surprise, not. Oh, I moved it too much. Okay, if we go through there then… Saba come on, be quick.

When she appeared unsure about what to do, she filled the space with 'Wait… wait…wait…' or 'oh… oh…oh' effectively cutting Saba out of the action. As the sessions progressed, Saba also assumed this style, with the effect of a rushed urgency to the play and the children vying for control of the tablet. Their talk was not co-constructive, as the girls rarely built on each other's ideas. Rather, it was a descriptive list of actions, with Saba's interjections directly to the characters, rather than to Molly. So, whilst it could be argued that Saba and Molly interacted in positive, immersive and affective ways with the characters of the game, their interactions with each other were more negative and at times disputational (Mercer 2000).

Analysis of the data shows that the children who took a more creative problem-solving approach were more successful at co-constructing meaning together, as they verbalised their thinking and could therefore 'interthink' (Littleton and Mercer 2013). Because Saba, Molly, Fred and Michael were more goal-orientated and reactive to situations that occurred within the game, and less exploratory in the diegetic world, they seemed to play alongside each other rather than with each other, taking control of the thinking when they had control of the iPad.

Conclusion

The examples in this chapter illustrate how 11-year-old children collaborated together in the strategic play of *Monument Valley*, whether through problem-solving to make progress, problem-solving to seek understanding about the story, or simply focusing on finishing and completing the game. The 'poem' (Rosenblatt 1994) created between player and game therefore was dependent on how the players positioned themselves, or their game and storyworld orientations. The children engaged in a dialogic interaction with the game, responding to it in either a reactive, goal-orientated way, or with a more creative problem-solving stance. Using reader response theories as a lens through which to view these stances highlighted the children's gameplay as a literacy practice, in which they sought to make meaning in a transaction with the text.

The game's dialogic interaction was formed through 'the space of future action' (Salen and Zimmerman 2004: 67) embedded in its design, so that different actions by the children prompted different responses by the game (perhaps blocking Ida's path with crows, or allowing her through a portal). That said, *Monument Valley* is not an open-world game, and only certain actions will enable progression, so whilst the route taken might vary the outcomes are the same.

In terms of the mobile device itself, I argue that the 'single-touch' feature of the tablet necessitated negotiation for successful collaborative and enhanced the dialogic interaction. Not all of the children were successful in this and there are implications here for classroom learning. In the same way that ground rules for talk (Littleton and Mercer 2007) can be seen as prerequisites for successful oral dialogic communication, some consideration should be given to how to establish successful collaborations when using a tool such as a tablet. However, that the tablet could be up-close and physically 'drawn-in' emphasised moments when the children were deeply immersed in the game as they huddled together bringing the iPad into their personal and collaborative space.

The children's dialogic interaction with the game was also linked to their immersion and investment in its diegetic world. The children imbued the characters with human qualities, and meshed (Gee 2015) their own goals with those of the game's characters, reacting in role and talking directly to the characters in a transparent response (Sipe 2008). They accepted the shifting geometry and physics of the virtual world and committed to the intentions of the game, trusting in its logic and expecting ultimately successful outcomes. This investment can be seen as affective, collaborative and dialogic, as the children accepted the terms of the diegetic world and responded to its actions and characters, drawing on their intertextual, domain-specific and general knowledge experiences to enrich their meaning-making. However, playing together potentially limited the immersion that the children experienced in the game, as their attention was drawn to their interactions with each other. Hence, the strategic engagement may have been more pronounced because of the shared play.

Some comment should be made about gender. The children were chosen as they were keen to be involved and already experienced iPad users. As a very small study, it would be inappropriate to make assumptions about the children's gameplay based on their gender, and indeed, all four pairs acted in some ways that were stereotypical, and other ways that were not. Wes and Stephen, for example, were by far the most detailed in their careful engagement in the storyworld, which might not be seen as typical of boy behaviour, and Fred and Michael were not interested in the narrative storyworld at all, which might be less surprising. Similarly, whereas Saba and Molly had an affective response to the characters in the game, they could be competitive and non-collaborative in their play. Alice and Kirsty, whilst collaborative and engaged in their gameplay, seemed less immersed in the actual storyworld. Rather than assign particular gameplay traits to the children as typical, it is more useful to attempt to build up a complex picture of engagement, orientation and collaboration.

Fleer (2014) describes 'flickering' as a movement between play and reality, or in the case of digital games, the virtual and real worlds. Similarly, Mackey (2007: 141) draws on the idea of 'diegetic border play' to capture the movement of children within and without the storyworld. In fact, the children here seemed to be simultaneously present within the world of *Monument Valley*; above it in their 'direction' of its action (most notable in Saba's interactions); and outside it as they called on their schematic knowledge of other texts (in terms of genre) and knowledge about gaming and expectations of the mode. Additionally they were positioned as paired players, in a specific literacy event and situation (Hymes 1972). Mackey (2007) as well as Douglas and Haragdon (2000) reference notions of 'flow' (Csikszentmihalyi 2002) to describe the unconscious movement between states or stances.

Analysing children's engagement and immersion in diegetic worlds, considering their collaborations and building a picture of this complexity, is a reminder about the importance of the 'close-up' view of children's literacy activities and illuminates language and the co-construction of meaning in action. Analysing literacy practices, which may sit outside mainstream education, is essential in the continuing push at the boundaries of how literacy is conceived in school.

The sophisticated approaches children bring with them from their experiences outside school reinforce the need for changing previous conceptions of literacy. This study enabled both analyses, and adds another tiny piece to the ever-growing jigsaw of research about children's literacy practices in an ever-changing technological world.

Acknowledgements Many thanks to the United Kingdom Literacy Association (www.ukla.org) who funded this research.

References

Alexander, Robin. 2008. *Towards dialogic teaching: Rethinking classroom talk*, 4th ed. London: Dialogos.

Anderson, Richard. C., and P. David Pearson. 1984. A schema-theoretic view of basic processes in reading comprehension. In *Handbook of reading research,* eds. P. David Pearson, Rebecca Barr and Michael L. Kamil, 255–291. New York: Longman.

Barnes, Douglas, and Frankie Todd. 1995. *Communication and learning revisited: Making meaning through talk.* Portsmouth, NH: Boynton Cook Publishers.

Bassey, Michael. 1999. *Case study research in educational settings*. Buckingham: Oxford University Press.

Beavis, Catherine. 2013. Multiliteracies in the wild. In *Virtual literacies: Interactive spaces for children and young people*, ed. Guy Merchant, Julia Gillen, Jackie Marsh, and Julia Davies, 57–74. London: Routledge.

Benton, Michael. 1992. *Secondary worlds: Literature teaching and the visual arts*. Buckingham: Open University Press.

Black, Rebecca, and Stephanie Reich. 2013. A sociocultural approach to exploring virtual worlds. In *Virtual literacies: Interactive spaces for children and young people*, ed. Guy Merchant, Julia Gillen, Jackie Marsh, and Julia Davies, 27–40. London: Routledge.

Burnett, Cathy, and Guy Merchant. 2014. Points of view: Reconceptualising literacies through an exploration of adult and child interactions in a virtual world. *Journal of Research in Reading* 37 (1): 36–50.

Cairney, Trevor. 1990. Intertextuality: Infectious echoes from the past. *The Reading Teacher* 43 (7): 478–484.

Craft, Anna. 2000. *Creativity across the primary curriculum: Framing and developing practice*. London: Routledge.

Csikszentmihalyi, Mihaly. 2002. *Flow: The classic work on how to achieve happiness*, 2nd ed. London: Rider.

Douglas, Yellowlees, and Andrew Hargadon. 2000. The pleasure principle: Immersion, engagement, flow. In *Proceedings of the eleventh ACM on hypertext and hypermedia*, 153–160. New York: ACM.

Escher, Maurits, C. 1953. *Relativity* [Lithograph]. Washington: National Gallery of Art.

Fleer, Marilyn. 2014. *Theorising play in the early years*. Cambridge: Cambridge University Press.

Gee, James P. 2007. *What video games have to teach us about learning and literacy*, 2nd ed. Basingstoke: Palgrave Macmillan.

Gee, James P. 2008. *Social linguistics and literacies: Ideology in discourses*, 3rd ed. London: Routledge.

Gee, James P. 2015. *Unified discourse analysis: Language, reality, virtual worlds, and video games*. London: Routledge.

Gee, James P., and Judith L. Green. 1998. Discourse analysis, learning, and social practice: A methodological study. *Review of Research in Education* 23: 119–169.

Glaser, Barney, and Anslem Strauss. 1967. *The discovery of grounded theory: Strategies for qualitative research*. Hawthorne, N.Y: Aldine de Gruyter.

Hymes, Dell H. 1972. Models of interaction in language and social life. In *Directions in sociolinguistics: the ethnography of communication*, eds. John. J. Gumperz, and Dell H. Hymes, 35–71. New York: Holt, Rinehart and Winston.

Iser, Wolfgang. 1980. *The act of reading: A theory of aesthetic response*. Baltimore: Johns Hopkins University Press.

Littleton, Karen, and Neil Mercer. 2013. *Interthinking: Putting talk to work*. London: Routledge.

Lyle, Sue. 1993. An investigation into ways in which children 'talk themselves into meaning'. *Language and Education* 7 (3): 181–197.

Mackey, Margaret. 2007. *Literacies across media: Playing the text*, 2nd ed. London: Routledge.

Maine, Fiona. 2014. 'I wonder if they are going up or down': Children's co-constructive talk across the primary years. *Education 3-13* 42(3): 298–312.

Maine, Fiona. 2015. *Dialogic readers: Children talking and thinking together about visual texts*. London: Routledge.

Maybin, Janet. 1994. Children's voices: talk, knowledge and identity. In *Researching language and literacy in social contexts*, ed. David Graddol, Janet Maybin, and Barry Stierer, 131–150. Clevedon: Multilingual Matters.

Mercer, Neil. 2000. *Words and minds: How we use language to think together*. London: Routledge.

Mercer, Neil. 2005. Sociocultural discourse analysis: Analysing classroom talk as a social mode of thinking. *Journal of Applied Linguistics* 1 (2): 137–168.

Mercer, Neil. 2010. The analysis of classroom talk: Methods and methodologies. *British Journal of Educational Psychology* 80 (1): 1–14.

Mercer, Neil, and Karen Littleton. 2007. *Dialogue and the development of children's thinking: A sociocultural approach*. London: Routledge.

Mukherjee, Souvik. 2015. *Video games and storytelling: Reading games and playing books*. New York: Palgrave Macmillan.

Rojas-Drummond, Sylvia, Nancy Mazon, Manuel Fernandez, and Rupert Wegerif. 2006. Explicit reasoning, creativity and co-construction in primary school children's collaborative activities. *Thinking Skills and Creativity* 1 (2): 84–94.

Rosenblatt, Louise. M. 1994. *The reader, the text, the poem: The transactional theory of the literary work*. Carbondale, Ill: Southern Illinois University Press.

Salen, Katie, and Eric Zimmerman. 2004. *Rules of play: Game design fundamentals*. Cambridge MA: MIT Press.

Sipe, Lawrence. 2008. *Storytime: Young children's literary understanding in the classroom*. New York: Teachers College Press.

Soter, Anna O., Ian A. Wilkinson, P. Karen Murphy, Lucila Rudge, Kristin Reninger, and Margaret Edwards. 2008. What the discourse tells us: Talk and indicators of high-level comprehension. *International Journal of Educational Research* 47 (6): 372–391.

Urquhart, Cathy. 2013. *Grounded theory for qualitative research: A practical guide*. London: Sage Publications.

ustwo. 2015. Monument Valley: An iOS and Android game by ustwo. http://monumentvalleygame.com. Accessed 11 August 2016.

Wegerif, Rupert. 2011. Towards a dialogic theory of how children learn to think. *Thinking Skills and Creativity* 6 (3): 179–190.

Author Biography

Fiona Maine is a lecturer in literacy education at the University of Cambridge in the UK. Her research investigates the dialogic interactions of children as they make meaning together from a variety of text modes, and she explores the language of their critical and creative thinking as they collaborate. She supports teachers to develop their literacy practices, encouraging a broad notion of literacy that incorporates visual, moving image and digital modes of text, and highlights the possibilities afforded by working with non-verbal and ambiguous texts.

Chapter 14
Relational Methodologies for Mobile Literacies: Intra-action, Rhythm, and Atmosphere

Ty Hollett and Christian Ehret

Introduction

In our first collaborative research project, we wanted to explore how youths' literacy practices with mobile devices moved with them across their everyday lives, and in particular how those literacy practices were influenced in the context of formal schooling (see Ehret and Hollett 2013, 2014). We designed and co-instructed a 12-week digital media and learning class for fifth grade students called stem3686 at a charter school in the Southeastern US, and we focused the course on teaching students to make new media using iPods. The course involved a number of 'challenges' that facilitated mobile composition across the school: creating QR code-based audio narratives of wordless graphic novels; photo walks relaying fictional accounts of found objects; augmented reality stories about Flat Stanley and Stella's adventures throughout the school.

When we think back to stem3686, we miss Yvette, Adela, Tiana, and Louie and the place we made together. We are also struck by how assiduously we worked to 'capture students' interactions with their screens. Audio recordings of our research debriefs were filled with discussions about new apps that might let us screen capture activity on students' iPods. When that proved too difficult, or too partial, we considered applications that would transmit screen activity to a nearby laptop—another screen we knew we could record—while simultaneously video recording each student with a stationary camera. Finally, we dropped the idea of recording screens altogether, opting instead for head cameras that could help us see students'

T. Hollett (✉)
The Pennsylvania State University, Pennsylvania, USA
e-mail: tyler.hollett@gmail.com

C. Ehret
McGill University, Montreal, Canada
e-mail: christian.ehret@mcgill.ca

C. Burnett et al. (eds.), *The Case of the iPad*,
DOI 10.1007/978-981-10-4364-2_14

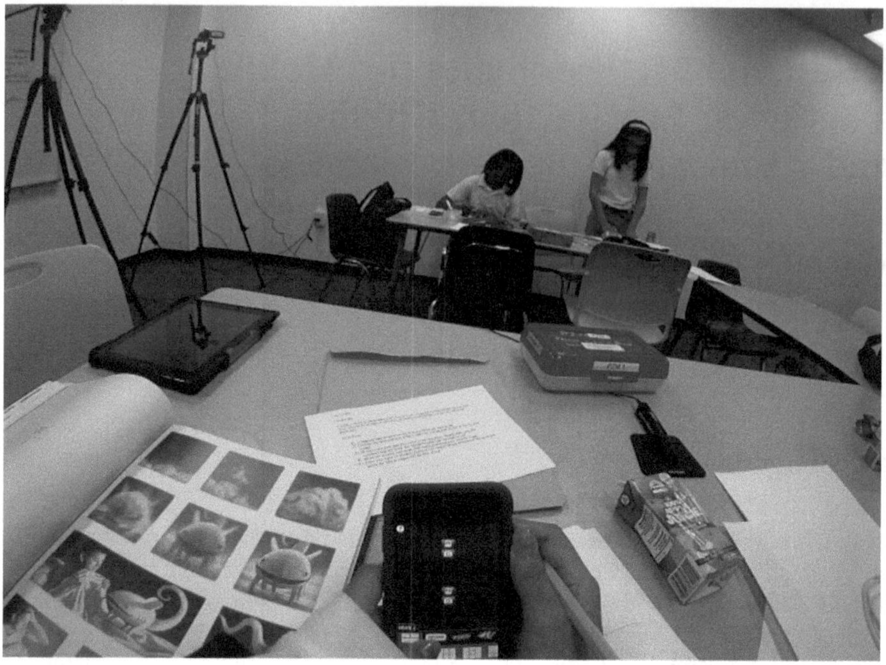

Fig. 14.1 Vantage point from Adela's head camera

interactions with their iPod screens—what apps students used, how they swiped, tapped, pinched, and rotated throughout their composition process (see Fig. 14.1).

It was never about the screen, though. In fact, what the head cameras helped us 'see' through students' perspectives was, no surprise, the school. But more than the material environment, we began to see the place that the school was for them, how they moved through place, and how place moved them. Through the head camera videos, through their digital videos, and through our experiences walking alongside our students, we experienced their continual remaking of their school as an everyday place: as they felt the atmosphere of an off-limits teacher workshop room, as they sensed creative potential in an electric outlet, as their feet clattered on tile. It was not the apps that deserved our analytic attention in this project. It was bodies' potential for meaning making, what bodies could do with mobile devices in this or that place, and how those potentials made place differently. And so we began to ask questions that continue to move us as researchers interested in mobile literacies: What can bodies do with mobile devices? How can bodies story and remake the everyday places of learning and schooling while they move with mobile devices? No number of GoPros can capture all that moving and making, all that feeling, whether head-mounted or not.

Moving Methodologies Forward

In this chapter, we illustrate methodologies we have developed since our overeager and misguided attempts to capture mobile literacies by focusing on students' interactions with apps, screens, and whatever-the-mobile device. The methodologies we demonstrate spring from a central theory of 'intra-action,' here described by Barad as distinct from 'interaction':

> The usual notion of interaction assumes that there are individual independently existing entities or agents that preexist their acting upon one another. By contrast, the notion of 'intra-action' queers the familiar sense of causality (where one or more causal agents precede and produce an effect), and more generally unsettles the metaphysics of individualism (the belief that there are individually constituted agents or entities, as well as times and places). (Barad 2012: 77)

Barad's agential realism, especially her theory of intra-action, has helped us to think about the experience of making new media beyond what is happening on screens alone, and to feel how those glassy, glossy screens are themselves only another part of the matter of new media making that is never simply directed by human actors, or human fingers touching and swiping (Ehret et al. 2016). Manning cogently describes the distorted perspective of agency that we forced ourselves into with head cameras: 'This is the problem with agency: It makes the subject the subject of the action. What if the act did not fully belong to us?' (Manning 2016: 16). What if the act of new media making did not fully belong to us?

Manning's posthuman proposition 'queers the familiar sense of causality' that has framed so much research on iPads in education, on mobile literacies, on literacies, on, well, most work in education research. And her proposition has moved us, the authors, beyond methodological perspectives that analyze subject-object relations: youth interacting with iPods to make new media out of an inert, material world. We have come to think about how place-iPod-genre-students-GoPros-researchers-and- intra-act to coproduce texts. Because youth are not separate or standing above the materials and places with which they make new media. Materials and places are not separate or standing above youth which *they* make new media. Place-youth-materials affect each other in making new media. There is not a subject, a prime mover, conducting the act. New media making is *of* the act, a relational unfolding among intra-actors, where agency is coproduced across bodies-materials as the act unfolds.

Moving methodologies forward, we have retrained ourselves, as intra-actors in the activities that we study, to attune to the movements of new media making in the act. Since our class with Yvette, Adela, Tiana, and Louie, we have been intra-actors in affective atmospheres of learning and care while playing Minecraft in a children's hospital (Hollett and Ehret 2015), and we have felt the rhythms of youth making a place for a learning and change in a library-based digital media and learning program (Ehret and Hollett 2016; Hollett and Ehret 2016). We use this chapter to illustrate the methodologies we have developed to know and express atmospheres and rhythms not because they are the only or primary foci that follow from propositions such as Manning's, but because they followed from propositions such as Manning's when, in our places of study, we opened ourselves to the proposition of intra-action, of posthumanism, of new media making in the act.

Moving Methodology from Interaction to Intra-action: The Case of the iPad in Education

We recognize that all this feels like a radical reorientation not only of methodology but of the privileged position of our own rationality. But for some time now scholarship outside of education research has wrestled with this reorientation, recognizing for instance the limits of human rationality and experience (Haraway 2013; Braidotti 2013). Radical as it may seem at first, consider all that is left out when we observe experience from the outside as something that human beings compose, as students act on their iPads to make something out of a world waiting for them to act upon it, when we see data though head cameras.

We do not situate a methodology of intra-action in contrast to the methodology (and methods) put forth by interaction analysis [IA] (Jordan and Henderson 1995). Instead, we build from guiding tenants of IA as an additional 'way forward' in terms of coming to know the so-called data of lived experience. Following Barad's distinction between interaction and intra-action, it is not our intention to reject interaction analytic methods, or necessarily to offer something completely new. Instead, like Barad, we 'renew ideas by turning them over and inside out, reading them deconstructively for aporias, and re-reading them through other ideas, queering their received meanings' (p. 34). Thus, as we move forward, we 'renew ideas' regarding IA, first by providing initial background for intra-action and then expanding that understanding through an explicit focus on rhythm and atmosphere.

Intra-action operates through an agential-realist ontology. 'Individuals,' Barad notes, 'only exist within phenomena…in their ongoing iteratively intra-acting reconfiguring.' (p. 77) Phenomena, literacies in the act, result from the entanglement of intra-acting agencies. In the act ourselves, we have evoked three key terms of intra-action: phenomena, entanglement, and agency. While IA might observe the interaction between humans in analytic 'hot spots,' intra-action follows the relational production of entangled phenomena. For instance, in an earlier intra-action analysis of the experiences featured below, we explored how a portion of the digital book trailer took shape within a stairwell of the students' middle school. Rather than using IA to analyze the ways in which, for example, student discourse and gesture partially facilitated the production of that specific scene, we questioned the various agencies that were at work in this emerging 'soundscape.' That is, we did not simply posit human 'bodies' as having agency; rather, we traced the entangled agencies of humans and nonhumans: students, shoes, floor tiles, walls, and energies that rose and fell as other students were moved to observe. As opposed to privileging the human bodies of students as having agency in the stairwell, we argued that agency was co-constituted in the intra-activity of bodies, materials, and place.

There are nuances to IA that are ripe for expansion, however, especially those emphasizing time, chronology and, especially, rhythm. Of rhythm, for example, Jordan and Henderson (1995) write:

> Many workplaces are tightly organized around more or less rigid schedules that impose repetitive activities. For example, at hub airports, one may find interaction in airlines operations rooms organized around complexes. The time during which a flock of connecting planes come in, exchange passengers and baggage, take on fuel and food, and take off again. During these complexes, activity in the operations room is highly energized, only to slow down to a more leisurely level in between (p. 63).

We wonder, for instance, how this room becomes 'highly energized.' On the one hand, through IA, we might think that the arrival of the planes leads to a sudden influx of baggage, which then leads to an increase in the tempo of workers and so on. Interaction, in short, seeks explanations of subject-object causality.

On the other hand, intra-action analysis may illuminate how charged atmospheric conditions result from entangled agencies producing the phenomenon. Workers are not predictable automatons, moving at a rapid pace because there is more baggage in need of sorting. Workers-baggage-departures are entangled: the physical bodies of co-workers are the luggage that needs to be lifted, the human baggage handlers, the concept of departing-on-time as pressured by a neoliberal atmosphere of market-driven realities. Place-materials, too, become entangled in this moment in the making—a flight from Vail, Colorado, one might assume, yields a different kind of luggage than that coming from Orlando, FL. And still more is entangled in this moment. The rhythm is in production with the time of day, the hours in a worker's shift (and how far into that shift they are), the size of plane, the weather on the ground and in other areas of the country that have led to this sudden influx of planes.

Project Background

Our illustration of rhythm and atmosphere below emerges from a 6-week study of youth production of a digital book trailer. Digital book trailers retain many characteristics of traditional book reports. For instance, trailer producers assume a persuasive and informed perspective, encouraging viewers to read the book. But digital trailers are also a visual-auditory experience, a narrative collage of film and soundtrack constructed by an invisible author to sell and tell a remixed film narrative. In the case featured here, five fifth grade students worked together to create a digital book trailer for the novel *Holes* (Sachar 2008): Domiana, Marcus, Ciera, Claudia, and Gerald. Students attended Heritage Middle School (HMS) in the Southeastern US, where they were selected by HMS English Language Arts teachers to work with two Reading Masters Candidates (RMCs), interning as part of their program at a local university, to create a sample book trailer over six, 2-h long sessions using a shared iPad that belonged to Karly. Students did not have access to iPads via HMS. The RMCs, Karly and Ginny helped students use the iPad to film video clips, to select images to help depict the landscape of the novel, to record sound effects, and finally, to edit the film using iMovie. The students took on, shared, adapted, and switched between various roles throughout the planning, enactment, and editing of the film trailer, such as director, actor, cinematographer, consume designer, etc. After completing their book trailer with the RMCs, the students would return to their class as production experts, acting in supportive roles for their classmates as the classmates, in turn, began their own digital book trailer project. Partly because our previous analysis of students' production process focused heavily on Domiana and Marcus, we reentered our data with an explicit focus on students who seemingly operated on the periphery of production: Gerald and Ciera. Seemingly on the periphery, these students are, of course, integral to the production of rhythm and atmosphere. And because agency not *in* any one person or thing, all bodies-materials are immanently responsible for the socio-material conditions that are productive of peripheries. Indeed, all bodies-materials are responsible for generating physical, conceptual, and affective boundaries that can be excluded across temporal scales of learning and making, from moment to moment, place to place. We reentered our data interested in how such peripheries are produced through the ongoing production of rhythms and atmospheres, because we are concerned that these affective dimensions of new media making are often overlooked in descriptions of inclusive digital literacies pedagogies. Understanding more about the production of rhythms and atmospheres in moments of digital literacies learning may therefore aid in feeling out, in the moment, how to move more youth in from the margins of ongoing activity.

Attempting to attune ourselves to the ongoing production of peripheries, we returned to our video data attempting to re-feel moments in which agencies became perceptively entangled in, what we have previously described as, felt focal moments (FFM) (Ehret et al. 2016; Hollett and Ehret 2014). FFMs, we have argued, are signaled by interruptions (Dawney 2013), or corporeal moments felt upon bodies, causing unexpected movements. Bodies, then, become 'site[s] of intensity through which feelings, textures, and resonances emerge' (p. 635). These moments disrupt the flow of experience as students produce with the iPad—but they also strike us—as researchers—interrupting the flow of our own analytic experience of our data. As Dawney writes:

> The researcher can, to a greater or lesser degree, respond and become attuned to these moments—make connections, argue for their significance, become self-consciously materialist through a reflexive and ongoing attention to the way in which philosophy and life can be thought and performed together. (Dawney 2013: 635)

By targeting felt focal moments, we make what Barad calls an agential cut. Agential cuts, she writes, 'enact a local resolution within the phenomenon.' We stop experience in order to attempt sense-making. Therefore, first identifying FFMs, we make an agential cut; then, we work to disentangle the various elements that are intra-acting, not to separate them out and parse them, but to try and understand the relations among them in composing the act which is part of the phenomena-in-the-making. Here, the phenomenon is new media making. Thus, as Barad writes: 'Cuts cut things together and apart' (2007: 178).

In particular, we were attuned to moments in which activity began to take on a new tempo, a flurry of moving bodies, hands, materials, and digital objects. But, as noted above, these intra-actions also produced affective boundaries: as things began to pick up speed for some, they also began to slow and stall for others. Thus, through the following accounts of rhythm and atmosphere, respectively, we question, first, how social rhythms were produced during the book trailer's production and, second, how an affective atmosphere emerged throughout the production of the digital book trailer, and we focus on how these rhythms and atmospheres were productive of excluding, affective peripheries.

Rhythms and Atmospheres of New Media Making with iPads

Rhythm

Lefebvre's (1991) study of the everyday dynamics of spatial encounters, his rhythmanalysis, informs our explorations of the rhythmic mobilities produced through new media making with mobile devices, like the iPad. The world, for Lefebvre, produces a multiplicity of rhythms in the flow of relations between things, places, bodies and acts—(McCormack 2013: 41). Rhythmanalysis necessitates cultivating a heightened awareness of—an attunement to the affects of—the ongoing rhythms of the everyday. The rhythmanalyst think-feels both with and through her body. Her aim is to 'mobilize the body as a set of rhythmic relations through which the spatiotemporal turbulence of everyday life registers as so many intensities of feeling' (McCormack 2013: 32). While remembering that rhythm is fungible and immanent to the unfolding of singular acts, we have found the following three characteristics of rhythm especially useful for attuning to its production in the becoming of literacy-in-the-act with iPads.

1. **Rhythms are harmonious as often as dissonant**. Various scales, pulses, and durations of rhythms may 'clash or harmonize, producing reliable moments of regularity or less consistence variance' (Edensor and Holloway 2008: 84). Lefebvre identifies both eurhythmia and arrhythmia as potential rhythms in the city, with the former signaling a kind of harmony and the latter a kind of dissonance. The various tempos and intensities of rhythms produce 'modulations of unpredictability and disruption' which, in turn, are felt as 'polyrhythmia, eurythmic synchronicity, or arrhythmia' (Edensor and Holloway 2008: 84).

2. **Rhythms are multiscalar**. Rhythms range from the scale of the body to that of institutions, regions, nations, and more. For instance, rhythm is always linked to 'such and such a place, to its place, be that the heart, the fluttering of the eyelids, the movement of a street or the tempo of a waltz' (Lefebvre 2004: 89). In any given space, the rhythms of disparate social actors intersect: suburbanites, shopkeepers, tourists, dog-walkers, police officers, school children, but so do those of seasons, for example, as well as neoliberal, market-driven entities.
3. **Rhythms affect the tonality of the act unfolding, and can affect esthetic judgment of the act**. Even before Lefebvre, artists and philosophers alike drew on rhythm to understand the artistic experience. Dewey (1934), for example, became enamored with rhythm. Rhythm, for Dewey, is central to the artistic experience: 'the first characteristic of the environing world that makes possible the existence of artistic form is rhythm. There is rhythm in nature before poetry, painting, architecture and music exist' (p. 147). Dewey's rhythm served as a counter to 'uniformly even flow, with no variations of intensity or speed' (p. 158). Thus, for Dewey, rhythm was critical to the experience of artistic production. Rhythm factored heavily into the 'building up of an integral experience out of the interaction of organic and environment conditions and energies' (p. 70). In the methodological illustration that follows, we attune ourselves not to the 'interaction' as Dewey writes, 'between organic and environment conditions and energies' but to the intra-actions between bodies—human and nonhuman—entangled in emergent rhythms of new media making.
4. **Touch, tap, friction, and flow: from micro to macro-rhythms**. Our focus on rhythm begins, incidentally, with friction, especially the rhythms produced as users intra-act with mobile devices. Fors (2015) describes mundane friction as 'the friction caused by habitually touching, rubbing, clicking, pinching through media technologies' (p. 1). Mundane frictions are an entry point to the rhythms of digital production—that digital production, especially with mobile devices, like iPads, is far from a visual, ocular-centric production: digital production is an emergent, form-taking process in which sensing, feeling, and touching are deeply integrated into the experience.

Mundane frictions are also rhythmic, however. Friction, for instance, changes the pace of production; it gradually slows down burgeoning velocity. These mundane frictions, we argue, foster the micro-rhythms of collaborative production around iPads. In the following, we first follow the mundane frictions of youth collaborative production by tracing those frictions that emerge as they select specific images for their book trailer. Then, we turn to the ways in which those micro-rhythms are entangled with macro-rhythms of embodied flows, or the fluid movements of students around the iPad.

We begin with this scene (Fig. 14.2). Domiana, Marcus, and Gerald work together at the iPad, selecting, inserting, and resizing images—including snakes, cacti, and other desert shots—that they can place in their digital book trailer. The students' energy is rhythmic, punctuated by the narrative possibility of certain

Fig. 14.2 Domiana, Marcus and Gerald choose and orient images together

images—the snake looks menacing (swipe to next image) the sunset looks beautiful. Mundane frictions, and the subtle manipulations produced by them, further fuel this rhythm.

Importantly, part of this energy is generated by the rhythmic movements of hands. Over a period of 20 min, hands produce mundane frictions as they tap, swipe, and pinch possibilities. These micro-rhythms consist of action and pause, of flurries of movement and lulls of reflection. That is, brief pauses emerge in between pinches and taps, short moments in which Domiana, Marcus, and Gerald examine the image and choose either to (1) select it and manipulate it or (2) jettison it in favor of another image. Figure 14.3, for example, follows the movements of Domiana's hands over the iPad as the group selects and manipulates an image.

Domiana's initial hand movements toward the iPad (1) signify a shift in the rhythm that is becoming among the students. Marcus senses this burgeoning energy, pulling his hand back, making way for Domiana's to enter (2), especially as her fingers begin to spread (3) in preparation to pinch (4). After her first manipulation, Domiana pulls back slightly (6–7), and reorients her fingers before pinching the screen one more time (8–9). This is the micro-rhythm of new media making. Fingers touch, tap, and pinch as they feel out how their images can contribute to the story they want to tell. These mundane frictions are rapid, subtly slowing down the process before it speeds up again as the group moves forward and on to a new image and a new rhythm.

Still, we wonder about the other agentive elements entangled in this rhythmic production. What about the app that houses the images? How easy is it for a finger to manipulate images? To change their shape, size, and even texture? How might students' bodies respond to forms of 'digital fatigue' that they may encounter when

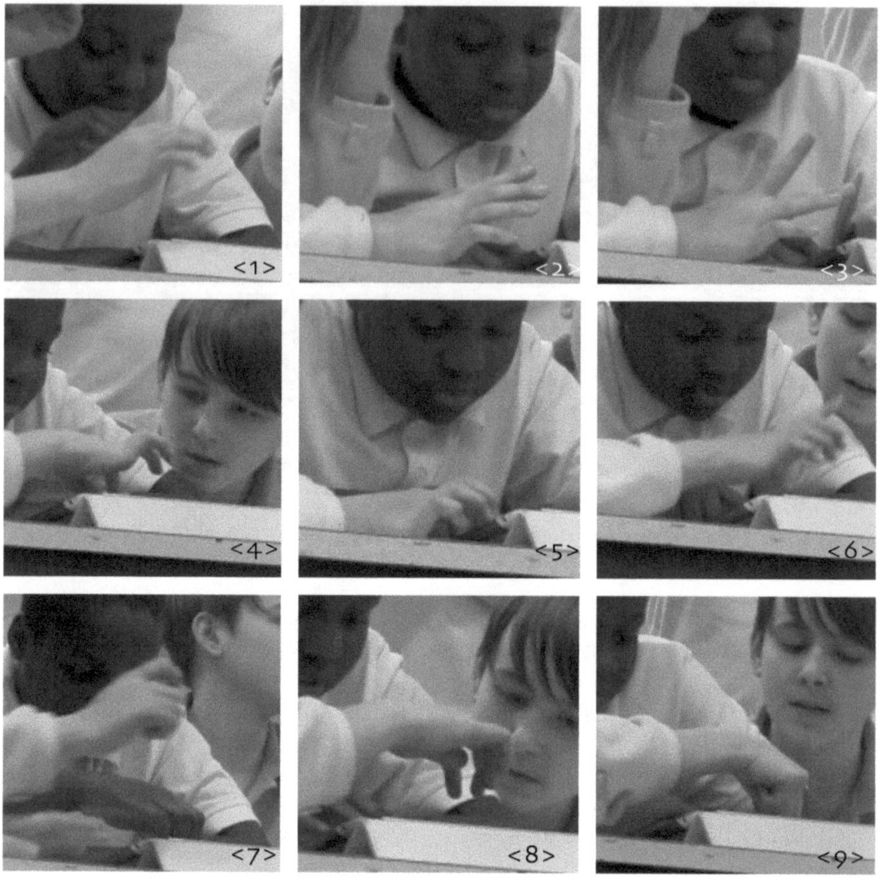

Fig. 14.3 Micro-rhythms of Domiana as she manipulates images

having to navigate within and beyond numerous apps? How is this 'fatigue' potentially felt by collaborators? How does this emergent feeling fuel—or syphon—the energy of the group?

Micro-rhythms do not exist by themselves, however. The rhythms of mundane frictions, and their concomitant movements of digital artefacts or through digital space, reverberate outward. These movements, in turn, affect the physical movements of others who are also copresent in the collaborative process of new media making with the iPad. In the above illustration, for example, Marcus pulls his hand back as Domiana begins to reach forward with her own. Marcus and Domiana fall into embodied rhythm with one another, feeling and sensing each other's movements while they manipulate images. They rhythmically flow toward, and away from, the iPad.

Embodied flows, we argue, denote the macro-rhythms at work as students collaboratively work around iPads. Bodies, becoming together in the act of new media making, affect one another—they move one another. That is, the affective intensities generated throughout making with new media—emanating from the entanglement of physical body and digital artefact—push and pull students to-and-from the iPad. In Fig. 14.4, for example, Domiana, Arthur, and Gerald all enter into an embodied flow with one another.

Their bodies enter into a kind of rhythmic dance, akin to Lefebvre's 'tempo of a waltz.' Domiana leans forward, hands pinching, as described above (1–2). Upon touching the iPad, Domiana then swings backwards, making room for Marcus to contemplate possibilities in response (3). Gerald, too, feels out (of) this rhythm, waiting for an opportunity move in toward the iPad. As Marcus leans back, and shifts his attention toward Karly, the RMC, Gerald seizes the opportunity to

Fig. 14.4 Embodied flows of Domiana, Marcus, Gerald and Ciera

contribute (4). He slightly shifts the iPad to give himself a better view before testing possible images. Domiana and Marcus both return to the iPad. Domiana orients herself to pinch the iPad screen while Gerald finishes his contribution (5).

Still there are other participants feeling out this rhythm. Karly observes over the shoulders of the students. Most notably, she feels and senses the rhythm that the students have fallen into—Marcus, Domiana, and Gerald all moving together. Karly, however, recognizes that Ciera has not entered into this embodied flow. Karly interrupts the rhythm that the students have established, by inserting herself between them and pushing the iPad toward Ciera (6).

These macro-rhythms, these embodied flows, are not separate from the aforementioned micro-rhythms. The touches, taps, pinches, and swipes produced through mundane frictions draw attention, primarily, to the subtle ways in which movement through digital space affects movement in physical space. This is real virtual intra-action. That is, our intra-active methodology does not simply orient us to the movements of hands, but attunes us to the entanglement of hands + digital images + physical bodies. Collaborative work around iPads, especially in settings that may not have a device for each student, are largely rhythmic productions. Students fall into—and out of—rhythm with one another. New media making, in the case of the digital book trailer's production, is less a visual enactment of seeing, choosing, and selecting specific images. Rather it is an emergent, form-taking production that brings together the real virtual entanglement of digital and physical bodies moving, and being moved by, students in rhythm with one another.

Atmosphere

Rhythms emerging in the act contribute to the continuous production of atmosphere. Consider the excitement-in-motion as Marcus, Domiana, and Gerald swipe through images with spikes in speed and stops for laughter and jest. It does not have a name yet, a distinguishing quality that students might recognize verbally as excitement. But something's happening, something's almost coming together. The pace quickens, and voices gain in tempo even when hands are still. Smiles smile. Eyes dart, shimmer, anticipate. Space begins to feel like *something*. Geographers and anthropologists, especially, have described how social space takes on a feeling, an atmosphere, in specific places ranging from annual community celebrations like the Blackpool Illuminations on the British seaside (Edensor 2012) to the home (Pink and Mackley 2016). Beyond any one place, cultural geographers have also described countries' contingent, collective atmospheres of nationalism, as in England during the London 2012 Olympic Games (Stephens 2016), or international atmospheres of neoliberalism as they move and morph at local and global scales (Anderson 2015). While remembering that atmospheres are also immanent to the unfolding of acts-in-the-making, we have found the following three characteristics of atmospheres especially useful for attuning to their production in the becoming of new media making with iPads.

1. **Atmospheres emerge as the concrescence of multisensory experience, movement, and place**. Pink and Mackley (2016) described how atmospheres emerge through the everyday rhythms and routines of home life, and are 'ongoingly co-constituted through flows of digital media and their affordances, people and other things and processes' (p. 358). In their study of the Ashton family, Pink and Mackley described Barbara's multisensory experience of her home, where she lived with her two children, her husband and their dog, 'feeling right:'

   > Because the sound of the TV, or of streamed YouTube videos would spill out of the rooms where they were used, Barbara, who was likely to be in the kitchen, could follow where people were and what they were doing…Their sounds contributed to the sensory, emotional and affective elements of the atmosphere of home. (p. 360)

   Through the everyday rhythms of home life that include digital media, atmospheres emerge from, and are materially grounded in, moving, multisensory experience. Family members' care for each other, and the shared sense of place 'feeling right,' is a relational experience of bodies' emergent capacities to move and be moved. Imagine these emergent capacities through Barbara sensing her children's movements and feeling potentials for their care, including moving to them if the soundscape shifts unexpectedly with laughter, a crash, quiet. The socio-material production of atmosphere is, in this instance, an emergent, affective attunement to place that is relational to the present and to histories of everyday rhythms.
2. **Atmospheres are experienced differently among different groups**. Although place holds atmospheric resonances related to routine rhythms, experiencing the atmospheres of place and event are contingent and perspectival. Edensor (2015) described how a Manchester City football game is experienced differently by aficionados than by newcomers. He further described how the intensifying commercialization of football on a national scale affected aficionados' and newcomers' relations with each other and therefore the coproduction of an emergent atmospheric experience of the event, a Premier League football match. Pink and Mackley (2016) argued that with such events, 'the analytical task of the researcher is not to ask if an atmosphere was generated, but rather to ask what it meant for a certain group of people' (p. 353). What does the atmosphere mean for our students on the periphery of new media making with iPads?
3. **Atmospheres are more-than-human productions**. Imagining how different groups experience and coproduce atmospheres requires admitting the agency of things. Things, like balloons, affect and are affected by circumstantial atmospheres, and circumstantial atmospheres are 'inflected by the properties of those things and by their capacities to move and be moved in different ways' (McCormack 2014: 607). For instance, consider the mundane reiterative practices of schooling in conjunction with the materiality of iPads. The iPad app momentarily locks up, and the iPad's materiality asserts itself into the production of frustrating feelings that become contagious, that become a feeling in the

air, a feeling that a teacher might mobilize herself in response to before saying to herself, 'these students are getting off track'; the iPad restarts itself and allows the flow of production to continue; teachers and students feel again an enthusiasm for the new media projects developing.

[Yawn]: Boring Atmospheres on the Periphery of Intermittent Excitement. In illustrating these characteristics of atmospheres, we contribute to the continued and necessary complication of numerous and pervasive popular assumptions related to technology in education, here specifically that iPads lead to automatic student excitement and engagement in project-based learning. To do so, we experiment with addressing the reader in the second person, attempting to invite you into the felt atmosphere we attempt to describe on the page.

If you could hear it while reading this chapter, you would feel uninspired by the squeaky overhead fan in the auditorium where our students made their book trailer. When no one was trying to talk over it during the episode describe above, when human voices were absent, the fan moved and infused the air with the feeling of an abandoned factory. A hybrid social space, the auditorium resisted the feeling of a factory, though: one day a place for special assembly, the next a place for jazz band practice, the next a place for an evening play performance. Today, it is a free place for researchers and RMCs to walk students to while their friends are still in class. So, there is perhaps a feeling of exceptionality that moves students to joke around, and even strut a bit, on the way to the auditorium. If only that fan would be more festive.

Our methodology orients us to the movements of bodies and how the capacities for those movements become in relation to a place for new media making not-yet made, not yet inviting of familiar social rhythms like, for example, the Ashton's home as described by Pink and Mackley. One entry point to understanding the place it is becoming, the place for new media making or not, is to ask: What does the atmosphere feel like as the concrescence of multisensory experience, movement, and place? There is not a right way for this not-yet-place to feel, however, so how is the place becoming as an experience of different groups? How are bodies beyond the human, and beyond the fan, affecting the feeling in the air?

A look back to Fig. 14.4 might remind you how small a single iPad becomes when three students collaborate on editing and producing a trailer. The iPad's diminutiveness asks you to turn it side to side so each of the three students can see—'This picture! Let's use this one!'—but it compels Karly, the RMC, more than it does Marcus and Domiana, who are exclaiming over the fan. Gerald, head in hand, is softer with his words and, as if wincing at the overexcitement too close to him, glances left at Ciera, head on arm on table, only to wince again at her exclusion. We wince with you and with Gerald. Exclusion feels. But the periphery in which Ceria is becoming bored is not the effect of Marcus and Domiana's excitement. When they realize her exclusion they become still and quiet for a moment, as if feeling awkwardness in the air, feeling in the air again the off-kilter-not-yet-in-place-in-the-making. Rhythmic flows of *not* coalesced into an atmosphere that feels like something *together*. Together and apart from the Ciera becomes bored, lulled by the fan, the iPad refusing to let her see. And she modulates the moment's tone in relation to the fan, the not yet place, the sideways glances, Gerald's acknowledgements and his becoming bored with her.

Although atmospheres are contagious, they are also contingent. In emergent relations, excitement in the air lulls when affected by a quick glance over at an atmosphere of disinterest and exclusion, evinced in Ciera's body. Boredom and excitement are equally valid perspectives, but each experience informs, reciprocally, the other, the atmosphere. A methodological perspective that opens questions around atmosphere is important analytically, as well as pedagogically, for feeling the peripheries of new media making in the moment. How can pedagogical attunement to atmospheres aid in adjusting them, in the moment, in making a place for making that *feels* more inclusive?

Relational Methodologies for Mobile Literacies: Moving Forward with the Past

> What is it…that makes us so certain that the act is volitionally directed by a human subject? What is it that gives us the strong sense that the act's effort belongs to us? (Manning 2016: 16).

Relational methodologies do not discount human agency; they are more fully attuned to agency becoming among the relations of multiple, material intra-actors. In this chapter, we have attempted to tell the story of our own coming to terms with the overly 'strong sense that the act's effort belongs to us.' No Ty, No Christian, the act cannot be 'captured' through any one perspective, through human eyes, through head cameras. But as young researchers the lure of scientism, of doing a particular brand of social science that positions human rationality above and over the world, was too much. But trying to push one another beyond ourselves, we have made efforts to expand our methodological orientations, especially as we continue to explore mobile literacies and move alongside youth, who move and make with mobile devices. Feeling-thinking through methodologies of intra-action has so far sustained our desire to push ourselves beyond the ego seemingly sedimented in our species, that the act is ours alone.

Just after our class with Yvette, Adela, Tiana, and Louie, we had the opportunity to work with youth making, playing, and creating with digital media in a children's hospital (Hollett and Ehret 2015). While playing *Minecraft* with one of these youth, Bean, we pushed each other to focus less on the screen where the game seemingly unfolded and to attune more to the felt-relations emerging in the act, on the affects moving bodies—digital and physical, material, and immaterial. We attuned ourselves, for instance, to how relaxed human bodies, lounging on bean bag chairs, resonated with one another, collectively producing an affective atmosphere of fear as digital zombies + humming the *Jaws* theme + lights off + AHHHHHHHHHHH! YOUJUSTDIED became entangled with one another.

Moving with the many bodies entangled with one another led us to also consider the rhythmic qualities of learning and literacy. Through studies of youth civic engagement when playing *Minecraft,* we explored the affectively charged ways of being in social flow with one another that emerge—and cohere—during gameplay (e.g., Hollett and Ehret 2016). We felt the emergence of social textures through rhythmic elements, like pulsation, or energetic spikes and lulls; reciprocation, or affectively charged 'call and response' among participants; and oscillation, or participants' repeated expansion and contraction from a unique location. Moving with these rhythms led us through the emergence of civic engagement, such as caring for collaborators and their *Minecraft* builds, and for the socially-just aims shared among the group and across build sites.

Across a range of research experiences, we have continued to return to the *places of learning and literacies* that have been produced through the entanglement of people, things, feelings, and more. We have observed—and felt—as places of learning and literacies have come together, as they have risked falling apart, and as they have held together over time (Ehret and Hollett 2016). Moreover, atmospheres and rhythm are essential affective dimensions of making place, and make new media *with* place as we continually remake place. Our shift from interaction to intra-action signals the inextricable relationship between place and the kinds of new media making that are possible with mobile technologies, like iPads.

It is not enough to say that literacy is material. Through our illustrations, we attune ourselves to the rhythms and atmospheres produced when students and things and materials and environmental factors *and* became together. Atmospheres and rhythm are essential affective dimensions of making place, and make new media *with* place as we continually remake place. We wonder what kind of place we could have made with Domiana, Marcus, Ciera, Claudia, and Gerald at Heritage had we stayed with them, imagined with them, and created with them in that place for a longer period of time? What stories could we have unearthed together? Instead, rather than producing a place, one that dissolved boundaries, one that generated a feeling of being in this moment together, we produced a digital book trailer (for the students) a research project (for us), in which we entered and exited after a pre-ordained period of time. Ultimately, if we are successful as education researchers, then we will have made a place alongside our participants. A place we can miss like that stem3686. A place where stories are still written on the (digital) walls.

References

Anderson, Ben. 2015. Neoliberal affects. *Progress in Human Geography.*

Barad, Karen. 2007. *Meeting the universe halfway: Quantum physics and the entanglement of matter and meaning*. Duke University Press.

Barad, Karen. 2012. Intra-actions: An interview with Karen Barad/Interviewer: Kleinmann, Adam. *Mousse Magazine* 32: 76–81.

Braidotti, Rosi. 2013. *The posthuman*. London: Wiley.
Dawney, Liela. 2013. The interruption: Investigating subjectivation and affect. *Environment and Planning D: Society and Space* 31 (4): 628–644.
Dewey, John. 1934. *Art as experience*. New York: Penguin.
Edensor, Tim, and Julian Holloway. 2008. Rhythmanalysing the coach tour: The ring of Kerry, Ireland. *Transactions of the Institute of British Geographers* 33 (4): 483–501.
Edensor, Tim. 2012. Illuminated atmospheres: Anticipating and reproducing the flow of affective experience in Blackpool. *Environment and Planning D: Society and Space* 30 (6): 1103–1122.
Edensor, Tim. 2015. Producing atmospheres at the match: Fan cultures, commercialisation and mood management in English football. *Emotion, Space and Society 15*: 82–89.
Ehret, Christian, and Ty Hollett. 2013. (Re)placing school: Fifth-graders' counter-mobilities while composing with mobile devices in a digital media enrichment class. *Journal of Adolescent & Adult Literacy* 57 (2): 110–119.
Ehret, Christian, and Ty Hollett. 2014. Embodied composition in real virtualities: Adolescents' literacy practices and felt experiences moving with digital, mobile devices in school. *Research in the Teaching of English* 48 (4): 428–452.
Ehret, Christian, and Ty Hollett. 2016. Affective dimensions of participatory design research in informal learning environments: Placemaking, belonging, and correspondence. *Cognition and Instruction* 34 (3): 250–258.
Ehret, Christian, Ty Hollett and Robin Jocius. 2016. The matter of new media making: An intra-action analysis of adolescents making a digital book trailer. *Journal of Literacy Research* 48 (3): 346–377.
Fors, Vaike. 2015. Sensory experiences of digital photo-sharing: 'Mundane frictions' and emerging learning strategies. *Journal of Aesthetics & Culture* 7.
Haraway, Donna. 2013. *Simians, cyborgs, and women: The reinvention of nature*. Routledge: Abingdon.
Hollett, Ty, and Christian Ehret. 2015. Bean's World: (Mine)crafting affective atmospheres for gameplay, learning and care in a children's hospital. *New Media & Society* 17 (11): 1849–1866.
Hollett, Ty and Christian Ehret. 2016. Civic rhythms in a media-rich, informal learning program. *Learning, Media and Technology*. Online before print.
Jordan, Brigitte, and A. Austin Henderson. 1995. Interaction analysis: Foundations and practice. *The Journal of the Learning Sciences* 4 (1): 39–103.
Lefebvre, Henri. 1991. *The production of space*. Oxford: Blackwell.
Lefebvre, Henri. 2004. *Rhythmanalysis: Space, time and everyday life*. London: Continnum.
Manning, Erin. 2016. *The minor gesture*. Durham, NC: Duke University Press.
McCormack, Derrick. 2013. *Refrains for moving bodies: Experience and experiment in affective spaces*. Durham, NC: Duke University Press.
McCormack, Derrick. 2014. Atmospheric things and circumstantial excursions. *Cultural Geographies* 21 (4): 605–625.
Pink, Sarah, and Kerstin Leder Mackley. 2016. Moving, making and atmosphere: Routines of home as sites for mundane improvisation. *Mobilities* 11 (2): 171–187.
Sachar, Louis. (2008). *Holes*. Macmillan: New York.
Stephens, Closs Angaharad. 2016. The affective atmospheres of nationalism. *Cultural Geographies* 23 (2): 181–198.

Author Biographies

Ty Hollett is an Assistant Professor at the Pennsylvania State University. He studies youth learning and literacies across formal, informal, and not-school settings in order to design equitable learning settings, opportunities, and arrangements for all youth.

Christian Ehret is an Assistant Professor at McGill University in Montréal. He investigates affective dimensions of learning, literacies, and digital culture through anthropological modes of inquiry across schools, communities, and children's hospitals. He recently received a 2016 Promising Researcher Award from the National Council of Teachers of English (NCTE) for his fictocritical exploration of writing and learning alongside youth in a children's hospital.

Chapter 15
Hands, Fingers and iPads

Guy Merchant

Introduction

Tablets buried in alluvial silt beneath the City of London attest to the long history of human entanglement with literacy and its technologies of production and consumption, indeed, recent archaeology pushes back the history of literacy in Roman Britain to the first century CE with the discovery of over four hundred such tablets, many traced with messages hinting at the personal lives of Londoners with their European connections. These tablets are described as being 'roughly the size of the modern iPad' (Smith 2016) portable enough to be a popular writing technology, and add to a catalogue that chronicles facets of everyday life—birthday party invitations, slave exchanges, family correspondence, business transactions and much more (see for example: CSAD 2003). The resurgence of tablets, roughly two thousand years later, is of course the result of many different influences including, amongst other things, the development of the silicon chip, glass with 'projected capacitance' for touchscreens, the availability of lightweight aluminium, small rechargeable battery cells and so on—not to mention the sophisticated transnational supply and distribution networks of companies like Apple—that, and our seemingly insatiable appetite for new gadgets.

Contemporary tablets are a far cry from those thought to be fashioned from recycled barrel staves filled with soot-stained beeswax. Technology has moved on; but yet there is still something striking in this very brief backward glance at the tablets of antiquity. It is this: tablets are made to be held, to be carried, to be transported from a to b. And not only this, they are designed to carry messages so that their users can create and display them; in short the generic description, mobile communication device, is quite fitting. Take the iPad Mini 4—only fractionally

G. Merchant (✉)
Sheffield Hallam University, Sheffield, UK
e-mail: g.h.merchant@shu.ac.uk

C. Burnett et al. (eds.), *The Case of the iPad*,
DOI 10.1007/978-981-10-4364-2_15

larger than the Roman tablet so carefully described by Tomlin (2004), although it is probably a little lighter; according to the manufacturer it puts 'uncompromising performance and potential in your hand' (Apple 2016), making it a handy device to own.

It is this notion of *handiness* that forms the initial focus of the current chapter; the handiness that connects the use of tablets new and old with the day-to-day business of literacy. I start, therefore, with an exploration of current literature on the significance of the human hand as a way of beginning to think about handiness, before turning to the subject of early literacy and what happens—or what might happen, when young children get hold of tablets in their early encounters with touchscreen technology. In doing this I attempt to come to an understanding of how handling tablets is part of the dense weave of growing up in social contexts that are now infused with new technology—technology with a reach and significance far wider than the manual dexterity required to operate them.

Handy Devices

They slide into your pocket, or disappear into the dark recesses of your bag, today's tablets may be slippery objects, but one thing that remains fairly constant in studies of mobile literacies is the 'new' work of hands and fingers. For example, Rowsell (2014) draws attention to gesture and touch; physical actions have been described (Crescenzi et al. 2014), holding and tapping have been examined (Merchant 2014); and Potter and Bryer (2017) develop the idea of 'finger flowment'. These studies sit alongside a growing interest in socio-materialism, the relationship between material and discursive practices (Lenz-Taguchi 2010; Kuby et al. 2015) and the ways in which they are imbricated in literacy in general, and early literacy learning in particular. From this perspective the co-mingling of things, bodies and semiotic resources might constitute a way of telling the history of literacy and, notwithstanding the fact that this privileges the able-bodied, it would be a history dominated by the work of the hands. As a basis for reflecting on what this might look like in the study of touchscreen tablets in early literacy, I turn now to two landmark studies of the hand, as a way of grounding this notion of handiness.

First, in the work of the neurologist Wilson (1998), we have a thorough exploration of what the hand does, the bone structure and muscular attachments that enable rotation, different intensities of gripping, holding, throwing and all the rest. Wilson shows that in precision movement, the eye works alongside the hand, and in a section that is surely of interest to literacy scholars, he focuses on the precision grips used in the manipulation of small tools—what he calls the 'writing/drawing cluster' (p. 158). Referencing the French psychologist Guiard, he notes how we use *both* hands in print literacy practices:

> Guiard showed that the nondominant hand plays a complementary, though largely covert, role by continuously repositioning the paper in anticipation of pen movement.
>
> (Wilson 1998: 159)

Of course a similar coordination of hands is also important in book reading, typing and text messaging. Although Wilson's central thesis about the hand-thought-language nexus and its origins in evolutionary biology are by nature speculative, he provides us with important insights into the anatomy of handiness and the role of hands in our experience of the body in context. Literacies, whether they involve the action of a stylus on wax, keyboard strokes, or the turning of a page all privilege manual dexterity.

Second, there is Tallis's philosophical anthropology of the hand (2003). Tallis sees the hand as the principal way in which consciousness extends out into the world, choosing what to grasp hold of, and of course what to manipulate or control. It is thus depicted as the leading edge of human agency. The pithy claim that 'the hand is an organ of cognition' (p. 28) is key to Tallis's thinking and one he uses to advance a unidirectional model. Human consciousness is central, and the hand, as its willing servant, operates at the interface between consciousness and the world. Tallis's study is something of a celebration of human exceptionalism—yet, however much this may be out of step with the current mood of posthumanism, his exploration of our dexterity is pertinent because it concerns the relationship between the brain and the hand. Although notions of feedback are hinted at by Tallis, this model is far-removed from the complex world of agential realism (Barad 2007) in which material and discursive, human and non-human forces act alongside natural and cultural phenomena. Still the fact remains, that this is another account that draws our attention to the precision and skill that is at our fingertips, that constitutes *handiness*—the sort of handiness that is crucial in holding a text, more or less at arm's length, navigating one's way through it, or indeed writing it oneself.

It should be fairly clear from this, that although the study of literacies is a wide and diverse enterprise, there is something central about the sort of *engaged material consciousness* (Sennett 2009) that involves, or arises from, careful co-ordination of hand and eye movement. Mackey (2016a) vividly illustrates this when she writes about the ways in which the hands connected literacy objects with the environment in her own literacy learning (for a fuller account see Mackey 2016b). This is not about any old hand–eye movement, however—precision matters—and of course that precision has to relate to what we might call an *inscription device*.[1] Herein lies an important difference between writing with pen and paper, or using a stylus and tablet, between reading a paperback or from a Kindle: that is the difference between the material affordances of the inscription device in question.

[1]In his exploration of the development of writing Harris argues that the 'presentation of writing most commonly depends on an artefact deliberately prepared for that purpose.' (2001, p. 86). Here, I use the term inscription device rather than artefact because it offers a little more specificity, but the basic definition still holds.

There is a subtle interplay, then, between materiality and literacy. It is not that literacy is anterior to technologies of inscription, that literacy is somehow waiting for the 'appearance of a suitable technology' (Harris 2001: 87); they develop together.[2] The popularity of the hashtag and its use on Twitter is a good contemporary example of this—it was handy to use a keyboard symbol to cross-reference tweets although it was not built into the design, but the hashtag was rapidly adopted by users, and it is now an established tweeting convention. A slightly different example is the use of the emoji. It would simply be impractical to use such a range of symbols alongside alphabetic writing on a wax tablet, or even with pencil and paper, but the menu-based selection which many of us are now accustomed to, makes it possible, with a quick swipe and a tap, to include our chosen emojis in rapid message exchange. Again, new work for the hands and fingers is required.

Thinking about handiness raises further questions, too. For instance, from an experiential point of view, ideas may emerge, whole sentences seem to write themselves as they move through our hands and fingers. Dexterity and touch recede into the background of consciousness. Rather like the example of the blind man's cane which 'has ceased to be an object for him' (Merleau-Ponty 2014: 144) we are in these moments, directly connected with meaning. Of course more unfamiliar or less-practised operations, like those required for a screenshot, interrupt this experience since they demand more focused attention on the hands. Perhaps this is why one may imagine that text is 'stuck' on the fingers when cut-and-pasting on a touchscreen. Fleeting impressions like these alert us to the often hidden work of the hands in everyday literacy.

It follows from all this that *part* of learning to be literate must be concerned with handling inscription devices, whether this is achieved through explicit instruction or informal interaction. And it is equally true for practices of the page and practices of the screen. It was as true for shorthand and typing as it is for computer-based graphic design. Literacy as a kind of engaged material consciousness is nothing short of a handy skill, and at this particular juncture, when such a wide range of inscription devices are available, there is of course plenty of learning to be done.

New Tablets in Young Hands

Public and professional reactions to the rapid advance of digital technology are nothing if not diverse, oscillating between unbridled enthusiasm and a persistent suspicion of their possible negative effects. It is perhaps only natural then, that such reactions are heightened when we think about the young children we care for, and what is right for them. In the face of this, touchscreen tablets have evoked a

[2]A fascinating historical example of this is provided by Lamarre's (2002) study of Japanese Heian calligraphy in which the text and the texture of the paper become part of the same poetic expression: 'papers of various colour are pieced together like a crazy-quilt [...] trails of dark ink run over lavenders, yellows, and reds that pool and stream...' (p. 150).

surprisingly favourable response from many parents and early childhood educators (Marsh et al. 2015). Ease of use and portability have no doubt contributed to this. Research, for its part, has tended to focus on the educational use of tablets (Lynch and Redpath 2012) and particularly on the use of story apps (Kucirkova et al. 2013; Merchant 2014, 2015).

As an inscription device, the iPad has quite specific operational features. Features that would, of course, be completely alien to the tablet users referred to in the introduction, but more or less unproblematic for the under-twos in the study reported on below. It might help to rehearse these operational features. First, assuming of course that the device is turned on, it must be held in focus, more or less at arm's length with at least one hand free to work at the touchscreen interface. Right away there are some challenges: how and where to place the tablet so that the screen is visible, how to keep it still, how to avoid too much glare on the screen and so on. Second, and assuming that the previous conditions have been met, you need it to display something you can interact with—an app. This of course requires the tap of a finger, contact of sufficient weight, accuracy and duration to open the app (it is easy to overlook how often we have to make minor readjustments, for instance, to tap again when the first attempt fails), and then those gestures and movements that are necessary to work with the app. I will not detail these, but they may include the preset touchscreen gestures (tapping, pinching and swiping), movement of the iPad (as registered by its accelerometer), and its audio-visual features (the use of microphone and camera). On the face of it, that is quite a lot for young children to work with, but then, they are quick to learn.

In previous work I looked at how under-twos responded to story apps on touchscreen tablets (Merchant 2014, 2015). Focusing on a number of story-sharing episodes that took place in an early years setting using an analysis of video-recordings,[3] I developed a simple typology of hand movements used by the children, all of whom were under 2 years of age at the time (see Table 15.1). Rather than starting from the operational features of the iPad-as-inscription-device, as outlined above, the typology derived from what was actually observable in these episodes. It is important to note, at this point, that these story-sharing episodes emerged out of the ongoing free flow of the setting, which included the movement of children and adults, the distribution of toys and games, nursery furniture, print texts and so on.

The typology took into account many of the ways in which the young children handled tablets, their largely successful attempts to hold them steady within sight in order to view the screens, or to use their folding cases on tabletops, categorizing these as *stabilizing movements*. It also enabled me to focus on the *controlling movements*—the taps and swipes that are part of the gestural economy of working at the interface of these particular inscription devices. Also noticeable within the story-sharing episodes was the work of arms, hands and fingers in pointing at the screen. These *deictic movements* are of course fundamental to shared meaning

[3]The video data was gathered by my colleague and co-researcher Karen Daniels.

Table 15.1 A provisional functional typology of hand movements used with the iPad (adapted from Merchant 2014)

1. Stablilizing movements
Holding—*using one or both hands to support the tablet as one might hold a tray*
Holding and resting—*as above but using the knees for additional support*
2. Control movements
General tapping—*using three or four fingers in a slapping motion*
Precision tapping—*using the forefinger (like the pointing gesture) or with the hand palm downwards slightly lowering one of the first three fingers so that it activates the screen*
Swiping—*hand palm downward using one or more fingers to drag across the screen*
Thumb pressing—*using the thumb to tap, swipe or operate the home button*
3. Deictic movements
Pointing, nodding and other gestures—*directing attention to the screen or visual items framed by the screen*

making, and they were woven into the choreographic texture of story-sharing as a multimodal ensemble. All this reveals so much about story work in general, and also about the specific nature of this sort of activity when it is mediated by a tablet —but, as we shall see, these episodes were also embedded within the ongoing life of the setting.

In general, the story-sharing was focused around adults, appearing like a brief *coalescence* of bodies, feelings, materials (particularly tablets themselves) accompanied by verbal exchanges. The stabilizing, control and deictic movement described how the hands worked in concert with other modes during story-sharing, often providing vivid instances of what Norris refers to as 'fluctuating modal hierarchies' (Norris 2012) in which one mode, such as a screen image, might briefly come to the fore only to give way to another, such as a gestural cue from a child. But even these movements were not always easy to isolate from ongoing action and interaction. Often it was a challenge to make clear-cut distinctions between categories—for example—when simple deictic finger-pointing gestures became control movements (taps) midway through their execution. Nevertheless, the iPads would come to rest, bodies would assume the proxemics of story-sharing, and adults would enact pedagogies. These typified moments of *coalescence.* But of course, there were also periods of *non-coalescence*, periods during which children wandered off, iPads displayed the wrong thing, adults were called upon for other duties and so on. Like other inscription devices—books, crayons, paper and all the rest, and like other bodies and things in the room they had a life of their own. This life is precisely what is hidden from view in an archaeology of literacy, and it is also what we miss with an exclusive focus on handiness.

A Different Story[4]

Focusing on story-sharing episodes was instructive in itself, but inevitably they were generated by a particular method assemblage (Law 2004) in which certain ways of seeing and certain ways of knowing are enacted. It seems important to acknowledge that one way of looking does not show the whole story, and remaining with material engagement is in itself insufficient. Despite the obvious limitations of video (see Maclure et al. 2010)—the disappearance of anything that is beyond the frame, things that are not captured, seen or heard, or even the semblance of a reality that is produced—there were other points of interest, too. For example, it was possible to notice where a particular child was recruited into the routine of story-sharing, moving close to an adult, perhaps pulling a screen into view, little fingers jabbing at the tablet, the physical contact between adult and child and so on. But something else was going on too, engulfing these episodes, swirling in and out of them, something that refuses the rather trite label 'context'. Something about the place, the setting with its cacophony of voices and things, the two segments of nearly-the-same-colour blue flooring, the children, unruly and unpredictable, and the adults performing various organizing or pedagogical moves.

I returned to the video data that had been discarded in the search for episodes of story-sharing in a mood of enchantment (Bennett 2001; Burnett and Merchant 2016), looking for alternative perspectives on how bodies, hands, fingers and iPads became part of the lively and emergent atmosphere of the setting. I located ten nodes that spoke to me, that evoked some strong affect—and took screen shots of them in order to think differently with them (Fig. 15.1). In summary part of what these ten nodes show includes:

1. An iPad on the blue carpet. Three children staring at the screen. Amie's bare foot dangling down (she has removed her sock).
2. A finger jabbing at an error message. Emma (the teacher) has Amie's pink sock bundled in her hand as she points at the screen.
3. Amie—her shoe is on the edge of the screen, making gentle contact. Emma rolls the sock on to her other foot, whilst a boy looks at the copyright page of an app.
4. Iona holding the iPad like a book. Her shoelaces are untied.
5. Iona walks away—crossing the threshold of the two blue sections of flooring. She is going away.
6. In the foreground: iPad action. In the background: Iona looks in a cupboard. She has taken off her shoe and holds it in her left hand.
7. Iona returns—there is a moment of physical intimacy with Emma (her teacher).

[4]I am indebted to my colleague Cathy Burnett for the idea of revealing multiplicity through generating different stories. We develop the notion of 'stacking stories' more thoroughly in Burnett and Merchant (2014, 2016).

Fig. 15.1 Ten nodes

8. Fingers are repeatedly tapping the touchscreen of an iPad. Amie has removed her sock, again (is it the same one?).
9. Another child is on all fours on a table top. Why? No one seems to notice (is this *OK*?).
10. On camera: a boy is looking directly at the video camera. He appears to know that he is becoming an image…

From these one begins to get the sense of multiple flows of activity, the shifting of interest and attention and a complex of concerns in which socks and footwear are as significant as hands, fingers and iPads, in which emotional warmth, physical care and pedagogical intent entwine. In contrast to the story-sharing episodes, on these occasions the tablet is one thing amongst many as it becomes absorbed into the more general to-and-fro of the social space. iPads are handled and carried by the youngsters who from time to time look at their screens; sometimes they are slapped or tapped and occasionally a tug-of-war ensues as young bodies struggle to take hold of them, to wrestle them from each other, or from the hands of adults. In all the tablets seem to slip between being slabs of metal and glass to be carried around, texts that invite attention (sometimes quite actively with a tune or recorded voice on an app), and part of the array of things, resources and equipment that populate the setting, different, but not by much, from the other inscription devices at hand—books, pencils and paper and whiteboards.

Lessons in Handiness

We know very little about how Roman Britons were inculcated into the use of wax tablets, but on the other hand there is plenty of more recent practice and debate that we can bring to bear on learning to use touchscreen tablets. Thinking about hands and tablets in the sort of ways explored in the early sections of this chapter could well lead one to suppose that young children should be trained, or should at least receive some sort of explicit instruction in the use of these devices. After all, if literacy as a socially prized form of engaged material consciousness is important, so is the specific work of the hands and fingers that are involved. But the observations referred to above showed that many of the young children concerned were already adept at handling tablets (Merchant 2014), and when this was not the case they were quick to learn through trial and error. In contrast, the ten episodes draw attention to the ways in which tablets, like the more traditional objects of literacy, are woven into the tapestry of classroom life, are handled in different ways and come in and out of focus in the unfolding of events.

Looking back over the recent history of literacy instruction shows how a lot of attention has been given to detailed and repetitive training in the use of inscription devices. 'Definite teaching of the right sequence of strokes' was the order of the day for writing instruction in the 1930s, and pupil progress from 'chalk to soft pencil, and thence to broad pen' was a matter of 'gradual training' (Board of Education 1937: 362). In a popular teachers' guide of the 1970s (Webb 1969) literacy learning depends upon 'systematic and quite formal instruction' (p. 40)—again practising handwriting is a focus of this work—although perhaps in keeping with the progressive ideas that were circulating at the time, it could 'be made interesting' (p. 48) through the use of a variety of different tools and surfaces. Shifts in educational priority in England continue of course, and as other aspects of literacy have come to the fore, such as phonics instruction and sentence grammar, less attention is now given to the work of the hand. Yet it remains the case that 'legible joined handwriting' is a prerequisite of performing at the expected standard at the end of primary schooling (Standards and Testing Agency 2016). Meanwhile, repeated calls for including keyboard skills, or instruction in touch-typing in writing curricula go unheeded.

Learning to be literate may well involve an education of the hand, and this is a central part of my argument, but this is by no means the whole story, and it certainly does not lead logically to the conclusion that touch and gesture should be the subject of direct instruction. Much has, in fact, been lost in successive attempts to identify specific skills that can then be placed in a learning sequence and used as a measure of progress. Education systems can end up reifying skills and routines, creating a reductive version of literacy—one in which bodies are schooled, and disciplined through literacy pedagogies. In the light of this, it is perhaps helpful to remember that 'school literacy is […] a discursive rather than a natural, practice' (Siegel 2016: 27).

Reflections on Touchscreens

Before the novelty begins to fade it may be time to reflect on what new technologies of literacy can teach us about older ones, and vice versa. Tablets, it turns out, are nothing new, and the evolution, design and use of inscription devices is always, and inevitably, shaped by the human hand. Furthermore, hands and fingers play a key role in communication. In literacy, more often than not they operate at the interface between bodies and meaning making. Touchscreens simply shed new light on this. But old technologies of literacy can also help to put newer technologies in perspective. Roman tablets were constructed from available materials and used to convey messages which were part of the conduct of everyday life. It is also the case that they were bound up with the lives of a ruling elite. In contrast, contemporary tablet technology is part of a global flow of materials, and in an unequal and divided world we cannot assume that everyone can enjoy the 'uncompromising performance and potential' that the Apple Corporation celebrates (Apple 2016). Young children, however, engage with what is at hand—the 'culture' that seems 'natural' to them. And for the young children in the study referred to in this chapter, touchscreens are a given part of that world.

As inscription devices go today's tablets are well-matched to complex communicative practices. Their screens display pin-sharp multimodal texts, they enable rapid interaction and message exchange, and they can store more than their predecessors ever could. They therefore challenge us to redefine literacy so that it can describe the ways in which we can tap to find information about almost anything, write legibly with our fingers, and interact with others simply by 'following', 'liking' or 'sharing'. This is contemporary meaning making which is literally at our fingertips—and yet its reach is far wider than the manual dexterity it requires. Reflecting on the changing nature of literacy, Brandt suggests that:

> we are just now entering an era of *deep writing*,in which more and more people write for prolonged periods of time from inside deeply interactive networks and in immersive cognitive states, driven not merely by the orchestration of memory, muscle, language and task but by the effects that writing can have on others and the self (Brandt 2015: 160).

For researchers and practitioners, looking at tablets on their own is not enough. They are, from one point of view, last in a long line of inscription devices. But just as we need to know more to reach a fuller understanding of how tablets were used in Roman London, so we need to be alert to the liveliness of children's interactions with iPads, and how the specific and essential work of hands and fingers is part of the power of meaning making in everyday life.

References

Apple Inc. 2016. iPad mini 4. http://www.apple.com/uk/ipad-mini-4/. Accessed August, 8 2016.

Brandt, Deborah. 2015. *The rise of writing: Redefining mass literacy*. Cambridge: Cambridge University Press.

CSAD [Centre for the Study of Ancient Documents]. 2003. Vindolanda Tablets Online. http://vindolanda.csad.ox.ac.uk/. Accessed August, 8 2016.

Barad, Karen. 2007. *Meeting the universe halfway: Quantum physics and the entanglement of matter and meaning*. London: Duke University Press.

Bennett, Jane. 2001. *The enchantment of modern life: Attachments, crossings, and ethics*. New Jersey: Princeton University Press.

Board of Education. 1937. *Handbook of suggestions: For the consideration of teachers and others concerned in the work of public elementary schools*. London: HMSO.

Burnett, Cathy, and Guy Merchant. 2014. Points of view: Reconceptualising literacies through an exploration of adult and child interactions in a virtual world. *Journal of Research in Reading* 37 (1): 36–50.

Burnett, Cathy, and Guy Merchant. 2016. Boxes of poison: Baroque technique as antidote to simple views of literacy. *Journal of Literacy Research* 48 (3): 258–279.

Crescenzi, Lucrezia, Cary Jewitt, and Sarah Price. 2014. The role of touch in preschool children's learning using iPad versus paper interaction. *Australian Journal of Language and Literacy* 37 (2): 86–95.

Lenz-Taguchi, Hilevi. 2010. *Going beyond the theory/practice divide in early childhood education: Introducing an intra-active pedagogy*. Abingdon: Routledge.

Harris, Roy. 2001. *Rethinking writing*. London: Continuum.

Kuby, Candace, Tara Rucker, and Jessica Kirchhofer. 2015. 'Go Be a Writer': Intra-activity with materials, time and space in literacy learning. *Journal of Early Childhood Literacy* 15 (3): 394–419.

Kucirkova, Natalia, David Messer, and Denise Whitelock. 2013. Parents reading with their toddlers: The role of personalization in book engagement. *Journal of Early Childhood Literacy* 13 (4): 445–470.

Lamarre, Thomas. 2002. Diagram, Inscription, Sensation. In *A shock to thought: Expression after Deleuze and Guattari*, ed. Brian Massumi, 149–170. Abingdon: Routledge.

Law, John. 2004. *After method: Mess in social science research*. Abingdon: Routledge.

Lynch, Julianne, and Terri Redpath. 2012. 'Smart' technologies in early years literacy education: A meta-narrative of paradigmatic tensions in iPad use in an Australian preparatory classroom. *Journal of Early Childhood Literacy* 14 (2): 147–174.

Mackey, Margaret. 2016a. Literacy as material engagement; the abstract, tangible and mundane ingredients of childhood reading. *Literacy* 50 (3): 166–172.

Mackey, Margaret. 2016b. *One child reading: My auto-bibliography*. Edmonton: University of Alberta Press.

MacLure, Maggie, Rachael Holmes, Christina Macrae, and Liz Jones. 2010. Animating classroom ethnography: Overcoming video-fear. *International Journal of Qualitative Studies in Education* 23 (5): 543–556.

Marsh, Jackie, Lydia Plowman, Dylan Yamada-Rice, Julia Bishop, Jamal Lahmar, and Fiona, Scott. 2015. Exploring play and creativity in pre-schoolers' use of apps: Final project report. www.techandplay.org. Accessed August, 8 2016.

Merchant, Guy. 2014. Keep taking the tablets: iPads, story apps and early literacy. *Australian Journal of Language and Literacy* 38 (1): 3–11.

Merchant, Guy. 2015. Apps, adults and young children: Researching digital literacy practices in context. In *Discourse and digital practices: Doing discourse analysis in the digital age*, ed. Rodney Jones, Alice Chik, and Christof Hafner, 144–158. Oxford: Taylor and Francis.

Merleau-Ponty, Maurice. 2014. *Phenomenology of perception*. Trans. D. Landes Abingdon.: Routledge.

Norris, Sigrid. 2012. Three hierarchical positions of deictic gesture in relation to spoken language: A multimodal interaction analysis. *Visual Communication* 10 (2): 129–147.

Potter, John, and Theo Bryer. 2017. Finger flowment and moving image language; learning and filmmaking with tablet devices. In *Literacy, media, technology: Past, present and future,* ed. Rebecca Parry, and Cathy Burnett, 11–127. London: Bloomsbury.

Rowsell, Jennifer. 2014. Towards a phenomenology of contemporary reading. *Australian Journal of Language and Literacy* 37 (2): 117–127.

Sennett, Richard. 2009. *The Craftsman*. London: Penguin.

Siegel, Marjorie. 2016. Inscription, erasure, embodiment: Literacy research and bodies of knowledge. In *Literacies, learning and the body: Putting theory and practice into pedagogical practice*, ed. Grace Enriquez, Elisabeth Johnson, Stavroula Kontovourki, and Christine Mallozi, 20–35. Abingdon: Routledge.

Smith, Roff. 2016. Ancient IOUs found beneath Bloomberg's new London HQ. National Geographic June 1, 2016. http://news.nationalgeographic.com/2016/05/ancient-rome-London-Londinum-Bloomberg-archaeology-Boudicca-archaeology/. Accessed August, 8 2016.

Standards and Testing Agency. 2016. *2016 Teacher assessment exemplification end of key stage two: English writing, working at the expected standard.* https://www.gov.uk/government/uploads/system/uploads/attachment_data/file/510832/STA-Ex2016-KS2-EW-MorganAnn_PDFA.pdf. Accessed August, 8 2016.

Tallis, Raymond. 2003. *The hand: A philosophical inquiry into human being*. Edinburgh: Edinburgh Press.

Webb, Lesley. 1969. *Modern practice in the infant school*. London: Blackwell.

Tomlin, Roger. 2004. The girl in question. *Centre for the Study of Ancient Documents Newsletter 11, Winter 2004–2005*: 1.

Wilson, Frank. 1998. *The hand: How its use shapes the brain, language and human culture*. New York: Pantheon.

Author Biography

Guy Merchant is Professor of Literacy in Education in the Sheffield Institute of Education at Sheffield Hallam University. He specialises in research into digital literacy and the inter-relations between children and young people, and new technologies of communication. He is widely published in international journals and is a founding editor of *Early Childhood Literacy*. The ground-breaking *Web 2.0 for Schools* was co-authored with Julia Davies, and he has since co-edited a number of collections including *Virtual Literacies* (2013), *New Literacies across the Globe* (2014) and *Literacy, Media, Technology: past, present, future* (2017). He is active in literacy education and professional work, including writing curriculum materials and professional publications.

Chapter 16
Mobile Literacies: Moving from the Word to the World

Alyson Simpson and Maureen Walsh

> *Reading the world always precedes reading the word, and reading the word implies continually reading the world. As I suggested earlier, this movement from the word to the world is always present; even when the spoken word flows from our reading of the world. In a way, however, we can go further and say that reading the word is not preceded merely by reading the world, but by a certain form of* writing *it or* rewriting *it, that is, of transforming it by means of conscious, practical work.*
> (Freire and Macedo 1987: 23)

We can find many definitions of literacy but the above description by Freire and Macedo is at the heart of this book. Literacy is always about 'reading' and 'writing' but how we read and how we write are constantly evolving as is 'the world'. The concept of 'mobile literacies' suggests a further potential in 'the movement from the word to the world' as new technologies have enabled the move from the boundaries of pen and paper. It accounts not only for development in literacies beyond print but also for increasingly interactive forms of communication, traversals within bounded structures and unbounded 'virtual' realities—hyperdomains. The concept 'mobile literacies' offers the potential of recognising transformations in human communication and learning while paradoxically there is a danger in being bounded with such concepts or definitions. Such paradoxes are explored in this final chapter as we weave our thoughts with those raised by authors through the previous chapters.

In the history of human civilisation, dramatic change has occurred with the movement of people across boundaries whether through exploration, war, geographical or economic events. As shown through the chapters of this book, the physical and nonphysical features of the iPad and similar devices have changed the

A. Simpson (✉)
University of Sydney, Sydney, Australia
e-mail: alyson.simpson@sydney.edu.au

M. Walsh
Australian Catholic University and University of Sydney, Sydney, Australia
e-mail: maureen.walsh44@gmail.com

C. Burnett et al. (eds.), *The Case of the iPad*,
DOI 10.1007/978-981-10-4364-2_16

boundaries for literacy and learning. In 1996, the New London Group found that the term 'multiliteracies' encapsulated the way literacy could no longer be bound by pen and paper forms of reading and writing. Computer technologies and globalisation required people to adapt to multiple forms of communication. Over two decades later, the fixed computer of the 1990s has been complemented by various mobile forms of technology including social media, augmented and virtual reality. Communication has always had mobility potential but it is now mobile in new physical and semiotic forms which, as explored in the first chapter, are tied inevitably to fluctuating economic and social realities.

How has the term mobile literacies been operationalised in this book? When, with Cathy Burnett and Guy Merchant, we used the term mobile literacies as part of the title for this book little did we realise how it would be interpreted by the various authors. Nor did we realise how unfixed the term is itself. Mobile literacies is not meant to be the latest, fashionable turn for 'literacy'. Rather, it helps us analogise and question what this movement across communication boundaries means for literacy in education as we explore what happens when literacies are in flux through the focal point of tablet use. The literacy practices described in the book raise questions about the schooled ways of doing literacy as Ng. (Chap. 7) demonstrates how reading and writing underpin activities such as curating and digital design in and out of school practices. They focus attention also on the 'classroom-ness' of technology use (Burnett, Chap. 2) through the orchestration of multimodal activity in diverse contexts such as early childhood settings, tutoring sessions and game clubs. Some reports suggest that use of technology in school is less cognitively challenging and more disciplined than the more exploratory usage seen outside of school (Rowsell, Maues, Moukperian, Colquhoun, Chap. 8). Our choice of the descriptor mobile literacies has provided authors with a prompt to describe how they saw literacies enacted in any context, as it simultaneously reminded them *of* the context in which devices might be placed. Knowing that 'literacy studies are never completely stable, and never completely able to be compartmentalised' (Mills 2016: xxiv) it is contradictory to keep trying to find definitions as they will never completely account for change; yet we wish to see through what Mills (2016) refers to as social, critical, multimodal, spatial, material and sensory lenses. In some ways then the concept of mobile literacies could be considered as a collective deictic, that stands for literacies AND…, what Marsh in Chap. 3 calls 'the interrelation of a range of factors which shape individuals' engagement with technology'.

The scenario below demonstrates the need to take account of context in socially situated and technologically mediated experiences of literacy. It shows how dealing with the portability of literacies may be challenging for learners as recontextualising meaning making in alternate modes makes meaning more difficult to make.

Place in Space: How Mobile Are My Literacies?

Episode 1

I am sitting on a plane flying from Australia to the US. Before I boarded I had planned to edit a journal article I wrote in Australia responding to the list of suggested revisions emailed to me from the UK. Already the activity I plan to complete has been aided by affordances of technology, which allow me to communicate with colleagues across the world. I aim to read the two documents on the computer screen and write up the changes in a word processing program. Again my activity depends on the affordances of technology, which allow me to access my draft word document and the email program using the mobile technology platform of my lap top. However, my plans are thwarted soon after take off. I can not open my lap top. My personal space has been compromised by the passenger in front of me reclining their seat to the full.

In this physical location where the materiality of the place I and others occupy is made very real, I am unable to negotiate additional space. Fortunately before I boarded I had planned ahead for this kind of situation predicting that I might need to call upon alternate literacies that are independent of screens at some stage of the journey (such as take off and landing). So I had printed off a hard copy of both the reviewers' notes and the draft paper before I left Australia. Smiling to myself I pull the paper copies out of my bag and set to work. First I reread the hard copy of the email and then, rationalising as I go my emotional and intellectual responses, I make hand written notes in the margins. I circle, I tick, I write suggested revisions while others around me watch movies on their in arm screens, read books using the overhead spot lights or hide from the air conditioning under their blankets. Each individual trying to create their own personal ecology for the 13 hour trip.

I am happily progressing with my work pleased that in my choice of hand writing I have found a solution to the limits placed on my mobile literacies. However, my complacency is soon broken when I complete the notes on the email and move on to transferring these thoughts to the journal article. If I was able to access a 'dynamic' copy of the text I would type up the changes directly but in my on board context – despite the fact that I am flying at thousands of kilometres an hour through the sky - the two texts I have are 'static'. I cannot cut and paste. So I take a second run at the task and realise that in transferring my writing from one text to the other I am reworking my ideas into new words and different phrases. In this space where I am hampered from using my powered devices I gratefully reflect that the use of pen and paper and the accessible literacy of writing on static text have prompted me to layer in an additional process of reading critically. I acknowledge that the lack of dynamic affordances for simply transferring my thoughts from one document to another has resulted in transformation of those thoughts into something new. Fortunately for me my literacies are mobile.

There are a number of possible reflections to make on Episode 1. One of the most salient to us is the reminder that 'literacy' is not dependent on technological devices. No matter how advanced the technology is, if the individual is capable of mobilising literate practices across a number of platforms as this academic writer is, then meaning making will be possible to achieve. In fact, in this case, the writer's lack of access to the affordances of a word processing program stimulated more critical thinking and rewriting. As 'literacy educators', we know that contemporary students are growing into learning and new forms of communication through interaction with new and mobile devices but we wish to acknowledge the dangers of the device becoming the focus of learning rather than its tool. Hence, the rationale of this book is to examine mobile literacies. New technologies will evolve and will determine our mode of communication but the capacity of being literate will always be mobile.

We need to consider the notion of mobility. While mobility means freedom of movement it is always, if paradoxically, related to a thing or time or place. For example, a hanging mobile decoration is both fixed and moving. A mobile phone is a physical device that needs to be held although it can be carried across places. Given the nature of the iPad as a digital device, it provides meaning making opportunities, which dynamically interact, interrupt and disrupt each other. However, the iPad is also an object, which can be acted upon in myriad ways including movement in the world. As Hammond, referring to Gibson's concept of affordance, states 'the world is full of potential not things' (Hammond 2010). Therefore, because people, devices and learning experiences are in a continual state of movement moving from, moving to, moving with (Pegrum 2014 in Ng, Chap. 7), we have adopted the concept of mobile literacies as an organising frame within which the iPad is located to examine the potential of this particular thing. In terms of the mobility of iPads, several of our authors have shown the importance of the place for their use—whether in the school, the home or the environment. They have accounted for mobility in different ways both physical and abstract explaining virtual 'wayfaring' (Rowsell, Maues, Moukperian, Colquhoun, Chap. 8) with a sense of dynamism that is value laden denoting freedom/engagement/open access/beyond systems as positive as opposed to statis/ limits/linearity as negatively bounded.

Place has long been acknowledged as a factor in literacy development (Leander and Sheehy 2004; Comber 2016) but not so well accounted for in critical explorations of mobility as it relates to iPads. Ingold's notion of 'em-placement' (see Chap. 2) is a helpful reminder of how quickly iPads have become placed resources deeply embedded in many learning contexts. As Marsh states in Chap. 3 'engagement with technology is never context-free'. Rather literacies need to be viewed as social practices 'constructed out of a constellation of social relations, meeting and weaving together at a particular locus' (Massey 1991: 28). With their strong focus on place, it is no surprise that ethnographic styles of research methodologies are common to the studies in the book as they take into account culture as key to meaning making processes. In order to explore the relationships constructed between humans and devices such as iPads in a dialectic fashion, we need to attend to what Gibson terms the 'complementarity of the animal and the environment' (Gibson 1986: 127). The role of context in creating open, closed or permeable boundaries within which mobility is made possible is important to note. In this book, the researchers are often 'in' the research space they have colonised. They openly acknowledge the multiple and partial perspectives provided as they present data collected from methods such as descriptive scenarios, digital artefacts, ethnographic interviews, narrated action, participant observation and video analysis.

The need for such variety of data collection methods indicates the complexity of trying to capture socialised relationships played out across space and time. To deal with the existence of ecological systems while acknowledging timescales where extended significance may be read from 'a series of isolated happenings' (Lemke 2000: 273), researchers record instances of literate engagement found at home, at school and out of school. Driven by the function of the task at hand literacies are mobilised during games, parent child interactions, school lessons, etc. as improvisations in meaning making occur using the appropriate affordances of technology. For example, in Marsh's study (Chap. 3), mobile technologies such as smart phones and GoPro Chest cams were used for young children as well as parents to film the children's tablet use and their interaction with parents and sometimes siblings during activities. These placed technologies enabled the researchers to develop ethnotheories about the attitudes of parents towards their children's table use. The digital dyad study of Kucirkova and Sakr (Chap. 11) allowed for a study of the concept of personalisation showing how one child's sense of self was developed through the sharing of a story making app on the iPad with her father. The link between reader response to literature and game theory was proposed and analysed through Maine's study of the dialogic interaction between two students in the story world of a game on an iPad (Chap. 13).

Just as place is important, similarly the physicality of iPads should be recognised as their materiality contributes to experiences of learning and meaning making. Merchant reminds us in Chap. 15 that learning to be literate in different ways depends on the material affordances of inscription devices. For example, the iPad has an external surface that can be experienced through embodied haptic awareness in a number of forms of 'thinging' (Ingold 2013). Previous research has examined the dynamic materiality of the touchscreen (Walsh and Simpson 2014) but the iPad device is more than just one of its parts. Socio-material approaches to literacy remind the reader that, in contrast with often touted perceptions of boundless opportunities for creating and communicating, the iPad should be viewed as a bounded object where design impacts on operationality and learner agency (Daniels, Chap. 12). As was noted in Chap. 1 and illustrated in Episode 2 below, the physicality of an iPad provides both opportunity and constraint (Hammond 2010) as objects may act and be enacted differently across locations becoming 'other' or different versions of the same thing (see Burnett, Chap. 2).

The scenario below demonstrates how digital space and physical space interrelate in the embodied mobility of the iPad. It also clearly illustrates the role personal engagement plays in literacy events as well as how the materiality of the device matters to the communication it makes possible.

Episode 2

On the back of the seat in front of me – angled oddly now due to the fully reclined chair of the passenger in front of me – is a tablet screen. When I tap it into life it reveals some bounded options. I may select from a range of enter- or info-tainment but only from the range that the airline has made available for this month. My tablet has been 'domesticated'. Tapping through various menus I can register a choice to change from listening to music now my writing task is done (see Episode 1) to watching a movie – not the one I was

> hoping to watch given the limited listings – but something to pass the time. This is a familiar scenario to me. Navigating through the use of touch and symbol I achieve my goal. My heightened awareness of my personal space reminds me to tap just hard enough that the tablet senses my physical interaction with the screen but softly enough that the passenger in front of me whose seat my screen is embedded in does not. I find myself wishing that someone had educated the young person behind me with the same communicative sensitivity of which I am aware. They have scrolled through the menus to the game section and selected what I sense to be a highly challenging activity. I sense this challenge in a number of modalities. First is the more obvious one of the strongly insistent tapping on the back of my seat that communicates itself directly to the back of my head. Second is the parallel vocalisation that accompanies each move in the game. This is communicated in loud and enthusiastic calls of affirmation 'Go!' or frustration 'No!' Moments of silence lull me into a false sense of relaxation but they don't last long. They are merely the signal that the player is concentrating hard on their next move, which is accompanied by renewed tapping and a new episode narrated with tones of excitement or disappointment. The player's facility with the technology has engaged them so deeply in the gaming 'space' that they seem unaware of the 'place' that they share with their fellow passengers. The connection the mobile literacies create in this instance between a private and a public social context (as felt through the back of my seat) are literally made material through the physicality of the interaction.

As seen above in Episode 2, there is a paradox where the sophistication of technology (tablet screen and game consoles on an international flight) is constrained by the choice in programs available and the physical limitations of the situation. It is an example of a bounded place and space where the enactment of the technology is limited. The iPad has become a fixed object to be acted upon by a passive consumer. In this instance, we remind ourselves of the contradiction that even though we may be mobile we are always confined by decisions of producers and deliverers of the technology. And yet, as examples earlier in the book show, although applications and technologies may have boundaries designed in, innovation and disruptive practice is always possible (Daniels, Chap. 12 and Ng, Chap. 7).

Our perspective on mobile literacies positions researchers to look beyond individualistic/private models of learning to community/participatory/public connectedness. It rejects the autonomous model of literacy identified by Street (1984) and presents literacies as social practices. Therefore the use of the iPad has been described in the book as a device that bridges the space of togetherness and apartness (Kucirkova and Sakr, Chap. 11). Many examples were given of how relational collaborations were made possible in ways that added to what was previously achieved and did not just replicate what could be done without the technology. Two are provided here. In the Simpson and Walsh study, the shared iPad use by pairs of students supported the development of a multimodal text from handwritten notes to a recording of an advertisement accompanied by theme music broadcast to a class. The shift from private to public interactions in this context showed increased semiotic complexity and high levels of motivation sustained over time. In Chap. 9, Caine, Davies and Williams explore how iPad usage supported the formation of new relationships as expertise and knowledge provided by students—who would not normally interact—fed into a collaborative project. The affective engagement produced through this process had long lasting impact on learners' social identity.

Parallel opportunities for shared interactions were seen to exist in an array of contexts common though globally distant. While social models of learning are not new (e.g. Vygotsky 1978), the way of 'reading the world' as viewed through Pokemon Go (Wohlwend, Chap. 4) pushes our understanding of literacies into complex accounts, which incorporate simultaneously the real/physical and the virtual/immaterial. The authors in this book are examining practices expanded through digital affordances as literacy AND not either or. In this, framing devices such as iPads are actants enacted, part of the flow of assemblages that operate in entangled networks of objects and practices (Chaps. 2 and 4). Resisting the tension of the need to work towards coherence, the authors are willing to encourage conceptualisations of chaos/rhizomatic connectedness that acknowledge the always in play/anytime/anywhere nature of meaning making. The chapters record instances when learning 'transcends the temporal and spatial boundaries of school' (Ng, Chap. 7). This work recognises the opportunities provided by the 'emergent properties' (Hammond 2010) of iPads to open boundaries, enable divergent discovery and encourage originality. However, chapters also record limits on access and equity created by closed boundaries, physicality, design logic, rules, policy, provision, limited cultural capital (O'Mara, Laidlaw and Blackmore, Chap. 6). In this way, the book accepts and problematises 'systems of regulation, surveillance and scheduling governing the organisation and control of mobilities' (Mills 2016: 5).

Where to Next and What Counts?

Undoubtedly future technologies will change the way we interact with texts and each other, yet they will not change our need to interact, learn and create. Bezemer and Kress (2008) describe literacy as 'the potential for learning and for expressing' (p. 168). Surely this is what 'literacy' includes. In moving from models of literacy that encompassed skills to current developments in coding languages, twenty-first-century expectations of learners' literacy options (Heydon 2013) have shifted. We need to distinguish between the technical skills and cognitive processes of using digital technologies and the affective need for human beings to be passionate about learning, creating and communicating. Most importantly, as we examine discursive practice in individual and communal activity, we need to contextualise our study in the world to acknowledge the entanglement of 'things, places, bodies and acts' (Hollett and Ehret, Chap. 14). Focussing on the case of the iPad has given us the chance to explore complex ecological systems in which the device plays only a small part. We have pointed the way to many other potential studies that could be undertaken to compare, contrast, challenge and dispute our findings. We note mobile literacies made available through a digital platform have brought abstract concepts into physical existence by the action of finger tips tapping on a keyboard. It is very clear in writing our account of the case of the iPad, the hand is positioned 'at the interface between consciousness and the world' (Merchant, Chap. 15). And now, as we prepare to type the last words of the chapter, email a copy to our colleagues across the world and put down the lid of the laptop as a material and allegorical sign of closure, we remind ourselves that our mental processes have been shaped into textual form through 'conscious, practical work' (Freire and Macedo 1987: 23) embodied in specific places and times. To help us transform our readings of the digitised world, we have read across instances of iPad use and contributed to critical accounts of its complexity through the framing concept of mobile literacies.

References

Bezemer, Jeff, and Gunther Kress. 2008. Writing in multimodal texts: A social semiotic account of designs for learning. *Written Communication* 25 (2): 166–195.
Comber, Barbara. 2016. *Literacy, place and pedagogies of possibility*. New York: Routledge.
Freire, Paulo, and Donaldo Macedo. 1987. *Literacy: Reading the word and the world*. Westport, U.S.: Bergin & Garvey.
Gibson, James. 1986. *The ecological approach to visual perception*. New York: Lawrence Erlbaum Associates.
Hammond, Michael. 2010. What is an affordance and can it help us understand the use of ICT in education? *Education and Information Technologies* 15 (3): 205–217.
Heydon, Rachel. 2013. *Learning at the ends of life: Children, elders, and literacies in intergenerational curriculum*. Toronto, Ontario, Canada: University of Toronto Press.
Ingold, T. 2013. *Making: Anthropology, archaeology, art and architecture*. London: Routledge.
Leander, Kevin M. and Margaret Sheehy (Eds.). 2004. *Spatializing literacy research and practice*. New York: Peter Lang Publishing Inc.
Lemke, Jay. 2000. Across the scales of time: Artifacts, activities, and meanings in ecosocial systems. *Mind, Culture, and Activity* 7 (4): 273–290.
Massey, D. 1991 A global sense of place. Marxism Today June, 24–29.
Mills, Kathy. 2016. *Literacy theories for the digital age: Social, critical, multimodal, spatial, material and sensory lenses*. Bristol: Multilingual Matters.
Pegrum, Mark. 2014. *Mobile learning: Languages, literacies and cultures*. UK: Palgrave Macmillan.
Street, Brian. 1984. *Literacy in theory and practice*. Cambridge: Cambridge University Press.
The New London Group. 1996. A pedagogy of multiliteracies: Designing social futures. *Harvard Educational Review* 66 (1): 60–93.
Vygotsky, Lev. 1978. *Mind in society: The development of higher psychological processes*. Cambridge MA: Harvard University Press.
Walsh, Maureen, and Alyson Simpson. 2014. Exploring embodied literacies through touch pad technologies: The dynamic materiality of modal interactions. *Australian Journal of Language and Literacy* 37 (2): 96–106.

Author Biographies

Alyson Simpson is an Associate Professor in the Sydney School of Education and Social Work at the University of Sydney, Australia. Current research projects in higher education and primary schools include work on the role of children's literature in education, the power of dialogic learning and the impact of digital technology on reading practices and pedagogy. She has served as a consultant to state and national education bodies across all sectors. She is the author of *The use of children's literature in teaching: A study of politics and professionalism within teacher education.*

Maureen Walsh is Honorary Professor in the Sydney School of Education and Social Work at the University of Sydney and Adjunct Professor in the Faculty of Education and Arts at the Australian Catholic University (ACU). Previously Professor of Literacy Education at ACU, she was the recipient of two national awards for university teaching. Maureen has published nationally and internationally in areas of TESOL, children's literature, reading education and visual literacy. For several years her work has focused on the impact of digital communication on literacy education and she developed a theoretical framework around multimodal literacy in several publications.

Index

A
Actants, 53, 61, 263
Action text, 50, 52, 53, 57–59, 63
Activity theory, 111
Actor-enactment, 15, 19, 20, 24–27
Affect, 33, 40, 132, 181, 186, 229, 234, 236, 237, 239, 251
Affective intensities, 237
Affordance, 23, 24, 55, 58, 67, 68, 73, 74, 77–80, 82, 90, 94, 97, 139, 160, 161, 164–166, 170, 174, 176, 197, 199, 208, 212, 239, 259, 261, 263
  afford, 97, 149, 165, 176, 179, 212
Agency, 15, 24–26, 113, 120, 121, 155, 156, 217, 229–232, 239, 241, 261
  cultural agency, 196
Agential realism, 229, 247
Algorithm, 6
App/Application, 2, 4, 11, 36, 37, 39–41, 49, 50, 54, 56, 60, 62, 67, 68, 93, 109, 110, 138, 139, 150, 153, 163, 179, 181, 183, 187, 190, 191, 198–200, 203, 205–207, 227, 239, 251, 262
Apple Corporation, 2, 3, 7, 254
Artefact, 16, 17, 18, 20, 23, 25–27, 185, 190, 236, 237, 260
Assemblage, 11, 12, 16, 18–21, 24, 25, 27, 33, 50, 53, 54, 61, 263
Assessment, 4, 6, 51, 79, 90, 91, 111, 116, 121, 133
At home, 171
Atmosphere, 228, 229, 231–233, 238–242, 251
Attunement, 181, 186, 233, 239, 241
Audio-recording *See also* Voice recording, 180
Augmented reality, 49, 106, 227
Autodidactic, 126, 128–131, 134, 135, 138

B
Barad, Karen, 61, 229, 230, 232, 233, 247
Bilingual, 159–163, 165–167, 169, 170, 172, 175, 176
Blackmore, Jill, 10, 87, 88, 91, 101, 263
Book, 2, 5, 12, 55, 80, 82, 163, 167, 172, 181, 230–234, 240, 247, 258, 260, 262
Bourdieu, Pierre, 31, 33, 38, 40, 44, 53
Bring Your Own Device (BYOD), 92, 94
Bronfenbrenner, Urie, 31–33, 40–42, 44
  ecological system, 31–33, 261, 263
  theory of human development, 31
    microsystem, 32, 35, 40
  mesosystem, 32, 40
    exosystem, 32, 41, 44
    macrosystem, 32, 41
  chronosystem, 33, 42, 45
Bruner, Jerome, 179–181, 188, 190, 191
Burnett, Cathy, 1, 11, 15, 16, 18, 20, 21, 24, 27, 40, 59, 61, 69, 106, 125, 149, 196, 197, 212, 251, 258, 261

C
Caine, Jamie, 7, 143, 262
Capital
  cultural capital, 33, 42, 263
  economic capital, 33, 42
  social capital, 31, 33, 38, 40, 44, 45
Cell phones *See also* Mobile phones, 164, 172
21st century, 9, 49, 68, 69, 88, 105, 106, 111, 120, 121, 212, 263
Classroom, 2, 5, 7, 15–17, 19, 21, 24, 26, 32, 54, 63, 67, 69, 73, 82, 88, 99, 101, 107, 110, 120, 121, 146, 149, 152, 154, 155, 159, 162, 164, 165, 168, 169, 172, 175, 195, 197, 203, 208, 258
Coding, 6, 59, 61, 71, 73, 146, 214, 220, 263
Collaboration, 57, 58, 155, 169, 212, 215, 220, 221, 262
Colquhoun, Chrystal, 125, 127, 260
Communicative repertoire, 196–198, 206, 208

C. Burnett et al. (eds.), *The Case of the iPad*,
DOI 10.1007/978-981-10-4364-2

Composing, 22, 57, 78, 139, 159–170, 172–175
Context, 17, 32, 33, 50, 58, 68, 72, 74, 81, 83, 92, 100, 107, 113, 126, 127, 150, 155, 162, 168, 174, 181, 191, 227, 251, 258, 260, 262
Corsaro, William, 196, 208
Cultural resource, 176, 197, 207, 209
Curriculum, 10, 17, 20, 45, 89, 90, 100, 108, 110, 116, 143, 144, 151, 173, 198, 207
Cybersafety, 100

D
Daniels, Karen, 16, 40, 196, 206, 208, 261, 262
Davies, Julia, 7, 143, 262
Deleuze, Gilles, 16, 26, 33
Design, 15, 21, 22, 61, 74, 83, 127, 130, 136, 149, 160–162, 168, 171, 187, 190, 197, 217, 221, 248, 258, 263
Device
- digital devices, 2, 8, 15, 87, 92, 93, 95, 97–99, 101, 179, 195, 206, 260
- inscription device, 247–250, 252–254, 261

Dialogism
- dialogic, 211, 214, 217, 218, 221, 222, 261

Digital
- digital cameras, 159, 160, 162–164, 171, 175, 176
- digital divide, 87, 91, 101
- digital media, 49, 52, 55, 145–155, 157, 229, 239

Discourse, 6, 16, 50–52, 54, 63, 88, 91, 156, 162, 212, 214, 230
Dynamic materiality, 68, 261

E
Early years setting, 22, 32, 40, 45, 87, 196, 197, 207, 249
EBook, 50, 55, 160–164, 166–170, 172–174, 176
Ecologies *See also* Bronfenbrenner, Urie, 7
Ehret, Christian, 24, 227, 229, 232, 241, 242, 263
Emergence, 3, 9, 72, 242
Emergent writing, 160, 161, 163–165
Emplacement, 128, 129, 140
Engagement, 3, 5, 24, 31–33, 35, 39, 44, 81, 82, 127, 147, 154, 184, 195, 196, 206, 212, 214, 217, 222, 240, 260–262
Engestrom, Yrjo, 111
- activity theory, 111

Entanglement, 16, 217, 230, 237, 238, 242, 245, 263
Environment, 2, 7, 10–12, 16, 32, 50, 59, 88, 100, 101, 108, 119–121, 125, 126, 153, 155, 160, 161, 167, 173, 175, 181, 182, 189, 198, 207, 228, 242, 247, 260
Ethnographic, 17, 31, 105, 107, 110, 198, 260

F
Flickering, 61, 215, 222
Foucault, Michel, 4, 52
Funds of knowledge, 144, 146, 154, 160, 195

G
Game, 40, 53, 133, 147, 152, 155, 199, 212, 214, 215, 217–222, 261
Gaming, 98, 145, 147, 151, 152, 212, 214, 222, 262
Gee, James Paul, 49, 51, 161, 211, 212, 214, 222
Global, 4, 8, 49–51, 57, 88, 91, 107, 159, 258
Global capitalism, 2
Go-pro, 35
Guattari, Felix, 16, 33

H
Hand
- hand movements, 235
  - typology of, 197, 199, 249, 250

Handiness, 246–248, 250, 252
Handwriting, 99, 205, 253
Haptic, 24, 61, 125, 132, 199, 200, 202, 205, 206, 261
Heritage language, 159–162, 165–170, 172, 173, 175
Hollett, Ty, 24, 227, 229, 241, 242, 263
Home, 2, 6, 32, 35, 40, 41, 56, 91, 126, 150, 154, 161, 163, 164, 166, 169–171, 173, 175, 179, 195, 201, 239, 261

I
ICT *See also* IT, 88, 90, 107, 108, 110, 112, 120, 121 *See also* IT
Identity, 53, 145, 151, 155, 176, 182, 183, 190, 191, 262
Immateriality, 69
Immersion, 211, 214, 217, 222
Ingold, Tim, 18, 26, 125, 126, 129, 130, 132, 260, 261
Interface, 2, 15, 16, 20, 26, 55, 58, 149, 150, 247, 249, 254, 263
Internet, 18, 37, 90, 113, 114, 120, 126, 150, 156
Intra-action, 61, 229, 230, 233, 241
iPad, 1, 2, 10–12, 16, 18, 20–26, 40, 50, 54, 57, 67, 70, 74, 79, 80, 82, 89, 93, 95, 99, 125–127, 130, 134, 144, 151, 154, 163, 179, 183, 187, 190, 191, 195, 197, 199,

205, 219, 222, 232, 236, 239, 245, 250, 251, 260–263
IT, 41, 147, 152

K
Kress, Gunther, 49, 58, 69, 70, 80, 125, 161, 183, 196, 197, 263
Kucirkova, Natalia, 4, 16, 31, 179, 180, 182, 197, 249, 261, 262

L
Laidlaw, Linda, 10, 31, 87, 89, 90, 99, 263
Law, John, 11, 15, 16, 19, 25–27, 251
Learning, 2, 9, 20, 36, 49, 50, 52, 55, 60, 62, 63, 67, 68, 70, 71, 73, 74, 81–83, 87, 90, 94, 95, 99, 101, 107, 110, 112, 113, 119–121, 129, 134, 145, 146, 150, 153, 155, 157, 160–162, 165, 176, 184, 195, 196, 199, 206, 208, 214, 221, 228, 240, 247, 248, 253, 257, 259, 261, 263
Lemke, Jay, 70, 181, 187, 261
Literacy events, 80, 111, 119, 121, 211, 261
Literacy practices, 5, 24, 50, 54, 55, 57, 69, 73, 77–79, 83, 100, 105, 108, 110, 120, 121, 126, 155, 196, 207, 211, 222, 227, 258

M
Macroanalysis, 53, 54
Maine, Fiona, 211, 214, 218, 220, 261
Marsh, Jackie, 4, 40–42, 44, 56, 59, 144, 195, 249, 260, 261
Mason, John, 5
Massey, Doreen, 260
Materiality, 12, 20, 25, 27, 80, 197, 239, 259, 261
Material resource, 98, 196, 197, 208
Maues, Fernando, 127, 260
Meaning making, 17, 69, 71, 72, 74, 80, 81, 126, 183, 196, 197, 206, 208, 214, 250, 258, 260, 263
Mediated discourse theory, 52, 53
Mediation, 37, 38
Merchant, Guy, 1, 4, 18, 27, 51, 59, 69, 105, 195, 197, 199, 207, 212, 246, 253, 263
Metacognitive strategies, 195
Microanalysis, 53, 54
Miller, Mary E., 149, 155, 160, 162, 168, 169
Mills, Kathy, 52, 106, 120, 258, 263
Minecraft, 125, 128, 131, 134–136, 150, 151, 229, 242
Mobile
mobile game, 211, 213, 217, 219
mobile literacies, 62, 63, 105, 106, 107, 108, 121, 228, 229, 241, 246, 257–260, 262–264
mobile phone *See also* Cell phone, 3, 8, 41, 49, 50, 92, 93, 95, 145, 150, 151, 260
mobile subjectivities, 4
mobile technologies, 3–5, 9, 50, 52, 63, 89–91, 93, 94, 102, 242, 261
Mobility, 9, 24, 89, 172, 260
Modal complexity, 58, 59, 68, 71, 73, 81
Modal density, 59, 70
Mol, Annemarie, 15, 16, 19, 26, 27
Moukperian, Sharon, 125, 127, 132, 260
Multilinear, 58, 59, 61
Multilingual, 159, 162, 163, 166, 168, 170, 175, 176
Multiliteracies, 258
Multimedia, 51, 179–181, 191
Multimodal
multimodal analysis, 73
multimodality, 25, 58, 69, 72, 90, 127, 183, 205
multimodal layering, 67–69, 71–76, 81, 83
Multiplayer, 50, 54, 56–59
Multiplicities *See also* Multiplicity, 16, 19, 26, 95, 196, 208, 233

N
Narrative, 6, 18, 60, 70, 112, 176, 180–182, 186, 188, 190, 191, 198, 213, 217, 218, 231
Neoliberal, 4, 96, 231, 234, 238
Network, 4, 50–53, 57, 89, 105, 108, 110, 116, 117, 120, 121, 179, 182, 187, 254, 263
New Literacy Studies, 49, 107
New London Group, 161, 258
New mobilities paradigm, 9
New technologies, 26, 49, 61, 88, 101, 146, 147, 155, 156, 193, 195, 210, 253, 257, 260
Ng Siew Hiang Sally, 105
Non-human, 5, 6, 9, 25, 26, 52, 230, 234, 247

O
Object, 11, 12, 20, 25, 111, 116, 126, 131, 176, 229, 231, 248, 261, 262
O'Mara, Jo, 10, 31, 87, 89, 91, 99, 263
Orchestration, 188, 199, 206, 207, 254, 258

P
Parent, 32, 38, 56, 98, 181–184, 186, 190, 191, 261
Participation, 50, 54, 57, 59, 151, 183, 186, 196, 208

Participatory cultures, 57
Pedagogical goal, 195, 198, 205–208
Pedagogy, 10, 49, 50, 52, 68, 72, 83, 90, 120, 121, 125, 232, 250, 253
Peer culture, 51, 53, 54, 175, 196, 207–209
Personalization, 3, 60, 180, 182, 184, 185, 187–192
  personalized stories, 179, 180
Photo, 1, 15, 22, 54, 56, 153, 163, 164, 170–172
Picture books, 7
Place, 3, 8, 11, 17, 22, 35, 39, 68, 121, 128, 134, 174, 197, 207, 228, 231, 239, 240, 242, 251, 260
Placed resource, 16, 162, 260
Play, 4, 11, 17, 23, 40, 41, 49, 50, 54, 56, 58, 60, 62, 129, 175, 183, 196, 208, 214, 222, 263
Pokemon Go, 17, 263
Policy, 2, 44, 88, 89, 91, 94–96, 99, 101, 107, 125, 205, 263
Portable device *See also* Portable, 105
Posthumanism, 230, 247
Power, 2, 5, 9, 33, 52, 62, 120, 144, 155, 186, 190
Problem-solving, 55, 115, 127, 214, 219–221

R
Rhizomatic, 21, 126, 128, 129, 134, 135, 263
Rhythm, 136, 139, 168, 230–235, 237, 238, 242
Risk, 88, 99, 101, 153, 173
Rowe, Deborah Wells, 51, 59, 161, 162, 197
Rowsell, Jennifer, 25, 51, 57, 58, 97, 141, 162, 246, 258, 260

S
Sakr, Mona, 179
Scaffolding, 38, 39, 51, 166
Screen, 3, 5–9, 17, 21, 38, 44, 49–51, 53, 55–61, 63, 67, 69, 75, 77–82, 87, 89, 94, 96, 100, 101, 109, 150, 159, 162, 164, 165, 167, 171, 173–176, 185, 195, 197, 200, 201, 203–205, 207, 208, 227, 229, 235, 245, 248, 249, 251, 252, 254, 259, 261, 262
Self-directed, 106, 113, 120, 129, 130, 135
Semiotics, 7, 69, 70, 183
  semiotic resource, 70, 179, 181, 182, 206, 208, 246
Simpson, Alyson, 21, 24, 125, 197
Sipe, Maurice, 235, 238, 239, 241
Slate PC, 108
Smart phone *See also* Mobile phone, 261
Social interaction, 4, 72–74, 77–79, 174, 184
Social media, 10, 39, 51, 55, 57, 116, 129, 130, 258
Social practice, 50, 51, 56, 59, 126, 162, 260, 262
Sociocultural framework, 211
  sociocultural theories, 179, 180
Socio-material, 50–52, 60, 61, 63, 232, 239, 261
Space, 5, 9, 21–23, 25, 42, 50, 53–55, 57, 58, 60–62, 70, 71, 73–75, 81–83, 89, 90, 110, 120, 134, 135, 144, 146, 148, 149, 154, 155, 159–161, 165, 167, 170, 172, 175, 180, 183, 190, 198, 207, 209, 220, 221, 236, 238, 252, 259–262
Storyworld, 211, 214, 217–219, 222
Street, Brian, 49, 195, 262
Surveillance, 5, 6, 99, 100, 263

T
Tablet *See also* Touchscreen, 1, 2, 5, 6–8, 10, 15–20, 22, 24–27, 31–42, 44, 45, 51, 55, 58, 68, 69, 73, 80, 91, 93, 96, 105, 109, 125, 149, 150, 156, 159, 160, 162, 164, 165, 167, 169–173, 175, 176, 219, 221, 245, 246, 249, 251, 253, 254, 258, 261, 262
  wax tablet, 248, 252
Testing, 4, 73, 90, 91, 93, 238
Third space, 159–161, 175
Time, 1, 4, 22, 25, 32, 33, 37, 38, 42, 49, 54, 62, 73, 93, 98, 110, 113, 130, 131, 135, 145, 151, 153, 155, 159, 171, 188, 200, 230, 242, 252, 254, 262
Touch, 5, 55, 61, 69, 78, 92, 128, 150, 197, 206, 221, 248, 262
Touchscreen *See also* Tablet, 30, 51, 53–59, 61, 150, 158, 162, 167, 175, 176, 195–197, 205, 207, 208, 245, 246, 248, 249, 252, 253, 254, 261
Transduction, 70
Translanguaging, 160, 161, 165, 168, 169, 172, 174
Travel, 53, 61, 129, 131, 145, 150, 153, 154, 159, 161, 164, 165, 170, 171, 175, 176

U
Urry, John, 9

V
Video, 17, 21, 35, 38, 51, 54, 56–58, 60, 67, 70, 71, 73, 77, 90, 115, 127, 134, 183, 212, 228, 232, 251, 252, 260
Virtual, 21, 23, 51, 57, 60–62, 109, 211, 218, 222, 238, 257, 263

Voice recording *See also* Audio recording, 56, 161, 163, 165–167, 169, 170, 172, 173, 175, 176
Vygotsky, Lev, 51, 52, 263

W
Walsh, Maureen, 68, 69, 71, 73, 81, 82, 125, 197, 210, 261, 262
Wayfaring, 126, 128–130, 132, 139, 260
Wi-fi, 89, 110, 153
Williams, Bronwyn, 143, 155, 262
Wohlwend, Karen, 49, 50, 53, 55, 57–59, 61, 63, 69, 138, 161, 263

Y
YouTube, 36, 38, 55, 57, 60, 126, 134, 239

Kolibri 360 GmbH
Ferdinand-Jühlke-Straße 7
99095 Erfurt, Deutschland
produktsicherheit@kolibri360.de